FILM, FORM, AND CULTURE

THIRD EDITION

Robert Kolker

Emeritus Professor, Department of English, University of Maryland

Adjunct Professor of Media Studies, University of Virginia

Boston   Burr Ridge, IL   Dubuque, IA   Madison, WI   New York   San Francisco   St. Louis
Bangkok   Bogotá   Caracas   Kuala Lumpur   Lisbon   London   Madrid   Mexico City
Milan   Montreal   New Delhi   Santiago   Seoul   Singapore   Sydney   Taipei   Toronto

The McGraw·Hill Companies

Higher Education

FILM, FORM, AND CULTURE
Published by McGraw-Hill, a business unit of The McGraw-Hill Companies, Inc., 1221 Avenue of the Americas, New York, NY, 10020. Copyright © 2006, 2002, 1999 by The McGraw-Hill Companies, Inc. All rights reserved. No part of this publication may be reproduced or distributed in any form or by any means, or stored in a database or retrieval system, without the prior written consent of The McGraw-Hill Companies, Inc., including, but not limited to, in any network or other electronic storage or transmission, or broadcast for distance learning.
Some ancillaries, including electronic and print components, may not be available to customers outside the United States.

This book is printed on acid-free paper.

1 2 3 4 5 6 7 8 9 0 DOC/DOC 0 9 8 7 6 5

ISBN 0-07-295392-6

Editor in Chief: *Emily Barrosse*
Publisher: *Lyn Uhl*
Senior Sponsoring Editor: *Melody Marcus*
Marketing Manager: *Lisa Berry*
Freelance Developmental Editor: *Martin Fox*
Managing Editor: *Jean Dal Porto*
Project Manager: *Catherine R. Iammartino*
Manuscript Editor: *Peter de Lissovoy*
Art Director: *Jeanne Schreiber*
Associate Designer: *Srdjan Savanovic*
Text Designer: *Srdjan Savanovic*
Cover Designer: *Srdjan Savanovic*
Art Editor: *Katherine McNab*
Photo Research Coordinator: *Natalia C. Peschiera*
Cover Credits: *2001: MGM/The Kobal Collection; Rio Grande: REPUBLIC/The Kobal Collection; Citizen Kane: © Courtesy Everett Collection; Vertigo: © Courtesy Everett Collection*
Associate Production Supervisor: *Jason I. Huls*
Lead Media Producer: *Shannon Gattens*
Composition: *10/12 Palatino by Cenveo*
Printing: *45 # New Era Matte, R.R. Donnelly and Sons Inc./Crawfordsville, IN.*

Library of Congress Cataloging-in-Publication Data

Kolker, Robert Phillip.
    Film, form, and culture / Robert Kolker.—3rd ed.
      p. cm.
    Includes bibliographical references and index.
    ISBN 0-07-295392-6 (softcover : alk. paper)
    1. Motion pictures. I. Title
  PN1994.K573 2006
  791.43—dc22

                         2004063184

The Internet addresses listed in the text were accurate at the time of publication. The inclusion of a website does not indicate an endorsement by the authors of McGraw-Hill, and McGraw-Hill does not guarantee the accuracy of the information presented at these sites.
www.mhhe.com

For Linda

ABOUT THE AUTHOR

"Teaching film is about getting control of the image and handing that control over to students." That has been Robert Kolker's goal in teaching and writing about film for the past 30 years. Combining his love of computers with his love of film, Kolker began experimenting with ways to deliver film in manageable, manipulable ways to an audience who could then watch carefully, see it analyzed, and interact with the moving image in a close and comfortable setting. The result is the DVD-ROM and textbook, *Film, Form, and Culture.* The textbook results from another overriding interest: to present a thorough grounding in film form and theory in readable prose that emphasizes not only the formal matters of film structure, but the larger cultural contexts in which film thrives.

ROBERT KOLKER is Emeritus Professor of English at the University of Maryland and Adjunct Professor of Media Studies at the University of Virginia. He is the author of many books on film. *A Cinema of Loneliness: Penn, Stone, Kubrick, Scorsese, Spielberg, Altman* is in its third edition. He has recently edited *Alfred Hitchcock's* Psycho: *A Casebook.* His book on European film, *The Altering Eye,* is now on the World Wide Web (http://otal.umd.edu/~rkolker/AlteringEye).

Contact the author at rkolker@mail.umd.edu

PREFACE

The response from colleagues and students who have used the second edition of *Film, Form, and Culture* continues to be both gratifying and helpful. Based on their comments, I have made a number of changes in the third edition that I believe will result in both textbook and DVD-ROM (replacing the two CD-ROMs of the previous edition) even more useful and comprehensible for your film course. The book has been expanded to nine chapters, and parts of it completely rewritten, in an accessible, readable style appropriate for undergraduate students.

NEW TO THE THIRD EDITION

Many users of the text asked for more detailed discussion of the shot, composition, editing, and genre. I've expanded discussion on all of these subjects and divided them into separate chapters. Because it is no longer possible to separate film from the digital—indeed, by the time you read this, film will be well on its way in its process of conversion from celluloid to digital design, cinematography or videography, and projection—it is important to think about the technical and aesthetic changes this will bring about, and therefore, elements of the former chapter on the digital are now part of the general discussion of film and its future.

The cultural context of film and film and media economics is treated throughout; it is the basic theme of this text that films never exist in a cultural vacuum and are always created in a culturally determined economic system. The cultural studies chapter, which introduces students to the methodologies of historical and cultural analysis, remains, along with the comparative reading of Hitchcock's *Vertigo* and McTiernan's *Die Hard* that colleagues tell me is particularly liked by students. It now serves as something of a focal point, pulling together the examination of film form on one side and the discussion of genres—the stories films tell us—on the other. I've expanded the treatment of genres, cinema's life blood, and so arranged two chapters devoted to the subject by returning to the auteur, especially foreign directors, and their influence on genres. I've balanced the *Vertigo/Die Hard* comparison at the end of the text with a comparative analysis of three films built on the same narrative, each of which corresponds to its cultural moments and national origins: Douglas Sirk's *All That Heaven Allows* (1955), the German director Rainer Werner Fassbinder's *Ali: Fear Eats the Soul* (1974), and Todd Haynes's *Far From Heaven* (2002). This allows for a useful conclusion to the study of genre and to the text as a whole. Throughout the book, many more stills now illustrate important points.

The Glossary has been expanded and more terms and their definitions within the text clarified. All words in boldface appear in the Glossary, in addition to terms used in the Glossary of the FFC DVD-ROM.

The *Film, Form, and Culture* DVD-ROM

Unique to this book from its beginning was an interactive CD-ROM in which clips from films are analyzed closely, more closely than can be imagined through the still images common to most film texts. That CD has now been redesigned and enlarged into an interactive *Film, Form, and Culture* DVD-ROM. Segments from more recent films have been added, and additional examples provided. Through moving images interactively designed with explanatory text, stills, and animations, students will become intimately familiar with the basic elements of editing, montage, shot structure, point of view, mise-en-scène, lighting, camera movement, film sound and music, and aspects of genre, focusing on film noir. The FFC DVD-ROM can be used alone or easily used in conjunction with the text.

Film, Form, and Culture remains a unique introduction to film for students in a variety of courses. It is one of the few that discusses not only the basic issues of film construction, but the way film is constructed for and by the culture in which it is made. It considers film as part of the world it inhabits. It is the first introductory text with a fully interactive FFC DVD-ROM. I hope it will remain a good reading (and viewing) experience for both instructors and students.

Robert Kolker

I would like to express my thanks for the many useful comments and suggestions provided by the following reviewers: Jeffrey Renard Allen, *City University of New York—Queens College*; Richard Ascough, *Queen's Theological College*; Anna Banks, *University of Idaho*; Jon G. Bentley, *Albuquerque TVI Community College*; Richard A. Blake, *Boston College*; Gerald Boyer, *Maryville University*; Bill Clemente, *Peru State College*; Robert A. Cole, *State University of New York—Oswego*; Jeffrey S. Cole, *King College*; Shekhar Deshpande, *Arcadia University*; Michel deBenedictis, *Miami–Dade Community College*; Carol Donelan, *Carleton College*; Pamela S. Ecker, *Cincinnati State Technical & Community College*; Susan Felleman, *Southern Illinois University*; Angelica Fenner, *University of Minnesota*; Cliff Fortenberry, *Mississippi College*; Eric Freedman, *Florida Atlantic University*; Mark Gallagher, *University of Oregon*; Mikhail Gershovich, *State University of New York—Old Westbury*; Marsha Gordon, *University of Maryland*; Melody

Graulich, *Utah State University*; Ann Green, *Jackson Community College*; Darren Harris-Fain, *Shawnee State University*; Bruce H. Hinrichs, *Century College*; Mark Hoeger, *University of Nebraska at Omaha*; Susan Hunt, *Pierce College*; Margot Starr Kernan, *Maryland Institute College of Art*; Salah Khan, *Pacific Lutheran University*; Tammy Kinsey, *University of Toledo*; William Klink, *Charles County Community College*; Börn Krondorfer, *St. Mary's College of Maryland*; Patricia Lacouture, *Salve Regina University*; Gerry LaFemina, *Kirtland Community College*; Sandi S. Landis, *St. Johns River Community College*; Christina Lane, *Ithaca College*; Peter Limbrick, *UC Santa Cruz*; Sandy Maliga, *Minneapolis College of Art and Design*; Gina Marchetti, *Ithaca College*; Gaetana Marrone-Puglia, *Princeton University*; James D. Marsden, *Bryant College*; Michael Minassian, *Broward Community College*; Susan Booker Morris, *Ferris State University*; Jerry Naylor, *Iowa Wesleyan College*; Devin A. Orgeron, *University of Maryland*; David J. Paterno, *State University of New York—Albany*; Reneé Pigeon, *CSU—San Bernardino*; David Popowski, *Minnesota State University—Mankato*; Don C. Postema, *Bethel College*; T. J. Rivard, *Indiana University East*; Brooks Robards, *Westfield State College*; Patricia C. Roby, *University of Wisconsin—Washington County*; Zoran Samardzija, *University of Wisconsin—Milwaukee*; George S. Semsel, *Ohio University*; Sharon R. Sherman, *University of Oregon*; Thomas J. Shoeneman, *Lewis and Clark College*; Greg Smith, *Western Michigan University*; Mark Smith, *Northwestern Michigan College*; Sherry S. Strain, *Keystone College*; Ralph Swain, *Briar Cliff College*; Kirsten Moana Thompson, *Wayne State University*; Stephanie A. Tingley, *Youngstown State University*; Frank P. Tomasulo, *Georgia State University*; Amy Villarejo, *Cornell University*; William Weiershauser, *Iowa Wesleyan College*; J. Emmett Winn, *Auburn University*; Andrew A. Workman, *Mills College*.

Many people were involved in the making of *Film, Form, and Culture*. My film students, patiently working with me over the year, helped me hone and clarify my ideas. Mike Mashon indirectly provided the name of the book. Marsha Orgeron did important research on its behalf, and Devin Orgeron helped check out the facts. David and Luke Wyatt read the manuscript, and their comments made it better. Stanley Plumly made me feel better with his encouragement. Other University of Maryland colleagues—particularly Joe Miller, Sharon Gerstel, Elizabeth Loiseaux, Barry Peterson, Jenny Preece, Ben Shneiderman—helped with conversation, ideas, and facts. Marta Braun, of the Ryerson Polytechnical Institute, Toronto, supplied the image by Etienne-Jules Marey that appears in the text. Paul Schrader, Oliver Stone, and William Blakefield helped make the FFC DVD-ROM possible. Jay Telotte and Angela Dalle Vaeche at Georgia Tech were endless sources of information and good humor. Robert Lieberman, my agent, saw the book's potential and helped bring it to publication. At McGraw-Hill, Allison McNamara, Cynthia Ward, Shannon Gattens, Catherine Schultz, Heather Burbridge, and David Patterson were extremely helpful through the first two editions. Melody Marcus, Martin Fox, Shannon Gattens, Beth Ebenstein, and Cathy Iammartino worked closely with me on the third. I am also grateful to Stephen Prince, who gave me technical support, and Patty Zimmerman, who offered invaluable information on independent women filmmakers.

CONTENTS

INTRODUCTION

Film, Form, and Culture asks you to think seriously about film, as seriously as you would about literature. It's a book about form and structure, content and contexts, history and business. It will give you some sense of film's history and its place in the greater scheme of things, especially in that envelope of words and deeds, money, art, artifacts, and daily life we live in that is called culture.

But why think seriously about film at all? Many people don't. Movies are among those things in our lives that we apparently don't *need* to take seriously. We go to the movies to be entertained, scared, grossed out; to make out, spend time, have something to discuss afterward. But we don't often want to think about movies as a serious part of our emotional or intellectual lives, or even treat them with the same intensity we use when we discuss sports or politics. Outside of a film studies course, we rarely hear people engaged in a discussion of films that goes much deeper than plot or characters.

Even the people who review movies on television or in the papers are not as serious about their subject as other journalists are about sports, music, or painting. They make jokes and puns, stick their thumbs up or down, tell us the plot and whether the characters are believable. Reviewers, in fact, are often part of the show, a kind of overture to the film we may go to see or bring home on video. They are another part of the entertainment.

The reason that attention must be paid to film is that most of us get our stories—our narratives and myths—from it, or from its close cousin, television. In other words, from the late nineteenth century onward, people have turned to film as entertainment, escape, *and* education—as an affirmation of the way they live or think they ought to live their lives. But even if film were "only" entertainment it would be important to find out how it works. Why does it entertain us? Why do we need to be entertained? And film is part of world politics and national policy. Some governments support filmmakers as a means to express their national culture to the world. Other governments have caused international incidents over film, particularly when copyright and piracy issues were at stake.

Hard to believe, but sometimes international policy concerning film can lead to aesthetic consequences. After the end of World War II, in 1946, for example, a major agreement was drawn up between France and the United States: the Blum-Byrnes Accords. This agreement came as an unequal compromise in the face of France's concern about getting its own films shown on its own screens. The French public wanted American films. The Accords forced France to accept American films in an uneven ratio: it could show sixteen weeks of its own films, thirty-six weeks of anything else. The Accords changed the way the French made films because some filmmakers decided that the best way to meet the quota was to make high-quality films through the adaptation of literary works. Other French filmmakers hated these adaptations and started to experiment with new cinematic forms, resulting in a revolution of filmmaking in the late 1950s that was called the French New Wave. The result, in turn, was a change in film form all over the world. French resentment over the influx of American film and other media surfaced again in the 1990s.

Issues of piracy of American films have changed distribution patterns, so that, instead of staging the release of a new movie first in the United States and then slowly releasing it around the world, many films are now released internationally. Film, politics, money, and culture are never separable.

The business of film ripples through the economy, the policies, and the technology of the world at large to this very day. In the coming years, the mergers of enormous media powers—most especially America Online and Time-Warner and the French company Vivendi and Universal pictures—may bring wide-reaching changes not only in the economics of film but in what film actually means. Media mergers may create a confluence of various delivery systems— film, digital video, print, music, and the World Wide Web—that will make film as we now understand it a different form and kind of entertainment. Or, as in the case of AOL Time-Warner, this convergence may fail. While still one company, the name "AOL" has been removed from its title.

All nations, our own included, understand the power of film and television to influence their people, to propagandize values and ideologies. Film may be a bargaining chip in foreign policy, always an economic commodity, sometimes the subject of the politician's wrath at home (as when candidates for office rail against the evil moral influence of Hollywood film, while Hollywood stars become politicians and influence our lives even more) and consequently film becomes the subject of study of many different kinds of academic courses in which its power and complexity are acknowledged and analyzed. We will talk some about the politics and the business, because film is big business and its creation, its form, and its content are about power, the core of politics. But mostly we will talk about the form—the way films are put together so that we, as viewers, understand what they are attempting to tell us—and the content of film. We will come to all of this from the perspective of textuality—studying the film itself and how all its parts work—and find out how film, its production and reception, its place in our culture, makes up a large, coherent construction of meaningful and interrelated elements that we can analyze—a text that we can read.

Let's go back for a moment to our straw men, the film reviewers. The first thing almost any reviewer does is talk about (usually summarize) the film's plot. "Charlie Kane is an unhappy newspaper man. His wife leaves him, and he loses all his friends." "2001 opens with a number of shots of animals out on the desert. Then one tribe of apes attacks another until, in the middle of the night, one of the tribes discovers this strange monolith in the middle of their camp. There isn't much dialogue, but the apes look real enough."

What film reviews almost always evade is one of the few realities of film itself, that it is an artificial construct, something made in a particular way for specific purposes, and that the plot or story of a film is a function of this construction, not necessarily its first principle. In other words, and as we'll see in more detail as we go along, the formal elements of film—the shot and the cut, for example—are unique to film. They are the basic forms of its construction—along with lighting, camera movement, music, sound, acting—and they themselves were and are determined by things going on in the development of film throughout its history and the development of the culture that filmmaking is one part of. When I speak of film as "artificial," I don't mean it's false; I'm using the term in its root sense, made by art or, often in the case of film, by craft. Film is an artifice, and it becomes an artifact, made in specific ways, using specific tools, fashioned to produce and create specific effects (one of which is the plot, which we often do have to revert to for convenience and to make a point about a movie) with the aim of pleasing the audience who pays to see it. Film reviewers and most everyday discussions of film try to ignore the artificial, constructed aspect of film—its form—and instead talk about it as pure story. The characters of its story become, somehow, "realistic," as if they might "really" exist rather than result from the way the film itself puts meaning together.

There is no doubt that filmmakers and the development of film form early in the last century play a role in this deception. Many filmmakers assume that most viewers are not interested in the construction principles of their work and have accomplished a remarkable feat, making the structure of their films invisible. In other words, one reason we don't pay attention to the form and structure of film is that the form and structure of film disappear behind the very story and characters they produce. This is a great act of prestidigitation and one of the main reasons film has become so popular. Movies have achieved a presence of being, an emotional immediacy that seems unmediated—simply there, without a history, without apparatus, without anything actually between us except the story.

In the discussion that follows, we will explain, analyze, and demystify this apparent act of magic. As we come to understand that film has a complex and flexible form and that story and characters are created by that form, we will become more comfortable with the notion of film as something carefully and seriously *made*. From that point we will be able to move on and understand that the making has a history and the history has a number of parts and branches. One branch—the largest—is the commercial narrative cinema of Hollywood, the major subject of our study. There are a number of national cinemas, some of them, like India's, almost as large as America's, but without much influence outside the nation's borders. Still another is a more experimental cinema—often found in Europe, Asia, Africa, the Middle East, and Latin America but occasionally cropping up in the United States—which explores and experiments with the potentials of film form in the way a good novelist or poet or computer programmer explores her language in order to create new meanings, new structures of thought and feeling.

Understanding film history will help us to understand the conventions of form and content. Clearly, films change over the course of time: they and their makers have a history, as we do, as the culture does. Visual structure, acting styles, story content, the way films *look*—all seem different now than ten or a hundred years ago. But, in many ways, these changes are only superficial. It would be only a small exaggeration to say that, with a few important exceptions, the structure of film and the stories and characters created by that structure have remained mostly unchanged, or have changed in only a gradual way, during the course of film history. Technical methods have indeed changed, and aspects of style (especially acting styles) have changed; but by and large the stories film tells and the ways it tells them follow a continuum almost from the very first images shown to the public. And yet film is always publicizing its uniqueness and originality. "For the first time on the screen . . ." was a popular publicity phrase in the 1940s and 1950s. "The funniest," "most unique," "unlike anything you've ever seen," "the best film," and "you've never seen anything like it" remain useful nonsense phrases for film advertisements. In truth, every commercial, theatrical film is in one way or another like every other commercial, theatrical film, and all are consciously created to be that way! In order to get a film made in Hollywood, an agent or a producer or a studio head has to be convinced that the film you have in mind is "just like" some other film "only different." Watch the first half-hour of Robert Altman's *The Player* (1992) for a hilarious representation of what "pitching a story" to a Hollywood producer is like, and see Albert Brooks's *The Muse* (1999) or Spike Jonze's *Adaptation* (2002) for an ironic fantasy about the search for an original film idea.

"Just like . . . only different" is the engine that drives film. Hollywood cinema in particular is based upon the conventions of genre, *kinds* of stories, told with styles and cinematic elements that are repeated with major and minor variations throughout the history of the genre. Through genres, films are influenced by history and, very rarely, influence history in return. Genres, as we will see in Chapters 8 and 9, are complex contractual events drawn between the filmmaker and the film viewer. We go to a horror film or a thriller, a romantic comedy or a science fiction movie, a Western or a melodrama with certain expectations that the film must meet. If it doesn't meet them, we will be disappointed and probably will not like the film. If a film masquerading as a genre turns out to attack or make fun of it, one of two things can happen. If other historical and cultural events are in sync with the attack or the parody, it is possible that the genre will wither and all but disappear. This happened to the Western in the late sixties and early seventies. Three moving and disturbing films that questioned the historical and formal elements of the Western—Sam Peckinpah's *The Wild Bunch* (1969), Arthur Penn's *Little Big Man* (1970), and Robert Altman's *McCabe and Mrs. Miller* (1971)—joined with the negative response to the Vietnam War and some profound questions about American imperial interests and the myths of "manifest destiny" to bring the Western down from its enormous popularity to a point from which it has barely recovered. These days, the Western is more likely to be a commentary on the genre rather than a repetition of it, or absorbed into other genres, like science fiction. Among the more interesting recent Westerns are those that use the genre as something like a cover for other investigations of character, history, and gender, such as Jim Jarmusch's *Dead Man* (1995) and Maggie Greenwald's *The Ballad of Little Jo* (1993).

The more likely response to a film that mocks its generic construction too forcefully is that no one will go to see it. This happened with Robert Altman's late seventies Western with Paul Newman, *Buffalo Bill and the Indians* (1976); the Bruce Willis action film *Hudson Hawk* (1991); and the Arnold Schwarzenegger film *The Last Action Hero* (1993). Of course, one ironic and self-mocking Bruce Willis action film, *Die Hard* (1988), was very popular (we will analyze it closely in Chapter 7). When Willis and then Schwarzenegger took the mockery too far, however, and the action hero stereotype was made too obviously like a cartoon and too self-conscious, viewers rebelled. Stereotypes, the expected character, the unsurprising story, the hoped-for conclusion, the invisible style are all part of our contract with the movies, what their makers believe we demand of them. Such demands are certainly not restricted to movies alone: in television, pop music, news reporting, and politics, we tend to be most comfortable with what we've most often heard. We are wary of the new. Our popular culture is, more often than not, an act of affirming already held ideas, of defining, delimiting, and limiting what we accept as the real. The "new" is either quickly absorbed by convention or ignored.

The worst thing we can say about a film is that it is "unrealistic." "The characters weren't real." "The story didn't strike me as being real." Reality is always our last resort. If someone thinks we're not being serious, we're told to "face reality." If our ideas are half-baked, overly narcissistic, or even just silly, we're told to "get real!" If we are college teachers or teenagers, we're told we'll find things different "in the real world." Reality can be a threat, the thing we're not facing, not in, or not dealing with. But it can also be a verbal gesture of approbation. "That was so real." And, of course, it's the greatest compliment we can give a film, even though—and this is the great paradox—in our media-wise world, we know deep down that what we are seeing has very, very little to do with reality.

The fact is that "reality," like all other aspects of culture, is not something out there, existing apart from us. Reality is an agreement we make with ourselves and between ourselves and the rest of the culture about what we will call real. Maybe, as some people have argued, the only dependable definition of reality is that it is something a lot of people agree upon. This is not to say that there aren't actual, "real" things in the world. Natural processes, states of matter (heat, cold, the relative solidity of physical things), the fact that, in temperate climates, plant life dies off in the fall and returns in the spring—these constitute a "reality," perhaps because they happen without our presence. But no matter what natural events and processes occur, they have little meaning without human interpretation, without our speaking about them within the contexts of our lives and our culture, without our giving them names and meanings.

We find films realistic because we have learned certain kinds of responses, gestures, attitudes from them; and when we see these gestures or feel these responses again in a film or a television show, we assume they are real, because we've felt them and seen them before. We've probably even imitated them. (Where do we learn the way to kiss someone? From the movies.) This is reality as an infinite loop, a recursion through various emotional and visual constructs, culturally approved, indeed culturally mandated, that we assume to be "real" because we see them over and over again, absorb them, and, for better or worse, live them. In an important sense, like films themselves, "reality" is made up of repetition and assent.

Here is where the reality factor is joined with genre, history, culture, convention, and the invisible structure of film that we talked about earlier. What we call "realistic" in film is, more often than not, only the familiar. The familiar is what we experience often, comfortably, clearly, as if it were always there. When we approve of the reality of a film, we are really affirming our comfort with it, our desire to accept what we see. Desire—simply wanting to see the familiar or a twist on the familiar and receive pleasure from the seeing—is an important idea, because filmgoers aren't fools. No one literally believes what they see on the screen; we all desire and in a certain sense covet, and in a greater sense *want*, what we see, despite what we know about its probability or, more likely, its improbability. We respond with a desire that things could be like this or, simply, that we might want to inhabit a world that looks and behaves like the one on the screen. We want to share, or just *have* the same feelings that the characters up there are having. We want to accept them uncritically, respond emotionally. Our culture keeps telling us over and over that emotions don't lie. If we feel it, it must be so.

In the discussion that follows, we will steer our way through the thickets of desire and try to find why we want so much from movies and how the movies deliver what they and we think we want. By examining form and the ways in which our responses are culturally determined, we will attempt to look at our responses in order to understand what we are really getting when we ask for realism, why we should be asking for it at all, and why our expectations keep changing. Remember that many of the most popular films—science fiction and action films, for example—are fantasies; and more and more of them, from the *Batman* films (Tim Burton, 1989, 1992, Joel Schumacher, 1995, 1997) through *Spider-Man* (Sam Rami, 2002, 2004) to *The Hulk* (Ang Lee, 2003) and *X-Men* (Bryan Singer, 2000, 2003), are based on comic books! Horror films and horror film parodies are fantasies that now openly depend on the viewers' understanding of horror film conventions and enjoying the ability to laugh at them. The film is proof that "reality" is not a given, but chosen.

Culture is another important idea in this book. Chapter 7 will cover in detail what the study of culture, and popular culture in particular, is and how our very ideas about culture keep changing, almost as much as the culture that's being studied. But since we will use the term before then, let me begin to introduce it here.

Culture is the sum total of the intricate ways we relate to ourselves, our peers, our community, our country, world, and universe. It is made up of the minutiae of our daily lives: from the toothpaste we use, and the fact we use toothpaste at all, to the music we like; the political ideas we hold; our gender; the image we have of ourselves; the models we want to emulate. Culture is more than ourselves, because our selves are formed by a variety of influences and agreements. So culture is also made up of the general ideological components, the web of beliefs and things we take for granted in the society we live in. Politics, law, religion, art, entertainment are all part of our culture: they form its ideological engine, the forces of assent, the values, images, and ideas we agree to embrace and follow or struggle against.

We will use culture here in a broad sense, perhaps close to what the French think about when they worry about their culture being at stake because of the influx and popularity of American movies. In our definition, culture doesn't mean "high-toned" or refer only to works of high art that are supposed to be good for us. Rather, culture is the complex totality of our daily lives and acts. Culture is the form and content of our selves in relation to our community, our country, our social and economic class, our entertainments, our politics and economics. Culture is the way we act out ideology.

Ideology is the way we agree to see ourselves, to behave, and to create the values of our lives. Ideology and culture are intertwined. When I decide to act calmly or angrily in a difficult situation, my reaction is determined by ideological and cultural demands of appropriate behavior. In this case it is determined by my gender, which culture forms in the course of my upbringing. Men are "supposed" to react strongly, if not violently, while women "should" be more passive, without an aggressiveness that would be perfectly acceptable in male behavior. Much of our culture calls "nerdy" any behavior that is intellectually driven and outside the norm. But "norms" are not created naturally. They are made by the ideological assent we give to—in this instance—what kind of behavior or personality type is considered "normal." Who determines the norm? We all do to the extent to which we assent to ideological and cultural givens. If we suddenly, as a culture, agreed that intellectual work was as meaningful and "manly" as physical work—athletics, for example—the ideological engine might shift gears and "nerds" would become as heroic as jocks.

The givens of ideology are actually created over the course of time and are changeable. For example, in older films, women were seen as needing to be saved by a heroic male, a reflection of the ideologies of the time. Today, we often see and cheer in film a strong female character. Contemporary horror films are a good example of the newly seen power of women over destructive forces, while contemporary action films often question male heroics, even while celebrating them.

Of course, when we speak of culture, it might be more accurate to think of cultures. Neither culture nor ideology is singular or monolithic. Let's move from film for a moment and take popular music as an example of how complex culture can be and how it can move in many directions. Hip-hop and rap emerged from African American popular culture in the seventies and eighties. Rap moved from the streets to the recording studios and into the wider population by the mid-1990s, and then separated into a number of strands. One strand, Gangsta Rap, became a way for male African American teenagers to express anger at middle-class white society. But its language of violence and misogyny also disturbed parts of African American culture and signified class and economic divisions within that culture. It brought down the wrath of some of the white establishment as well. Rap as a whole quickly transcended the music world into the larger cultural arena where art, industry, politics, and promotion are intertwined. It became sound, fashion, aggression, record sales, movie deals, police busts, highway noise, and big business. Attraction for many and irritant to some, rap became a phenomenon of the culture, a practice of one subculture (a term used to define one active part of the entire culture) and a representation of all of the culture.

The point is that culture is made up of expressions and intersections, representations, images, sounds, and stories, almost always influences of or even formed by gender, race, and economics. It is local and global, moving and changing, depending upon the needs of individuals and groups. It can be as peaceful as family churchgoing or as violent as Serbian weekend warriors, who, during the wars of the nineties, dressed up like the movie character Rambo and set out to kill those they believed were their ancient enemies.

In *Film, Form, and Culture*, we will look closely at all the contexts of film (with some references to television and new media): where it fits in the culture, what constitutes its popularity, and why popularity is sometimes used to condemn it.

Finally, a word about the films we will discuss. We will be thinking about and analyzing theatrical, narrative, fiction film—films that tell stories that are meant to be seen by relatively large numbers of people. While we will refer to documentary and to some avant-garde practice, our concern here is with the kinds of film that most people see most of the time. We will talk a lot about American film, because that is the dominant cinema around the world. But there are other very important and very wonderful cinemas and individual filmmakers outside Hollywood, many of whom make their films in response to Hollywood. We will, therefore, also address world cinema, the roles it plays, its individual filmmakers and their films.

But doing all this raises a problem. What particular films should we discuss? Within the context of a book, it is impossible to mention (not to say analyze) everyone's favorites, or to deal with films that everyone has seen or wants to see. Adding to the problem is that there is not really an established canon in film studies as there is in literature. Of course, there are great films. Everyone agrees that *Citizen Kane* (Orson Welles, 1941) is among the most important films ever made, and we will discuss it here. But every film scholar and film teacher, like every filmgoer, has his or her favorites. I am no exception. The choice of films I discuss and analyze is often very subjective. I've tried to follow the principle of part for whole. Rather than drown you in names and titles, my hope is that the analyses of the films I do discuss can provide tools for thinking, talking, and writing about other films; and that each discussion of film, genre, or larger theoretic principle will serve as a template for work on other films, other genres, and other related interests. This is one reason that a few filmmakers are referred to a number of times in different contexts.

One more word on the selection of films. Because film has a history, I have included many older films, even (especially) black and white films. Black and white was the norm—the reality and the mark of realism!—before the late sixties. My hope is that you will want to see the films referred to and get a sense of how wonderful they were and still are.

No matter what the film, you will be asked to connect things and to refuse to believe that the experience of any one thing exists in isolation from any other experience. This book therefore invites you to look at the movies, and, by extension and example, television and the computer screen, as one item in the enormous palette of your own experience and the wider experiences of the culture we all belong to. It invites you to think of a film narrative as seriously as a literary narrative and to understand that the array of images and stories, beliefs and prejudices, love and rejection, peace and violence that we learn about in literature we can learn in very different ways from film. In effect, this book is about the end of film innocence; it is an invitation to discover a world in which nothing is simple, nothing is "just there," and nothing can be dismissed without, at least, your being conscious that dismissal has consequences.

The FFC DVD-ROM is a companion to the text: it covers many films, but not every film that's in the text, and it occasionally goes beyond the text to demonstrate what can only be shown with moving images. The films excerpted in the DVD-ROM complement, more than duplicate, the examples used in the text. Sections in the text that are directly explicated on the DVD-ROM are so noted. For a complete table of contents for the DVD-ROM, see the inside front cover.

1 IMAGE AND REALITY

IMAGES OF IMAGES

Oliver Stone's violent, hallucinatory film *Natural Born Killers* (1994) contains a scene in which the homicidal Mickey is caught by the police in front of a drug-store. The media are present; television is capturing Mickey's capture. The police get Mickey on the ground and viciously beat him with their clubs. The camera assumes a position at some distance from the action, observing it. Before our eyes, Stone re-creates, in a fictional space, the infamous videotape of the beating of Rodney King by the Los Angeles police that took place in 1991. In that event—which, at the time, became a major controversial issue in our society that continues to this day—Rodney King, an African American, was stopped by the police for a traffic violation and brutally beaten. The videotape of the beating, which was shown over and over again on television news, seen by millions of people, was an eloquent example of how a simple image can communicate a violent truth. Or so everybody thought.

When the police who took part in the King beating were first brought to trial, their lawyers used the videotape as evidence against the prosecution. The defense lawyers turned themselves into a parody of film scholars, teaching the jury how they should read the images in a way that was favorable to the defense. They showed the tape in slow motion, backwards and forwards, frame by frame. They instructed the jury in the methods of close visual analysis, and they used their analysis to prove to the members of the jury that they weren't seeing what they thought they were seeing. What was really on the videotape, the

FIGURE 1.1 A still from the videotape of Rodney King being beaten by the police.

FIGURE 1.2 Oliver Stone's re-creation of the beating in his film, *Natural Born Killers* (1994).

defense said, was an offender violently resisting arrest. What the police were doing was actually part of an "escalation of force." The jury, perhaps predisposed against the victim in the first place, believed it.

Ron Shelton's *Dark Blue* (2002), a strong film about police corruption, the Rodney King beating, and the 1991 uprisings in Los Angeles, does not allude to the King footage, as in *Natural Born Killers*. Rather, it re-creates it, in grainy color. No irony is intended as it is in Stone's film, no "double take" at what we are seeing in the film and what we know the actual footage looks like, or, more importantly, means. After a decade, the images become part of a plot line, reality is turned into fiction; fiction is made to take the place of reality. Representation and the thing represented begin to dissolve into each other.

This is taken as a theme in the *Matrix* movies (Wachowski brothers, 1999, 2003), in which a conscious playing with illusion versus reality becomes part of the weave of the worlds of the films. This old literary theme has been brought up to date especially in recent film whose subject is the digital world. Hollywood filmmakers, aware that they create "virtual" worlds anyway—that is, visual representations of things that may or may not exist—are intrigued by that other virtuality: worlds created digitally online, in computer games, and in the very creation of films themselves that use computer graphics to create the environment of their characters. We will talk about this in some more detail later, but for now it's important to know that the overwhelming majority of films, whether or not their subject is digital virtuality, *use* it for everything from backgrounds, to cityscapes, ocean scenes, crowd scenes. George Lucas, in the most recent *Star Wars* sequels, boasts that relatively little of the films contain "live" action and most of that was photographed against a **blue screen,** in which the "live" characters perform against a blue background that will be filled by other, digitally made, images later. More and more filmmakers are using more and more digital graphics, while some, like the Wachowski brothers, use digital graphics to warn us about the dangers of virtual worlds. In such cases, the digital itself becomes a

FIGURE 1.3 Ron Shelton's re-creation of the event in *Dark Blue* (2002).

version of the monster in older horror films, cautioning us against the terrors of computers out of control, an idea we'll trace in Chapter 9 when we look at science fiction film.

Where Oliver Stone, in *Natural Born Killers*, plays with the ways that the real and the illusory break down each other's boundaries and seep into one another—thereby creating a complex and ambiguous film—the Wachowskis are marking good and evil rather sharply, by indicating that the false can appear more real than reality and that what we think is reality isn't and must be destroyed before it destroys us. Stone speaks about an everyday world so mediated that "reality" and fiction slide into one another. The *Matrix* films attempt to divide reality from its simulacrum, which is a mock-up of something that looks as if it could exist somewhere else—the Matrix itself. Both are telling us interesting things about the nature of images and the cinematic image in particular. They are not what they seem.

The "Truth" of the Image

There is a curious cliché that says pictures don't lie. It's part of that greater cliché that says seeing is believing. Somehow a thing seen directly—or through a visual representation like a painting, a photograph, or a film—brings us closer to some actual reality. Words are too obviously not things themselves; words are made-up sounds, developed throughout the life of a culture, represented by made-up letters, put together in a contrived grammar that everyone in a culture uses to communicate through a decision that the particular words will refer to particular things. Language is clearly cultural and not natural: it is human made and accepted with some variations throughout a particular culture. Every English speaker understands what the word "food" refers to, even though the particular kind of food that comes to mind to each individual may vary. More abstract words, like "cool," may have a range of meanings that keep changing. But seeing a thing seems to bring us something very close to the thing itself—to "reality." Things that are *seen* appear to be and even feel as if they are unmediated; that is, they seem to be conveyed directly to us, not conveyed indirectly. Nothing stands in their way. They are true.

But, in fact, an image, whether photographed, painted, or digitized, is not the thing itself. It is a representation of a mediated transmission—composed, lit, pushed through the camera lens, or a computer, and transferred onto film or through binary code onto the computer screen, appearing to be the thing itself, though, in reality, only its image. But even when we acknowledge the intervention of optics, chemistry, computer science, and the human hand and eye of the photographer in the recording and developing of the photographic image, we still haven't considered all the **mediation** that goes on. An image of the thing is not the thing. The subject of a photograph is not neutral: the subject—a person or a thing—is first chosen to be a subject, and then poses or is posed for the camera, often assuming a camera-ready attitude dictated by the culture (smiling, for example). Even a subject caught unawares by the camera has been changed by the very act of having been caught unawares. In the act of being captured on film, a subject who may be unaware of the presence of a camera is frozen in photographic time and space, turned into an image, made into something she wasn't when the camera snapped her picture. The natural object—a landscape, for example—is marked by the fact of its being chosen, as well as by the time of day during which it is photographed, the way the photographer composes it for shooting, chooses an appropriate lens, and manipulates the quality of light, first with the camera and then in the darkroom or in an image manipulation program on a computer.

Here is a core issue for everything discussed in this book. People wish to perceive "the thing itself," but it is a wish impossible to come true. Whether in a photograph, or the series of photographs that make up a movie, or the electronic scanning of objects that create a television image, or from a computer's binary code; whether on the page, from someone's own mouth, or from a teacher and her textbook; what we hear, see, read, and know is mediated by other things. The Rodney King video, a videographed record of "the thing itself," a man being beaten, was made to mean what various people, in various contexts, decided it should mean.

But the artificiality of the image is a hard concept to accept, because evidence seems to go against it. "Seeing is believing." The image looks too much like the thing. Unlike words, which interpret or mediate experience ("let me describe what happened," we say, and then give a verbal interpretation of what we've seen, sort of like summarizing the plot of a movie), images appear to be present and immediate: there, whole, and real. Of course we know they are not exactly the thing itself. A picture of a cat is no more a cat than the word "cat." It just looks more like a cat than the word cat sounds like one. Animals believe the image—notice how a dog perks up when it sees a dog on television! Even "in reality" when we look at something out in the world, we aren't seeing the thing itself either but an image of it, in fact two images, focused upside down by the lens of each of our eyes onto their retina, righted and merged in the brain to create the sensation of an object in space. The point is that everything we do is mediated, and everything we see is some kind of representation. We *choose* how close to reality—which is itself something built upon complex, often unconscious, but always learned agreements we have made with our culture—an image might be. Often, having made the choice, we revel in it, because the image seems to be delivering the thing itself to our eyes. Yet, when it comes to special effects movies, we are delighted to learn how the illusion was created to appear so *real.*

Images entrance us because they provide a powerful illusion of owning reality. If we can photograph reality or paint or copy it, we have exercised an important kind of magical power. This power is clear in the linguistic tracings of "image": "imagination," "imaginary," and "imagining" are all related to "image" and indicate how the taking, making, or thinking of a picture is an integral part of understanding. Through the image we can approach, understand, and play with the material of the external world in ways that both humanize it and make it our own. At the same time, the image allows us to maintain a real connection with the external world, a solid, visual connection.

We love to look and see. It's part of our curiosity about the world and our desire to know. There's even an erotic component to our desire to see, which films depend on so much that critics have adopted a term for it: **scopophilia,** the love of looking. The term is slightly more benign than "voyeurism," the act of looking at a person who is unaware of our look, but it is still erotically charged. We love to look and we especially love to look at the pictures of people and things, and often we do it to satisfy a variety of desires. We take and look at photographs, make videos, and create digital images; we do it as amateurs, often allowing the camera to be our intermediary amidst the chaos of real events, or we enjoy the work of professionals. Images are our memory, the basis of our stories, our artistic expression, our advertising, and our journalism. Images have become an integral part of popular music since MTV, and they are, of course, the core of movies.

We so believe in the presence and reality of images that we may take them at face value. They are, we often think, exactly what they are (or what someone tells us they are). Journalism and politics are infamous for doing this: picking out some aspect of an event, editorializing on a public figure by choosing a particularly unflattering pose, and then manipulating and describing it to present only one part, one perspective of the event itself—all the easier now with digital manipulation. Television news, by concentrating endlessly on murder and violence, uses images of a small part of what is in the world, which, in their selection and repetition, may convince some that this is what most of the world is about. In *JFK* (1991), Oliver Stone is at pains to make sure we understand that seeing is *not* believing, that the images given us by the media, molded by politics, make us think that we are seeing what is, but may, actually, may not be.

We invest images with emotion and meaning; we may forget that they are *images*—mediations—and create a kind of short circuit: if the image of a thing is close enough to the thing itself, perhaps we may be in some danger of neglecting the thing itself—those events actually going on in the world—and merely believe the image. The emotions we attach to an image or to the images that make up a film can be simply set in motion by the images themselves, and we can ignore the origin as well the formal properties—the **composition,** what is chosen to be in the shot and how these elements are arranged in the frame, **editing,** the placement of the shot in relation to others, the lighting—all the imaginative things that went into the making of the single image or a motion picture. We can cut ourselves off from the events that made the image possible—the material of the external world, the computer, and various acts of illusion making—and make that short circuit, accepting the cliché that pictures never lie. If pictures never lie and are worth a thousand words, they must be dependable, true, and, if not the thing itself, at least a suitable substitute.

This is what Oliver Stone was thinking about when he imitated the Rodney King videotape in *Natural Born Killers* and what the Wachowski brothers have turned into a theme about those who exist in the flesh and those who create a digital imitation of the flesh. The Rodney King videotape contained an image of an event, taken without the knowledge of those who were participating in it, which is the closest image making can get to objective recording, an argument used by documentary filmmakers, who try to maintain the illusion that their images are closer to objective reality than those made by fiction filmmakers. But, as Stone shows, such footage is not "objective"; it exists because of the economics of video recording, the relative cheapness and ubiquity of amateur equipment; the willingness of an onlooker with a camera to turn it on as the beating was in progress, rather than do something to stop the beating; the willingness of television news programs to show over and over again any kind of novel, violent imagery they can find. The footage exists not merely because there was someone there to tape it, but because on the other end there was a desire of people to watch it and use it. Stone re-creates the image, this time with all the expensive, professional apparatus available to Hollywood filmmaking, and turns it into an ironic commentary. Just as with the original footage, where we felt sympathy for the victim of a vicious beating, here we feel sympathy for the trapped and beaten Mickey. But in the fiction of *Natural Born Killers,* Mickey is a vicious, psychotic killer who needs capturing. He is, at the same time, something of a sympathetic figure. The reference to the "actual" Rodney King footage serves, therefore, to complicate our response and to make us wonder about how objective images can actually be. In many ways, Stone is expanding the experiment he began in *JFK,* a film that is not only about a presidential assassination but also about how images and the history they try to create can be read in multiple ways.

What about the "objectivity" of the image itself? Anyone who took to heart the cliché "seeing is believing" saw, in the King video, a man being beaten by the police, in the fuzzy gray wash of an underexposed, amateur videotape taken at night. The trial lawyers, however, who analyzed the image from their own perspective in their desire to debunk the evidence in order to free their clients, proved to a jury—willing to believe them—that they didn't quite see a man being beaten but an aggressive person the police were trying to restrain. The evidence held in those images was a matter of political and racial conviction, not of any self-evident "truth." In Oliver Stone's re-creation, the police are brutally restraining a brutal, aggressive person, an unthinking, amoral killer. The image is a complete fabrication, done in the studio or in a carefully controlled location. Most likely the actor, Woody Harrelson, isn't even in the shot, replaced by a stunt man. There is, in a sense, nothing there, only a studio or location fabrication of an image within a narrative fiction, fully exaggerated as representatives from television news (including Japanese television, with an excited commentator whose remarks are translated through subtitles) look on, make their images, make comments, while the sound track is filled with the music of Carl Orff's *Carmina Burana*. The re-creation is, as I said, twisted with irony, begging us to provide a more complex reaction than we might have given to the original King videotape or the trial lawyers' interpretation of it.

The *Matrix* films, on the other hand, are lacking in irony: they take very seriously the split between the good "real" and the evil digital manipulators of the real. They often try to confuse us as to what is what, who is who; they excite us with their choreographed, digitally and cinematographically enhanced fight sequences. In the end, they don't so much question the reality of the image, but assure us that all images are carefully crafted mediations of what may or may not exist. The images are so carefully constructed that both real and unreal are made to look equally real. This *should* be ironic commentary, but it all becomes, as the sequels progress, background to spectacle and violence.

Stone asks us to think about the construction of images, something that few films attempt to do because their value is built upon our desire not to ask what images are made of and what they might really mean, or, in the case of special effects movies, to wonder at the realism of the fake. We love to look; movies love to show us things. Maybe we don't want to know what we're looking at and want to simply enjoy the illusion, or enjoy the illusion even knowing how it was created. In the case of *Natural Born Killers* Stone's ironies were lost on many people, who found the film too violent. Unwilling to decipher the complex visual structure of the film and understand what that structure was trying to say—that images of violence are manufactured to play upon our desire to see and enjoy violence at a safe distance—they took the images too literally and were repelled. They believed what they saw.

All of which leads us to the central question of this chapter: When we look at an image, and especially when we look at the images that make up a movie, what do we see? What's there, what do we think is there, and what do we want to be there? We can begin an answer by turning very briefly to the development of painting and photography, because film is so much an extension of the latter and borrows many effects from the former.

The Urge to Represent "Reality"

People painted before they wrote. Painting is among the earliest artifacts we have of prehistoric civilizations: a hand, a deer, images of the human figure and the naturalized world, even sculptures of animals, things caught and seen and then, in the case of the deer, eaten. There's elemental magic in these early images, the kind of magic that says if you own a part of or representation of a thing, you have power over that thing. In this case, the "thing" is nature itself. These early cave paintings show that humans wanted imaginative control over the natural world and wanted to make permanent representations of it. The painted image, in different ways in different cultures, came to express not merely seeing but an interpretation and a desire to own what is seen. Painting, along with story telling, grew from the same urge to interpret and control the world—to give it a human and humanized shape. "Primitive" art is simple and direct. Painting moved from the primitive in interesting ways.

Perspective and the Pleasures of Tricking the Eye

"Primitive" art is never, of course, simple and direct, not even primitive, but seems that way because of the major changes that occurred as painting moved from a desire to capture the world through simple images to a scientific and technology-driven desire to remanufacture images of the world for the viewer's pleasure. We must understand that, no matter what a painting represents (or, in the case of abstract painting, doesn't represent), it is an interpretation of something seen that has been executed by the artist's hand and imagination. A painting is pigment on canvas articulated through a combination of color, shape, volume, and spatial organization. The way space is organized and the subject represented in a painting is very specific to a given culture and time, though it also bears traces of a particular artist's style and personality. Perspective, for example—the illusion of depth on a two-dimensional surface—is hardly a universal way of organizing space on canvas and did not always exist. Traditional Asian painting has never used it. Western painting didn't use it until the early fifteenth century. It was developed by the Florentine architect Filippo Brunelleschi (1377–1446) and the painter Masaccio (1401–1428). Perspective is based on mathematical principles of linear convergence, the way lines can be drawn so they appear to vanish at a single point in space.

FIGURE 1.4 Perspective was a mathematical invention that allowed a vanishing line to be created on a canvas and thus presented the illusion of depth on a two-dimensional surface. Photography and film adopted the principle. Photographers and cinematographers set up their cameras to show the vanishing line, and we can see it at work here, in one of the earliest films we have, the Lumière brothers' 1895 film of a train arriving at a station.

People have theorized that perspective was invented for ideological and cultural reasons, because it allowed the wealthy patrons who sponsored artists to be given a privileged place in viewing the canvas. That is, perspective allowed the viewer a

FIGURE 1.5   Drawing of a camera obscura.

sense of ownership, a sense of standing before a space that was made for his gaze. He stood outside the painting, occupying a position that seemed to be at the convergence of an imaginary set of lines that opened into the canvas and then appeared to converge again behind the canvas. These "vanishing lines" created the illusion that the space of the painting completed the patron's gaze— indeed any viewer's gaze. The double convergence creates an important effect, for if sight lines converge toward the back of the image on the canvas, they also converge in the imaginary space in front of the canvas, a space that is filled by the controlling look of the spectator. This phenomenon would have tremendous repercussions in the development of film in the twentieth century.

By the neoclassical period (from the late seventeenth to the mid-eighteenth centuries in most of Europe) the ideological thrust of painting was to be as "true" to the natural world as possible. Interpretation and inspiration were, in theory at least, subordinated to imitation and to the capturing of the image, to reproducing it, proclaiming that nature could be taken and owned whole by the imagination. Many artists approached the imitation of nature through technology. The camera obscura came to prominence in the seventeenth century: a box with a pinhole through which light could pass, it projected an upside-down image on its opposite side. A painter would enter the box and literally trace the image of the outside world that was reflected through the pinhole. Another version of this contraption, called a "Claude Glass," after the admired French landscape painter Claude Lorrain (1600–1682), was also put to use by painters. It had a convex black mirror that concentrated an image of the landscape that could be painted over or copied. The Dutch painter Jan Vermeer (1632–1675) actually reproduced in his paintings the lighting effects that were created by the camera obscura.

Photography and Reality

The camera obscura was a sort of prephotographic device, designed to make possible the urge to capture the real world with as little apparent mediation as possible. Photography was invented in the nineteenth century out of experiments that, like those involving perspective, were both scientific and aesthetic. At its most basic, photography is a chemical process, during which a light-sensitive material is altered when exposed to light. When this altered material is chemically treated, the exposed particles wash away, creating transparent or translucent spaces where the light fell. The negative image (light for dark) is reversed during printing. The chemistry hasn't changed very much since the middle of the nineteenth century, though the optics have, and faster, more light-sensitive film stock was developed that made nighttime shooting possible. Within the past few years digital imaging has begun to render chemical processing obsolete. The aesthetics and ideology of photographic mediation are a different matter. Photography became a major factor in the ways we observed and perceived the world around us.

The great French film theorist André Bazin speaks about the inevitability of photography. What he means is that art has always been motivated to capture and maintain the reality of the world, to hold its images eternally. Photography is the climax of that desire because, Bazin believes, it is the first art in which, at the exact instant during which the image is transferred to film, the human hand is not involved. For Bazin, the taking of a photograph is a pure, objective act. He puns in French on the word *objectif*, which means both "objective" and "lens." Bazin was deeply committed to the concept of film and photography as the arts of the real, but he was also aware that the reality of film and photography was "artificial," made by art. He was intrigued by the paradox. He was well aware that in the seemingly automatic passing of a thing to its image, some human intervention always occurs. So, of course, even though the image passes through the lens to the film in the camera without the intervention of the human hand, that intervention has already occurred: in the crafting of the lens and the chemical manufacture of the light-sensitive film emulsion, by the photographer who chooses a particular lens and a particular film for a particular shot, in the way the photographer lights and composes the shot. Every photographer is a composer: think of the basic, practically universal gesture of an amateur picture taker, waving her arm to signal people in front of the lens to move closer together, to get in the frame. Think of the ramifications if this photographer purposively moved the camera slightly to the right to remove one member of the party from the frame. The professional photographer and the photographer as artist make more elaborate preparations for a shot and, after the shot is composed and taken, manipulate the image in the darkroom or on the computer screen. They reframe and crop, alter the exposure so the image is darker or lighter. They play with color. They make the image their own.

When photography came along in the nineteenth century, painting was put in crisis. The photograph, it seemed, did the work of imitating nature better than the painter ever could. Some painters made pragmatic use of the invention.

There were Impressionist painters who used a photograph in place of the model or landscape they were painting. But by and large, the photograph was a challenge to painting and was one cause of painting's move away from direct representation and reproduction to the abstract painting of the twentieth century. Since photographs did such a good job representing things as they existed in the world, painters were freed to look inward and represent things as they were in their imagination, rendering emotion in the color, volume, line, and spatial configurations native to the painter's art.

Photography was not wholly responsible for the development of abstract painting, which fit well with other movements both in the world and in the art of the late nineteenth and early twentieth century, movements that began to call attention to form and away from an apparently simple representation of "reality." The very inventions of the age—photography, movies, railroads, the telephone—along with the coming apart of old political alliances and traditional class and family connections pushed artists to embrace new forms that would speak to the changes in the old concepts of space and time, of religious and political allegiances. The important point here is that photography introduced to modern culture another form of image making, of visual representation, one apparently more "real" than painting because it seemed to capture an image of the world out there and bring it—framed, composed, and contained—before our eyes.

It's worth repeating again that the principle of representation (and mediation) is that an image is not the thing itself but a thing in itself with its own formal properties and methods of interpreting something else. This sounds perfectly obvious until we recall the phenomenon of short circuiting we discussed earlier. We tend to look at a representational painting or a photograph as something that uniquely represents another original object and that acts as a trigger mechanism for an appropriate emotional response. The surrealist painter René Magritte made a famous picture, *La Trahison des images (The Betrayal of Images)*. It's a very "realistic" painting of a pipe, the smoking kind. Magritte paints a title directly onto the canvas: *"Ceci n'est pas une pipe"* ("This is not a pipe"). Within his own painting, he creates a concise lesson about representation. The image is not the thing. But it remains a hard lesson, harder still when it comes to photography.

When we look at the family photo album, we don't ask how the images were constructed and what the construction is saying about the subject of the photograph. We don't wonder why the photographer chose to be outside the frame, behind the camera, or to time the shutter and leap into the picture; we may not question why one aunt is not smiling, or why some relatives have been cut out of the composition, or why father is way in the back, barely visible. We desire to see and feel something through the image. So we look at the images and feel nostalgia or joy or pain about the family represented in the photographs.

However, when the transparency of the image is closed off, when the photograph is of something unrecognizable, or the painting is abstract, or an avant-garde film denies recognizable plot, our first question is, "What is this about?" We want our images to be transparent, to seem to relate some kind of story that we understand, to allow us to look through them to the meanings they seem to convey. They exist to transmit the real world to our eyes and to trigger emotional response.

Manipulation of the Image

During its relatively brief existence, photography has taken on many culturally and economically determined forms. In the very early days, in order to overcome a perceived inferiority to painting, photographers adopted a painterly style. Some of them hand-colored their work, after composing a figure or landscape in poses or compositions similar to those used by the Impressionist painters. As photography found its independent path, many other styles emerged, all of them depending upon some kind of manipulation of the image during the picture-making process. These included the creation of "abstract" photographs, images that reveal only patterns, shapes, and volume. This style flourished in the 1920s at the same time that Dadaist and Surrealist artists incorporated the photographic image into their work. During this period, the photographer Man Ray created abstract patterns by putting actual objects directly onto photographic paper and exposing them to light. The resulting "rayograms" parody Bazin's notion of the objective lens. Here there is no lens and the "real" is turned into the abstract.

When, again in the 1920s, photography became more common in journalism and advertising, manipulation of the image became extreme. Removed from the status of art—with all its implications of personal style, subjective vision, and revelation—the photograph became a tool for representing specific commercial and political points of view with the purpose of selling commodities and focusing opinions. Shifting from a cultural realm of style and ideological determination in which individual expression counted strongly, photography became part of another, a corporate style in which the image of a politician making a speech, or a group of strikers in a menacing posture, or a woman assuming a conventional pose of seduction while wearing a particular brand of makeup or clothing has specific designs on the viewer and asks for specific responses, to make a political point or show a hamburger in the best light—especially when the hamburger is painted, sprayed, lit, and in general "styled" to make it look the best it can.

Images like these are obviously determined by external, cultural, economic, and political needs. But the image in the cause of economics and politics is different from the image in the cause of art only in its purpose. All images, all stories, all creations made by people have designs, in all senses of the term. The particular designs of journalism and advertising photography are narrow and focused, wanting the viewer to respond with a political action, hatred for a dictator, putting money into circulation by purchasing a product, in a word, buying into something—an attitude, idea, commodity, or ideology (which subsumes the rest). This kind of photography does not primarily imitate, reveal, or show. Rather, it exhorts, cajoles, and manipulates. It exploits fully the one abiding reality of representation and mediation: a call for some kind of response from the viewer. Something does indeed come between the thing itself and the image. In the case of the work of art, that "something" is a form and structure that ask of us an emotional and intellectual response meant to help us understand the artist and the way she understands the world. In the case of the journalistic, advertising, or political image, that something is a form and structure that ask us to agree to the general values of our culture and the various commodities it creates, to form an opinion, to spend money or cast a vote. In the case of movies, form and structure ask us to respond to many of these same requests simultaneously.

Reality as Image

The argument of this book is that reality is always a mutually agreed upon social construct, a more or less common consensus about what is out there and what it all means to most people. Our shared ideas of truth, beauty, morality, sexuality, politics, and religion; the ways we interpret the world and make decisions on how we act in it are determined by a complex process of education, assimilation, acculturation, and assent that begins at birth. It is a cliché that human beings are out of touch with nature, and that more than a few of us are out of touch with reality. The fact is, even when we are in touch, it's not with some given natural world or some objective, existing reality. Being in touch with nature means acting upon a learned response to the natural world. In fact, responding with awe in the face of natural beauty dates back only to the eighteenth century and became a major cultural event only in the nineteenth. Before the late seventeenth century, people in Western Europe did not pay much attention to nature's grandeur; they were not moved by it nor did they care much to contemplate it. A mountain range was something in the way. A complex shift in sociological and aesthetic responses occurred in the early eighteenth century and can be traced in its development through travel literature and then in poetry, fiction, and philosophy. By the mid-eighteenth century, wild, mountainous landscapes became the site of grand, overwhelming emotional response. The mountains had not, themselves, changed; cultural response had. The "Sublime," the effect of being transported before nature's wildness and in front of representations of that wildness in painting and poetry, was born. With it came nineteenth-century romanticism and attitudes toward the natural world that remain with us still.

Reality is not an objective, geophysical phenomenon like a mountain. Reality is always something said or understood about the world. The physical world is "there," but reality is always a polymorphous, shifting complex of mediations, a kind of multifaceted lens, constructed by the changing attitudes and desires of a culture. Reality is a complex image of the world that many of us choose to agree to. The photographic and cinematic image is one of the ways we use this "lens" (here in a quite literal sense) to interpret the complexities of the world.

The Wachowski brothers attempt to simplify this complexity. Stone and others represent it with clarity and, paradoxically, all its ambiguities.

Reality becomes a kind of cultural baseline upon which we can build a variety of responses. One response is a feeling of security. We feel safe in front of something that strikes us as "real" or realistic. Another response is to dismiss someone who doesn't seem to be operating from this same base. We bless something (a film, a painting, a novel, a political program, a way of life) with the name of realism if it comforts us with something we desire or are familiar with, or have been told we should desire or be familiar with. We are asked or we ask someone to face reality when we or someone else acts in unfamiliar ways. We say "that's not realistic" to dismiss someone or something that does not fit into our range of beliefs, hopes, or desires. "Get real," we say. "Get a life."

So, when the critic André Bazin said that the history of art is equal to the history of people's desire to save an image of the real world, he quickly modified this idea by saying that the desire to capture reality is in fact the desire "to give significant expression to the world." In that phrase "significant expression" lies the key. It's not the world we see in the image but its significant, mediated expression. For Bazin, such expression becomes very significant in photography and film because of the apparent lack of interference from a human agent. This is a peculiar paradox. The image is a significant expression of the real world; it almost *is* the real world because its image is formed without human interference. Recall Bazin's theory that, at the instant of transferring the image to the film, the photograph occurs without human intervention. As we have seen, this theory has a kernel of truth but is deeply compromised by all the manipulation that goes on before and after the image is actually made (and even while the image is being made, because lenses are not neutral). Out of the paradox come many of our confusions over what the photographic and cinematic image actually is and actually does.

FROM THE PHOTOGRAPHIC TO THE CINEMATIC IMAGE

The alleged reality of the cinematic image is, in reality, a mechanical event. In a sense, film itself is a reality machine. Time and space—the coordinates of Western art, story, and life—are represented by the vertical strip of images that travels through the projector. Twenty-four photographs, or frames, go past the projector lens each second. A simple, very nineteenth-century mechanical process pulls the filmstrip down, one frame at a time, while a shutter in the shape of a Maltese cross opens and closes the lens so that each frame is projected on the screen in its turn. The resulting illusion is extraordinary. Because of the operation of the shutter, the screen is actually dark for a total of almost thirty minutes during an average two-hour film. And because of a cognitive desire to attach the events of one image to the next, and thanks to perceptual optics that cause our eyes to see images fused together above a certain rate of flicker, the

FIGURE 1.6 Reading through the code to see the simulated digital world. *The Matrix* (Andy Wachowski, Larry Wachowski, 1999).

series of stills projected on the screen is interpreted by our brains as a continuous flow. Space and time appear unified and ongoing. Even on video or DVD the images scan in sequence across the screen. Analog mechanics have become transformed into digital electronics and will soon replace the filmstrip. But the result is still the illusion of a unified and temporally progressive series of spaces, not the thing itself, but its analog representation. Remember the character in the *Matrix* who could actually read the digital stream that made up the simulated world? He—in the fiction of that particular film—was getting close to "reality," despite the fact that the "reality" created by the code was not reality at all.

Moving Images

The search for "reality" in photographic images moved with some speed in the nineteenth century when it joined with the invention (or, more appropriately, the inventions) of cinema. Before the very late nineteenth century, the moving image and the photograph developed along separate lines. Projections of painted images, sometimes called magic lanterns, had been around since the seventeenth century. Various devices that created an illusion of figures in motion, or the sense of moving images in a large space surrounding the viewer—devices with wonderful names like zoetropes, phenakistoscopes, thaumatropes, cycloramas, and panoramic views—had been around since the eighteenth century and reached their apogee in the nineteenth. These were mostly toys or sideshows that in various ways placed painted images in progressively different positions of movement on the inside of a revolving drum. By peering through slits in the side of the turning drum, or—in the case of cycloramas—standing in front of an unrolling canvas, the figures or painted landscapes seemed to elide into each other in a semblance of continuous motion.

Magic lanterns, zoetropes, and photography intersected in the late nineteenth century in a quasi-scientific way through the work of two photographers,

Eadweard Muybridge and Etienne-Jules Marey. Muybridge was born in England and did much of his work in America. Marey was French. In their work, the nineteenth-century curiosity about mechanical invention, industry, and the ways in which both could overcome the limitations of time and space met and pointed to the development of movies—a time and space machine that rivaled the locomotive and the telegraph.

Muybridge and Marey photographed human and animal movements in ways that analyzed the motion into its component parts. Marey actually used a gunlike photographic mechanism to "shoot" his photographs (and the terms "shooting a picture" and a "shot" originate from that machine). With its aura of scientific investigation, their work situates one branch of photography in that tradition of Western culture that seeks to analyze and quantify nature. It very roughly duplicates the discovery and implementation of perspective in painting during the fourteenth century; both are part of the larger movement to comprehend, own, and control the natural world, to become the visual owner of the image, even enter it imaginatively. With the advent of film, science and technology and imagination merged to make the reality machine.

Leland Stanford, a former governor of California who liked both horses and science, invited Eadweard Muybridge to help him settle a wager concerning whether or not at one point in a horse's gallop all four hoofs leave the ground. Muybridge proved that they do by taking a series of photographs at high speeds. Muybridge and Stanford went on to publish photographs of animals in motion in *Scientific American,* and Muybridge parlayed this into a career of

FIGURE 1.7 Before the moving picture, photographers began analyzing motion into its component parts through multiple exposure. One of the most important of these experimenters was Etienne-Jules Marey (1890).

public lectures in which he demonstrated his analytic series of shots of animals—as well as naked people—in motion. He published a version of his work in 1887, the eleven-volume *Animal Locomotion*. (Marey had published his animal locomotion studies, called *La machine animale*, in France in 1873.) Muybridge further combined his analytic photographs with the old kinetoscope-zoetrope toy to create an illusion of movement of his animals and people and, by 1881, he was projecting them on a wall to a large audience. Scientific investigation, commerce, and spectacle merged in the projected image.

The image was becoming a commodity. The rapidity of this event was accelerated during the last decade of the nineteenth century when Thomas Alva Edison's employee, William K. L. Dickson, developed a way to record moving images on a Kinetograph and show them on a Kinetoscope. Edison had wanted to make moving images as an accompaniment for his phonograph, but decided to concentrate on the image alone, thereby holding back the development of sound film for almost thirty years. The work of Edison's company in the late nineteenth century led to a slow but steady proliferation of moving images in peep shows, in which "flip cards" or a film loop was viewed through a viewer in a machine; in nickelodeons, where working-class people paid a nickel to go into a small room and see a short film projected on a sheet; and finally by the 1920s in the movie palaces built as part of the successful attempt of moviemakers to create a "respectable" middle-class audience for their images. By the late twenties, in an economic slump, the movie studios revived Edison's original notion of synchronizing image to sound and made "talking pictures" to the delight of audiences and a resulting rise in box office receipts.

The steady progression from the individual photographers, inventors, and entrepreneurs who developed the moving image up to the film studios, which were actually large-scale factory operations that mass-produced these images, may seem, at first, a big leap, but it took less than twenty-five years.

The immediate and almost instantaneous emergence around the world of movies as a popular commercial art was just slightly in advance of the great boom of popular culture that would take place in the 1920s. Film's invention came with the great nineteenth-century technologies that included telegraphy and the railroads. Its beginnings coincided with the growing influence of newspapers. It completed its growth as a mass medium in the twenties, at the same time as radio, and each shared in the other's popularity, radio shows often consisting of spoken versions of film. In the end, film infiltrated the imagination more than any other nineteenth-century invention because it told stories with images. It also made its storytellers rich.

The popularity of movies was so great that, soon after 1900, demand for films exceeded supply. Various theater-owner entrepreneurs on the East Coast, most of them first-generation immigrants from Eastern Europe who had engaged in wholesale and retail selling before entering the business of film exhibition, decided that the best way to supply their theaters with product was to manufacture it themselves. They would make the images they needed to sell. They fought with Edison, who attempted to control the patents on his motion picture machines and who sometimes employed thugs to beat up the filmmakers and take their equipment away (constituting what film historians call the "patent wars" of 1910 to 1913). The filmmakers went to California to escape Edison's reach, settled in Los Angeles, and rather quickly established their own tightly knit companies that by the 1920s had evolved into the studios that centralized all facets of motion picture production and exist, if only in name, to this day.

In the history of film, the first quarter of the twentieth century was a particularly active period of creativity on all levels and in many countries: the development of film's visual narrative structure; the creation, the buying and the selling of studios and human talent; the invention of the star system; the integration of the entire production and distribution of images through theaters owned by the studios, which guaranteed that the studios had an automatic outlet for their products. This is—in very compressed form that we will open up in the next chapter—the history of production that moved from an individual, director-based activity into a huge industrial operation headed by an executive who delegated individual films to producers and peopled by an enormous in-house staff of writers, directors, composers, designers, electricians, actors, and other craftspeople.

The speed of the process by which moviemaking developed into commerce was driven by the willingness of audiences to look and look and look and want to see more and more. Movies supplied a visual imagination and narrative flow for the culture at large. They extended basic stories of popular culture—stories of sexuality and romance, captivity and release, family and heroism, individualism and community—into visual worlds that were immediately comprehensible, almost tactile, *there*, in front of the viewers' eyes. In the movies, time and space appeared as if intact. Human figures moved and had emotions. Life seemed to be occurring. The moving image was a vibrant, story-generating, meaning-generating thing. More than literature, painting, or the photograph, moving images eloquently expressed what many, almost most, of the people across economic and social classes wanted to hear and see. That what they were hearing and seeing was an illusion in every respect seemed not to matter. It might, in fact, have contributed to film's popularity. Seeing and feeling in the secure knowledge that no obvious consequences are involved is an important aspect of our response to any aesthetic experience. The moving image was a particular attraction to everyone who wanted to see more, feel more, and do it in the safe embrace of an irresistible story. It still is.

In the following chapters, we will analyze the endurance of the desire to see and how the desire is created and maintained. We will examine the elements of image, motion, story, creator, and creation, and the culture they and we inhabit. We will examine how and why moving images work and speculate about why we respond to them. In the course of that examination, we will try to account for a great number of kinds of films and filmmakers, and film viewers, too.

NOTES AND REFERENCES

The Truth of the Image   Some of the best analysis of the use of digital
imagery in filmmaking is by Lev Manovish, *The Language of New Media*
(Cambridge, MA: MIT Press, 2003). Basic resources for information on the
way we perceive image and reality include Rudolf Arnheim, *Art and Visual
Perception* (Berkeley and Los Angeles: University of California Press, 1974)
and E. H. Gombrich, *Art and Illusion* (London: Phaidon, 1977).

Perspective and the Pleasures of Tricking the Eye   Professor Sharon Gerstel
of the University of Maryland supplied information about the history of
perspective. Erwin Panofsky's *Perspective as Symbolic Form,* trans.
Christopher S. Wood (New York: Zone Books, 1991), is a good source for the
theory of perspective. Professor Elizabeth Loizeaux of the University of
Maryland offered ideas about the camera obscura. Michel Foucault's essay
"Las Meninas" argues the theory of perspective as a means of owning the
space of a painting. It is in *The Order of Things* (New York: Random House,
1970), pp. 3–16.

Photograph and Reality   The references to and quotations from André Bazin
are from *What Is Cinema?* vol. I, trans. Hugh Gray (Los Angeles and
Berkeley: University of California Press, 1968), p. 12. This is an invaluable
book for understanding the theories of reality and the moving image. See
also Bill Nichols, *Ideology and the Image* (Bloomington: Indiana University
Press, 1981). For an emotional and theoretical discussion of photography,
see Roland Barthes, *Camera Lucida : Reflections on Photography,* trans. Richard
Howard (New York: Hill and Wang, 1981). A classic work on the Sublime in
literature is M. S. Abrams, *The Mirror and the Lamp: Romantic Theory and the
Critical Tradition* (New York: Oxford University Press, 1985). In the 1970s
and 1980s painters called photorealists took Polaroids of their subjects—a
human face, a city street, a diner, a motorcycle. They placed a grid over the
photograph and a corresponding grid over the canvas and then copied the
photograph, square by corresponding square, onto the canvas. When you
look at a photographic reproduction of a photorealist painting, you often
can't tell that it's a painting.

Moving Images   Material on early movie machines, Marey, Muybridge, and
Edison can be found in Charles Musser, *The Emergence of Cinema: The
American Screen to 1907* (New York: Charles Scribner's Sons, 1990),
pp. 15–132. For Etienne-Jules Marey, see Marta Braun, *Picturing Time: The
Work of Etienne-Jules Marey (1830–1904)* (Chicago: University of Chicago
Press, 1992). David A. Cook's *A History of Narrative Film* 3rd Edition (New
York: W. W. Norton & Company, 1996) and Kristin Thompson and David
Bordwell's *Film History: An Introduction* 6th ed. (New York: McGraw-Hill,
2003) are excellent sources for information about the development of film as
art and industry. See also Scott Bukatman, "Gibson's Typewriter," in *Flame*

Wars: The Discourse of Cyberculture, ed. Mark Dery (Durham: North Carolina University Press, 1994), pp. 73–74. Anne Friedberg, *Window Shopping: Cinema and the Postmodern* (Los Angeles and Berkeley: University of California Press, 1993), offers a good reading of nineteenth-century technology and the development of mass media.

FORMAL STRUCTURES: HOW FILMS TELL THEIR STORIES

THE IMAGE, THE WORLD, AND THE FILM STUDIO

The evolution of the photographic image into the moving narrative image is it-self a narrative of the making and comprehension of illusions. It is a narrative that runs almost as smoothly as a good Hollywood film. And it is a narrative that is tightly linked to the economic history of filmmaking. Almost from the be-ginning, filmmaking and moneymaking went hand in hand, one determining the other. Filmmakers, from very early on, understood on an intuitive level that images were profoundly manipulable. Even more, the filmmakers knew that by their manipulating the image, the image in turn would manipulate how and what people saw and the way they responded to what they saw. This would in its turn create the desire to see more images and to pay to see more. As sophis-ticated as the Renaissance painters, who plotted the sight lines in their paintings to create the illusion of depth and presence, filmmakers could plot all aspects of the image for very similar purposes. Sight lines, plot lines, character, spectator positioning—how an ideal viewer is literally created by the images and the nar-rative going on on the screen—all are planned to reduce the sense of distance between spectator and image and to optimize an illusion of participation.

From Image to Narrative

Let us take a moment and stay with the early development of the moving image and its stories in order to more easily understand the structuring of illusions and the formation of conventions—those structures of form and content that, once invented, are used over and over again. This chapter will start with an examination of how image and narrative structure were formed and then move into a discussion of how that form and its variations were perpetuated throughout the history of film. We need to understand the formation of image and story and then go on to its meanings.

Moving-picture projection was developed almost at the same time in the United States, France, England, Germany, and other countries around the world. In 1888, Eadweard Muybridge, the photographer, visited Thomas Alva Edison, the inventor. Muybridge urged Edison to combine Muybridge's image projector, the zoopraxiscope, with Edison's phonograph. In 1889, Edison met Etienne-Jules Marey, who had developed a moving-image filmstrip, in Paris. In 1891, Thomas Edison's assistant, William K. L. Dickson, demonstrated a viewing machine in which could be seen a smoothly moving image of a man— Dickson himself. In France, in 1895, Auguste and Louis Lumière projected a short film they had made of workers leaving their factory. The French magician Georges Méliès, who had watched the films of the Lumière brothers, projected his first film in 1896.

The Edison Company's early attempts at filmmaking were of single, staged events: a co-worker sneezing, a couple kissing —the erotic image emerging in cinema at its very start. The Lumière brothers shot events going on in the world: their workers leaving their factory, a train arriving at a station. But they soon began staging incidents: a child squirting a gardener with a water hose, brother Auguste feeding his baby. The magician, Méliès, on the other hand, worked largely inside his studio, mocking up images, creating trick shots on film. He showed people disappearing in the middle of a scene, people underwater, men traveling to the moon. Before distributing the finished film, Méliès had his factory workers hand-paint each frame, creating an illusion of color.

This greatly reduced history may give a faulty impression. While we know the history of Edison's work, as well as what was happening in France and in other countries where inventions similar to Edison's were appearing at the end of the nineteenth century, it grows increasingly difficult to develop a coherent history of film's very rapid early development after this point. It is especially hard to say who was the "first" to do anything for the simple reason that approximately three-quarters of all films made during the **silent era** (roughly 1895–1927) are lost. But the Lumière brothers, Méliès, and the Edison factory

FIGURE 2.1   Film and the erotic are linked in some of the earliest images we have. *The Kiss* (1896).

FIGURE 2.2 The Lumière brothers filmed things happening in the world and also made things happen for the benefit of their cameras. From its earliest moments, film was attracted to slapstick comedy, based on physical interaction of people and objects. Louis Lumière, *Watering the Gardener* (1895).

do provide us with models for certain lines of development in film, lines by no means straight or uncomplicated. What they developed leads to a notion—a theory, actually—that three fundamental conventions of filmmaking emerged from their work. From the Edison factory came both the Hollywood studio system, with its division of labor, and the **classical Hollywood** or **classical narrative style**, based on character and action. The Lumières pointed the direction to the **documentary,** to film's power to record events that would occur anyway, even if the camera were not present (we will talk in some detail about documentary filmmaking in Chapter 8). From Georges Méliès' magic trick films came the cinema of fantasy, of science fiction and the wondrous voyage, which would, of course, become an important part of Hollywood filmmaking.

Another, much later, French filmmaker, Jean-Luc Godard, who throughout his career as critic and director from the 1950s to the present has been interrogating the nature of the film and television image, came to a different conclusion. He suggested (through a character in his 1967 film, *La Chinoise*) that the Lumière brothers, those presumed documentarians and makers of *actualités*—events filmed as they were happening, events that *would* be happening even if the camera weren't there—did not in fact give us documentaries of late nineteenth-century Parisian life. From the prospect of a century, Godard suggested that what the Lumières really made constitutes our fantasy images of what Paris looked like in the late nineteenth century. Their images constitute the imaginary—the shared image fantasy—of the way things were, through the images of film. Méliès, Godard suggests, seems to be the documentarian of the fantasies of late nineteenth-century, middle-class France.

This is a neat turning of things on their heads. More than an intellectual puzzle, Godard's proposition gets to the root of the question of the image. Just because the Lumière brothers turned their cameras on events in the street or the railway station does not make them recorders of things as they were. Indeed, we know that they set up many of their shots in advance. They composed their images carefully, often employing the fundamentals of perspective invented during the Renaissance. Because Méliès made trick shots in his studio does not make him a mere fantasist. Each was involved in different kinds of early cinematic mediation, of putting on the screen images that were not about reality but about different ways of constructing reality cinematically, different ways of seeing and interpreting the world. The same is true of the work of the Edison factory. Edison's film inventor, William K. L. Dickson, made moving images that, like the French, moved people's imaginations, all the while working toward the commercial exploitation of his inventions. The work of the Edison factory prefigures the Hollywood process in which commodities demonstrating the imagination's ability to fashion images that are eloquent and moving can be manufactured for profit.

Ultimately, cinema did not evolve simply into two or three separate paths, but into various branches, growing out of basic impulses, almost never pure, to see, manipulate, and represent the world in images. "Documentary" and "fiction" intertwine in curious ways. Film sees the world from a variety of perspectives, which often intersect. Whatever the origin of the moving image—whether it is a recording of what is already there in the world or made up in the studio—imagination, culture, ideology, and economics intervene. They mediate and form what we finally see on the screen; we, as viewers, mediate in turn, interpreting the images to make them meaningful to us.

THE ECONOMICS OF THE IMAGE

As cinema developed, the impulses of the Lumières, Méliès, and Edison were joined in intriguing ways. From the Edison factory came the economic impulse, the urge to treat the image as commodity, to own it, rent it, sell it, profit from it. From the Lumière brothers came the urge to reveal, to present an image of what appears to be the world as it is, but always turns out to be the world as it is seen in a particular way in film and the other visual arts. They also sold and profited from their images. From Méliès came a sense of the image as the space of fantasy; he also developed a concept and methods of image fabrication that finally came to form the basis of American film production, part of its economy of manufacture. Méliès also sold his images and profited from them.

FIGURE 2.3 The triumph of artifice. Human figures (on the right) are combined with drawings. Georges Méliès, *A Trip to the Moon* (1902).

The work of Méliès was about control, crafting every element of the image, putting it together, element by element, for specific effect. Whereas Auguste and Louis Lumière allowed a certain serendipity to occur when they exposed motion picture film to the outside world, Méliès arranged and accounted for every element in the shot. Working in the studio, using **stop action** (shutting off the camera, removing or putting something in the scene, then starting the camera, so

the person or object seemed to pop into or out of view), working with minia-
tures, painted backdrops, and then hand-coloring the film, he and his factory allowed nothing to occur by chance and little of the outside world to intrude.
Even though legend has it that the first stop-action event in a Méliès film occurred by accident, in fact the elements of his image making were calculated,
created, and circulated by the filmmaker and seen by the viewer in a closed ac-
counting system in which nothing appeared by chance. This was to prove to be
the future of the Hollywood system of image making, where "reality" is a product manufactured in the studio, and economy means not only the calculation of
profit and loss but the entire circulation of imagination, production, distribution,
and exhibition, each calculated to create the maximum return of emotion and
grosses at the box office. We cannot understand film, American film in particular, without understanding this complex economic system.

The System Develops: Buster Keaton and Charlie Chaplin

As an example of the way these various threads became woven into the kinds
of films we watch today, I want to remain in the early history of cinema and
concentrate on two comic filmmakers, Buster Keaton and Charlie Chaplin,
whose films and working methods remain a model for current film.

Before the **studio system,** filmmakers experimented with different attitudes
toward the external world and the economics of the image. Many filmed outdoors, where light was available and backgrounds were ready-made. Much of
the pleasure of watching the films of the silent comedian Buster Keaton, for example, comes from seeing images go by of the world of early twentieth-century
America. This world is not foregrounded, however. Keaton's images are not
documentary, not about chance, but rather about his body in flight, running,
falling, endangered, engineered into precarious situations. One of the great moments in silent film comedy comes in Keaton's *Steamboat Bill, Jr.* (1928). Keaton
stands in the midst of a terrific storm and the facade of a house behind him suddenly falls. It is a full-sized house, or at least the front of one, towering over the
still figure of Keaton. When it falls, the sense of his fragility is marked. He will
be crushed. But the engineering of the trick is such that when the facade of the
house falls straight over him, the cutout of the window in the middle of the top
floor neatly falls around his body. He stands stock-still without a flinch, and
then runs away.

The essential physicality of this stunt is unthinkable in any other medium because none other, not even live theater, could create the illusion of the *thereness*
of the actor's body and the house falling on him within a space that is so obviously in the world. Only film can make things look "real" by means of fabricat-
ing and composing reality out of a trick occurring in the way it configures, and
we perceive, space. In the case of the Keaton gag, the two-dimensionality of the
image (like all images, film has no depth, so things can be hidden, angles and

points of view can trick our eye, depth and volume can be manufactured), the obvious weight of the building—which was, in fact, a set and probably extremely light—the presence of the body, that figure in a landscape that film depends upon like no other medium other than painting, make the stunt startling, funny, and in the peculiar manner of film, "real."

Manipulated, used, and also *there*, the human figure and the landscape are part of the mise-en-scène of a film by Keaton or any other great physical comedian, including the much maligned Jerry Lewis. **Mise-en-scène**—originally a theatrical term that literally means "put in the scene"—is an element of any film, comic or not, and refers to the way space is organized and perceived in a film, including the way figure and background are composed. Mise-en-scène also includes lighting and movement, the use of black and white or color, the distance between camera and figure—everything that happens within the frame, including the frame itself. In almost any Keaton film we see Buster and the streets, curbs, houses, cars, and people around him. Space is used generously; it is open and wide and many things occur in the frame other than the main action. Keaton himself becomes one of the many elements that occur within that space. At any time, any one of these elements may be called upon to become a prop for a gag or a stunt. As in the case of the house facade in *Steamboat Bill, Jr.*, parts of the world may be built specifically for the gag. But even the apparently spontaneous appearance of people and streets in a Keaton film is part of its preconceived presence, its mise-en-scène. Our response to Keaton's images is—as Jean-Luc Godard said of the Lumières—the response of our fantasy of what the world might have looked like. Even in Keaton, we do not see the world itself. We see its image. Its visual memory. And that remains strong enough, present enough to surprise and delight us.

Keaton's great rival in silent comedy, Charlie Chaplin, worked somewhat closer to Méliès' method of studio shooting. Chaplin had less use for the outside world than did Keaton. He worked almost exclusively in the studio and reduced the mise-en-scène to himself. The main signifying element in a Chaplin film is Chaplin. He might indeed engineer a complex gag, as when he gets caught in the gears of an elaborate machine in *Modern Times*. (*Modern Times* is a post–silent film made in 1936, but Chaplin doesn't talk.) Constructed in the studio, the process of the gag highlights Chaplin and his combat with the guts of the machine rather than the mad confluence of physical structure and the body as in Keaton and the falling house.

Foregrounding his own persona and making that persona, the Tramp, a representation of character, attitude, and sentiment, a figure onto which the viewer could overlay his or her own desires, vulnerabilities, and feelings of social or economic inadequacy, Chaplin could demand that focus be kept on his body. Here he was quite unlike either the Lumière brothers or Méliès and closer, perhaps, to the tradition of Edison. The latter foregrounded characters and faces in his early films; Méliès and the Lumières worked with a larger mise-en-scène in which human figures were often only one element of many. For them, the

FIGURE 2.4 Keaton loved to place himself within the physical world, allowing the camera to observe the body caught and triumphing. Buster Keaton and Clyde Bruckman, *The General* (1927).

FIGURE 2.5 The subject of his own mise-en-scène, Chaplin understood that viewers were interested in seeing him; and he obliged. Charles Chaplin, *Modern Times* (1936).

moving image represented intersections between subject, foreground, and background. For Méliès, those intersections were crafted together in the studio, parts of them literally by hand, whereas Chaplin's studio work uses little of the potential sleight of hand (or eye) offered by the camera, by paintings, and by trick shots. His was the cinema of personality, of the star.

The different styles of Keaton and Chaplin represent, in a sense, the next level in the culture of the image, in the processes of cinematic representation and the transition from film as craft to film as commodity. Their work also puts another turn on our investigation of the reality of the image. As comedians, the images they made and the stories they told exaggerated the world and the place of the human figure in it. Though both filmmakers indulged in the comic movements of falls and chases, pursuits and being hit by blunt instruments, their styles were quite different. Keaton saw his cinematic world as a place for combat between his body and the physical things of the world. Chaplin saw his as a site of sentimental triumph, of the cleverness of the "little guy," conquering odds and winning the heart of a simple woman. Image making for him provided the vehicle to carry his character of the Tramp through misadventures to redemption and the triumph over class, from despair to a measure of self-possession. He wanted all this to take place in a world whose presence was immediate and apparently unmediated. He wanted his audience's hearts.

But we can find a delightful paradox when we compare Chaplin with Keaton that makes the parallels with Méliès even more interesting. As much as he liked to work his gags in the middle of the ongoing, outside world, Keaton, like Méliès, also understood how he could manipulate the components of the shot to best effect. Keaton liked to make the artificiality of the image part of the joke of his films. In *The Playhouse* (1921), Keaton plays with multiple exposure, performing an entire vaudeville act by himself, with himself as every member of the audience. In *Sherlock, Jr.* (1924), Keaton is a movie projectionist who dreams himself into the screen, into the image, and is overcome by its conjuries. Scenes change; the weather changes; the flow of images confuses him and causes him to take pratfalls.

This sequence in *Sherlock, Jr.* is among the great statements and admissions of how artificial the film image actually is. Keaton, in all his films, is either doing or being undone by things that happen around him. Objects and people in the image conspire; Buster flees and then cleverly gets the better of them. In *Sherlock, Jr.*, he is conspired against by the very medium in which he works. The image itself turns against him. Chaplin, however, appears as the master of the image and intends to subdue it to his comic persona. He tends to battle people more than things, as Keaton does, or use things for simple, heart-tugging comic effect, as when he sticks a fork in two rolls and makes them perform a ballet or delicately eats his shoe in *The Gold Rush* (1925).

The Growth of Corporate Filmmaking

Together, Chaplin and Keaton indicate what is happening as filmmaking grows to industrial proportions and, in the course of that growth, reconciles or fudges the boundaries between illusion, realism, audience response, and corporate need. Both very independent filmmakers, their styles reflected and incorporated the complex, sometimes contradictory parts of art and commerce that would form filmmaking both in America and abroad. Even their professional careers pointed to the directions filmmaking moved in the 1920s.

Late in the twenties, Keaton, who successfully operated his own production company, signed with MGM, already one of the giants among film studios. By doing so, by signing with a studio that developed and promoted the producer system in which the director had only a small role, Keaton lost much of his creative control and creative edge. The films he made for MGM were not as good as his previous independent work, and he disappeared into obscurity until rediscovered in the 1960s. Earlier, in 1919, Charlie Chaplin, together with two of the biggest stars of the silent period, Douglas Fairbanks and Mary Pickford, along with D. W. Griffith, the great film director, formed United Artists. They first formed the company for their own films, but as financial problems grew, and the actors and directors turned control over to an important management figure in the early studio days, Joseph Schenck, UA became a major studio, though one that acted as a financing and distribution, rather than a production, company. Artists' control of the means and economics of production may have been short lived, and it never quite came back, but the origins of United Artists did indicate that some in early Hollywood understood the direction filmmaking was moving.

Chaplin and Keaton were used by the Hollywood system in different ways. Chaplin's privileging of his own star presence, making his figure the sentimental focus of a studio-bound construction in which everything is made in order to foreground the star and his story, became, in fact, the dominant mode in

American filmmaking. Becoming part owner—with two other big movie stars and a pioneering director—of a studio, Chaplin further helped the studio system to come into dominance. (Ironically, later in his life, during the U.S. government's and the film studios' anticommunist purges in the fifties, Chaplin's career and reputation were all but ruined.) Keaton's individual talent was swallowed by the studio system. Later in his life, after the old studio system collapsed, Keaton emerged from oblivion and reentered film and television, a rediscovered comic talent. Within the studios, the image that represented the world outside was subdued to the image of the world made within the studio's confines. The image made in the studio became, in turn, subdued to the attractiveness of story, star, and, always, economics. Mediated by story and star, and by the viewer's willingness to see what the story asked her to see, the image became "realistic." That is, it became transparent, invisible. It became the classical Hollywood style.

The Classical Hollywood Style

Fabricating the Image

Let's first repeat and then elaborate some basic principles. What you see when you look at a movie is not what you actually see. What you are actually seeing on the movie screen is the reflection of a strong beam of light sent through a moving ribbon of plastic. Embedded in this plastic are dark and clear areas formed by the chemical residue of a previous exposure to light. These make up the images. The screen reflects the projected images back to you, and you interpret them as objects and figures, still or in motion. This means of projecting and perceiving moving images has not changed much since the late nineteenth century when it was invented. Newer technologies, the ones employed when a film becomes a videotape or DVD, are more complicated. The original images have been transformed into analog electromagnetic waves, which are then recorded onto tape or digitized and burned into pits on a DVD, which are then read and reconverted into electrons. When they bombard the red, green, and blue phosphors of a television screen, or light the appropriate diodes of an LCD screen, a representation of the original image is created on the reverse side of the tube: an electronic representation of what was originally a representation made from light and chemicals. Soon, "film" will be digitally recorded from the outset—many already are—and the old chemical process will disappear entirely. The analog process will occur only on the decoding end, when the film is exhibited. From photography through distribution there won't be small frames of images on a ribbon of plastic, but the ones and zeros of digital code.

Our perception of cinematic narratives is an illusion, made up of fragmentary elements of light and shadow, pieced together and then interpreted as coherent, ongoing wholes. The studios who make the films were pieced together from a number of small moviemaking and movie distributing businesses in the 1910s and 1920s. Self-contained filmmaking "factories"—with employees who included everyone from writers, directors, and actors to set decorators and elec-tricians—the studios created an economy of the visible, an organized, rational-ized, commodity-driven form of production that depended upon the manufacture of a film out of various pieces, each one made by different groups of people in the studio hierarchy. The finished product depended upon the au-dience's willingness to interpret and decode those pieces, reading and respond-ing to the story they told.

In order to accomplish the manufacture of up to two films a week during the peak years of studio production, from the late twenties through the late forties, the studios had to streamline production processes. They followed essential manufacturing processes, begun in the twenties, by dividing up the work. At the top, the studio boss in Hollywood communicated with his financial officers in New York, who, by controlling the money, actually held the reins of the studio. The studio head in Hollywood settled on the stars and properties (books, plays, scripts) that were handed along to the producers. The producers, in collaboration with the studio head, in turn assigned writers, a director, and other crew to the film. By the time shooting was begun, everyone's role was laid out: shots were sketched on storyboards, sets were built, the script, usually the product of many hands, was largely finished. The work of making the film was and remains largely a process of executing a plan in precise, piecemeal fashion, so well deter-mined as to allow as few mistakes, as few time and cost overruns, as possible. We will look at the various people involved in the process in Chapter 5.

Part of the planning involves creating the images themselves as a staged process. Very often, a **shot**—which is any length of an unedited, or uncut, piece of exposed film (a close-up, or a long tracking movement of the camera, for ex-ample)—is actually put together bit by bit over a course of time, with many dif-ferent hands contributing to the construction process. In studio filmmaking, very few of the various elements of a shot—the human figures, the background, foreground, sky, scenery, buildings—need to be present at any one time in its creation. The economics of the image require that the studio break the shot ele-ments into the smallest, most manageable units, just as they break the entire production process down into manageable units. Everything that can be done indoors is. Whole sets or parts of them are put together on a sound stage or on the back lot. It's not possible to put up tall buildings in a studio, but it is possi-ble to build the lower part of a building facade and compose the shot so that the character is standing in front of a structure that appears to be large because we are inclined to want to imagine a whole even though we see only a part. In any given shot, if more of the building needs to appear, it can be added in the spe-cial effects lab, or painted on glass and put in front of the camera (recall our ear-lier discussion of the two-dimensional image; in this instance, a *background* placed in the *foreground* can, through the trick of perspective and our own ex-pectations of how space should be arranged, appear in the background when we watch the movie). Swamps are difficult places to shoot in; but a mound of dirt, a pool of water, some vegetation strewn carefully about, combined with careful lighting and composition, will convey the appropriate image. The

FIGURE 2.6 The lyricism of artificiality. Within the studio, filmmakers can pull resources together to create images that suggest more than they show. Here, the idea of a moon and some water, with the camera that starts behind the man's back (in the film, the camera gently tracks behind the man as he walks), has a lyrical and foreboding effect. F. W. Murnau, *Sunrise* (1927).

swamp sequence in the German director F. W. Murnau's American film, *Sunrise* (1927), with a spotlight standing in for the moon and the camera gracefully moving around the characters on a movie set, remains one of the most lyrical shots in the history of film, despite its utter artificiality.

Going to sea to shoot a film is an expensive and tactically difficult proposition. It is cheaper to send a second unit crew out to shoot some boats in the ocean and then do the rest in the studio. A large tank of water with a skillfully built model boat can substitute for the full-scale event out in the vagaries of the natural world. A set of the captain's deck constructed on hydraulic lifts that rocks back and forth will serve for the dialogue shots in which the characters need to be seen talking. For added realism, the set can be placed in front of a large movie screen with a projector behind it. On the screen, a film of waves and stormy sky shot by the **second unit** or taken from the studio library of stock shots can be projected while the dialogue scene is being shot. (In *Titanic*, 1997, James Cameron had most of the ship created digitally.) **Rear-screen projection** is the most common means studios used—and still use—for scenes shot in moving cars. A cutout model of a car is put in front of the screen, the driver and passenger sit and deliver their dialogue, and the street is projected on the screen behind them. In older studio films, rear-screen projection would sometimes be used to show two people simply walking down a street. The actors would be put on a treadmill.

These are relatively straightforward image manipulations. More complicated are the paintings or models or mattes of backgrounds and foregrounds that, well executed and well lit and integrated with the human figures in the frame, give the illusion of a complex and articulated world. The paintings, the models, and the actors need not be in the same place at the same time, and the painting may have openings cut out for the human figures to be projected into. A process called a "blue screen **matte**" or "traveling matte" allows the parts of the shot to be photographed in front of a blue screen. The various shots that will eventually make up one completed shot are projected one after the other through an optical printer, which is simply a projector and camera that can be carefully calibrated and synchronized with each other. The blue color is dropped out, the components of the shot merge, resulting in an image of illusory wholeness, even of illusory motion when the matte shot includes a figure in motion: Superman flying, Bruce Willis falling down an elevator shaft in *Die Hard* (1988), the SAC bomber flying over Arctic wastes in *Dr. Strangelove* (1964)—indeed almost any sequence in which a figure or object is foregrounded in front of a complicated background.

We usually think of such highly wrought special effects in relation to action or science fiction films, and we take a special pleasure in seeing the results of "f/x." We enjoy the reality effect of such shots while acknowledging their artificiality. But the fact is that all Hollywood studio films, no matter what their genre, use special effects much of the time.

And it is an old tradition. In 1903, Edwin S. Porter made a short film called *The Great Train Robbery.* An early Western and among the first films in which the story shifts back and forth between narrative sequences, it contains a scene in a railroad car where the scenery going by outside is actually processed in—taken at another time and then matched with the set of the railroad car through either rear-screen projection or optical printing. The difference between this sequence and a film by Méliès is that the trickery is not supposed to be noticed. It is not meant to be part of the visible appeal of the film. This peculiar **process shot**—as rear-screen projections or matte shots are called—is a forerunner of all those shots of people driving their cars in front of movie screens showing images of passing roads and streets, or people walking up roads whose surroundings

FIGURE 2.7 A model plane matted against a traveling matte process shot. Stanley Kubrick, *Dr. Strangelove Or: How I Learned to Stop Worrying and Love the Bomb* (1964).

FIGURE 2.8 This railroad car is a set. The image of the outside rushing by is probably created by projecting the image on a screen, or matting it in later, just behind the cutout of the door in the railroad car. Edwin S. Porter, *The Great Train Robbery* (1903).

have been painted or computed and matted into the image long after the actors have gone on to other films.

Are there shots in films in which everything we see was present when the shot was made? Certainly. This is part of the appeal of documentary films, for example, in which the camera observes, with a minimum of intrusion, a sequence of events that might have occurred had the camera not been there. The documentarist looks for or tries to re-create a whole ongoing event, and we will examine this work in Chapter 8. The post–World War II **Italian neorealist** movement was based on making films in the street, observing people in their surroundings with an immediacy that was powerful and sometimes shocking. Hollywood took immediate notice. In the late forties and early fifties, American films used some exterior, on-location shooting, especially in low-budget gangster films. American theatrical films in the sixties and seventies, responding to yet another European innovation, the films of the **French New Wave**, tended to move away from the synthetic image, at least for a while. Sequences in cars were actually shot in cars moving along the street. Crews spent more time at locations, with actors and their surroundings present within the shot as the shot was taken. Historically, in European cinema, there has been almost as much dependence on constructing an image from component parts as there is in American filmmaking. But abroad and at home, there have been and continue to be individual filmmakers willing to go outside the studio and shoot in the world. When that happens—in the streets and countryside of Calcutta in Satyajit Ray's Apu trilogy (*Pather Panchali*, 1955; *Aparajito*, 1956; *The World of Apu*, 1959), or in the streets of New York in so many American gangster films of the 1950s, and in Martin Scorsese's best work—the image and our relationship to it change. The reality effect becomes even stronger, and the sense of seeing a world as it might actually exist makes the image stronger. Recently, a Scandinavian group of filmmakers, calling themselves "Dogma 95," have vowed, like the Italian neorealists before them, to do away with studio fabrication of the shot—to do away with the studio altogether. In their work and that of other filmmakers, both European and American, the response to the closed and secure world generated by the studio offers the opportunity of opening into a more detailed, textured, less manageable image of the world outside.

In Hollywood today, the artificial construction of the image has made a major comeback. All the old practices of rear-screen projection, matte work, and

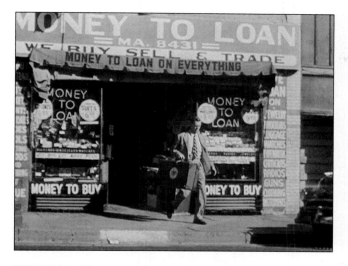

FIGURE 2.9 The gangster on the street. In Stanley Kubrick's *The Killing* (1956), Johnny Clay gets a suitcase to pack the stolen cash. The move to on-location shooting in the fifties marked an important break with the studio tradition. Many independent filmmakers, like Kubrick, working on a small budget, took their cameras outside, away from the studios. The visual texture of the mise-en-scène began to change.

FIGURE 2.10 Shot on location in Calcutta, Satyajit Ray's *The World of Apu* (1959) is the last of a trilogy of films (including *Pather Panchali*, 1955, and *Aparajito*, 1956) in which a culture is explored by seeing characters in their landscape.

other forms of image manufacture are now being done by computer. Through digital manipulation, the image is put together bit by bit. Backgrounds are rendered in three-dimensional graphics programs. Characters are pasted into the middle of crowds, the members of which are digitally duplicated (think of Mr. Smith in *The Matrix Reloaded*, 2003), or on mountaintops, or in outer space. Dinosaurs are graphically rendered and made to leap across a plain as humans look at them; a gigantic spaceship hovers over New York; a huge ocean liner hits an iceberg and sinks; an atomic bomb or a meteor destroys a city; incredible acts of transformation and destruction are possible with no location necessary other than a computer terminal. Anything and anyone can be placed anywhere and made to do anything—even in an apparently simple, "realistic" shot. The same holds true for sound. Digital sound allows intricate sonic mixes to be made in which every single sound, from footsteps to the human voice, is built and processed to achieve the best effect. The purpose of digital image and sound manipulation is the same as old-fashioned optical work: to save the filmmakers money while achieving the greatest reality effect.

Paradoxically, major digital effects are very expensive and time-consuming, but they give the studios the greatest amount of control possible and engineer the viewer into the image and then beyond it into the story. With the digital, there is a seemingly unlimited possibility to substitute spectacle for substance. There are times in the economy of filmmaking when expense is born for the sake of control. But even this is changing. The more common the use of digital composition, the cheaper it will become, and in a few

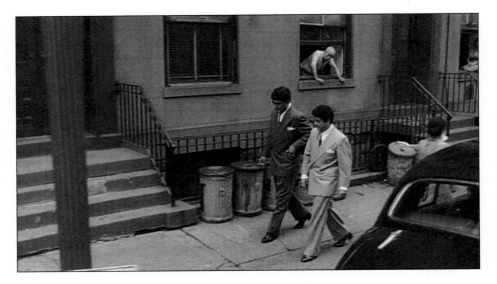

FIGURE 2.11   In almost neorealist style, Scorsese shoots his characters in the city streets
(*Raging Bull*, 1980).

years, the old filmmaking process will disappear altogether and digital cameras
will directly transform the image into the abstractions of binary code, which will
be delivered via digital tape or DVD or satellite to theaters or high-definition
television. The recent *Star Wars* episodes, for example, are made digitally, with
actors inserted into a computer-generated mise-en-scène and the whole film
recorded directly onto digital tape.

The Whole and Its Parts

The construction of shots, including all the choices that go into how many elements will appear in the shot at any one time of its manufacture, and how the
shots will be edited together, is a combination of economics and aesthetics. The
economy of the image is entwined with the economy of production and the economy of perception. While the studios change, while production practices alter to
incorporate new technologies, even while some experimentation in form and content is allowed to occur as the culture surrounding filmmaking changes, the basic
structures of shot making tend to remain the same. The formal structures, the
very substructure of film construction and film viewing, are largely unchanged,
or changed so subtly that they are hardly noticeable. The production process is executed in bits and pieces, from the selection of a story to the writing of a screenplay—often by many hands—to the creation of sets, the direction of scenes, and
the **editing** of the scenes into a whole. Film is made in bits and pieces. And that is
what we see on the screen: bits and pieces of image and story so cunningly put together that they appear as if they were an ongoing whole.

Film acting, for example, is built shot by shot. A performance in a film is not a
continuous process as it is on the stage but is put together out of many parts. A

film is not shot in sequence, nor is a sequence made completely in one **take.** (For convenience, we use the term **"scene"** as the unit of action or a segment of a story, while a "sequence" is a related series of scenes or shots. In many cases, scene and sequence are used interchangeably.) Therefore, an actor has to perform in spurts, in short spasms of emotion, guided by the director and a staff member called the continuity person (or, in older Hollywood parlance, the script girl), whose job is to keep tabs on everything from the hands on a clock that may be in the shot, to the position of a necktie, to a half-completed gesture, to a facial expression or the direction of a gaze that must be held from shot to shot.

Any given part of a film can be made at any time. The middle may be shot first, the third sequence last, the end at the beginning, the next-to-last sequence just before the middle. For example, if a number of scenes throughout a film take place in the same room, it is more economical to shoot all those shots at the same time, rather than leave the set unused and then return to relight or rebuild it. If a high-priced, in-demand actor is involved in a film, it is more economical to shoot all the scenes in which that actor is involved rather than recall the actor to the set again to shoot a scene that will occur later in the narrative. If a **location**—that is, a site, usually out of doors, at a distance from the studio—is involved, all the scenes that take place at that location will be shot together, no matter where or when they appear in the film. There is a story about the making of the film *Blow-Up* (1966), directed by the Italian filmmaker Michelangelo Antonioni. He wished to film in chronological order. Two major parts of the film, one early, the other at the end, took place a day or two apart in the story, in a London park. Actual filming began in spring and concluded in the fall. When director and crew returned to the park for the last sequence, the leaves had changed color. They had to spray them green to re-create the earlier effect. An American filmmaker would have shot all the sequences in the park at one time and worked out the temporal arrangements during the editing process. Or, instead of shooting outside at all, the American filmmaker might have had a tree and some grass put up in the studio, matting in the rest of the environment in the effects lab or, these days, on a computer.

Making the Parts Invisible

Creation through bits and pieces is a production procedure, not a reception problem. In other words, as viewers we are not supposed to see the fragmentary, stop and start process that filmmaking is. With relatively few and important exceptions, films from all over the world are constructed on a principle of radical self-effacement—of rendering their form invisible while causing few economic difficulties during the creative and manufacturing process and *no* obstacle at all for the viewers during the process of reception. This is made possible through a set of conventions and assumptions by means of which the viewer will accept the illusion of transparency and see the film as an unmediated, ongoing whole, a story played out in front of her eyes. Form and structure, the artifice of the image, and the fragmentary nature of screen acting will all melt away and merge together in apparent wholeness.

This effect is not unique to movies. Recall our discussion of perspective. Although perspective is based on carefully calculated mathematical structures, the result of perspective in painting was to naturalize the image, to give the illusion of three dimensions on a two-dimensional surface and, by so doing, provide a window through which the viewer's gaze could own the contents of the image. Painting presented "content," represented things in the outside world, until late in the nineteenth century. When photography and film took over this job, painting began to represent its own form, to speak about surface, color, form, and texture. When it did, it created obstacles. Looking at abstract art, people keep wanting to know "what is it trying to show?"

Music depends upon its ability to link itself effortlessly to emotional response. Few people understand the mathematical complexities of harmony and counterpoint, know what a hemidemisemiquaver is (a musical note that is one sixty-fourth the length of a whole note), or can explain the sonata form. In the early twentieth century, a group of composers rebelled against the transparency of musical form and wrote atonal music based on the mathematical principles of the twelve-tone scale. They sought less a pathway to emotion than an expression of musical form. Their work demanded knowledge of how music works and attention to something other than the emotions of the sounds. This music was not very easy to listen to or very popular.

Prose writing also has its version of an invisible form. Reading some books requires little attention to the structure of language. The style of the book may ask the reader to concentrate instead on what the writer is saying and what his characters are doing, which correlates with our desire to see what the painting is about or feel the emotions of the music. Those writers who concentrate on form, who foreground the structure of their prose and how it makes meaning—Henry James, James Joyce, Samuel Beckett, Jorge Luis Borges, Toni Morrison, to name a few—become the focus of academic study. In ordinary reading, though, the greatest compliment many will give to a book is that it is a "page turner." The phrase implies the reader moves past page, prose, form, and style into the movement of story and character.

There is no equivalent phrase for film, probably because there are relatively few films that are *not* the equivalent of "page turners" and because, while we are watching, the "pages," the images, are turned for us. The assumption is that the structure and style of any film will be invisible, allowing the viewer to enter and move into the story and the emotions of the characters. The point is for us to be carried away by plot and the motivations of the characters. Image structure and editing, the way the story is put together, are subservient to the story and the characters' lives.

Story, Plot, and Narration

Our task, now that we have an inkling of how a film is put together and its parts made invisible (which we will examine in greater detail in the following chapters), is to bring the form and structure of film—its means of production, construction, and comprehension—back into consciousness and make them visible again. To start, let's redefine "story." This is what the film tells us, the process of events the characters go through and enact. Plot is the abstract scheme of that story, what we summarize after we've seen the film, what film reviewers on TV and in newspapers give us. Narrative is the actual telling of the story, the way the story is put together, formed, and articulated.

Narrative is the structure of the story. Take Steven Spielberg's *Jaws* (1975) as an example. Here's some plot: a great white shark terrorizes a beach town, kills people, and is finally hunted down by three men in a boat. I could elaborate that into something closer to the story, although it would be more description than story and in any case would be *my* story, derived from the film, because I am giving it narrative structure: Sheriff Brody is pulled from a peaceful domestic life by the intrusion of the terrible creature into the town he has been hired to protect. The shark attacks people, but the elders of the town want it kept quiet so as not to ruin holiday tourist business. There is tension between Brody and the elders, and also uncertainty. Brody has been hired to do the bidding of the town, but he has a moral responsibility to protect the innocent. And so forth.

I could also elaborate this in a way that comes closer to the film's narrative: the presence of the shark is indicated by music—low, almost staccato chords played on bass fiddles, a mirror of the high staccato strings used in Hitchcock's *Psycho*. When the shark is ready to attack, the film allows us to look as if through the shark's eyes, moving in the water toward its prey. Suspense is further created by playing with the gaze of Sheriff Brody on the beach. He looks and looks at the water. People move in front of him, and he has to bend and rise to see. There are false alarms, and our tension keeps rising. The intercutting of **shot/reverse shot** from Brody (the shot) to what he sees (the **reverse shot**) reaches a climax when Brody finally does see something in the water. At this point, Spielberg uses a device that Alfred Hitchcock developed. By combining two movements of the camera—a **tracking** shot in one direction and a **zoom** in the opposite—he shows Brody as if space were collapsing around him, thereby heightening our awareness of some exciting and terrifying event.

In this brief analysis, I began by recounting plot and then moved from plot to structure, that is, from content to form, describing some of the ways the narrative is put together to tell us its story. This analysis also puts the structure into a context by revealing that Spielberg didn't invent everything but borrowed and developed some stylistic devices from another filmmaker. The point is that all aspects of a film are based on formal, structural principles and that meaning and emotion as well are always communicated by structure. We see, understand, and feel by the way we are manipulated by the shot and the arrangement of shots edited into a narrative structure that tells a story. Meaning or emotion does not exist without a form to communicate it. We never simply "know" something, or see something, or are told something. When we respond to a film, there is always a formal structure driving that response. The development of that structure occurred intuitively during film's early history, beginning with very short "one-reelers" that showed one event—a couple kissing, a train

FIGURE 2.12 On the level of plot, Brody is looking out for the shark. But the structure of this sequence does more than tell us that: it draws our gaze to the character's and, by alternately looking at him and assuming his own point of view, creates expectation and excitement— especially when that point of view is blocked. Steven Spielberg, *Jaws* (1975).

entering a station—and within a few years, in films such as *The Great Train Robbery* (1903), directors began combining shots, leading to the long period of experimentation undertaken by D. W. Griffith that led to what we now refer to as the classical Hollywood style.

Convention and Consciousness

The classical Hollywood (or continuity) style forms the basis of almost all American film since the early twenties. With the exception of the work of a very few directors who try different means of cinematic expression, and overseas filmmakers who battle against it in order to find their own visual statement, it is the way films make us see. Perhaps the complexities of the classical Hollywood style and the responses to it can be summed up by a notion of unconsciousness and consciousness. The classical style asks that we be unconscious of form and structure but conscious of their effects. That is, most films want us to understand them immediately, directly, without mediation. Filmmakers who wish to explore the language of cinema and make its form and structure expressive in their own right—the way some painters and novelists use the language of their art to draw attention to its own devices—want us to be conscious at all levels. They want us to know when they are cutting and to ask how the editing pattern is creating narrative meaning; to be aware of a camera movement and think about its purpose; to look *at* the way people and objects are arranged in the frame and not look *through* that frame as if it were some kind of open window or mirror.

In the end, we have to be conscious of everything in every film. To be lulled by the classical continuity style into a trance of identification with light and shadow on a white screen is not useful. Assenting to the ideology of the invisible may be relaxing, but, in an important way, it is not safe. To look through form and structure does not mean that form and structure have actually disappeared. They *are* present, working to create the meaning and generate the feelings you experience during a movie. To ignore them means that they and the corporate communities that created them are given permission to continue on their way doing what they want, telling stories that may or may not be beneficial to us in our dealings with the world. But to *read* them, consciously, analytically, with as much attention as we read those films that do not use the classical style, means that we not only are entertained, but understand why and how we are entertained.

Analyzing the illusory nature of film does not discredit it or diminish the pleasure of watching. Quite the contrary. The more you know about what you are and are not seeing, the richer the experience is, and the more reflective. It's exciting to respond emotionally and intellectually to film; to feel the story and understand how that story is being constructed; to see through the images to the characters and their turmoil and at the same time observe and understand what the images themselves are doing. It's possible and important to feel and understand, to synthesize and analyze.

We can extend this process of analysis and synthesis beyond the individual film to the individuals who are responsible for making them and then to a wider context and consider the role of film and other popular forms of entertainment in the culture at large. How do films reflect larger cultural events? Why does the culture support the conventions of story telling in film and other forms of mass entertainment? Why do films keep telling us the same stories? Who is doing the telling? First, we need to look closely at how the stories are told and examine the complexities of shot composition and editing in order to see how much work goes into making the form of film invisible.

NOTES AND REFERENCES

From Image to Narrative   The story of Muybridge and Edison and the information about early projection is from Charles Musser, *The Emergence of Cinema: The American Screen to 1907* (New York: Charles Scribner's Sons, 1990), pp. 62–68, 91. Linda Williams discusses the early development of the image and its relationship to the body in *Hard Core: Power, Pleasure, and the "Frenzy of the Visible"* (Berkeley and Los Angeles: University of California, 1989), pp. 34–57.

The Growth of Corporate Filmmaking   A complete history of United Artists can be found in Tino Balio, *United Artists: The Company Built by the Stars* (Madison: University of Wisconsin Press, 1976). Thomas Elsaesser's collection of essays, *Early Cinema: Space, Frame, Narrative* (London: British Film Institute, 1990), is a good source of information on the formation of the early film industry. See especially pp. 153–59.

3 BUILDING BLOCKS I: THE SHOT

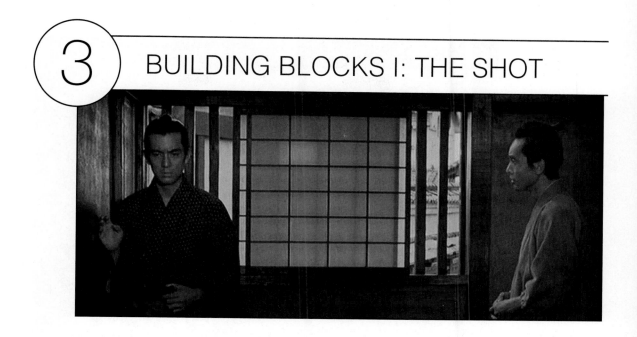

THE SHOT

Film form can be reduced to two basic elements, each of which is complex and can be used in a great variety of ways. They are the shot and the cut. A *shot* is any unbroken, unedited length of film. That length can be the entire magazine of film in a 35 mm camera (twenty minutes or more) or the much longer length of tape in a video camera. A shot can also be made in the editing room when an otherwise unedited length of film has some unwanted material trimmed from either end. The shot is determined by its physical existence as an unbroken entity—or its appearance as such.

Despite the fact that it may be made up of many parts photographed separately, the shot is cinema's unit of internal continuity. It allows film to represent space and time as connected and ongoing: it composes space and either guides the viewer's eye within that space, or offers a reflective, meditative gaze at the space. What happens in a shot can be as simple as the camera gazing at a character or as complex as a movement in which the camera follows a character across a long and articulated space. In Orson Welles's *The Magnificent Ambersons* (1942), the camera watches for many minutes as characters in a darkly lit, turn-of-the-century kitchen talk about the decline of their family and home. This is a classic example of the **long take**, in which the filmmaker allows action to proceed at length without cutting into it. The intensity of the sequence grows from the camera's unflinching gaze and the power of the actors' performance—one stuffing his face with strawberry shortcake, the other getting more and more upset. This

51

FIGURE 3.1 This shot from Orson Welles's *The Magnificent Ambersons* (1942) lasts 4 minutes, 27 seconds. Except for a camera movement at its beginning and one at its end, and the entrance of a third character, it holds on these two characters for its duration. In addition to the acting, the shot holds our attention through its lighting and its breaking of the picture plane into four parts: the table in front, the characters talking, the pots and pans in shadow behind them, and the lighted rear wall in back.

is a rare moment in film in which a performance—in the usual sense of an ongoing and developing process—is allowed to continue on its own, and Welles's unwillingness to give us any other view, to cut into or away from the action, gives us no option but to watch it unfold. Welles's *Citizen Kane* (1941), the film that preceded *Ambersons,* also uses long takes, but is even more interesting than *Ambersons* in its use of composition. *Composition* is the most important element of the shot, but to understand it, we must first consider the limitations imposed on it.

COMPOSITION: THE SIZE OF THE FRAME

Composition—the arrangement of characters and objects within the screen **frame**—is, first of all, about that frame, which is constituted by the borders that contain the image. The structure of the image in painting, photography, or a movie depends, to begin with, on the size of the frame, the boundaries of where the image will begin and end. In painting and photography, the frame is flexible. A painter can choose a small frame, a large one, the entire ceiling of a chapel, like Michaelangelo's dome of the Sistine Chapel, or a gigantic mural, covering many walls, like those of the great Mexican muralist, Diego Rivera. It's hard to get a photograph quite that large, but the photographer too has a choice about the size of the image and therefore how much can be included and where the viewer's eye will be focused. Through cropping and reframing during the developing of the film, or its manipulation on the computer, she can determine the composition as much as she did when the picture is taken. The prime purpose for framing and composing is to direct the viewer's eye in ways that, for the artist, make the most sense for his vision and the narrative the visuals are telling. All art is about control: the artist controls what is seen in order that the viewer will see it expressed exactly the way the artist wants it to be seen.

We can never forget that film is a technological art and that its technology is a function of its economics. Therefore, filmmakers have never quite had the options available to other visual artists. Frame sizes (or, more correctly, the ratio of height to length) were rarely up to the filmmaker. In the silent period, many filmmakers could vary the frame internally, by masking off parts of it, using an **iris shot**, for example—a circular mask that would open out or close down the frame, concentrating on a character or an action without cutting. Even the gauge, or the physical size of the celluloid, varied in the early years, as did the placement of the sprocket holes, by means of which the camera and projector pull down the film strip, exposing one frame after an another. But shortly after the coming of sound, a frame size that would incorporate the soundtrack was established as the industry standard, with dimensions of four units wide and three units high. It was called the "standard ratio" and lasted almost thirty years. This was the frame the filmmaker had to work with, and the best thing about it, as with any standard, was that it was dependable. The cinematographer and the director could compose within that frame with the knowledge that their composition would be faithfully reproduced in

FIGURE 3.2 An iris shot from a battle scene in D. W. Griffith's *Birth of a Nation* (1915).

FIGURE 3.3 This is a frame from a strip of 35 mm film, in which you can see the sound track and the sprocket holes. Film unknown, probably from the 1930s.

the movie theater, where the proportions of the screen were more or less the same as the film image, even though the physical size of the screen varied according to the size of the theater.

Wide Screen

All this changed in the 1950s, when film began competing with television for an audience. Rather than working on making better films, studio executives decided that the offer of an enormous image would give them the competitive edge against the machine that was drawing audiences away from theaters and keeping them at home. Wide screen was not invented in the fifties—various experiments had been attempted since the twenties—but, as with sound, which the studios also experimented with before the famous *Jazz Singer* in 1927, the studios had no economic need to exploit it. In the fifties, need emerged, and filmmakers slowly lost their control over the frame. First there was **Cinerama**, a cumbersome process in which the image was captured on three cameras and then projected from three projectors onto a gigantic curved screen—a kind of clumsy precursor of Imax (which uses only one very large gauged film strip). The seams between three panels were always visible, but Cinerama was as much a method for foregrounding form rather than content. Rather than conveying story, as in the classical Hollywood style, Cinerama conveyed the size potentials of cinematic exhibition, attempting to create an immersive experience by wrapping the audience within the image—a precursor, perhaps, of current immersive reality experiments in the digital world. In other words, one went to see and be amazed by Cinerama, not any story that might be told by this particular form.

Three-strip Cinerama was used mainly for travelogues—sight-seeing films, roller-coaster rides—and therefore the emphasis was on the spectacle of its huge curved screen and its potential to overwhelm the viewer. Except for its size, it was a return to the very earliest beginnings of cinema, with its emphasis on amazing views—an update of early cinema's representation of spectacular events. Only one narrative film, the multi-director *How the West Was Won* (1962), was filmed in the three-strip process.

Anamorphic and "Flat" Wide Screen Processes

Cinerama was only the beginning of the end of film frame standards. In 1954, Twentieth-Century Fox introduced a proprietary format that they had originally played with in the twenties, **Cinemascope**. It was an **anamorphic** process, meaning that, with a special lens on the camera, it squeezed a wide image into a distorted form onto standard 35 mm film. Another lens on the projector unsqueezed the image to a ratio of 1:2.35.

Cinemascope introduced distortion on the sides of the frame. For this and other reasons, another anamorphic process, Panavision, slowly took over and the company is now the dominant supplier of lenses for anamorphic and other wide-screen processes, which are now the dominant means of framing.

FIGURES 3.4–3.5 The first is the squeezed, anamorphic image as it would look on the filmstrip. The second is the unsqueezed image after being projected through an anamorphic lens. The film is *No Down Payment* (Martin Ritt, 1957).

Anamorphic wide screen introduced problems that are only now beginning to be solved. A few directors, such as the Japanese filmmaker Akira Kurosawa and the American Robert Altman, took full advantage of the screen width, placing characters and actions at the peripheries, emphasizing the horizontal line. Some directors fought against wide screen. Alfred Hitchcock said it was like

FIGURE 3.6 Akira Kurosawa used anamorphic wide screen in ways that took full advantage of its width (*Red Beard*, 1965).

FIGURE 3.7 Robert Altman is an American filmmaker who uses the anamorphic process as a canvas to paint on end to end (*McCabe and Mrs. Miller*, 1971).

looking through a letter box and never used it (although in *Dial M for Murder*, 1954, he did use one short-lived 1950s' process, 3-D, with the audience wearing glasses to filter out the double image on the screen, producing a cardboard 3-D effect). The German director Fritz Lang said that wide-screen processes were only good for photographing snakes and funerals. But such resistance was futile. In the early fifties all the studios were attempting varieties of wide screen. To compete with Fox's Cinemascope, Paramount Pictures developed **"VistaVision."** Picking up on a major fad of fifties music recording and playback, they called it "Motion Picture High Fidelity." And today anamorphic and "flat" (non-anamorphic) wide screen are the industry standards.

VistaVision was originally photographed on reels of 65 mm film running horizontally through the camera. It was then printed down vertically on standard 35 mm, but the width of the image, even though reduced, allowed it to be projected at various ratios. VistaVision—the aesthetics of which we will discuss again when we analyze Hitchcock's *Vertigo* in Chapter 7—was part of the movement toward "flat" ratios. **"Flat" wide screen** can be made and projected in a number of ways. The film can be matted in the camera—that is, black bars are placed at the top and bottom of the image. Another matte in the projector allows the image to fill a wide screen. Alternately, and increasingly more rare, a film can be shot "full frame" filling the 35 mm frame. When projected, the film is matted down to wide-screen proportions. You may have noticed this process on videotape, where lights and microphones can sometimes be seen dangling from the top of the frame.

By the mid-fifties, "standard ratio" was finished and all films were composed in one form of wide screen or another: the 1:2.35 ratio of Cinemascope and Panavision or the 1:1.66 or 1:1.85 of flat wide screen. Interestingly, the 1:1.66 ratio goes all the way back to the ancient Greeks, who produced it (as the Renaissance would perspective hundreds of years later) mathematically and called it the "golden section," representing the perfect proportion. It needs to be said that, soon after the standard compositional bounds of the screen disappeared, at the time when television went to all color and all films wound up on television, black and white cinematography also disappeared. This, too, will become part of our story.

Loss of Standards

These technological shifts, like so much in film production, remove a great deal of control from the filmmaker's hands. Wide screen has made careful composition all but impossible. Videotape very rarely transferred anamorphic wide screen with the black bars necessary to represent the width of the image. Instead a film is **"panned and scanned,"** with a lab technician determining what he or she might consider the most important action in the frame—you know that this has happened when a card appears before the movie, stating "this film has been formatted to fit your television," or if a DVD says "full screen." The viewfinders used by directors and cinematographers to frame the image for the camera may contain many frame lines: anamorphic and flat wide screen, and television ratio—which is almost square.

Shopping mall movie theaters size their screens not according to the ratios in which the films might be shot, but rather to fit the often small and oddly shaped auditoriums in which they will be exhibited. So, even a film shot in anamorphic wide screen might be cropped at the sides, reducing its width. DVDs and wide-screen televisions are bringing more and more films to home viewers in something approaching the ratio in which they were shot. Still, the filmmaker is

FIGURES 3.8–3.9 Examine these images from David Fincher's *The Game* (1997). They are almost identical frames from the film, one in the anamorphic ratio of 1:2.35, the other panned and scanned into the almost square television ratio. There are obviously figures missing from the cropped shot; but more important, Fincher's intent, to place the Michael Douglas character in a kind of cage, surrounded by the horizontal lines Fincher so much likes as a compositional anchor, is replaced by something approaching a close-up in which mise-en-scène vanishes.

stymied: the edges of the frame are not dependable. Anything put there might not be seen in a theater or on television.

How Composition Works

It may seem odd to speak about the restrictions placed upon the shot before explaining how the shot is actually composed. But all works of the imagination are based upon the artist wrestling with her material, and in film, where the material is often based on economic necessity, the filmmaker has to be very imaginative to overcome its limitations. Filmmakers (directors, cinematographers, even producers) must follow technology, which must follow what the studio and distributor need to turn a profit. We have to understand this interaction.

Composition in Early Cinema

Much of so-called "primitive" cinema was show without telling. Single shots, often of spectacular, erotic, or sometimes disgusting events (Edison's infamous *Electrocuting an Elephant* (1903), for example) demonstrated what has been called a "Cinema of Attractions." At the early moments of its life, much film depended entirely on the shot: frontal, eye level, offering the viewer something unusual, exciting, even arousing, like Edison's *The Kiss* (see Figure 2.1). It was a kind of representational extension of vaudeville, the music hall entertainments popular through the turn of the last century, and for some years after. But as we've already seen in the Lumière brothers' *Arrival of a Train at La Ciotat* (see Figure 1.4), there were also very early attempts to compose along the lines of Renaissance perspective. And, in fact, once film moved ahead and developed narrative structure, the perspectival line became more and more important.

One aspect of the early "cinema of attractions" has remained. In most films, the main action is centered, the sight lines of the audience aimed at the middle of the screen, bearing the weight of the image. The peripheries may produce atmosphere, even be carefully set and lit to provide the right environment. But the eye will almost always be led to the center, with perspective used to create an illusion of depth.

D. W. Griffith

There were exceptions to centering images in the frame even in film's early years. D. W. Griffith is best known for *The Birth of a Nation* (1915) and *Intolerance* (1916). Before these two large and controversial works, Griffith served a kind of apprenticeship at the Biograph company, from 1908 to 1913, where he turned out in the neighborhood of 500 short narrative films. In the course of this tremendous output, Griffith, like all other filmmakers of the time, taught himself cinema. There were no rules, but plenty of room to experiment, both in composition and in cutting. We'll focus on the first here. Griffith, like most of his contemporaries, used the frontal, eye-level style and, like a classical painter,

FIGURE 3.10   D. W. Griffith, *The Unchanging Sea* (1910).

FIGURE 3.11   D. W. Griffith, *The Musketeers of Pig Alley* (1912).

some perspective, all to the purpose of focusing the viewer's attention on the most important element in the frame, the human figure.

But not all the time. From film to film, Griffith would experiment with composition. In some instances he would put the characters in a lower corner of the frame, so that the viewer's eye would have to find them out and, even more important, understand them as part of the landscape they are inhabiting. The shot in Figure 3.10 from *The Unchanging Sea* (1910) makes the sea itself the immediate focus of our attention. We don't have to look hard to see the characters. They are dark against the light, and in the foreground. But, placing them in the lower left of the frame, Griffith's composition represents an early attempt to make the human figure only one part of the landscape.

Griffith is well known for using the **close-up** to achieve dramatic effect. It became a standard compositional strategy to bring the viewer close to a character and allow that character to communicate an intense reaction to events, and Griffith, especially in his later work, used it for intense effect. Earlier, in this famous image from his 1912 Biograph gangster film, *The Musketeers of Pig Alley*, Griffith uses the close-up without giving up the environment surrounding the characters. The gangsters are pressed against the wall, moving forward with menace, almost threatening the boundaries of the frame itself.

The 90-Degree Rule

Griffith's experimentation with composition had great influence—but not, ultimately, on the Hollywood style. His work on editing did, as we'll see. But in the development of the Hollywood style, the essential notion of centering the important elements of the image held sway well through the coming of sound

FIGURES 3.12–3.13   The very first shot of *The Mothman Prophecies* (Mark Pellington, 2002) is unusual because it is a 90-degree shot, straight on, looking at the character. The second shot of the film is more like the norm, as the two main characters, who are being addressed by the man in the first shot, are shown off the 90-degree angle, but also slightly below eye level. As this is a horror film, the director is permitted to try unusual angles.

where importance shifted to characters talking. Characters were centered, but not viewed straight on. Primarily to avoid the obvious flatness of the two-dimensional screen space and so give the illusion of depth, directors and cinematographers, rather early, centered the figure in the frame, but almost always put their camera off the 90-degree axis. The center of the frame bears the weight of the viewer's gaze. That is where we are asked to look. The **90-degree rule** doesn't alter this, and, in fact, accentuates it. By photographing any scene off dead center, off the 90-degree angle, some perspective is introduced and therefore, because of the illusion of depth, a further ability to guide the viewer to what is important in the frame is gained.

The Studios and the Shot

Experimentation with compositional effects continued throughout the history of film and is still going on. In most cases, the emphasis remains on the human figure, and this became accentuated in the early sound period, when, it was assumed, people wanted to see the actors talking. The thirties were years of **"shallow focus,"** where the background was often in soft focus, the camera concentrating on brightly lit characters. As always in the history of film, there are no universals. Universal Pictures, using techniques of German Expressionism in its extraordinarily popular cycle of Frankenstein and Dracula films during the thirties, paid much attention to light and dark and the placement of figures within strange surroundings and sometimes in unusual compositions.

We might say that the shallow focus, **high-key** (that is, brightly) lit, dialogue-centered films of the thirties define the mise-en-scène of that decade—their method of composing the shots of their films. Yet despite the commonalities of composition and lighting, each studio developed its own variety of this mise-en-scène. The thirties saw the studio system at full throttle, each with its own craftspeople, its own producers, directors, cinematographers, and production designers, generating their own general style. So, if MGM epitomized the bright, shallow focus that was the general rule of the decade, Warner Brothers often used different compositional strategies, lower lighting, a more mobile camera—especially in the famous Busby Berkeley

FIGURE 3.14 One of the great stars of the 1930s, Greta Garbo, in *Grand Hotel* (Edmund Goulding, 1932). Her face is the major point of the composition. The background is in soft focus, and so is she. It was common in the thirties to photograph a female star so that no blemishes would be seen. You can just see the key light in Garbo's eyes and clearly see the backlighting on her hair and reflected on the piece of furniture behind her.

FIGURE 3.15 Busby Berkeley was Warner Bros. choreographer of the thirties. His song and dance numbers usually begin on a theater stage, but wind up in an abstract space in which the dancers become patterns rather than individual figures (Mervyn Leroy, *Gold Diggers of 1933*).

FIGURE 3.16 The gangster in the dark. The early Warner Bros. gangster films composed their characters in darkness, cowering, guns at the ready (*Little Caesar*, Mervyn Leroy, 1931).

musicals that not only choreographed dancers and characters, but composed them so that the bodies of the dancers made strange, erotic patterns.

MGM prided itself on the high style: it was the visual lift from the economic and cultural depression of the thirties. Warners, on the other hand, found itself more comfortable with darker subjects—both thematically and visually. Warner Bros. was the studio of the earliest sound gangster films (Mervyn LeRoy's *Little Caesar* and William Wellman's *Public Enemy*, both 1931). LeRoy's *I Am a Fugitive of a Chain Gang* (1932) was perhaps the darkest of them all. Condemning the work gang brutalities of Southern jails,

FIGURES 3.17–18 In *Public Enemy* (William Wellman, 1931), Warner Bros. could copy the high-key glamour of an MGM film, even creating an interestingly layered composition with the glamour star of the day, Jean Harlow, in the foreground; the gangster, James Cagney in the middle plane of the image; and the strange statue averting its eyes in the rear. But when the gangster gets his due, Wellman reverts to the dark, rainy streets that foreshadow the film noir style of the forties.

the film wrung sympathy for the unjustly accused, not only in its narrative movement, but in its visual treatment that moves from the relatively bright, open compositions that show its central character, James Allen (Paul Muni) at the peak of his powers as an engineer, to the last shot of the film, still among the most chilling, in which light disappears. Allen, escaped again, arranges a furtive meeting with his girlfriend. "How do you live?" she asks. He pulls back into the dark: "I steal."

In all these cases, composition is used to create a concentration of the viewers' gaze, or lack of it in the case of *I Am a Fugitive of a Chain Gang*, and, in many instances, to use lighting and different parts of the frame, side to side and front to back, to create the needed effect.

Mise-en-Scène, German Expressionism, Exceptions to the Rules

The exceptions to the rules—the Universal horror films, for example, and the work of director Josef von Sternberg, who sculpted his films with light—were the result of borrowing methods from one of the most influential movements in film, German Expressionism. The movement flourished in Germany during and right after World War I, and it was one of the earliest film styles that used composition, and everything that makes it up, to create a mood—in this case of darkness, despair, and madness. Its influence was profound, particularly because many of its practitioners came to the United States.

In order to understand Expressionism and its influence, we must return to the concept of mise-en-scène. In an earlier chapter I spoke about mise-en-scène as the way space is articulated within the image. Mise-en-scène encompasses everything that happens in the frame, including character placement, camera position, camera movement, lighting, how grayscale tonalities in a black and

FIGURE 3.19 In this still from Josef von Sternberg's *Shanghai Express* (1932), we can clearly see a number of thirties' compositional and lighting effects come together. Sternberg puts his favorite actress, Marlene Dietrich, in mildly soft focus, and at the same time marks the exoticism of the frame with the Chinese banner and stripes the whole image with dark bands.

white film are used, or color in a color film. Even sound and music might be considered an aspect of mise-en-scène. The term is also evaluative. That is, we can say that a film made with high-key lighting, in which everything in the frame is lit evenly, composed with an eye-level camera with little movement, concentrating on the characters, who are placed centrally in the frame, has no mise-en-scène that adds anything to what we learn from the dialogue or cutting. A director who creates a consistent visual atmosphere, who uses black and white or color expressively, moves the camera in relation to the characters, and, in short, creates spaces that relate as much about the film as what the characters say is a mise-en-scène director. Such

FIGURE 3.20 Expressionist tendencies in the *Bride of Frankenstein* (James Whale, 1935)

FIGURE 3.21 A forerunner of Frankenstein in the Expressionist film, *The Cabinet of Dr. Caligari* (Robert Weine, 1919). The actor playing the somnambulist, Conrad Veidt, came to Hollywood and one of his roles was Major Strasser in *Casablanca*.

work is rare, because doing all these things requires imagination and time, but is present throughout the history of film, and a film with a strong mise-en-scène cannot be mistaken for any other film.

German Expressionism is about mise-en-scène, precisely because it extrapolates the stressed emotional states of individuals into the environment. This required such control that the various elements of the composition were not left to chance or actual sets, but sets that were literally painted with representations of buildings that were distorted and threatening, streets that zigzagged to nowhere, all the way to the shadows cast by lampposts. Madness, the grotesque, and the emotionally oppressed were major narrative themes of Expressionism, which very much reflected the state of German culture following World War I. This was carried forward into the Frankenstein and Dracula films that resonated with the public because, as some have suggested, they reminded people of the horrible wounds and deformities that had resulted from the war.

Mise-en-scène in Sternberg, Murnau, and Hitchcock

Josef von Sternberg, an American filmmaker, who made *The Blue Angel* in Germany in 1930, further developed a mise-en-scène based on shadow more than light and, under the influence of Expressionism, created carefully composed images when he returned to the United States. His films, very much in contrast to the brightly lit norm of thirties filmmaking, were *about* composition, lighting, and the general construction of mise-en-scène as much as they were about story. The way they looked was their story. Atmosphere and eroticism were their narrative. (See Figure 3.19.)

Many German filmmakers emigrated to America in the 1920s and 30s, especially in the face of Nazism, bringing their vision with them. One of the earliest was F. W. Murnau, who made the very first Dracula film, *Nosferatu*, in 1922, while still in Germany. His first American film, *Sunrise* (1927), brought Expressionist techniques to late American silent films. *Sunrise* is a magical work. We've seen in the previous chapter how he could create a mood in the studio with some lights and a moving camera. He could also combine images within one composition and superimpose his characters in fantastic city scenes expressing their happiness or their despair. Murnau used every trick in the late-twenties book, even using small people for background figures to force the

FIGURES 3.22–3.23 F. W. Murnau's *Sunrise* (1927) used every cinematic trick in the book. This multiple exposure and matted shot creates a vision of a city holiday that seduces the young man from the country. And in the country house, the seductive City Woman in the background seems to knock everything off kilter in a typical Expressionist shot that distorts spatial expectations.

perspective of his shots. *Sunrise* is a source book of compositional styles, as well as one of the most perfect melodramas we have in film.

Alfred Hitchcock moved in the opposite direction from Sternberg. He was a British director who created a large body of work before emigrating to the United States. Early in his British period, he went to work in Germany and directed some films there, learning much from the Expressionist style. Even in a film as late as *Psycho* (1960), we can see Expressionist composition in which emotion is expressed by the mise-en-scène. But Hitchcock's work goes even further in its compositional control and extends the Expressionist mise-en-scène by bringing it close to modern painting. *Psycho* is a tightly constructed film, wound like a machine, and, whenever you see it, it continues to open surprises that you know are no longer surprises. The tightness of its construction that creates its dark vision of the inevitability of madness is based on composition and camera movement—as well as editing in the infamous shower murder. It achieves expressiveness by constructing a closed, isolated, threatening, black and white world which is based upon an abstract compositional pattern. In other words, Hitchcock and his designer, Saul Bass, construct *Psycho* along controlled compositional patterns of vertical and horizontal lines, the slashing movement of a knife, and high angle shots that indicate a character in danger. As we can see in the accompanying stills, the film depends upon the control of our eye as we are allowed to approach, but never pierce, the curtain of madness.

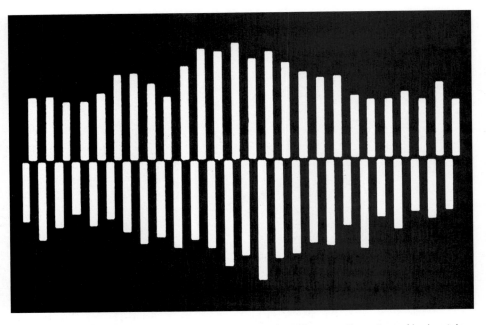

FIGURE 3.24 Saul Bass's credit sequence for *Psycho* (1960) sets up the pattern of horizontals and verticals, as well as the disrupting curve that will form the pattern for the film.

FIGURE 3.25 The dissolve from the credit sequence to the beginning of the narrative overlays the abstract pattern onto the image.

FIGURE 3.27 The structure allows Hitchcock to create an almost abstract pattern, as in this shot that occurs just after the shower sequence.

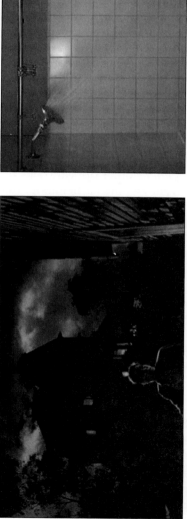

FIGURE 3.26 The motel and the old Gothic house are the most concrete examples of the compositional structure set up by the film. This particular shot fully reveals Hitchcock's Expressionist roots.

FIGURE 3.29 The shower scene breaks the horizontal/vertical composition with an arcing, slashing motion.

FIGURE 3.28 The high-angle shot is a favorite of Hitchcock's. It shows a character in danger and creates unease in the viewer.

Orson Welles and the Reinvention of Composition

The influence of Expressionism was, as I have said, widespread, and no one showed it to better advantage than Orson Welles in *Citizen Kane* (1941), a film which forced a rethinking of cinematic composition. Welles came to film from a background in radio and theater. He wanted his composition to have the depth of a theatrical set while at the same time exhibit the movement and flexibility that was possible in film. He and his cinematographer, Gregg Toland, used a technique called **deep focus** that had been used occasionally in other films, and turned it into a compositional imperative. Deep focus, or "depth of field," is a result of camera optics. A lot of light and a very small aperture opening (which translates as a high f-stop) create the effect. It is hard to do, expensive, and tends to call attention to itself, three reasons why it is rarely used in filmmaking.

There are occasional examples of faked depth of field, in which a special lens is used to focus two spatial planes. You can see it in Martin Scorsese's *Cape Fear* (1991). For *Kane*, Toland had special lenses ground to obtain the effect he wanted; but, if that didn't work, he used good old-fashioned special effects— placing characters behind a glass painting to achieve forced perspective (on the screen's two-dimensional surface, a painting correctly placed in front of characters will give the impression of the reverse), or other optical tricks to achieve what he and Welles wanted. Remember what we said earlier about the general rule of not putting everything that will finally be there in the shot at the time the shot is first taken.

But many of the shots in *Kane* are done with most elements present, and the result is astonishing. Welles forces the viewer to look: there are items in front, in the middle, in the rear of a given shot, each one demanding attention. No longer is the person talking the main focus of the composition. In fact, at a crucial moment in the narrative, when Kane is reading his "Declaration of Principles" for his newspaper, he is in total shadow. This may not sound terribly subtle, but it is striking when seen, and it plays a double narrative role by bringing into question Kane's sincerity about his "principles" and foreshadowing a scene, much later in the film, when Kane receives the torn pieces of the "declaration" from Jed Leland, his one-time friend.

Deep Focus and the Long Take

Welles played with perspective in *Citizen Kane* and in all his subsequent films, in ways that were not entirely different from what many contemporary painters were doing. Far from the simple vanishing point that the Lumière brothers' cinematographer borrowed from classical painting, Welles, like other visual artists, understood that perspective was a convention—something invented and then naturalized as the only way to represent the "real" world. But, as we've been saying, the "real" is what we or an artist makes of the world, and Welles saw the world cinematically as a dark, enigmatic place, where the true character of an

FIGURE 3.30   This image of Susan Alexander Kane's suicide attempt divides the image into three layers receding to the back of the frame. It is, by the way, a fake. The medicine bottle and glass are models, and may have been matted in.

FIGURE 3.31   Filming by the book will always demand that the central, speaking character is in full light. Here, Kane, reading his "Declaration of Principles," is in darkness, foreshadowing the fact that he will not follow them too closely.

individual depended upon who was talking about him. The space the characters inhabited was not only dark, in deep focus, but composed in such a way that the perspective lines were out of joint, forcing the eye in a number of directions at once, giving it ownership of nothing.

A visual example of this is shown in Figure 3.32. It takes place early in the film, when the reporter, Thompson, makes his first visit to the dead Kane's second wife, Susan. She is silent and Thompson calls his editor. The scene is shot in one very long take, in deep focus, and by the time Thompson enters the phone both, the composition is divided into a triptych, or three-paneled layout in which each panel is related to the other. Susan sits in despair in the rear of the left part of the first frame. The waiter is in the center, and Thompson, in silhouette, in the foreground, is on the phone, between the middle and right panels. He's doing the talking and should be the center of attention, but the waiter, in the middle distance, and especially Susan, although in the background, also demand our attention. Where is the perspective of this composition? The answer is that there are not merely two, but many perspective lines, each drawing our eyes in various directions. Figure 3.33 diagrams some of them.

There is a sequence in *Citizen Kane* that tells us about Kane's childhood, concentrating on the moment when his mother signs over his care to the rich Mr. Thatcher. The sequence concerns the shifting relationships between mother, son, father, and a new patriarchal figure, who will take the son from his parents and introduce him to the world of wealth and personal isolation. Welles describes these relational changes not so much through what the characters say to each other as through the way the camera and characters move through the space of

FIGURE 3.32 The viewer has to do the work in such an image, because Welles does not cut between the various figures, but frames them off internally, keeping them all in view.

FIGURE 3.33 Here we can see how Welles skews perspective and makes our eyes travel through the different planes of the shot, complicating the mise-en-scène.

the sequence. The sequence begins with Mrs. Kane looking out the window and calling to her son, who is playing with his sled in the snow (the sled that, at the end of the film, will be revealed as "Rosebud," Kane's dying memory). The camera pulls up and back as Mrs. Kane turns around, and as the camera moves, it reveals a figure to her right. This is the new guardian, Mr. Thatcher. The camera tracks backward in front of them as they move to the other side of the room, talking about signing the papers that will give Thatcher custody of Kane. Through all of this, the child outside in the snow remains visible and audible through the window even as the camera moves back. As a result of deep focus and the long backward track of the camera, space expands to the rear of the frame. The small cabin in which all this takes place is expanded into a larger area of psychological change and uprooting, which is underscored by the appearance of the father in the shot.

As Mrs. Kane and Thatcher continue to move toward the opposite end of the room, Mr. Kane is revealed on the left side of the frame. Throughout the shot, he remains always slightly behind his wife as she and Mr. Thatcher approach the table where the papers are. In their movement to the table, the child, still playing outside the window, is sometimes blocked out by the figure of his mother or father, but throughout the shot a triangulated dynamic is maintained between the three adults and the child. After withdrawing her gaze from Kane out in the snow, the mother looks straight ahead and then down at the table. Thatcher's and Mr. Kane's gazes remain fixed on Mrs. Kane. She is the pivotal figure, the one making the choice. The two men are dependent upon her actions while the child is separated from her, almost literally pulled away by the visual effect created as the camera moves from the window to the table.

After Mrs. Kane and Thatcher sit down at the table and Mr. Kane comes closer to the two of them, the camera tilts up, causing the father to appear for a moment as a slightly threatening figure—threatening, at least, to those ready to sign away his child. Note that an unusually low camera position often has the effect of making a character loom over the frame in a threatening manner. However, Welles will sometimes use this position ironically to indicate that the imposing figure is about to fall from power. An unusually high camera position diminishes a character. Hitchcock will often use a disorienting high angle shot to show a character in physical or moral jeopardy. In our sequence from *Kane,* the father's power is weak and diminishing. He's about to lose his son to a man who is practically buying him from his mother. The three adults talk about their business deal while young Kane remains clearly visible through the window, on the other side, far behind them, now forming the apex of the triangle. Mr. Kane relents in his opposition to the deal the moment he understands how much money is at stake. He then goes to the back of the room and shuts the window—as if shutting his son out of his life. Mrs. Kane and Thatcher follow; she opens the window again, and, finally, after about two minutes and thirty seconds, there is a 180-degree reverse shot of Mrs. Kane from outside the window.

This complex arrangement and rearrangement of space and figures create a kind of Oedipal ballet in a small room, a dance of shifting parental relationships and authority that results in both gain and loss for the child. The ballet of camera and character in their dynamic spatial confines is more eloquent than the spoken dialogue and much more descriptive of narrative events.

Another less complex long take in *Citizen Kane* occurs right after Kane's electoral defeat. It is a long dialogue between Kane and his friend Jed Leland. The camera is set below the level of the floor and looks up at these two figures, one a giant just cut down to size by his election loss, the other an obsequious friend who is beginning to find his own power. The camera moves with them, but there is no cutting. Its position is ironic; the power lies in our observation of these two figures whose place in their world is changing before our eyes.

For Welles, in *Kane* and all the other films he made in the course of an active career, the screen became a highly malleable space, a demanding space in which we, as viewers, must actively seek out the various elements in the composition. *Kane*, along with other influences, was a forerunner of **film noir**. I will speak in detail about this particular genre later on. But it is important to note here that its dependence on darkness, on compositions that were off center, that complicated the perspectival line, came directly from *Kane* as well as from modern art. Darkness became its theme as well as its visual

FIGURE 3.34 This low angle, deep focus, long take indicates changing positions in the character's situation and power. Kane has lost his election bid for governor, and his friend, Jed Leland, is leaving New York. The mise-en-scène provides as much information as the dialogue.

construction. Composition—as in *Psycho*—is used to create anxiety rather than composure.

WORKING AGAINST THE RULES

Other filmmakers make use of the long take, which is particularly embraced by a director who wishes to work against the Hollywood style. Films as diverse as Murnau's *Sunrise* (1927); Howard Hawks's *The Big Sleep* (1946); Bernardo Bertolucci's *Last Tango in Paris* (1972), whose compositions are based on the work of the British painter, Francis Bacon; Chantal Akerman's *Jeanne Dielman, 23 Quai du Commerce, 1080 Bruxelles* (1975, discussed in detail in Chapter 6); all the work of French director Jean-Luc Godard; Terence Davies's *The Long Day Closes* (1992); Alexander Sokurov's *Russian Ark* (2002); and any film by the Greek director, Theo Angelopoulos or the Russian Andrei Tarkovsky—to name only a very, very few—illustrate the ways filmmakers can work against the rules of continuity, using long takes, alternative cutting patterns, and unusual visual and dramatic rhythms to achieve results that differ from those of standard Hollywood practice. In films such as these, the viewer's gaze is, in a sense, unlocked, cut away from the story and made instead to look at how story is being created.

Some filmmakers, as noted, want to exploit and expose the two-dimensional compositional space of the screen by using 180-degree shots, focusing our attention on the image. Stanley Kubrick was one who not only employed straight-on shots, but also made symmetrical compositions, just slightly off to unbalance the image and the composition. The contemporary director P. T. Anderson also experimented with 90-degree shots in *Punch Drunk Love* (2002), creating compositions that put his figures—Adam Sandler in particular—in almost abstract settings, removed from the realism of most narrative film.

The Italian filmmaker Michelangelo Antonioni revised notions of composition entirely. His films—*L'avventura* (1960), *La Notte* (1961), *The Eclipse* (1962), *Red Desert* (1964), and *Blow-Up* (1966), among others—sometimes moved close to Abstract Expressionist painting, always using composition to express his characters' states of mind, reducing them to figures in a landscape, in which the latter often dominated the characters. Abstract Expressionist painting did away with the figure entirely, something that narrative film cannot do. But in Antonioni's work, the figure and the landscape merge, often in abstract patterns that express their state of being in the modern world.

FIGURE 3.35 During the opening long take of Kubrick's *A Clockwork Orange* (1971), the camera pulls back, revealing a fearful symmetry, artificial, strange, threatening—exactly the opposite of the usual style of a Hollywood film.

FIGURE 3.36 In his 2002 film, *Punch Drunk Love*, Paul Thomas Anderson experiments with the straight-on, 90-degree shot.

FIGURE 3.37 Michelangelo Antonioni refigured the possibilities of composition as radically—and differently—as did Welles in *Citizen Kane*. In this shot from *L'avventura* (1960) the figures become part of the horizontal lines of the composition of sea and island. But, come to think of it, how far is this composition from Griffith's in *The Unchanging Sea* (see Figure 3.10)?

LIGHTING AND COLOR

The lighting of *Citizen Kane* is different, not only from the general high-keyed lighting of the thirties, but of film lighting in general. With the exception of film noir, shadow and darkness are used mainly as drivers of the story: a nighttime chase, the old dark house of a horror film, a dimly lit parking garage where danger lurks. Basic, **three-point lighting** remains the convention: a **key light** on the characters talking, catching their eyes (look at any film and you will notice a glint in the eyes of the characters in the foreground, as in Figure 3-14); a **back-light** behind the characters to set them off from the background and provide an illusion of depth; **fill light**, perhaps the most subtle kind of lighting, that gives texture, provides depth, and provides visual cues and defines the mise-en-scène.

Color presents very different lighting problems from black and white. Color was always present, even in the earliest films, which were tinted, toned, and sometimes hand-stenciled. Various processes to capture color were tried, until three-color **Technicolor** was established. Technicolor actually began in 1917; but it wasn't until 1932 that the "three color" process was perfected. This was a complicated process that used three strips of black and white negative, filtered so that each would capture one of the primary yellow, green, and cyan colors. The negatives were then literally printed onto the positive in ways that allowed dyes, corresponding to the colors filtered on the negative, to be transferred to the film. The process was expensive, the equipment huge (if you visit the Smithsonian in Washington, D.C., you can see an enormous, old Technicolor camera on display), and the lighting demands enormous. Also, Technicolor was a proprietary process so that each studio had to lease equipment and a Technicolor consultant. The consultant, usually Natalie Kalmus, former wife of the man who owned the process, had a particular idea of what color on the screen should look like: bright, with a tendency to vibrant pastels.

The point is that, today, some of us consider black and white "unrealistic" and color the opposite. From the 1930s through the fifties, however, exactly the reverse was true, and color was reserved almost exclusively for some musicals and fantasy films. In the sixties, as we noted earlier, when films were ultimately aimed at television, which was going to color, black and white cinematography, and the compositional effects that could only be achieved with grey scale, disappeared. So did Technicolor. Eastman Kodak's "monopack" process, in which all the color dyes were embedded in one negative, took over. It was cheaper, and there were no strings attached, but the color of a **release print** was completely unstable. When filmmakers began complaining in the 1970s that their films turned an irreversible pink in about five years, Kodak made a more stable formula.

Despite these problems, and the demands for uniform shooting in color, a few directors experimented, sometimes cooling the colors down; some "flashed" or otherwise pre-exposed their film stock so that the image would have uniform color tone, such as the sallow yellow-green that pervades David Fincher's *Seven* (1995). And many directors subtly choose color combinations that relate emotions and express their characters' states of mind. Stanley Kubrick's last film, *Eyes Wide Shut* (1999), uses blue and gold-yellow lighting throughout the film so that it renders an almost painterly coherence of color. Michelangelo Antonioni, already noted for his intricate composition, turned color in *Red Desert* (1964) to an even more painterly use so that the film's palette forms the canvas of the almost inarticulate characters' emotions. Creating another kind of expressionism, Antonioni used color to express emotional values, perhaps those of the character or those of the film as a large canvas itself.

Black and white or color, lighting can either flatten a scene or literally sculpt it in light. It produces a narrative effect, silently directing us as to how we should interpret a character and his or her actions, or the direction of the entire film. In film noir, dark rather than light is dominant. Noir's world encloses its characters in the dark and we sometimes have to search them out through the darkness and often through canted, tilted, very low or high compositions.

In general, lighting, as part of composition, helps give the two-dimensional space of the movie screen depth and texture, directing our attention or diverting it, leading us into image—making the viewer the recipient or even a part of the total mise-en-scène.

Composing in Wide Screen

Lighting can add depth. The size of the screen provides width. Welles could take full advantage of a standard film frame and compose right to its edges. Most directors, as we discussed earlier, now compose toward the center of the screen in order to make their framing safe for television, videotape, and mall theaters. But, as we saw, there have been and still are important exceptions, filmmakers who literally think in wide screen—as any good artist thinks and sees his world in terms of the media he uses to represent it (see Figures 3.6 and 3.7). It was said that the advent of Cinemascope and Panavision would destroy the close-up, because the full face could never be made to fill the wide rectangle. The Italian filmmaker Sergio Leone, in his so-called "Spaghetti Westerns" (*A Fistful of Dollars*, 1964, *The Good, the Bad, and the Ugly*, 1966, *For a Few Dollars More*, 1967, and *Once Upon a Time in the West*, 1968), made the close-up the

FIGURE 3.38 In this shot from the final sequence of Joseph L. Lewis's *The Big Combo* (1955), light becomes an intruder on the villain's darkness. The film was photographed by the great noir cinematographer John Alton.

FIGURE 3.39 Sergio Leone solved the problem of the close-up in the Panavision frame by turning it into a frame-filling landscape (*Once Upon a Time in the West*, 1968).

FIGURE 3.40   The rigidity of the horizontal line in anamorphic wide screen. In this shot from David Fincher's *Seven* (1995), the figures all but disappear into the enclosed horizon.

central point of his compositional strategy, holding his characters' faces at length, creating a veritable aria of gazes.

Robert Altman crowds his wide-screen compositions with figures from left to right, front to back, and then uses a *zoom* lens to pick out important (or not important) events in the crowds. Even Altman's soundtrack is "wide screen" and deep aural focus. Rather than having individuals talk and stop, waiting for the other character to say her line, everyone in an Altman film—as they often did in the films of Howard Hawks and Orson Welles—talks at once. The audience needs to be the sound mixer in an Altman film.

David Fincher is almost visually obsessed with the horizontal line of the Panavision screen and composes his images over and over again against the horizontal. In the end, the most expert and talented of filmmakers work just like this: they compose against a pattern, perhaps less interested about directing the viewer's gaze toward the figures who are speaking and more inclined to create an overall compositional strategy in which all components of the mise-en-scène work toward expressing emotions, ideas, and, most important, *visual* information.

THE MOVING CAMERA

It is almost impossible to write descriptions of moving camera. But camera movement is one of the most important compositional elements in film and needs to be considered as best we can here. It is important because it allows a filmmaker to create and traverse space. The moving camera becomes an extension of the director's inquisitive eye—if, that is, the director is inquisitive. It can even be an exclamation of the director's bravura, as is the almost four-minute take in Scorsese's *GoodFellas*, when Henry and Karen visit the Copacabana. To the music of the Crystals, they start on the street, wind down the steps to and then through the kitchen, into the club, as a table is set for them; they sit and talk, until the camera moves again to pick up first another group of people across from them, and then a comedian performing on stage. Bravura, but also a definition of character. Henry is at the top of his game here, and will start to slide. The moving camera expresses the composition of character: strong, in control, space giving way before his approach.

Kubrick does a similar gambit with Alex in the record boutique in *A Clockwork Orange* (1971). Rather than follow the character, the camera here precedes him as he walks through the shopping mall, Beethoven sounding triumphantly on the soundtrack, Alex in full command, the camera and the space it creates giving way before him, his servant.

Sometimes a moving camera can be threatening, recomposing space to indicate a character's entrapment or diminishment. Welles does this, weaving his camera through the dark, fleeing in front of a character—as he does in *The Trial*, where Joseph K. runs through a kind of tunnel made up of wooden slats. A moving camera can, on rare occasions and in talented hands, indicate time. The Greek director, Theo Angelopolous, in his film *Traveling Players* (1975), has a group of people walking down the street, in an extremely **long shot**. As they walk, and the camera moves, the street around them changes, moving back in history. Alexander Sokurov creates an even more dramatic example in *Russian Ark*. Filmed on digital video, it is a continuous, ninety-six minute take in which

FIGURE 3.41   A still from the tracking shot through the record boutique in *A Clockwork Orange* (1971). The image shows other compositional techniques that Kubrick often employed: lighting permitted to shine directly into the camera; a wide-angle lens that creates deep focus and distorts the image.

the most contradictory thing— a montage made without cutting that covers three centuries of Russian history—is created in the halls and galleries of the St. Petersburg's Hermitage museum.

Even in less dramatic examples, a moving camera, especially when used with a **long take**, is a temporal event. Unlike the short takes of conventional cinema, long, moving camera sequences indicate duration and permit performers to act, almost as if on stage, making a temporal process out of the development of their emotions.

Clearly, the elements that make up composition are numerous and complex. After all, they constitute the immediate visual presence of any film. Combined with cutting, a narrative is created. We now cut to the editing process.

Notes and References

Composition: The Size of the Frame   For the early film as spectacle, see Tom Gunning, "An Aesthetic of Astonishment: Early Film and the (In)Credulous Spectator," in Leo Braudy and Marshall Cohen, eds., *Film Theory and Criticism*, 6th ed. (New York: Oxford University Press, 2004), pp. 862–77. John Belton, *Widescreen Cinema* (Cambridge, MA: Harvard University Press, 1992), is an excellent source for the techniques and aesthetics of wide screen. For information on the Golden Mean, see Ocvirk, Stinson, Wigg, Bone, and Cayton, *Art Fundamentals*, 9th ed. (New York: McGraw-Hill, 2002), pp. 62–65. Lotte H. Eisner, *The Haunted Screen* (Berkeley and Los Angeles: University of California Press, 1974), remains the best work on German Expressionism. The theory that horror films emerged as a response to World War I is presented in Robert Skal, *The Monster Show: A Cultural History of Horror* (New York: Faber & Faber, 2001).

The Studios And The Shot   For an excellent study of Busby Berkeley and his treatment of the human figure, see Lucy Fischer, *Cinematernity: Film, Motherhood*, Genre (Princeton, NJ: Princeton University Press, 1996), pp. 37–55.

Mise-en-Scène in Sternberg, Murnau, and Hitchcock   For an extended visual analysis of *Psycho*, see Robert Kolker, "The Man Who Knew More Than Enough," in Robert Kolker, ed., *Alfred Hitchcock's* Psycho: *A Casebook* (New York: Oxford University Press, 2004), pp. 205–58.

Deep Focus and The Long   Andrè Bazin addresses the contemplative nature of deep focus and the long shot throughout his essays in *What Is Cinema?* cited in Chapter 1.

Lighting and Color   See James L. Limbacher, *Four Aspects of the Film* (New York: Arno Press, 1977). Limbacher also analyzes screen sizes.

4 BUILDING BLOCKS II: THE CUT

The long take is a rarity in traditional Hollywood filmmaking. What we see on the screen in an average Hollywood film *appears* to be an ongoing, transparent process of narration, but this is not, by any stretch, created with a long take. Here's an experiment: begin counting the number of seconds each shot lasts on the screen—in other words, start when a new image takes the place of the previous one and count the seconds until another image takes its place. I promise you the results will be amazing. You will discover that the average shot length of an American film is about nine seconds, usually shorter, occasionally longer. This does not necessarily mean that the take made during production was only nine seconds long, but it does point out the deep, abiding illusion of film called the classical Hollywood style: short pieces of film are spliced together to create the impression of an ongoing process of story.

But we need to back up a bit to understand this fully. The shot and its composition are what you see on the screen. A cut or edit is invisible; the only thing you see is its result: another shot. But the purpose and possibilities of what the cut produces are as complex and varied as the elements that make up the shot itself—which itself will partially determine where a cut will occur. Like the shot, editing also addresses time and space by building the temporal structure—the movement of characters and events across the narrative of a film—and directing our gaze, and that of the characters, to those things and events the filmmakers deem important. Editing also creates transitions, movements from one place or time to another. A **dissolve**, for example, in which one shot fades out while another fades in, is an editing effect, as is the fade to black of a sequence

FIGURE 4.1 By means of this dissolve, Rick (Humphrey Bogart) moves into a flashback of happier days in Paris. The camera has moved close to him and, in this instance, slowly goes out of focus as the Paris landmark is dissolved over him (*Casablanca*, Michael Curtiz, 1942).

to mark the end of a narrative moment. This was a favorite device of Alfred Hitchcock, who would, in effect, squelch a scene with a fast fade to black, leaving the viewer in a state of suspension and expectation as to what might follow. Even though such techniques are created optically, either in the camera or in the **optical printer,** which allows multiple images to be projected onto an undeveloped piece of film, they are still editing techniques. Some varieties have become cinematic conventions such as when the dissolve is created by using wavy lines, and we know a **flashback** is occurring. It became a convention by being repeated over and over again until the audience knew immediately what it signified. Today, this and other transition devices—like the dissolve or the **wipe**—have been replaced by the **direct cut.**

The formal expression and method of editing is the cut, a literal—or today, digital—severing of the shot. A shot is an actual or apparent unbroken length of film—editing is what breaks it. But editing joins together as well as cuts apart. Through editing, filmmakers build the structure of a movie by arranging its shots. Editing is what is done to a shot. Editing is cutting; but *an* edit usually refers to the joining together of two shots. There are a number of editing styles, the most dominant of which is the classic **continuity style** of American filmmaking.

A reasonable question at this point might be, why edit at all? Why not just create the sequences of film each in one shot, so the unity of time and space would be maintained without having to trick the viewer's eye into believing that parts are wholes? The answer to the question lies deep within the history and culture of Hollywood studio filmmaking and speaks to the development of the classical style. Very early in film history—at the time of Edison, the Lumière brothers, and Georges Méliès, and lasting until just after the turn of the twentieth century—films were short and usually made in one or a few shots. There was not much camera movement, and the space defined by the composition of the shot was often frontal and static. People have theorized that this frontal, static gaze was an attempt to represent the view of a stage from the point of view of the auditorium, a perspective most early filmgoers would have understood and found comforting. More recent theories, as I've mentioned, have emphasized the aspect of spectacle in early film: one shot that shows an amazing and attractive event—President McKinley receiving a message, a fan dancer, two people kissing. Over the course of a relatively few years, as spectators became more comfortable with the spatial arrangement of the shot and the composition of the image, filmmakers began experimenting with the construction of story—the narrative—of films. The single shot seemed not to provide enough flexibility. Flexibility was a key reason for editing: filmmakers began cutting to alter points of view, keep the viewer's eyes engaged, and find ways of creating a **narrative** that could be more easily achieved by cutting scenes and sequences together.

This was not done easily or without concern. Nothing in filmmaking then or now is done without concern or even anxiety. Would spectators understand what was happening when two shots were cut together or a cut from a long shot to a close-up was made? The audience did. Film is perhaps the greatest

FIGURES 4.2–4.5 Four of the spaces cut together to form a narrative, in addition to the robbery itself: the dance; a woman praying over a victim of the robbery; the townspeople who were at the dance, riding in pursuit. These examples don't follow each other directly, but indicate the way Porter manipulated the narrative to encompass a number of actions (*The Great Train Robbery*, Edwin S. Porter, 1903).

self-teacher of all the arts. New methods of building stories were taken in by audiences with apparent ease, and, as they were accepted, more editing techniques were tried out. By the early part of the twentieth century, further experiments were made. Edwin S. Porter's *The Great Train Robbery*, made in 1903, is an early example of a film that intercuts sequences—of the robbery itself, of the townspeople at a dance—and it pointed the way to great flexibility in narrative construction. For a short time in the early part of the twentieth century, control of this flexibility extended to film exhibitors—the owners of the movie houses! *The Great Train Robbery* includes a famous shot of one of the robbers pointing a gun toward the camera and firing as if at the audience. Exhibitors were at liberty to put this shot at the beginning or at the end of the film. Some eighty years later, near the end of *GoodFellas* (1990), Martin Scorsese splices in a shot of Joe Pesci's Jimmy, firing his gun directly at the audience, in direct reference to Porter's early film.

FIGURE 4.6   The robber shooting at the camera *(The Great Train Robbery*, Edwin S. Porter, 1903).

FIGURE 4.7   Scorsese redoes Porter by placing this shot of Jimmy (Joe Pesci) shooting at the audience at the end of *GoodFellas* (1990).

THE DEVELOPMENT OF CONTINUITY CUTTING

Imagine this problem: A film calls for two events to happen simultaneously. A woman is held captive by a man of evil intent. Her fiancé knows where she is and is coming to rescue her. As we will see in Chapter 8, this is a master narrative of film (and literature), the **"captivity" narrative**. Versions of it are still with us—think of David Fincher's *Panic Room* (2002). How can this information be structured for maximum effect? One method might be to show each action in a single shot, each complete in itself, one after the other. This method would extend the single-shot construction that was the mainstay of early cinema, but it would not provide temporal control. In other words, the action of the story would be at the mercy of the linearity of the shots, not the rhythm of the action: the heroine is held captive, the hero rides to her rescue, the hero arrives and saves the heroine.

The successful solution of this problem creates an illusion of simultaneity by editing the sequences together so that a shot of the woman in captivity and a shot of the fiancé coming to her rescue are intercut in an alternating sequence. Intercutting two sequences, often called **cross cutting** or **parallel editing**, provides a means to integrate story parts with finesse and flexibility. Early filmmakers—we see it in *The Great Train Robbery*—discovered that suspense could be created by changing the lengths of these alternating shots, perhaps shortening them as the hero approached the captive heroine to increase tension. Audiences accepted this structure with ease, and it became one of the foundations of the classical American style.

Other, very important, elements of cutting were developed during the period between 1905 and the early 1910s, all of them crucial to the continuity style and to cinema being created to entice and hold the viewer's gaze. One element was a solution to a seemingly simple problem. A filmmaker might need to get a character up from a chair and out of a room, catching her again from the outside of the room as she passes through the door. With a mobile camera, it would be quite possible, and very dramatic, to do a backward track, **dollying** the camera (moving it on tracks or another device) away from the person as she gets up and moves through the door. During the early period, however, cameras were not very mobile. Since they had no electric motor and needed to be hand-cranked, they couldn't be moved easily, unless apparatus and operator were placed in a moving vehicle—which Griffith did in *Birth of a Nation* and *Intolerance*—but this would not be useful for the closed space of a room. Beyond the physical limitations, there was, as I said, a desire for a rhythmical structure in film that could only be attained by cutting, a rhythm that would keep the viewer's attention through changing shots as opposed to continuous unbroken shots. Narrative rhythm became an important driving force in the development of editing.

Cinema, early and late, is full of shots of people getting up from seated positions, leaving a room, getting into a car, going to their destinations. These are essential narrative transitions. During the pre-1910 period, however, these movements were not always cut together in consistent ways. In an early film, it is quite possible to see a person rising from a chair in the first shot and, in the second, the person rising from the same position she had already occupied before the cut. The effect is seeing the person getting up from the chair twice. This is not incompetence but rather the sign of a cinematic grammar incompletely standardized, as if one didn't know (or care) that the clause on either side of a coordinate conjunction should be different and instead saying, "She got up out of the chair and she got up out of the chair." There were no conventions of continuity cutting, no rules; they had to be invented and used over and over again before they became conventions. But as we noted earlier, "invented" is not quite accurate. The individuals who developed the grammar of continuity cutting were not theorists and were certainly not scientific.

Griffith and Cutting

The process was an intuitive one, and you can see it developing across the period and especially in the short films D. W. Griffith made for Biograph, which we discussed earlier in the section on composition. Griffith and others learned how to match shots, so that the analysis of a single movement—the person getting out of a chair and leaving the room—would appear not to be the fragments of an action that they actually are but the illusion of one continuous action. Even the hard part, synchronizing the cut of the woman leaving the room to the shot of her exiting the door on the other side, becomes smoothed and timed to achieve the right sense of forward, purposive motion, not only of the character but of her story as well. Coordinates become, in effect, commas. Hiding the cut by editing on a continuous movement, distracting the viewer with something else going on in the frame, and, from 1930 on, using dialogue or sound as a cover became a major function of the continuity style.

Here is an example of an almost perfect continuity shot from Griffith's *The Lonedale Operator* (1911), another train robbery film. This is a brief sequence from the film that entails the telegraph operator receiving a message, getting up, and going out to greet the arriving train. The first shot frames the operator, giving a lot of space for her to actually get up and move. He then offers a **point of view** shot of the message before cutting to her getting up and leaving the room. He then cuts to her coming out the other side of the door. As she goes to the door that leads to the train station, she begins to wave, and Griffith cuts again, as she exits on the other side of the door, where she once again waves. Now, this may be a **mismatched cut**, though there is always the possibility that Griffith intended for the actress to wave going out the door and wave once more when she got outside.

FIGURE 4.8 The Lonedale operator sits at her desk in medium close-up, copying a message.

FIGURE 4.9 Griffith cuts in the message she's writing.

FIGURE 4.10 The operator, in a wide shot, leaves her desk to deliver her message to the arriving train and begins exiting through the door.

FIGURE 4.11 There is a continuity cut to the other side of the door, where she continues her exit.

FIGURE 4.12 She goes through the next door, waving.

FIGURE 4.13 Griffith then cuts to pick her up outside, where she continues to wave (*The Lonedale Operator*, D. W. Griffith, 1911).

Although one can still sometimes spot a continuity error in a film, seamless continuity cutting has became the norm and filmmakers have developed a set of conventions that allow them to cut invisibly: cuts on action, where the beginning of the action is completed on the other side of shot; cuts on music or dialogue, so that either or both smother the obviousness of the cut; cuts to a different scene which is telegraphed by the dialogue in either the scene before or the scene following. All these techniques are formal properties of movies. They aren't natural or "given"; the cuts are made to be invisible and we therefore learn to ignore them. The story is moved forward. There are always glorious exceptions. Perhaps the greatest noncontinuity cut in film history occurs in *2001: A Space Odyssey*. The edit is made from a bone, hurled in the air by an ape who has just learned to use the tool to kill, to a spaceship in an astral ballet with a space station circling the moon. This is a discontinuity created on purpose, a temporal cut that literally cuts hundreds of thousands of years, all of which are hidden in the edit. Such audaciousness proves that there will always be filmmakers who go against the rules to create, even within something as complex as continuity cutting, something more complex, and more visible—something that makes us take notice that the structures of film can themselves say as much as any other narrative element.

Shot/Reverse Shot

One element of continuity cutting is, in many ways, the most important, because it establishes a basic structural principle for the way narrative is created in film. We approached this in our discussion of *Jaws* in Chapter 2. This kind of cutting involves the concept of the gaze, the way characters look at one another and the way we look at, and get caught up in, the looks of the characters on screen. We are connected to a filmic story largely through the orchestration of these looks, and the prime conductor of the process is the shot/reverse shot: one character looks (shot) and we cut to what the character is looking at (reverse shot, which, if it is exactly what the character is looking at, is a *point of view* shot). Making the fragments of the editing structure invisible and creating the illusion of an ongoing action depend upon building the gaze of the spectator into the story telling or narrative space of the film. Our glance is directed, woven, sewn into the visual structure so that we forget the act of cutting and become involved in what each cut reveals. In fact, critics often use a surgical metaphor, calling the process in which our gaze is stitched into the narrative the **"suture effect."** We become part of the telling of the story as well as the one to whom the story is told.

Perhaps the most insistent, unvarying version of the shot/reverse pattern occurs in the presentation of a simple dialogue sequence between two characters. This structure has been so common for so many years (the pattern was developed *before* the coming of sound) that if you watch a movie or any drama or news interview program on television, you are guaranteed to see the following: two people begin a conversation with the camera framing them together in a **two-shot.** This shot will last perhaps ten or twelve seconds. The sequence will

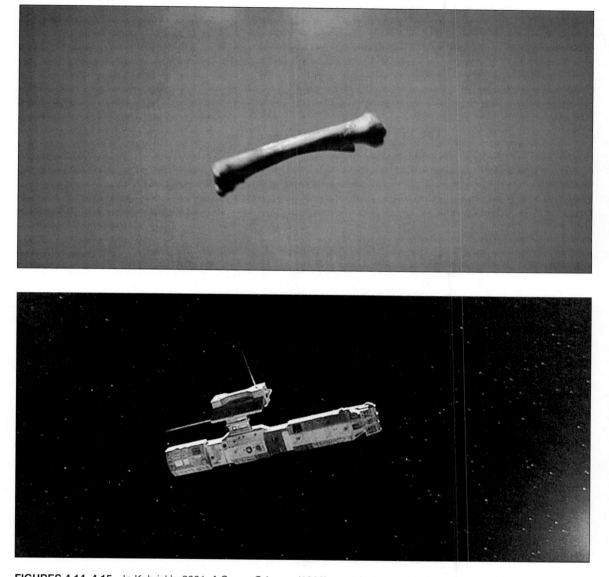

FIGURES 4.14–4.15 In Kubrick's *2001: A Space Odyssey* (1968), a cut is made from the bone hurled in the air by a prehistoric, proto-human to a spaceship going to a space station on its way to the moon, eons later.

then cut to a shot over the shoulder of one of the participants looking at the other. After a very few seconds, the sequence will cut to a reverse shot of this, over the shoulder of the second participant, looking at the first. These reverses, each one lasting perhaps three to six seconds, will continue, perhaps punctuated with **one-shots**—that is, shots of one or the other participant alone in the frame—for as long as it takes the dialogue to conclude. And it will conclude with the original two-shot of both figures.

We can illustrate this pattern in almost any film. But because this cutting pattern is so universal, we can create a verbal description, a template that can be applied to any movie that you are likely to see. Imagine the following scene: a man walks into a room, sits down across the table from a woman, and starts a conversation. A third person in the room is standing and listening. The editing structure might be as follows. Each item indicates a shot you might see on the screen:

1. The woman looks up toward the door.
2. Shot of the door opening as man enters.
3. The woman looks up, surprised.
4. The man approaches and sits down at the table.
5. Shot of the third person in the room, who raises his eyebrows.
6. The man and the woman talk in two-shot (both are together in the frame).
7. Cut to an **over-the-shoulder shot** from the woman to the man.
8. Reverse shot over the shoulder from the man to the woman.
9. Repeat this pattern three times, perhaps inserting a one-shot of each, then return to
10. The two-shot of the two people talking.
11. A shot of the third person smiling.

The core of this sequence might actually have been constructed out of eight separate shots. For example, the woman looking toward the door, registering surprise, and then smiling might have been filmed in one shot. The man entering the room, approaching the table, and sitting down might constitute the second. The two-shot of the man and woman talking at the table would make up a third; the change in camera position from over the shoulder of one of the participants to the other would make up the fourth and fifth shots; the one-shots of each would make up two more. All of the onlooker's reactions would be shot together, as would the two-shots of the couple at the table and the over-the-shoulder shots. Although eight shots are used to construct the sequence, many more would actually have been taken (they are called "**takes**" of the same shot). Each of the shots actually used would be chosen from a number of takes, in which the same setup, dialogue, and action were repeated, over and over, until the director felt she had enough good ones to choose from. (Bear in mind that, traditionally, only one camera is used in filmmaking, so that each **wide shot** (showing the whole group), one-shot, two-shot, or close-up is done separately.) Out of all these takes, the shots are chosen and cut together to create the continuity of the sequence.

Some of these shots might not require all the participants to be present. The shot of the man entering the room might include all three people, as would the initial two-shot of the conversation. But the shot of the woman looking up would not necessarily require the presence of the other two actors, nor would the shot of the onlooker responding to the conversation (especially if these shots were done in **medium** or full **close-up**). In the over-the-shoulder shots that make up the dialogue at the table, it might not be necessary to have present the actor over whose shoulder the camera is gazing. If the shot shows only a little bit of one actor's face, a stand-in performer will do, and will certainly be less expensive. In television interview programs, it is common practice to shoot reaction shots of the interviewer after the person interviewed has left. These are then cut in to give the impression that the interviewer is responding to the answers given by his subject.

In the editing of a sequence, as in the composing of a single shot from different elements, the filmmakers create and we read what we need in order to understand the forward momentum of the story. In our made-up sequence, it is easy to imagine that a look of anticipation from the woman toward the door makes us anticipate something, and our anticipation is fulfilled by the cut to the man entering. The looks from the bystander serve to seal the participants and the viewer into the content of the sequence and create a dramatic context for what is going on. If the bystander smiles warmly, we believe everything is fine; if the bystander sneers or grimaces, we might suspect an evil deed is about to occur. This, however, goes beyond editing into the issue of **"coding"** in which certain looks and actions, repeated over and over again throughout the history of film, telegraph meaning to us, thereby allowing a narrative economy—a way for the visual narrative to communicate quickly and cheaply—to occur.

Point of View

Point of view is part of this narrative economy and in cinema means the representation of what a character sees. It is built out of the basic cinematic units of shot and cut. If a shot of a character looking at something is followed by a shot of an object or another person, we assume (because film almost never gives us reason to assume otherwise) that what we are now seeing is what the character is seeing. This is the closest film ever gets to the first-person effect in written fiction. The "I" in cinema becomes, almost literally, the "eye." We are asked to believe that we are seeing through the eyes of the gazing character. There have been very few experiments in creating film that is structured entirely in the first person. Welles wanted to make his first film—an adaptation of Joseph Conrad's novella *Heart of Darkness*—a first-person narrative, but couldn't make it work. The actor Robert Montgomery attempted to mimic the detective novelist Raymond Chandler's first-person style in his film adaptation *Lady in the Lake* (1946). The result was a wooden, silly-looking film in which the camera gets punched in the nose and coffee cups are lifted up to the lens to mimic the character drinking. The only time the main character is seen is when he looks into a mirror.

The first-person effect in film is best achieved by means of the interplay of gazes created through the intercutting of characters who look and the people or things they're looking at. Film, therefore, is mostly narrated by a mute third-person voice, the overseeing eye of the director and his camera and the controlling movements of the cutting. First-person point of view is built into this general third-person structure, articulating it with the intensity of the individual gaze.

Sight Lines

Remember that each of the shots for a dialogue sequence, or any sequence in a film, is made independently and then cut together during the editing process to create the sequence. It is important for the purposes of constructing the sequence, and for maintaining continuity when the sequence is viewed by an audience, that the sight lines maintained by the characters remain constant. The characters must look in the same direction in each shot, for fear of breaking the rhythm of the viewer's own gaze at the scene. This is called an **eye-line match,** and it is another constituent of the continuity style. If a character is looking to the left in one shot, that eye line must be maintained in the succeeding shots of the sequence, and the other character must be continually looking to the right. What's more, as the cutting moves our gaze from one character to the other, the position of the camera must remain along the same plane in front of the characters. This is the critical and, like everything else in this process, absolutely arbitrary **180-degree rule.**

The 180-Degree Rule

One of the most ironclad rules of the classical Hollywood style is the 180-degree rule. It is even stricter than the 90-degree rule in composing the image. Basically, the camera may not be allowed to cross a 180-degree line imagined to stretch from left to right across the scene. You can visualize this by imagining that you can look straight down at a scene of two people and see a line drawn directly behind, or even over them. The camera may be placed at any point on one side of that line, never behind it (and, as pointed out, never exactly 90 degrees in front of it because the space would appear too two dimensional). Such rules came into being out of fear that, if the characters were looking in different directions from shot to shot, if the camera moved to the other side of the 180-degree line or was positioned at a direct 90 degrees to the figures, audiences would be confused and the artificial structure of cinematic space would be revealed.

When these and other conventions are followed with such regularity in film after film, we begin to take them for granted. Our gaze is so woven that a two- or three-way pattern is formed in which we, like the viewer of a perspective painting, are given pride of place and the illusion of ownership of the narrative space. Things happen for our eyes, and as our eyes are entangled with the gazes of the characters in the film, we feel a part of events, an element in the narrative. Like every other aspect of continuity cutting, the shot/reverse shot sequence achieves complex results from quite simple means.

The shot/reverse shot is, of course, not restricted to dialogue sequences alone, and it can be fodder for unexpected results. Near the end of *Psycho*, Lila Crane, the sister of Marion, who was brutally murdered in the shower, goes into Norman's mother's old, dark house to visit with the old lady. From the moment she starts up the stairway leading to the house, Hitchcock constructs the sequence from a series of shot/reverse shots during which we look at Lila as she registers a response of fear or curiosity and then cut to the object of her gaze: the house, a room, a fixture, a bed. Through this construction, Hitchcock so synchronizes our expectations and fears with Lila's that he can play two jokes. The first one is on both the character and us. Lila enters Mrs. Bates's room and approaches the bureau, her eyes caught by—as the camera, in reverse shot, zooms in on—a bronze sculpture of two folded, smothering hands. As she stands by the bureau, her reflection in the mirror is bounced back from another mirror behind the one she is looking at, so that there are actually three Lilas. We look from behind and see Lila's back. In the mirror before her, we see her reflection and, in the second reflection, we see her back. These images occur very quickly, so that before we can actually make out her reflections, she is startled by them, shrieks, turns, and we shriek with her. As she turns, Hitchcock cuts to the mirror behind her, now object of her gaze and ours; she sees that the figure who startled her was her reflection, so do we, and we both relax.

The joke that's played on us alone occurs when Lila examines Norman's room. Again, Hitchcock cuts from Lila looking to what Lila sees: Norman's bed, a stuffed doll, a record of Beethoven's *Eroica* Symphony on Norman's phonograph. Lila takes a book off the shelf and registers the fact, which we see in the reverse shot, that the book has no title on its spine. She looks at the pages and registers surprise tinged with a bit of horror in the reaction shot that follows. But Hitchcock refuses a final reverse shot. He does not show us what Lila has just seen in the book. For a moment, the suture is cut, and we are left on our own.

The shot/reverse shot convention is such a powerfully established part of the institution of making and watching cinema that a clever filmmaker can tinker with it to provoke a specific reaction. But the tinkering is rare enough, especially in Hollywood cinema. Its normalization is what allows filmmakers to work quickly and within budget and us to understand the narrative easily and quickly without our attention being diverted by the way the narrative is formed.

FIGURE 4.16 During her exploration of *Psycho*'s old, dark house, Hitchcock uses the shot/reverse shot to trick both Lila and the viewer, as she frightens herself with her own reflection in the mirror.

FIGURE 4.17 When she looks through Norman's room, Hitchcock again uses the shot/reverse shot sequence to play a joke. Lila Crane examines Norman Bates's room. Her gaze is caught by something.

FIGURE 4.18 She goes to the bookcase, pulls out a book, and looks at it. As she is about to turn the page . . .

FIGURE 4.19 There is a reaction shot—a shot of her reacting to what she sees.

FIGURE 4.20 But, instead of cutting to the point-of-view shot that would show us what Lila is seeing, Hitchcock cuts to an action occurring elsewhere in the motel, where Sam is confronting Norman. We never get to see what's in the book. (*Psycho*, Alfred Hitchcock, 1960).

CONVENTION, CULTURE, RESISTANCE

It is important to note that ideology is at work in the construction of the classical style. Most film viewers have assented, across our culture and, increasingly, across the world, to what film is supposed to be and not supposed to be—what it should look like and, to a large extent, what it should say. They have agreed that film is the transparent communication of story: no work should be involved in getting access to that story, and no conscious process of reading and interpreting that story should be required. Film should give all and demand little. It should not—we mentioned earlier—be serious, demanding, or "deep." There are many levels of assumptions here, and they need to be unpacked.

FIGURES 4.21–4.22   The illogic of the 180-degree rule. The "rule" is supposed to keep us from getting confused by wondering how the camera could have leapt to the other side of the screen. When filmmakers break the rule, as Stanley Kubrick does in the infamous bathroom scene in *The Shining* (1980), done in bright red and white, and cut strictly against the rules, it produces surprise, but hardly confusion.

FIGURES 4.23–4.24   Back in the heyday of the Hollywood style, nobody seemed to worry that the viewer might wonder what happened to the wall in this over-the-shoulder shot that follows the 180-degree rule (*Casablanca*, Michel Curtiz, 1942).

As I have said, the work of imagination, no matter what its face—painting, music, novel, or film—is not a simple mirror image of reality, pure emotion, or pure story. Imagination requires mediation, of color and shape, of sound (carefully, even mathematically determined, in the case of music), of words, of moving images. In all cases content—story, characters, emotions—is never simply there, waiting for us to see it. Content is generated by the form and structure of the imagination's work and is specific to the kind of work being done. The form and structure of painting are different from that of novel writing or filmmaking. In all cases, some kind of interpretive work is involved on the part of the viewer or listener. On some level, reading is involved, reading in its most general sense of engaging the form of a work, comprehending it, interpreting it, comparing it with other, similar examples of its kind, contextualizing it, in short, making sense of it. Sense is not a given. It must be made.

Making sense out of film is not automatic. We have to learn how to read shots and cuts and the narrative images they create. But this job is easily and quickly accomplished at an early age. Around the turn of the twentieth century, early filmmakers had to begin learning how to make images and editing legible, how to structure them so that they would be easy to read and the stories they told immediately comprehensible. "Learning," though, as I pointed out, is not quite precise, because early filmmakers did not have a body of knowledge to absorb. "Intuiting" is better, because these filmmakers were really guessing, in a haphazard manner, how image and narrative structure would work best. By the late 1910s, their guesswork was largely done. They had accomplished a task they had not even known they were beginning: the creation of a universal, legible structure of image, movement, and narrative that would dissolve into pure story in front of its viewers. The components of that structure have not changed very much. They are, with rare exceptions, routine and repeated in film after film. As with any routine, the more we do it, the less we are aware of it, and the more automatic our responses to it become.

When we watch a film, we are part of a great process of assent to its presence and wholeness, even though it is absent and made up of fragmented shots, which are themselves most often put together at different stages of production. The assent is an ideological event: what we *want* to see and what we are *asked* to see are mutually agreed upon and take precedence over the "reality" of what we are actually seeing so that we usually do not question it—or even see it. Earlier, we defined ideology as the way we agree to see ourselves, to behave, and to create the values of our lives. Here we can expand that definition of ideology to include the idea of—as one writer put it—assenting to the "obviousness" of things. We take the conventions of cinematic form as "obvious" and, therefore—as we are doing here—have to work through their obviousness to the structures that create the effect of that "obviousness" in order to understand how they work and how we respond to them.

Shot/reverse shot structures and over-the-shoulder dialogue sequences have to be parsed like a sentence in order to see their artificiality and understand how they work their "obvious" forms on us, without our even being aware. With this in mind, we can understand that under the ideological banner of pleasure without toil, of leisure activity that demands only a positive emotional response, filmmakers and filmgoers have been joined in the process of making images and stories that are immediately understood and enjoyed, so immediately that they appear there, ready-made and unique—obvious—even though they are not there and are made with a great deal of artifice, put together in bits and pieces, and so far from unique that they have been repeating themselves, form and content, for over a century. No other dramatic, visual, or narrative form uses these conventions (although they have been modified for use in comic strips and have been varied for television), nor does anything like them exist in ordinary experience. No one leaps from one side to the other when watching two people talking. The conventions have lasted over 100 years and are ubiquitous, so much so that the first thing a filmmaker usually does when he wishes to explore alternatives to the Hollywood continuity style is refuse to do over-the-shoulder shots or obey the 180- and 90-degree rules.

Continuity cutting is an industrial standard, like driver-side and passenger-side doors on a car, like the exact tolerances that enable a nut and a bolt to fit together. Like any standard, continuity cutting creates functionality and universality and becomes the means that permit filmmaker and audience to ignore the details of structure while they go about the work of communicating emotions and advancing a story. From the principles of continuity cutting, narrative is generated and a story is told. The key element is that the story is told with the least interference from the structure that creates it. Creative energies and viewer comprehension need not be absorbed with formal complexity because the form—as complex as it is—is so conventionalized that viewers look through it, as if observing a story unfolding on its own. As we saw in the example from *Psycho,* an innovative director may exploit these techniques and make them yield different responses. Most filmmakers do them by rote. As viewers, we are so acculturated to these compositional and cutting techniques that we don't know they are happening—which is exactly the point. To film a dialogue sequence is to create an over-the-shoulder cutting pattern. Therefore, to watch a dialogue sequence is to watch the over-the-shoulder, shot/reverse shot cutting pattern. We take it as a given and essentially don't notice it—we see right through it. More precisely, we don't respond to the cutting except to move within its secure and comforting pattern, imagining ourselves between the glances of the participants on screen.

The classical Hollywood continuity style is incredibly economical. Since every filmmaker must know how to shoot a dialogue sequence, or a suspense sequence, or a sequence in which a woman looks at a man and knows she's in love, the setups (lighting, camera position, marks on the floor where the actors need to stand) are relatively easy to make. They are shot simply and inexpressively in a shallow space, with bright, even high-key lighting, the camera set quite still at eye level to the characters. Much of the burden of narrative is carried by the dialogue. The rest is carried by facial gestures, body language, props, and other elements of the mise-en-scène—all of which are fit to make a sequence and entire film. Almost always, they are determined by a thousand such sequences made in other films. Fragmenting a sequence into many different shots makes it possible, as we've seen, not to have all the actors present at the same time or the entire set built at once. If an intense confrontation between a good guy and a bad guy in a warehouse calls for individual shots (one-shots) of each character threatening the other, only the character in the particular shot need be present. Someone out of camera range (usually the person responsible for keeping track of the continuity from one shot to another) can read the lines of the good guy while a shot is made of the bad guy yelling threats and brandishing his gun. The two parts of the sequence can be cut together in the editing room, where a better reaction from one of the actors, taken at a different time and from a different scene, can be cut in if needed. **Coverage**, shooting the sequence from different angles and making numerous takes of those angles, ensures that the film can be put together to the producer's liking, in line with conventional cutting procedures in the inexpensive confines of the editing suite. As long as attention was paid to where the eyes of each of the antagonists were looking, as long as the lighting was consistent and nothing changed in the background—a clock, for example, which must not be permitted to indicate the passage of shooting time but only the passage of narrative time—the editor can match movement, dialogue, and sound so that the intercutting between the two characters will be subordinated to what they are saying.

As we've seen, the economy of the continuity style operates on the side of reception as well as production. As viewers, we have been so acculturated to the style's nuances that a mere exchange of glances, edited across the gaze of two characters, can tell us volumes. Suspense and horror films, for example, depend absolutely on a character's look of surprise or fright that prepares us to expect to see the object of this agitated gaze. That object can be shown in the following shot or a few shots later. But shown it must be to close the circulation of the look, the expectation, and to satisfy that expectation. Even new cinematic ideas quickly become conventionalized when they prove popular.

Contemporary thrillers and horror or science fiction films made in the classical style may use an expressive dark-blue, smoke-filled lighting for nighttime. Some horror films use exaggerated point-of-view shots to allow us to "see with" the eyes of the monster. But these, too, have all become conventions; we expect to see them and we know what they mean when we do. These elements of the classical style have become, like all the others, invisible and, at the same time, heavily coded. Especially in the horror film, we are wise enough about these codes to laugh at their obviousness, even while enjoying them: the recent *Scream* (1996, 1997, 2000) and *I Know What You Did Last Summer* (1997, 1998) series, as well as *The Blair Witch Project* (1999), depend upon our understanding of the codes, the genres that are formed from them, and our continued willingness to be taken in by them.

On one level, we take no notice of them, but on another level, these conventions communicate to us, succinctly, economically, what we need to know to understand the story being told and to feel the emotions that must be felt. When the camera dollies in to a close-up of a character whose eyes are slightly raised and, after the dolly in, there is a dissolve with wavy lines from one shot to another, we know what's coming: a dream, a daydream, a memory, or a fantasy sequence (see Figure 4.1). Someone steals into an apartment or underground parking garage and hides in the shadows. A woman follows, going about her business as if nothing has happened. Our gaze is privileged by so many other sequences just like this that we see and know more than the woman does. Trained to move across the cuts, we know that women in dark spaces inhabited by a villain unseen by them are vulnerable. We experience unease and fright in anticipation of what might happen. No matter what is going on in the rest of the story, this combination of shots tells a story of its own. The characters' point of view doesn't matter, only ours. Whenever a camera moves around in an arc or rapidly dollies forward toward an object, our emotions surge (perhaps because the camera is otherwise so often still). Facial expressions or body movements, edited in counterpoint to each other, tell volumes. A nod of a head, a stiff smile, parted lips, narrowing eyes, hands held up to a wide-eyed face with mouth agape; a shot of a hand moving down toward a pocket; shoulders hunched or hands held away from the body; a head buried in open hands or a hand cupping a chin—these and dozens of other stock movements and gestures make up a rhetoric of narrative codes used by film.

Gender

Gender drives many cinematic conventions. Gender-specific stereotypes of the strong man saving the weak and passive woman informed the early development of cross cutting—the editing of captivity/rescue sequences by intercutting shots of the woman in peril with shots of her approaching rescuer. In general, the structure of the gaze in film is really the structure of the male character and of the male viewer, gazing at the female character, who is built into the narrative as the object of desire. The exchange of looks in film is very often erotic, and so the structure of the gaze drives the narrative, drives our emotions, and propels the characters across the cutting and into each other's arms. Even small gestures are gender marked, and much narrative material is expressed through the gender of the person who uses it. Only women put their hands up to their faces to express horror, fear, sadness. Men may jerk their shoulders back or put an arm out—often a protective arm if a woman is with him. A man will allow his head to fall on his forearm in a moment of stress or pull it down between his shoulders to express anger. Women cast eyes upward for a variety of sexually related reasons; men work their mouths, usually in a self-contained smile or smirk. Men may raise their eyes, but usually as a look of annoyance. In almost every instance, from the editing structure to the slightest movement of an actor's arm or face, form dictates content and almost always sexual desire dictates both (see Figure 8.3).

Coding

Directed by the looks of the characters and, on a higher level, by the structure of looks and cuts that are used uniformly over all of cinema, the viewer need be shown and told quite little. Events, responses, emotions, narrative movements become coded. Having seen films and television, we know how to read the structure. Like a computer code, it runs our responses and, within given limits, can be assigned variables. So, it would be absurd to say that *all* films are alike, that they all communicate the same meanings and garner from us exactly the same response. But the ways they order our responses, code them, and communicate them are indeed quite uniform—so much so that radical variations from the established patterns become visible to us and are accepted or rejected to the extent that they disturb us with their visibility. A large part of this coding process occurs generically, that is, according to the film's genre, and this will be discussed at length as we proceed. But much of it also is the result of cutting and composing.

Viewers and reviewers remarked how director Quentin Tarantino played with narrative chronology in his 1994 film *Pulp Fiction*. Chronology is an important aspect of the classical style, and it has not advanced very far from Aristotle's classic notion that dramatic narrative construction should consist of a beginning, middle, and end. (Jean-Luc Godard once commented that Aristotle was quite right; narrative should have a beginning, middle, and end, but not necessarily in that order.) A film narrative must proceed along a recognizable path of development and must come to closure. Any dissonance, any disruption to the lives of the characters generated at the beginning and worsened toward the middle, must be resolved by film's end. *Pulp Fiction* seems to disrupt this movement. The end of the very first sequence of the film, in which the two gunmen are caught in the middle of a holdup in a diner, takes place at the end of the film. In the middle of the film, one of the gunmen, John Travolta's Vincent, is shot to death, coming out of a toilet—meaningless, violent death being a main narrative anchor of Tarantino's movies. There he is, alive again, at the end of the film in a sequence the beginning of which we have already seen.

Responses to Conventional Cutting

The structure of *Pulp Fiction* is less radical than jokey and actually helps Tarantino tie up his film and leave audience members less queasy than they might have been. It gives Vincent a reprise, while also sending him back to the toilet in an attempt at ironic counterpoint to the event that occurred earlier and to further emphasize the anal references throughout the film. It also offers a mock redemption to Samuel L. Jackson's Jules, who decides to leave his life of crime and take up religious work. The minor break in narrative continuity is amusing, only provocative enough to make an audience curious. More serious efforts are found in the work of other filmmakers, most often from outside the United States, where experiments began early and still continue. There is, for example, a British film called *Betrayal* (David Jones, 1983), written by the playwright Harold Pinter, whose narrative runs backwards, starting at the end and ending at the beginning. An episode of *Seinfeld* parodied this narrative trick, and a similar experiment occurs in Christopher Nolan's *Memento* (2000). Mike Figgis's *Time Code* (2000) breaks its narrative into four quadrants on the screen, using sound to focus the viewer's attention on one or the other of the four interlocking events taking place (see Figure 5.3). In the classic *Last Year at Marienbad* (1961), by the French director Alain Resnais, normal continuity cutting is made noncontinuous, and the entire convention of linear chronology in film narrative is called into question. Any reverse shot, in this film about the uncertainty of memory, could possibly take place at another time than the shot that preceded it and therefore not be a reverse shot in the normal sense at all.

Other alternatives to the classical style, classical continuity, and conventional narrative development have occurred throughout the history of film. They were occurring even as the classical style was in the process of inventing itself.

Eisensteinian Montage

There was an important moment in the history of film when continuity cutting was challenged as the best way to make a film. It arose out of political turmoil. The Russian Revolution of 1917 unleashed enormous creative energies across the arts in the new U.S.S.R. Revolutionary artists were driven by a desire to make aesthetics, culture, ideology, and politics interact on a visible, formal level and make them accessible to as many people as possible. In filmmaking, artists such as Lev Kuleshov, Alexander Dovzhenko, Vsevolod Pudovkin, Sergei Eisenstein, Dziga Vertov, and Esther Shub looked to editing—or **montage**, as it is more accurately called when applied to their work—as the means by which the raw material of film, the shot, could be turned into a statement charged with revolutionary energy. They looked closely at Hollywood films, particularly at D. W. Griffith's, to find out how they worked. What they discovered was that the continuity cutting being developed in the West was a form that led to reconciliation or redemption: men rescued endangered women, bad guys were overtaken by good. There was always climax and closure, in which "good" prevailed. In *Intolerance* (1916), Griffith was not averse to having Christ and the angels descend over the scene to close the narrative and unify it for eternity. The revolutionary Soviet filmmakers had something else in mind. They were looking for perception, not redemption; they wanted to pass on the charge of history to their viewers, not the calm of eternity. They found the way through montage.

Eisenstein in particular was fascinated by the ways in which montage could be used as an aesthetic and an ideological tool. In his films (*Strike*, 1925; *The Battleship Potemkin*, 1925; *October*, aka *Ten Days That Shook the World*, 1928; *Old and New*, 1929; *Alexander Nevsky*, 1938; *Ivan the Terrible*, 1943, 1946) and the essays he wrote about them, he formulated a structure of filmmaking that was more than montage; it was an attempt to generate the pulse of revolutionary history in his viewers. Eisenstein believed that the basic unit of film structure was not the shot but at least two shots cut together. The process of cutting shots together was not to be an operation that repressed the visibility of what was happening in the name of continuity. Rather, montage was form hurled at the viewer. It was to be visible, legible, and powerful, a way of making the viewer sit up and take notice. Eisenstein's filmmaking colleague, Dziga Vertov—who, among many other films, made twenty-three issues of a newsreel called *Kino Pravda* between 1922 and 1925 and *Man with a Movie Camera* in 1929—referred to his own method of filming and editing as the "kino eye"—the cinematic eye. Dziga Vertov believes in the kino eye, said Eisenstein. I believe in the kino fist! (See Figure 8.4.)

For Eisenstein, the shot was raw material and montage the film artist's tool that allowed him to cut images together in ways that would cause conflict and visual dissonance. Eisenstein would play shots off one another in order to make the viewer see something greater than the individual shots alone. A montage sequence might be built from the rhythmic or dynamic elements of the individual shots: conflicting diagonal lines, the movement of figures in one shot placed against an opposite movement in another; conflicting *ideas*, a woman calling for peace and calm cut against the chaos of advancing soldiers and hysterical crowds. This interaction makes up part of the montage pattern of the great "Odessa Steps" sequence in *The Battleship Potemkin,* in which the Czarist navy attacks civilians on shore in retaliation for a mutiny aboard one of their ships. The sequence builds from shots of the people of Odessa demonstrating support for the mutiny to the attack itself, which is rendered in rapid, often shocking cuts of gunfire, the crowd, a lone woman carrying her dead child up the steps as soldiers marching with their rifles toward her in the opposite direction. Masses of people, soldiers, civilians, seen collectively, in groups, one, a few, or many, moving in opposite directions and cut together in a montage that defines the outrage of the attack and its brutality. In the most famous montage in the film, which has been parodied by Woody Allen in *Bananas* (1971) and Brian De Palma in *The Untouchables* (1987), not to mention the crazy *Naked Gun 33⅓: The Final Insult* (1994), a woman with a baby carriage at the top of the Odessa steps is shot by the troops. As the sequence proceeds, and the montage returns to her every few seconds, she sinks lower to the ground. But these successive shots are not in continuity with one another. That is, each time we see a shot of her falling, she is not in exactly the same position as she was in the previous shot. Usually, she is in a more upright position than she was at the end of the last shot. The suspense and agony of her fall are therefore discontinuous, stretched out, repeated.

Working against the codes of continuity cutting being developed in Hollywood, Eisenstein refused to indulge in an illusion of linear time, replacing it instead with an emotional time, the time of suspense and of thought, extending the woman's fall so that the viewer understands the enormity of the crime against her (echoed elsewhere in the Odessa Steps sequence by a brief and stunning shot of an old woman in close-up, who, having exhorted the crowd to reason with their attackers, is shot in the eye). As the woman finally falls, she loses her grip on the baby carriage, which, finally, is released to roll down the steps, against the tide of the oncoming troops and the fleeing crowds, in a montage of accelerated speed toward destruction.

Eisenstein's was a cinema of ideas and huge political emotion, in which the conflicting patterns of images attempt to represent the conflict of history itself—a Marxist history of class struggle, the overturning of oppression, and the victory of the proletariat. Eisenstein wanted nothing less than to give cinema the form of dialectical materialism, that philosophy of history which sees events and ideas churning in conflict with each other, negating one another, creating new syntheses, constructing the new out of conflicting elements of the old. Nothing suited Eisenstein better than to create Soviet montage as the dialectic to Hollywood editing.

His ambitions outstripped political reality. Eisenstein visited America in the late twenties, shot footage in Mexico, and negotiated with Paramount Pictures to make a film of Theodore Dreiser's novel *An American Tragedy*. He lost ownership of the Mexican footage, and his ideas and politics were too radical for Paramount, which reneged on the deal. He returned to a Soviet Union in the throes of a violent retrenchment. The arts were undergoing the revisions of Socialist Realism, a state-ordered aesthetic that cut back formal experimentation and promoted a transparent representation of worker and peasant heroes. Eisenstein had already run afoul of Stalin, who was partially responsible for stopping his Mexican film. This avant-garde communist filmmaker—who also happened to be gay and Jewish, working in an anti-Semitic, anti-gay culture and finding himself suddenly in an anti–avant-garde political atmosphere— was permitted to make fewer and fewer films. He spent much of the rest of his life writing and teaching.

Eisenstein's films have left only the most sporadic influence in Russian cinema or any other. His style can be recognized in some of the documentary films of the thirties, including those financed by the American government, films such as Pare Lorentz's *The Plow That Broke the Plains* (1936) and *The River* (1937). In Hollywood, Eisensteinian montage was mostly turned into another variety of special effects and then largely forgotten. But his films and his theories of montage remain an important force in the history of cinema as a response to the Hollywood style. Flashes of Eisenstein are suddenly breaking out in cutting styles of MTV music videos (hardly a revolutionary form) and, in more interesting ways, in the work of Oliver Stone, especially in *JFK* (1991), *Natural Born Killers* (1994), and *Nixon* (1995). Here, as Eisenstein did, Stone will cut against temporal expectations. He will repeat a motion or a character's comment. Like Eisenstein, he turns time into an emotional and political force, a way to express an idea rather than a simple trajectory for the story to follow.

The Narrative of the Classical Style

Despite Eisenstein and so many other exceptions, which demand viewer attention and response, the classical style holds sway. It speeds narrative along and places us squarely in the story. But, in a curious way, Hollywood conventions tell another story. In many ways the classical style constitutes its own narrative. It tells its own story of stimulus and effect, action and reaction, our desire to see and respond to the continuous stream of images and movements, characters, and stories that satisfy our seemingly endless desire. The formal devices of the classical style communicate meanings, transitions, elements of story that are the same from film to film. Facial expression, hands and body movements, props, camera movement, lighting, and cutting patterns are used over and over again to ensure that we understand perfectly what is going on. The curious and fascinating thing about all of this is that these repetitions of style and gesture are not taken as a joke when they are seen in context, unless they are self-conscious, stilted, their timing is off, or some other ineptitude is committed by the filmmaker, or they

FIGURES 4.25–4.26   In *Nixon* (1995), Oliver Stone plays a variation on Eisensteinian techniques. These two images follow each other. The first is in color, the second in black and white. The juxtaposition represents a character—here delivering an almost psychotic political statement—whose internal and external lives are fractured from each other.

are being used to parody their own conventionality, as in those recent horror films. The reason, in part at least, is that we are not about to laugh at something that helps us so easily understand what's going on in the scene and in the film. We are not about to laugh when these stock gestures and movements are carrying us forward through a story that has captured our attention to itself and away from the ways it is being created.

   The classical style is therefore invisible and highly visible at the same time. Its visibility and invisibility can play counterpoint. A film dependent on ordinary structures of shot/reverse shot, eye-line matches, conventionally expressive gestures may suddenly indulge in a surprising camera movement or an unusual spatial composition. A filmmaker may wrench the invisible into the foreground by exaggerating a movement or a gesture, as Hitchcock does with the **cross-tracking** effect in which a character in motion is intercut with a point of view shot of what she is looking at, also in motion, or with the leap to a high-angle shot that he so often uses to express the diminished, vulnerable state of a character who has just made a terrible discovery or is in terrible danger. As we've seen, some filmmakers, in and out of the Hollywood system, make up new codes, give new meanings to movement and gestures, shots and cuts, or turn the old ones on their heads. Orson Welles and Stanley Kubrick use tracking shots to turn space into expressive containers of their characters' loss of power and diminishment. Oliver Stone revived Eisensteinian montage to mold time, character, narrative, and culture into alternative views of history. As we'll see Mary Harron in *American Psycho* (2000) and Julie Dash in *Daughters of the Dust* (1991) turn mise-en-scène into a reflection of misogyny in the first instance, and the shifting moments of family memory in the second.

Avant-Garde Film

The **Avant-Garde** movement, which started in the 1920s in Europe and continues worldwide to this day, is a noncommercial, extremely personal and idiosyncratic style that foregrounds cinematic style instead of story telling. Avant-garde is a difficult term to define and worth a brief digression. In popular usage, almost any form of cinema or the other arts that refuses a linear plot line, simple realism, and the narrative conventions of the mainstream can be called by that term. But, more precisely, avant-garde usually refers to an artist or work committed entirely to small, subjective, even private musings in a medium that is bent and refigured to the artist's aesthetic desire. Avant-garde art is not aimed at a wide audience, does not cost much money to create, and can be perfectly, even maddeningly personal and obscure.

In film, 16 mm photography, repetition, abstraction, single frame shots, outrageous takes on sexuality, or pure aesthetic pleasure marked the avant-garde. It flourished from the late forties through the sixties, often in small cinema clubs. Some of its practitioners, like Stan VanDerBeek, took academic posts, as poets and novelists often do. Others, like John Whitney, made early experiments in computer-generated imagery that had an influence on the "Stargate" sequence in Stanley Kubrick's *2001: A Space Odyssey* and that has now become the norm in contemporary filmmaking. Avant-garde art is almost always eventually incorporated into the popular, sometimes—as in television commercials—in ways that would make its originators cringe.

These days, video is the chosen medium for much avant-garde subjective and political filmmaking because of the reduced production costs (with digital production quickly catching up), and it is in video that women filmmakers have come into their own. Women's films will be discussed in detail in Chapter 6.

Working Creatively within and against Conventions

All this shows that though the classical style remains triumphant, it is not invulnerable. Very few filmmakers, even American filmmakers, depend solely upon shot length and shot content to articulate the narrative space of their films.

Many directors—and we have referred to them already—combine the shot and the cut together to create a mise-en-scène of space and time that enables them to develop narrative subtleties. This, in turn, permits the viewer to comprehend a range of meaning and emotion in the frame and across the cut. In Chapter 6, we will discuss a number of individual filmmakers, concentrating on their styles as well as the stories they tell with those styles. This will allow us to see how filmmakers use the basic building blocks of cinema to create unique, imaginative works that prove that conventions and rules exist for two purposes: to permit the Hollywood system to work smoothly and to allow filmmakers of imagination to break the rules and explore the boundaries of cinema.

NOTES AND REFERENCES

For an interesting analysis of very early film and audience response, see Jonathan Auerbach, "McKinley at Home: How Early American Cinema Made News," *American Quarterly* 51, no. 4 (December 1999), pp. 797–832.

The Development of Continuity Cutting   In addition to Thomas Elsaesser's collection of essays, *Early Cinema,* cited in Chapter 1, two other books present a broad and stimulating examination of the early developments of the classical Hollywood style, concentrating on the development of cutting and narrative patterns: Noël Burch, *Life to Those Shadows,* trans. and ed. Ben Brewster (Berkeley and Los Angeles: University of California Press, 1990); and Tom Gunning, *D. W. Griffith and the Origins of American Narrative Film* (Urbana and Chicago: University of Illinois Press, 1991). Porter's 1903 film *The Life of an American Fireman* used to be considered the "first" film to intercut sequences. In fact, a more reliable print of the film was discovered in which the scenes were linked in a linear fashion, leading to the conclusion that the intercut version was a *later* edition, made by someone after intercutting had become the norm. See Stephen Bottomore's essay "Shots in the Dark—The Real Origins of Film Editing" and André Gaudreault's "Detours in Film Narrative: The Development of Cross-Cutting" in Elsaesser's *Early Cinema.* The standard work on the concept of the "suture," the stitching of the viewer's gaze into the narrative, is Daniel Dayan's "The Tutor Code in Classical American Cinema," in *Film Theory and Criticism,* pp. 106–17. An excellent treatment of sound in cinema can be found in Rick Altman, ed., *Cinema/Sound* (New Haven: Yale French Studies, 1980) and *Sound Theory, Sound Practice* (New York: Routledge, 1992).

Shot/Reverse Shot   The notion that cutting on a look to the thing looked at will create the appropriate emotional response is an old one. The story of the "Kuleshov effect" has it that, in the early 1920s, the Russian filmmaker Lev Kuleshov took a strip of film showing a neutral close-up of an actor. He then intercut that shot with one of a plate of food, a coffin, and children playing. When the film was shown, people were amazed at the versatility of the actor, who showed hunger at the food, sadness at the coffin, pleasure at the children.

Convention, Culture, Resistance   There are a number of essays and books that discuss the ideology of the classical Hollywood style. Two excellent and accessible essays are Robin Wood's "Ideology, Genre, Auteur" and Colin McCabe's "Theory and Film: Principles of Realism and Pleasure" in *Film Theory and Criticism*, pp. 717–26. Bill Nichols, *Ideology and the Image*, cited in Chapter 1, is another good resource. The concept of "obviousness" is from Louis Althusser, "Ideology and Ideological State Apparatuses," *Lenin and Philosophy*, trans. Ben Brewster (New York and London: Monthly Review Press, 2001), pp. 172–73. For a detailed history of the classical Hollywood Style, see David Bordwell, Janet Staiger, and Kristin Thompson, *The Classical Hollywood Cinema: Film Style and Mode of Production to 1960* (New York: Columbia University Press, 1985).

Gender   For the male gaze, read Laura Mulvey, "Visual Pleasure and Narrative Cinema," in *Film Theory and Criticism*, pp. 837–48, and widely reprinted elsewhere.

Eisensteinian Montage   Eisenstein's essays are collected in two volumes, *The Film Form: Essays in Film Theory*, ed. and trans. Jay Leyda (San Diego: Harcourt Brace Jovanovich, 1977); and *The Film Sense*, ed. and trans. Jay Leyda (New York: Harcourt Brace Jovanovich, 1975).

Avant-Garde Film   Two excellent books on avant-garde cinema are P. Adams Sitney, *Visionary Film: The American Avant-Garde in the Twentieth Century*, 3rd ed. (New York: Oxford University Press, 2002); and Gene Youngblood, *Expanded Cinema* (New York: E. P. Dutton, 1970).

5 THE STORY TELLERS OF FILM I

Who makes movies? We've looked at the structural stuff of which film is made, at the economics that are part and parcel of the structure, and at the work of a few directors—and will look at more, especially at those who have gone beyond the Hollywood style. But it remains very difficult to pin a precise creative entity to a Hollywood film, like we can to a poem, painting, or piece of music. In the world of criticism, the very concept of the individual creator has come under examination in recent years. Some theorists hold that the notion of human individuality in general is just that, a notion: individuality isn't a thing that every person automatically has, hard-wired into the brain, but an idea that a culture creates and maintains about itself and its members. An ideology. One of the dominant fictions of movies and the culture at large is the importance of the individual and "individual freedom." Films are always telling us stories about the process of discovering and "being true" to ourselves, to the individuality we each have.

But recent thinking holds that this is just part of a story we have been telling ourselves over the past six centuries. What we think of as individuality is really a complicated set of social relationships, in which "I" and "you," "we," "them," and "it" are continually shifting arrangements or positions that we all take up from moment to moment according to where we are, to whom we're speaking, or about whom we're speaking. The self, in other words, is neither innate nor permanent. The individual really is a shifting thing. The "I" writing this book is not exactly the same "I" watching *Dumb and Dumber,* teaching a class, or complaining about life to a friend. In fact, all the "I's" I am are constructed over a long life of being in the world, a "you" to the person talking to me, "he" to someone talking about me. Individuality is a function of moment and the place. Think of Travis Bickle's "You talkin' to me?" in dialogue with his reflection in *Taxi Driver.*

If this is true about individuality in general, what can we then say about individual creativity? The theories that tell us that individuality and subjectivity are cultural formations rather than objective realities are powerful and persuasive precisely because they take culture and history into consideration. They counter individuality with larger forces in which the individual is one particle, always being altered. But even if all this is true and individuality in the abstract is a cultural and ideological formation, we still believe in its existence and have proof of it whenever we or others act. After all, we do feel, think, and create. Therefore, we can consider various ideas about the individual: individuality is a shared, cultural belief; acts, including creative acts, performed by an individual are always also formed by many forces, internal and external; a creative work—including and especially the creative work of filmmaking—has in fact many authors, including the audience and the culture that surrounds and infiltrates it, not to mention the economic forces that put it into shape. Individual contributions are finally determined when they are discovered *in* the work, or a collection of works by one hand, rather than beforehand. The author is, in a sense, created backward from the work to the person.

With this in mind, we can ourselves work backward to discover what some individuals do in making a film possible on the production side, always keeping in mind that these people were a part of and partly created by the historical and cultural moment. This will be useful because, if we understand the individual contributions to a film, we can continue to understand that a film does not come out of nothing but is the result of craft, calculation, and—sometimes—art, all of which are the result of human activity. We can understand as well that creative imagination need not be thought of in the romantic sense, as the unique working of an inspired individual, creating alone and calling upon the forces of solitary emotions. We can understand imagination as a collective event, the result of a collaborative project.

COLLABORATION AS CREATIVITY

Collaboration is the core of cinematic creativity. From the most independent filmmaker to the largest studio production, people work together, divide the labor, contribute their particular expertise. There may be one single, guiding intelligence that integrates or orchestrates all the collaborations, or there may be many. There may even be an external, abstract force that is doing the orchestration on the economic level: the force of the box office, which is the representative of the audience and its willingness to pay. We must understand, once again, that the Hollywood imagination is an economic system, an economics of the imagination. And this system now works across the world, infiltrating the filmmaking of other countries where individual creativity used to be more easily identified.

Filmmaking began in America as the work of what we like to call rugged individualists, despite the fact that Edison was a company that created many things besides film. We discussed how William Dickson, an employee of the Edison factory in the United States, and the Lumière brothers and Georges Méliès in France worked to invent the apparatus of filmmaking and film exhibition and develop some of the basic narrative structures that survive to this day—as well as methods of distribution. Early in the twentieth century, other individuals battled (sometimes physically) with the goons that Edison sent out to protect his equipment patents, and finally set up shop in Los Angeles. For a while, production in Hollywood and New York was the work of individual filmmakers working with small companies, developing, helping to invent their craft. D. W. Griffith was one of them. In collaboration with his cinematographer, Billy Bitzer, and working for five years for the Biograph Company, he made major contributions to the development of the continuity style. He then struck out on his own to create *The Birth of a Nation* (1915) and *Intolerance* (1916), two films that solidified the position of film as a social and cultural form.

But such independence was short-lived. Even Griffith understood the economic advantage of incorporation, of joining his work to that of a larger economic entity. We discussed in the second chapter how, in 1919, along with Charlie Chaplin and two other enormously popular actors, Douglas Fairbanks and Mary Pickford, he formed United Artists, a studio whose main purpose was to distribute the independent productions of various filmmakers. The arrangement never worked to Griffith's economic advantage—he was hopeless when it came to money—but it is indicative of what was happening to filmmaking at the time. The economics of production absorbed the imagination of individuals, ultimately allowing it only to push against its constraints. The studio system evolved as a means of industrializing the imagination—making it economically viable—and turning individual activity into collaborative effort that enabled industrial filmmaking.

As in any manufacturing effort, speed and efficiency, established with the least cost, are essential in the mass production of film. The studios became self-contained entities, with facilities, technical staff, producers, actors, writers, composers, directors, all working within their physical bounds, all of them under contract. Some of these workers, from electricians to writers to directors, formed unions, and as a result, clear divisions of labor were marked out. (If you are a fan of credits, you might notice the line at the end of many current films, whose narrative is set in a U.S. city, indicating that they were shot in Toronto or elsewhere in Canada, in an attempt—this the credits don't say—to escape American unions.) In short, every job had on-site personnel to carry it out, and every staff member knew his or her job. There is a temptation to reduce the outcome of this

work—the films that the studios produced—to the anonymity of its mass production. Indeed, in the 1950s, criticism of popular culture did just that, imply-
ing that work of the imagination produced in a factory, for mass consumption
and economic gain, could not attain the complexity and status of art. But an opposing argument would be more valid, that a new kind of art, created out of collaboration, emerged from the studio system. We can also argue that there are
indeed important individuals involved in cinema's creative process, individuals who develop and use their talents in a collaborative effort in which individual skill becomes absorbed in group effort and assumes anonymity in the
resulting films.

CREATIVE CRAFTSPEOPLE

On the level of the physical apparatus itself, a number of people plied their
skills and talent in the studios, and still do, though more often as independent
suppliers: electricians, camera operators, sound recorders, set designers,
painters, greens people, film lab technicians, assistant editors. These people rig
the lights; set up the camera (as well as turn it on and off and keep it focused on
the scene being shot); dress and paint the sets; put up greenery; create the special effects that synthesize actors, backdrops, painted scenery, and models into
a single image; develop the film; mix the sound; assist in the complex process of
editing the shots; and then match the edits on the master negative that will be
used to strike exhibition prints.

There is yet another cadre of individuals that has been growing since the
mid-1990s: computer graphics designers, software engineers, members of a
large variety of companies like George Lucas's Industrial Light and Magic and
smaller digital effects houses like Rhythm and Hues. Again, a look at the credits at the end of a film will reveal just how many people are involved in the digital work that has taken over from the studios' special effects units.

The following are among the most important of the creative personnel and
craftspeople who collaborate on a film's production. I've tried to group them in
relationship to both their importance and whether the role they play takes place
during or after a film. However, I've left screenwriters, actors, and producers
near the end. They are not simply "craftspeople," and their creative talents are
crucial to the entire process of a film's creation.

Cinematographer

The **cinematographer** is among the most important creative people involved in
the production of a film. He (in a notoriously male-centric industry, there have
been few women cinematographers, though recently their numbers are slowly
growing) handles the lighting, chooses the appropriate lenses and film stock,
decides on all the elements that determine the size of the image, its spatial qualities, density, color values or gray scale that will result in an image appearing,
first on the film stock and finally on the screen, when the light of the projector is

focused through it. If the director wants a wide shot or to introduce some distortion into the image, the cinematographer may choose to put a 28 mm lens on the camera, which will produce a very wide, deep effect. The cinematographer will choose the correct combination of lights to produce the appropriate mood of the scene, and will even tinker with the color to create an overall visual effect. The cinematographer and the director make the compositions we analyzed in a previous chapter.

At his best, the cinematographer is a close collaborator with, and an adviser and consultant to, the film's director. In the days of the studios, some major stars had their own cinematographers assigned to them in film after film. William H. Daniels, for example, worked consistently with Greta Garbo, MGM's glamorous and mysterious star of the thirties, because Garbo and the studio felt he could light her to best advantage. This was not an act of mere vanity but of the studio's and the audience's desire to have a consistent image of its star, which the cinematographer could best provide (see Figure 3.14).

In some instances, a cinematographer exercises extraordinary creative license, expanding upon what the producer or director wants to see on film. This was the case in Gregg Toland's collaboration with Orson Welles on *Citizen Kane*. Toland signed on to the project because he felt that working with a new, young, imaginative director would give him the opportunity to experiment, which it did. He ground and coated new lenses, experimented with lighting, and figured out ways to create the deep field compositions and expressionist style that both he and Welles envisioned. The way *Citizen Kane* looks—its dynamic articulation of space, light, and composition—had more influence on filmmaking than anything else since *The Birth of a Nation*, which like many of Griffith's films was photographed by Billy Bitzer (see Figures 3.10–3.11). In *Citizen Kane*, that articulation is the result of the Welles and Toland collaboration, which Welles credited (see Figures 3.30–3.34). *Citizen Kane* is perhaps the only American studio film in which the names of both the cinematographer and the director appear together at the end of the film. Some would argue that on many films the cinematographer should get similar or even greater credit as the originator and developer of a film's visual style.

In many instances, directors and cinematographers remain together as a team. This is more usual in Europe and in the **post-studio period** in American filmmaking, where it is less likely that individuals will be assigned to a film and more likely that writer, director, and producer will choose whom they want to work with. Among the most famous director-cinematographer teams in film history was Swedish director Ingmar Bergman and cinematographer Sven Nykvist. When Bergman quit his filmmaking career—after he had become the most widely known European director of the sixties and seventies—Nykvist began working in the United States. He lends his rich style, in which he sculpts fine details of interiors in carefully modulated light and shadow, to an unlikely film, the popular *Sleepless in Seattle* (Nora Ephron, 1993).

Alfred Hitchcock worked with one cinematographer, Robert Burks, on twelve films. Hitchcock, who predetermined the structure of every shot before filming ever began, needed a cinematographer he could depend upon to accurately interpret his instructions. Carlo Di Palma, who photographed two of the Italian director Michelangelo Antonioni's extraordinary color films, *Red Desert* (1964) and *Blow-Up* (1966), has worked with Woody Allen on most of his films since the late eighties. In Hollywood today, some directors and cinematographers remain close collaborators: Steven Spielberg and Allen Daviau or Janusz Kaminski, Oliver Stone and Robert Richardson, Martin Scorsese and Michael Ballhaus (who was cinematographer for the German filmmaker, Rainer Werner Fassbinder), for example.

Production Designer

Craftspeople are the creative workers of the technical and physical apparatus of filmmaking. Others work on a more conceptual level, closer to our conventional notion of artists, developing the words, the design, and the images that make the film. The **production designer** (usually called "art director" during the studio period), for example, conceives and elaborates the settings, rooms, and exteriors that together help to give a film its physical texture, its spatial and temporal orientation, and that mark its setting in the past or present as recognizable, even giving the illusion of being "authentic." If the film takes place in a particular historical era, the work of the production designer—along with that of the costume designer—takes on a special importance. During the studio period, each company had a head production designer—Cedric Gibbons at MGM, Lyle Wheeler at Twentieth-Century Fox, Hans Dreier (who began his career in the late 1910s at Germany's UFA studios) at Paramount, Robert Clatworthy at Universal, for example—who had great responsibility for creating the general style of a particular studio.

Since the days when studios exercised complete control, production designers have developed individual styles and can sometimes be linked with the work of certain directors. There is the careful re-creation of thirties and fifties spaces and objects that Dean Tavoularis develops in Arthur Penn's *Bonnie and Clyde* (1967) and Francis Ford Coppola's *Godfather* films (1972, 1974, 1990). Cars and dusty Midwestern towns in the former film; tables, chairs, carpets, wall hangings in the latter films are chosen and placed to evoke and represent the domestic space of a certain class and time. In *Godfather I*, a newsstand on the street is arrayed with period papers and magazines, which are laid out as they might have been in the fifties. A room in *Godfather II* is laid out to reflect the decorative style of the fifties and sixties. In *Apocalypse Now* (1979), Tavoularis creates for Coppola the nightmare jungle of Vietnam (in the Philippines).

Recall the dark, fantastic urban future designed by the late Anton Furst for *Batman* (1989). Those sets—consisting mostly of hand-painted mattes that were processed into the shots of the film to give them a physical presence—help create the atmosphere of despair and unspoken terror that supplies much of the subtext for director Tim Burton's film. Italian production designer Dante Ferretti has worked on many of Scorsese's recent films. In Europe, the late

FIGURE 5.1 In this image from Todd Haynes's *Far From Heaven* (2002), a film we will closely examine in Chapter 9, we can see the art of the production designer and cinematographer (Mark Friedberg and Ed Lachman for this film). Lighting emanates from 1950s style lamps and dominates the right side of the frame. The figure on the left is in shadow, looking into the empty spaces of the room.

production designer Alexandre Trauner began work in the twenties and helped develop the "look" of French cinema, especially the thirties school of "poetic realism" that climaxed with Marcel Carné's *Children of Paradise* (1945). He went on to work with Orson Welles on his film of *Othello* (1952) and, in Hollywood, with the German émigré Billy Wilder. Like the work of any good production designer, his design can be detailed and crafted to catch the viewer's attention, or made invisible, not calling attention to itself, but adding incalculably to the director's mise-en-scène.

Production designers combine the talents of graphic artist, which today includes computer-generated design, interior decorator, architect, art historian, or futurist, to create ideas that—once executed and organized by the set designer, matte painter, carpenter, greens person, and special effects people—fashion a world that the camera can photograph, or the computer generate, and the editor can assemble into a coherent representation of time and place. The production designer readies the space for the actors to inhabit and for the cinematographer, or director of photography, to film.

Computer Designer

I spoke earlier about the ways in which a shot, in almost any studio film, is built from a number of elements, including rear-screen projection, *matte* shots, and any number of optical devices that added images to the still undeveloped piece of film. Beginning in the mid-eighties, when John Lassiter—who went on to direct the *Toy Story* films (1995, 1999) and acted as executive producer on *Finding Nemo* (2003)—created the digital knight in Barry Levinson's *Young Sherlock Holmes* (1985), and continuing in the hands of a growing cadre of digital artists through James Cameron's *The Abyss* (1989) and Spielberg's *Jurassic Park* (1993), **computer graphics imaging (CGI)** has replaced most of the older forms of optical effects. As in sound design, few major figures have emerged in this field, mostly because the companies that create the effects employ dozens of people involved in a complex enterprise requiring a great deal of collaborative knowledge and work that combines imagination and computer science.

Obviously special effects films, or computer-animated films, like *Toy Story* or *Finding Nemo* (Andrew Stanton, Lee Unkrich, 2003), productions of Disney and Pixar Studios, run by Apple executive, Steve Jobs, are completely computer generated. 3-D animation is an enormously difficult task, requiring not only complex software, but the ability of the designers and animators to visualize three dimensions in a two-dimensional space. Old-fashioned animation involved drawing successive "cells" in which the action changed slightly from one cell to the other. Each cell was photographed separately. Computer animation requires generating a figure, either from scratch, but often, as in old-fashioned animation, **rotoscoping**, having a live action figure filmed and then used as a reference for the computer-generated figure, building paths for it to follow, and marrying it with three-dimensional backgrounds before the whole is transferred to film.

FIGURE 5.2   The digital domain (*Men in Black II*, Barry Sonnenfeld, 2002).

Special effects films, anything from *Jurassic Park* to the latest *Star Wars* (1999, 2002), *Spider-Man* (Sam Raimi, 2002), the *Men in Black* series (Barry Sonnenfeld, 1997, 2002), mix live and computer-generated figures almost seamlessly.

But beyond these obvious special effects and computer-animated films are the domestic melodramas, gangster films, any of the traditional genres that, like their predecessors, are, as they almost always have been, created virtually. Only now, their virtuality is not created with models or paint, but with computer code creating pixels on the screen. These are currently transferred to film; but soon, perhaps as you read this, changes will occur. "Films" will continue to use digital design, but they will be recorded and projected digitally from start to finish. We have passed through one major technological change with computer-generated design; we are about to move through a major passage from celluloid using digital imagery to the totally digital.

Sound Designers

The coming of sound to film was not an overnight event. Warner Brothers' *The Jazz Singer* (Alan Crosland) did not appear from nowhere in 1927. The studios had been experimenting with sound for some time, but it wasn't until Warner Bros. found itself in financial difficulties and began looking for a novelty to bring large audiences back to theaters that they offered a full-length silent film accompanied with synchronized sound. "Synchronized" is, of course, the operative term. As I've noted, films always had a musical accompaniment, but making words that match the movement of the actors' mouths was another problem altogether. At first, phonograph records were used, but these proved difficult to synchronize. The **optical sound track**—literally a photographed strip of sound waves next to the **image track**—made synchronization all but foolproof (see Figure 3.3).

Again, it must be emphasized that this was not a simple chronological process. For one thing, roughly synchronized sound was born at the beginnings of film. Edison wanted sound to accompany his early film inventions, and his film inventor employee, William Dixon, worked on this in the late 1880s. So did others in Europe. Technical difficulties and lack of interest put sound to rest until the 1920s. And when it was revived, with the success of *The Jazz Singer*, each studio employed a slightly different technique, until it was obvious that standardization was necessary.

There are few "stars" in the realm of sound recording, few who quite match in renown some cinematographers or production designers. One reason for this is that sound people are largely engineers and technicians, working quietly to perfect their specialty. They work hard, inventively, and largely anonymously. Another reason is that sound has never received quite as much attention as the more prominent visual aspect of film. A few gifted individuals have received recognition—Douglas Shearer at MGM, who was prominent in the early years of sound, and more recently, Walter Murch, who did extraordinary sound work for Francis Ford Coppola. An individual whose name has become a term of art,

Jack Foley, was an effects pioneer from the early days of sound film. His name has become an adjective, and you will see it in every film made during the past fifteen or more years: **foley** artist, foley design. The term indicates that, like the production designer, films now employ a sound designer, someone who will build the film's sonic structure, from footsteps to specific effects, to the **ambient sound** that accompanies all the shots and binds them together, helping to create the narrative.

The sound technician is responsible, obviously, for recording the dialogue. But even this is not a straightforward process. What dialogue do we hear? How do we hear it? How is dimensionality of sound achieved? In fact, just as the cinematographer must give the illusion of depth to a two-dimensional surface, so too the sound engineer must provide a dimensionality to the sound track, which, without it, would be flat and lifeless. Placement of microphones and mixing sound to achieve the right balance and depth is a complex job, as is dubbing dialogue and adding and enhancing sound during editing, supplying background noise and sound effects, which is the major work of recording sound today. Dialogue can be focused by the way it is mixed so that it directs our attention, as much as composition or editing does. An obvious example is Mike Figgis's recent experiment, *Timecode* (2000), shot in digital video—the title referring to the time and frame stamp on strips of exposed film or tape. The film consists of four long takes shown simultaneously in four quadrants of the screen. The only thing that draws the viewers' attention to one quadrant or another is that Figgis turns up the sound on the square he thinks is most important in the narrative flow. But in all films, dialogue is mixed to complement or hide the cutting or to keep our attention focused in the shot itself. There are exceptions: filmmakers as different as Orson Welles, Howard Hawks, or Robert Altman will mix sound in ways that allow many voices to be heard simultaneously, creating a complex aural canvas to complement the visual one.

These days, most sound, including dialogue, is added during editing, especially with the advent of digital sound. **Automatic dialogue replacement (ADR)** dubs in dialogue without the dead sound and unsynchronized lip movements associated with the earlier version of dubbing. Dubbing sound after filming is called "**looping**." Digital sound and more sophisticated understanding of the ways in which sound, along with music, can affect the ways an audience responds to a film have produced extraordinary sonic effects made up from a variety of found sounds as well as sounds generated by the computer. Think only of the dinosaurs' roar in *Jurassic Park* (Steven Spielberg, 1993). More important, listen beyond the dialogue in a contemporary film. In older films, dialogue was surrounded mostly with silence, unless a scene was outdoors or in a large space. But now there is almost always something there behind the dialogue: **room tone** or **world tone**, to use older film production jargon, refers to the background sounds behind the dialogue. Filmmakers carefully complement the visual atmosphere of the shot with an aural atmosphere, sometimes in the background, heard almost subliminally, but just as often brought forward; sometimes used for shock; always to create an aural space.

FIGURE 5.3   *Timecode* (Mike Figgis, 2000) uses four frames throughout the film, each containing a continuous long take, and draws viewers' attention to them by variously lowering the sound on three so that we pay attention to the fourth.

Editor

The cinematographer is the individual with great responsibility for the overall character of a film's visual style. He or she works closely with the production designer, the digital designers, and, especially, the director. The cinematographer is present throughout preproduction and shooting. After shooting, when everyone but the director and producer have gone on to other projects, the **editor** assembles the pieces of footage into a coherent whole, in the variety of ways discussed in the previous chapter. Editing has been one of the few major roles in filmmaking open to women, a fact that is all the more significant because the editor is the person who gives a film its final shape, makes it conform to the will of the producer (during and after the studio period) or the director (who, in the post-studio period, helps oversee the editing process). A cynical view might hold that, because the editor takes orders, producers felt quite comfortable having a woman in a passive role. But the primary talents of an editor are far more important than passivity and patience. A film editor needs great dexterity, a sharp eye for detail and rhythm, a prodigious visual memory. In the studio days, the editor was the one who managed to structure pieces of exposed film into the patterns of the continuity style. Under the producer's eye, she made the film the audience would see—and often remade it if previews went badly. Few directors, then and now, shoot with the precision and economy that could dictate and control the final shape of their material. Many directors still shoot a great deal of footage, and very few "edit in the camera," thereby giving the editor little footage and therefore fewer choices. Producers are nervous when there is either too much to work with, or too little to cut, giving the editor too much material, too much to put into comprehensible shape, or too little.

Many films are still saved in the editing process. Bad acting can be covered up by cutting away from a talentless actor, or even a good actor who could not deliver a particular line, to something or someone else in the scene, with newly recorded lines dubbed in to create a better performance. Many films are invented during editing. The violent stunts of action films are constructed by editing. Sequences in which people knock each other down, fall off buildings, bash their cars into each other are constructed out of shots—themselves manufactured out of various image elements—carefully cut together to create the illusion of fists meeting faces and bodies falling through glass doors. In most films, the various pieces of shots put together in the editing process do not necessarily have to have occurred at one time. If a close-up is needed, for example, and a good one is discovered earlier in the shooting than in the finished film, an editor will cut it in. This, by the way, should not imply that all editors and their directors succeed. There are films whose editing is completely flatfooted, containing shots that last too long after they should have been cut; editing decisions that create no sense of coherent action; no narrative rhythm. When these missteps occur and there is no attractive mise-en-scène to hold the eye, then none of the constituent parts of film hold together or hold our interest. But all this needs to be put in the larger perspective of the continuity style, in which all motion, progression, movement, and unity are illusions built out of the ways small fragments of exposed film are cut together—and that is the editor's task.

In American cinema during the studio period, editors have had major responsibilities for executing the cutting style of the studio, and some important editorial names are attached to their respective companies, rather than to directors: Viola Lawrence at Columbia, George Amy at Warner Brothers. Dorothy Spencer worked at a number of studios on films as different as *Stagecoach* (1939), *The Snake Pit* (1948), *Cleopatra* (1963), and *Earthquake* (1974). Like cinematographers, some editors have worked consistently with particular directors: George Tomasini with Hitchcock, Dede Allen with Arthur Penn, Thelma Schoonmaker with Martin Scorsese, Michael Kahn with Steven Spielberg. Some of these are creative collaborations. In others, the editor helps the director keep his film coherent, and in all cases they provide the narrative structure the audience sees.

Composer

The composer of a film's musical **sound track** is only peripherally involved with the actual production of the film. He may not necessarily spend a great deal of time on the set. He is not directly connected with the construction of the film's visual elements, as are the production designer and cinematographer. Like the editor, he is more involved with fragments than wholes. The composer may confer with a film's producer and director, read the script, and make some melodies in advance. Even during editing, the director may use some found music to provide a temporary background, until the producer, director, and editor get a sense of the film's shape and the composer steps in to assist, through his music, organizing final narrative and emotional direction.

Only the title score and music for the final credits are written as complete, if miniature, musical compositions. The rest of the music is written as "music cues," brief snatches of melody, sometimes only seconds long, that are composed to fit sequences or transitions between sequences, to distract from editing effects (or even bad acting the editing can't hide), and in general to create emotional responses from the audience, sometimes greater than the narrative, the mise-en-scène, or the acting can. Music can carry a film that may be otherwise weak, and in melodramas and thrillers (but not exclusively in those genres) provide cues to us, as viewers, as to when and how to react.

The history of music in film marks some of the major trends in moviemaking and the cultural forces that influence it. During the studio period, composers, like all creative people and crafts persons, were under contract to individual studios. They—like writers, cinematographers, editors, production designers, and directors—were paid labor, who worked under orders from the producer of the film, who, in turn, worked under the studio bosses. Many early composers, such as Erich Wolfgang Korngold, Max Steiner, and Miklos Rozsa, had distinguished composing and conducting careers in Europe before moving to Hollywood and becoming contract composers with various studios. Along with others such as Franz Waxman and Dimitri Tiomkin they made their fame and fortune writing for movies. Some worked closely with a single director. Bernard Herrmann, who started his broadcast and theatrical work in New York with Orson Welles's Mercury Players, came to Hollywood with Welles and composed the score for *Citizen Kane* (1941). He continued working with various directors and in 1956 began an eight-year collaboration with Alfred Hitchcock. His music for Hitchcock is so intensely involved with the narrative images Hitchcock creates that you can listen to a recording of Bernard Herrmann's music and experience the emotions of the film it comes from.

Herrmann's work with Hitchcock coincided with the end of the first era of the symphonic score and a period of change in the constitution of the studios. As movie attendance fell during the late forties and throughout the following decades, and as contracts with staff and players ran out, the studios changed from complete in-house manufacturers of narratives, with a ready, salaried staff always on hand, to less centralized production facilities and distributors. These days, the studios may assist in initiating a project, provide financing, and distribute the completed product to theaters, but leave the details and the staffing to the individual production group formed for the particular film. By the 1960s, an in-house composer and a studio orchestra were among those dependable, off-the-shelf services studios could no longer afford. The same period saw a rise in popular music—rock and roll especially—and a change in film marketing procedures.

Movie audiences had always been segmented to some degree. Studios produced "women's pictures," more accurately known as domestic melodramas, to appeal to the female audience and action films and Westerns to appeal to women or men. But, at least until 1946, the studios had an audience they could depend upon—an audience eager for their products. By the sixties, the studios had to seek out their audience and then discovered that the most attractive group was those between their late teens and mid-thirties. Since this group proved to be a lucrative market, and because pop and rock music were very popular among them, the symphonic score lost favor. Many films since the sixties use existing pop or rock music as background. Robert Altman's great Western, *McCabe and Mrs. Miller* (1971), uses the music of Leonard Cohen in ways that make it so integral to the images that it might as well have been written for the film. Martin Scorsese creates such complex scores out of old rock and roll—especially for *Mean Streets* (1973), *Goodfellas* (1990), and *Raging Bull* (1980)—that some have referred to the films as visual jukeboxes. At the same time, Scorsese is sensitive to the power of the symphonic score. He commissioned Bernard Herrmann to create the music for *Taxi Driver* (1976). It turned out to be that composer's last and, except for the music he wrote for Welles and Hitchcock, his greatest score. Unsatisfied that Herrmann was no longer available, Scorsese commissioned another older Hollywood composer, Elmer Bernstein, to redo Herrmann's score for his remake of *Cape Fear* (1991) as well as compose original music for many of his later films.

By the sixties the large studio symphony orchestra all but disappeared, as did the great names of film music composition. In Europe during the same period, some directors still collaborated with individual composers and carried on a sense of textual coherence between image, narrative, and score. Federico Fellini and Nino Rota, Michelangelo Antonioni and Giovanni Fusco, Sergio Leone and Ennio Morricone are some examples from Italy. Ennio Morricone, who wrote the scores for Sergio Leone's great Spaghetti Westerns, also composes for American film.

One film score convention remained. Almost from the introduction of sound, music associated with a film was turned into a commodity that could be marketed separately from the film. A song or score might become popular and be sold as a phonograph record, or a film's producer might specifically commission or license a song for a film with plans to sell it as a single after the film's release. Fifties songs like "The Tender Trap" and "Three Coins in the Fountain" are examples of this practice, which is now extended to various tie-ins like MTV videos. The video will plug the song and show sequences from the film. If a film score is made up of a collection of songs, the producers will certainly have them packaged as a CD for separate sale and extra income and may advertise the music on the **trailers**—the coming attractions—for the film.

In America, the cycle shifted back to the symphonic score in the late seventies, partly because of nostalgia, partly because young filmmakers, who had been studying film history, were intrigued by the use of music during the studio period, and mainly because of the successful collaboration of Steven Spielberg and John Williams in *Jaws* (1975) and, subsequently, all of Spielberg's films. Today, whether an elaborate score is prepared specifically for a film or a series of rock or rap tunes are selected for the sound track, music remains an important part of a film's narrative flow, part of its emotional dynamic and, in clever hands, an integral part of the film's structure. A film composer can become known for work in many fields, like Henry Mancini, and can also do wildly different kinds of scoring in different media. Danny Elfman wrote the music for the two *Batman* films and others by Tim Burton as well as the theme for television's *The Simpsons*. John Williams continues to compose for Spielberg and spent time as conductor of the Boston Pops, and Randy Newman, cousin of the famous Hollywood composer Alfred Newman, has largely turned from writing popular songs to creating musical scores for such films as *Seabiscuit* (Gary Ross, 2003) or *Monsters, Inc.* (Peter Docter, David Silverman, 2001). The end of the studio period seems to have released the composer into activity in many fields.

The role of the composer is oddly secure, because he can remain somewhat aloof from the production. The composer knows his role, knows that he must write to order. Little is left to speculation or temperament. There is a funny, perhaps apocryphal, story of a conference held many years ago between the famous Russian émigré composer Igor Stravinsky and the studio executive Samuel Goldwyn about the composer's working for films. There was some mutual accord until the studio executive asked Stravinsky how long it would take him to deliver a score. "A year," he responded. The meeting and the collaboration were over. For the composer, like the cinematographer, "individual genius" is subordinated to collaborative imagination. Art is put into the service of the manufactured narrative, and everything is subordinated to budget and schedule.

Screenwriter

Every film begins with the written word. Yet, despite this truism, the screenwriter's task has not been so clear or easy. He (and sometimes she) is the one figure in the talent pool of filmmaking who, certainly in the thirties and forties, was wracked with doubts, ambiguities, uncertainties, self-hatred, and mistrust. There is no great mystery as to why the screenwriter has been such a tormented figure or why we, as viewers, can have little confidence about exactly how much the person we see listed in the credits as writer was actually responsible for the film. American and European culture maintain the nineteenth-century image of the writer working in splendid isolation, with complete control over his or her work. Even when subsidiary myths are bracketed off—the Hemingway myth of the brawling, hard-drinking, adventurous writer—we still think of the process of writing itself as being carried out in a sacred isolation, where the creator is the controller of his or her production. Most writers believe this story, too, even though, like all cultural myths, it is only somewhat true. While much writing is, indeed, done alone, not all of it is (think of coauthorship, even in fiction). And there are few writers who are free of editorial intervention—few whose work gets into the bookstores exactly as it was written, almost as few as there are film directors who see their own version of a film on the screen. There is, finally, nothing very romantic about writing: only people attempting to put good words on paper. If writers and their culture need to maintain their myths of isolated inviolability, film executives know better.

Writers had always worked in film, but in the late twenties and early thirties, when actors began speaking dialogue, the studios needed writers to do more than create a story and write intertitles between scenes, or written versions of what the actors were supposed to be saying, and instead write the actual dialogue the actors would speak. Studios had few places to turn. Hollywood, at that moment, was not a great literary Mecca, and the studios began importing often well-known writers from New York—novelists, playwrights, essayists— at high salaries. When these writers arrived in L.A., the studio bosses put them in offices and told them to make words from nine to five. The writers found themselves used as common labor. The studio executives loved it, because, semiliterate as some of them were, they were delighted to have intellectuals under their control. Besides, they were offering a lot of money and expected their control to be heeded.

To add insult to injury, the executives rarely allowed one writer to produce all the words for a given film. The studio bosses enforced the collaborative nature of film on all levels, whether the writers were willing or not. Studio executives put scripts through many hands, some of them specializing in very particular kinds of writing: comedy dialogue, romantic interludes, dramatic exchanges, mid-story plot and character complications ("**back stories**" in current Hollywood parlance). Some scriptwriters, then and now, are known to be good "script doctors." They don't originate material: they fix the words others have written that a producer or director thinks aren't working or won't transfer well when filmed. The names of any of these writers may or may not appear in the credits. In fact, the writing credits are the least dependable of all, because so many hands may go into the creating of a shootable script. The screenwriting process echoes the fragmentary nature of the making of the film itself, moving through an outline, treatment, and character analysis, through scenario and screenplay, each one filling in the material with various hands playing a role at various points. The process is so rigid, in fact, that budding screenwriters can buy software that will put their ideas and words in the proper form for each stage.

Some major authors in the past, like F. Scott Fitzgerald, couldn't quite manage the process. The few who could did it on a grand scale. William Faulkner contracted with Warner Brothers and worked with director Howard Hawks on such fine films as *Air Force* (1943), for which he did not receive screen credit, and *The Big Sleep* (1946), for which he did. He asked Jack Warner, head of the studio, if he could receive a special dispensation and work at home. Warner agreed, and Faulkner promptly left Hollywood for his home in Oxford, Mississippi. He wrote scripts for "them"; he wrote novels for himself and his public, and everyone, including himself, profited in many ways from both. This was a rare freedom, but it was not based on Faulkner's fame alone. Rather, it was a demonstration of a half-truth on Faulkner's and a rare amount of good faith, understanding, and self-possession on everyone's part.

Hollywood moviemaking, like any large business enterprise, is not usually based on self-possession and understanding. Power and money are the motivating forces, and power depends upon generating insecurity, resentment, and fear in order to work. That's why writers often felt miserable under the studio system. In the studio days, executives took all of this for granted, but the writers did not. An unpleasant culture was created for them, and many felt they were working in bad faith. But two good events emerged from this. One was the Screen Writers Guild, a powerful and, in its early days, left-of-center union that the writers formed in the thirties to help protect their interests, as best they could be protected. An important job of the SWG was and is to arbitrate what writer gets credit on a film. During the thirties, it also provided a base where writers could discuss the political and intellectual matters they couldn't deal with in their films.

The other, long lasting, series of events were the great studio films created between the early thirties and the mid-fifties, films that prove the old cultural myths wrong: that it is possible to get good writing and strong narrative structure through a group effort. While few films have shining, imaginative dialogue, many of them have good dialogue. Some of it captures the rhythms of the language of the day (even though, because of the Production Code and a general fear of offense, profanity was not heard in film until the sixties). Much of it delineates character and propels story and expresses emotions. Like the continuity style of which it is an essential part, dialogue becomes integrated within the seamless web of story and action. If a film coheres, the viewer cannot recognize the fragments of writing that come from various hands. Like the editing, like the music, it becomes unified and coherent, part of the story's presence.

There is somewhat less resentment and self-hatred among screenwriters these days. One reason is that there is little innocence left about the process. Most writers who go into the business know that it will be a collaborative event and that egos and romantic myths about independence and control won't work. Perhaps more important, a screenwriter stands to make a great deal of money. A quarter-million dollars is not unheard of for a first effort, millions for an established screenwriter, someone like Robert Towne (the writer of *Chinatown*, Roman Polanski, 1974) or Joe Eszterhas, who was paid three million dollars for his script for *Basic Instinct* (Paul Verhoeven, 1992).

The cynical view would be that sanctimony disappears in the face of profit; a kinder view is that more and more writers, who consciously choose screenwriting as their profession, understand what movie writing is all about and are able to join in the collaborative mix we've been discussing, doing their jobs with few fantasies about individual creativity. They *are* creative, but in ways that don't usually fit in with our preconceptions.

Actors

Early in the history of film, both filmmakers and audiences found a way to ignore the entire issue of the creative individual behind the camera by focusing on the visible figures in front of them, the movie actors. Actors are, after all, the most recognizable, most promotable, sometimes the most memorable elements of a film. They create an illusion of embodiment, of giving story flesh and bone. They are turned into simulacra of our desire—representations of what we think we want to be and know we want to see. They are our collective imaginary—the cultural repository of images of beauty, sexuality, romance, strength, and power. Filmmakers, who at first (long ago, at the turn of the twentieth century) tried to keep their players anonymous so they wouldn't have to pay them a lot of money, soon had to yield to public curiosity—public *desire*—and actively promote the people who turned out to be their most valuable commodity.

A strong argument can be made that film as we know it—with all its attendant apparatus of publicity, fandom, expectation, identification, and desire—was born when public recognition and admiration of stars forced filmmakers to acknowledge that they could extend their profits by extending the stories they told about the people in front of the camera beyond the films themselves. The film narrative became only one in a larger constellation of stories. The star system became a great attraction and convenience for everyone. Audiences could live out fantasy and desire through their favorite players both on and off the screen. Sexual promise, so much at the core of what movies are about, could be expanded from film narrative to publicity narrative, and journalism became one more extension of the studio system. They could all feed one another. A studio's filmmaking and publicity machines meshed gears with newspapers, magazines, radio, and television to author a supernarrative of sex, wealth, and fantastic irresponsibility. This narrative continues today through radio and television movie reviews, through *Entertainment Tonight,* the *E!* cable network and website, *People Magazine,* the tabloids, and the tourists' drive through Bel Air to see "the homes of the stars."

But what is the reality of the actor's role as creative individual? Film acting, and the very bodies who do the acting, should be understood as part of a film's mise-en-scène. A player is one element of the film's narrative space. How an actor looks, gestures, talks, moves, gazes can be understood in relation to everything else that's going on in the shot or from one shot to another, and becomes an important element of the film's total design. If the actor is well known and his or her gestures are part of a career-long development from film to film, an interplay of recollection is added to this mix. Coherence and continuity are the keys. A good actor can maintain, within one film and across a number of films, an intensity of style. She can create a performance that grows out of the particular film and is marked by a style that can be recognized from one film to another. Gesture, response, and delivery of dialogue propel the narrative of any one film and propel the actor through a number of films.

This may seem obvious, until one considers exactly what film acting is, which is precisely the reverse of stage acting or any other idea we hold about a performance. Acting in film doesn't involve a coherent, ongoing, developing representation of narrative-driven emotion—at least not on the actor's part. A performance is created *by* the film's structure, its mise-en-scène and editing. The actor actually "performs" in relatively short spurts and in multiple takes of relatively short pieces of business, usually shot out of sequence. (Stanley Kubrick

demanded his actors deliver take after take after take until, all inhibition and resistance gone, they produced the effects the director found useful.) The actual
process of film acting is part of the continuity style, composed out of fragments
in the editing room. In reality, the producer, the director, and the editor create
the performance, if we define performance as a process in which a character and
situation are developed. They emphasize what they want and hide what they
don't, sometimes by no more complicated means than cutting away to something or someone else when a particular character is talking, or mixing parts of
various takes of a scene, or cutting a reaction shot into one scene that might
have been filmed for another. The filmmaker can provide accents to a scene by
lighting, camera angle, and movement when the scene is being filmed and by
music and editing rhythm when the film is being assembled. The actor must be
able to call upon his or her tricks or talents for emotional delivery on demand
and without a real sense of connection to what was going on before or may go
on after, when the final cut is assembled. Like the composer, the actor creates on
demand and in disconnected bits—a look, a gesture, a piece of dialogue. The
continuity style creates the illusion of physical and emotional presence and continuity. The actor's body is given, if not flesh, then the immediacy of appearance, and it expresses the illusion of emotions deeply felt.

I noted that very good film actors and actresses have the talent to create a
role within a film and a style that is carried from one film to another. These are
the ones whose presence and style may either transcend the subservience to directorial and editorial manipulation or allow it to be used to everyone's best advantage. Some screen players create personae, versions of themselves that are
made up of attitudes, gestures, and facial expressions so coherent and main-
tainable that they become instantly recognizable and sometimes more interesting than the particular film they are in. When this is combined with the
elaboration of a cultural myth about the actor's persona, a story built up in the
collective popular consciousness from the actor's roles and publicity, a figure is
created that transcends his or her individual films. John Wayne is more than the
character in this or that film; he is, even dead, an evolving idea of a hero (we
will note Wayne's career in Westerns in Chapter 9). Marilyn Monroe transcends
The Seven Year Itch (1955) or *Some Like It Hot* (1959)—both directed by Billy
Wilder—becoming part of the culture's collective sexual insecurity and its
mythologies of the sexually active, self-destructive woman. Others take up
somewhat less cultural space, but demand our attention in and out of their films
nonetheless: Humphrey Bogart, Henry Fonda, Katharine Hepburn, Robert De
Niro, Kevin Spacey, Julia Roberts, Bruce Willis, Samuel Jackson, Cameron Diaz,
Ben Affleck, Uma Thurman, and many others are actors with a reputation for
intensity, grace, a peculiarity of gesture and gaze that draws us to them from
film to film. So also the great comedians, old and recent: Chaplin, Keaton, the
Marx Brothers, Laurel and Hardy, Jerry Lewis, Alan Arkin, Rodney Dangerfield,
Jack Lemmon, John Candy, Joan Cusack, Steve Martin.

Some actors can both transcend and inhabit a role. Marlon Brando had a recognizable class of attributes, subtle ways in which he moves a hand, tilts his

head, inflects his despair. In his best films, such as *A Streetcar Named Desire* (Elia Kazan, 1951), *On the Waterfront* (Elia Kazan, 1954), *The Wild One* (László Benedek, 1953), *The Godfather* (1972), and *Last Tango in Paris* (Bernardo Bertolucci, 1972), Brando was a camera-riveting presence—the way he is able to focus the viewer's gaze on the character he is making and the processes he's using to make the character foreground his presence as the central point of the film's mise-en-scène. The cliché about "taking up a lot of space" is quite appropriate to Brando. He was, with the help of a good director, able to put his resources in the service of the narrative. He could develop a role and allow the viewer to observe how he develops it. He anchors the narrative and then moves with it. But, while doing all of this, he focuses every action within the film and every perception of the viewer on his presence (see Figure 7.3).

Some current film actors—Billy Bob Thornton, Bridget Fonda, William H. Macy, Bill Patton, Glenn Close, Parker Posey, John Cusack, Edward Norton, for example—can change their styles, shifting, chameleonlike, into different personae in different films. And there has always been a huge store of character and bit players, anonymous people with instantly recognizable faces who populate television and film and act as anchors. They are more than extras, less than stars, filling out the scene, transmitting important narrative information, securing our gaze. They give us comfort, like a genre—always present, always changing.

A talented player, who can sustain an illusion of performance and build a coherent character across the film's narrative, can be thought of as a creative figure *in* a film rather than a creator *of* the film. The actor whose persona transcends a film can be considered the cocreator of another narrative: her or his mythic life, articulated in films by the studio's public relations people, newspapers, and television. The strong supporting or bit player works for hire, does her job, helps fill the screen and the narrative, and moves quietly on to the next role. All of this demands an act of recognition by another creative figure: the viewer. The viewer enjoys the actor's work in a film and observes and responds to celebrity, taking part in a story of desire, fulfillment, eventual loss, and sometimes pathetic death of the figure who is partly real human being and mostly illusory construct, the imaginary figure of the movie star.

Let's take stock. There is the group of creative people involved in various stages of film production, from writers to composer, from production designer to cinematographer and computer designer. There is the creative presence of the actor in front of the camera. It is clear that filmmaking is collaborative work in which each individual contributes a part of the imaginative component that goes to construct the whole. Collaborative, however, is not quite the same as communal. Decisions about how the imaginative pieces are going to fit are rarely made by committee and never through full consensus among the participants. Someone is always in charge during a film's production, pulling things together, giving orders, keeping the hierarchy working—exercising power. We are left with two figures who might still be counted as the major creative forces of a film, and who fit the roles of head of the hierarchy: the producer and the director. Between these two figures, the power, creativity, and the myths of creativity are held in contention.

Producer

Orson Welles once said that no one can figure out exactly what a producer does. At the Academy Awards, the "Best Film" award is given in the name of the winning film's producer. In the credits of a film, the producer's title is prominent, though often subdivided among many individuals: executive producer, coproducer, associate producer, line producer. What do these people actually do? Depending upon a number of factors, a **producer** is an initiator of projects, a fund-raiser, a deal maker, an administrator. The producer is also a cajoler, a protector of egos, often enough a tyrannical ego him or herself. The producer and her associates get the money and represent it. She oversees the writing, casting, design, and direction. More often than not, the producer is on the set during shooting and in the editing room when the film is being assembled. All this control bestows a right on the producer to leave an aesthetic mark on the film itself. Even if it's just suggesting a camera angle or an actor's reading, or cutting a few frames or entire sequences during editing, or to get the appropriate rating from the **Motion Picture Association of America (MPAA),** the producer likes to think that administrative creativity should also extend to the artistic.

The amount of power that a producer has cannot be underestimated and never is in Hollywood. From the time that Irving Thalberg was appointed executive producer at MGM by Louis B. Mayer in 1923 and reorganized the film production process, demoting the role of director to another contract worker, the producer has been the focal point of the American filmmaking system. Mayer and Thalberg were the ones who established the film studio as an artistic version of the factory assembly line. The studio head, through his executive in charge of production, oversaw production in Hollywood. In New York, the studio owners (sometimes relatives of the studio head) controlled the finances. At the studio, the executive producer worked with the studio head in choosing stories and stars and assigning producers to individual films. Staffing for each production was done according to which writers, stars, director, and cinematographer best suited the project, were available, or whose contracts and schedules indicated that they were in line for some work. The executive producer assigned a producer to each film, and that producer oversaw the day-to-day operations of the film, ran interference for the cast and crew to and from the executive producer and the studio head. His word was law. His creativity lay in marshaling the forces, getting them to work according to plan and schedule, and conforming the film to the studio's style and standards.

The producer system created a perfect hierarchy for order and control. It put someone in charge whose main obligation was to get things done the way management wanted them done. The system mediated and moderated creativity, because the studio's representative was always there to make sure the film was made the studio's way. If this system repressed great flights of imagination, it permitted small ones and, by creating something of a uniform style for each studio, allowed room for variations. From such volume came much mediocrity, but also a certain leeway for experimentation. When Orson Welles was invited to Hollywood by RKO in 1939, he was offered a multipicture deal with the right to final cut. The film he made would be the film RKO released. It was the kind of contract few directors have received before or since. It was one of the things that made Welles disliked in Hollywood from the start. But, as a recent biography of Welles has pointed out, the studio never totally gave up its control. They insisted on consultation at all times and held the right to cut the films for censorship purposes. Though Welles produced and directed *Citizen Kane*, RKO never gave up anything. The fact that RKO threw Welles out when management changed and promoted a new slogan for the studio, "Showmanship in place of genius at RKO," indicates that experimentation was never safe in the studio system; it only had its moments. Welles was fired after beginning work on a documentary, *It's All True*, which he was filming in Brazil for the U.S. government. The editing of his second film for RKO, *The Magnificent Ambersons*, along with the reshooting of its final sequence and throwing out much wonderful footage, was done by the studio.

In the post-studio period, the producer's role has changed only slightly. While some producers still work for studios and sometimes run them, many are freelancers (and women, like the action-film producer Gale Ann Hurd, are finally taking the producer's chair). The studios themselves are no longer self-contained factories but part of large, often multinational corporations that have nothing to do with filmmaking, except that one of their holdings happens to be a film studio. But reduced or not, the studio still has power. Although a producer may no longer have one boss to whom she must answer, she still remains the mediator between the money and the production, which the producer often puts together (though not always: a film can now be organized by an agent, a director, or a star, who will then hire a producer, or, often enough these days in the case of a star, be listed as a coproducer). Unlike the old studio days, few things are "off the shelf" and few personnel are available down the hall or across the lot. An array of service businesses has grown around the filmmaking process: equipment renters, sound recording studios, casting agencies, digital special effects companies, caterers, and powerful talent agencies who represent all those people—writers, cinematographers, composers, production designers, and the like—who used to be under contract. The business of putting together the pieces has become complex, and the producer has to work her way through the complexity and turn out a product that will turn a profit.

Have there been great producers? Certainly John Houston, who was Orson Welles's producer before Welles came to Hollywood and was then the producer of *Citizen Kane* and many other fine films after that, was a man sensitive to the director's work. Currently, an individual perhaps not as sensitive, but, in his way, just as talented, Jerry Bruckheimer, the master of the action film, is dependable for well-paced, high energy films and television (he is executive producer of the *CSI* series, among others). Bob and Harvey Weinstein, who ran the Disney subsidiary, Miramax films, have had enormous success with semi-independent films, which they produce or distribute, like *Pulp Fiction* (Quentin Tarantino, 1994), *The Hours* (Stephen Daldry, 2002), *Chicago* (Rob Marshall, 2002), *Gangs of New York* (Martin Scorsese, 2002), and *Fahrenheit 9/11* (Michael Moore, 2004).

But, in the end as in the beginning, the producer's creativity is that of a manager. He has to know how to initiate, negotiate, mediate. He must believe that he possesses an excellent intuition of what constitutes popular success and impose that intuition upon the entire production, with the control of a stern administrator. He has to believe that he knows "what the public wants" and get a film made that delivers it along with what the studio or the distributor wants, in the only form his bosses understand: box office receipts, cable deals, and videotape rentals. If not, Sony (owners of Columbia Pictures), or newspaper mogul Rupert Murdoch (whose News Corporation owns 20th Century Fox), or Time-Warner, or Viacom (owners of Paramount Pictures, as well as CBS, not to mention MTV and Blockbuster Video), or the latest conglomerate—as of this writing—Vivendi Universal Entertainment (which includes Universal Pictures, General Electric, and the National Broadcasting Company) may not want him to produce any more films for them.

We have not quite yet answered the question: Who makes movies? That is, we haven't answered it if we are still looking for filmmaking to fit within the tradition of the creative individual. Even if we can comprehend the idea of collective creativity, that ideological relay switch almost always trips on, forcing us to say that anything made by a group can't be very creative. So we keep looking for answers even though the answers that come along never quite satisfy our longing for the romantic myths of creativity. Still, the cultural desire to find the creative person dwelling inside of and existing as an aura around a work of imagination is very strong, so strong that, without it, a work is in danger of getting no respect. As long as film remains a product of "them," instead of her or him, it is unmanageable by the critical mind; a handle can't be put on it. For film and the study of film to be taken seriously, a single, identifiable author (who is not a manager, a figure held in little respect in intellectual and academic circles) has to be identified. And, indeed, such a person has been identified, or perhaps imagined, in a curious, roundabout fashion. That figure takes up the next chapter.

NOTES AND REFERENCES

An excellent, though challenging, source of information on the individual subject and its shifting positions is Kaja Silverman's *The Subject of Semiotics* (New York: Oxford University Press, 1983).

A brave reader may want to tackle Jean-Louis Baudry's essay, "Ideological Effects of the Basic Cinematographic Apparatus," in *Film Theory and Criticism*, pp. 355–66. The best and clearest theorizing about the existence of the author is Michel Foucault, "What Is an Author?" in Vassilis

Lambropoulos and David Neal Miller, eds., *Twentieth-Century Literary Theory* (Albany: State University Press of New York, 1987), pp. 124-42.

Cinematographer One of the finest works on cinematographers is a compilation film called *Visions of Light* (Arnold Glassman, Todd McCarty, Stuart Samuels, 1992) available on VHS and (preferably) DVD. It contains good commentary and excellent visual examples.

Computer Designer Lev Manovich covers in detail the work of computer design in film in his previously cited (Chapter 1) *The Language of New Media*.

Sound For the early history of sound, see Cook, *A Narrative History of Film*, cited in Chapter 1. A collection of essays on recent theories of sound can be found in Rick Altman, ed., *Sound Theory, Sound Practice* (New York and London: Routledge, 1992).

Editor One of the best books on film editing is by the director Karel Reisz, *The Technique of Film Editing* (New York: Hastings House, 1968).

Composer Because few people combine the talents of a film critic and music expert, there has not been a great deal of work on film music. Two recent books are Kathryn Kalinak's *Settling the Score: Music and the Classical Hollywood Film* (Madison: University of Wisconsin Press, 1992) and Royal S. Brown, *Overtones and Undertones: Reading Film Music* (Berkeley, Los Angeles, London: University of California Press, 1994). For the use of popular music in film, see Jonathan Romney and Adrian Wootton, eds., *Celluloid Jukebox: Popular Music and the Movies since the 50s* (London: British Film Institute, 1995) and I. Penman, "Juke Box and Johnny-Boy," *Sight and Sound* 3, no. 1 (April 1993), pp. 10–11. Stories of Stravinsky in Hollywood can be found in Otto Friedrich, *City of Nets: A Portrait of Hollywood in the 1940's* (New York: Harper & Row, 1986), pp. 38–39; and John Baxter, *The Hollywood Exiles* (New York: Taplinger, 1976), pp. 220–21.

Screenwriter Here is a story that demonstrates how difficult it sometimes is to arbitrate a screenwriting credit. In 1995, a film named *Bulletproof* appeared. The screenwriting credit was given to one Gordon Melbourne, a Canadian. In fact, the film was written by Mark Malone, an American. The bogus name was put on the film in order to register it for a Canadian tax shelter. (See *New York Times*, May 21, 1995, pp. H11–12.) For a good survey of Hollywood screenwriters, see Richard Corliss, *Talking Pictures: Screenwriters in the American Cinema* (New York: Penguin Books, 1975). For some stories about writers in Hollywood, see Tom Dardis, *Some Time in the Sun* (New York and Middlesex, England: Penguin, 1981).

Actors There have been two recent books on acting: James Naremore's *Acting in the Cinema* (Berkeley and Los Angeles: University of California Press, 1988); and Christine Gledhill's edition of essays, *Stardom: Industry of Desire* (London and New York: Routledge, 1991). See also Richard Dyer's *Stars* (London: British Film Institute, 1979). For Kubrick's work with actors, see Vincent LoBrutto, *Stanley Kubrick: A Biography* (New York: Donald I. Fine, 1997); and John Baxter, *Stanley Kubrick: A Biography* (New York: Carroll & Graf, 1997). The cultural historian Garry Wills has written an important book on John Wayne: *John Wayne's America: The Politics of Celebrity* (New York: Simon & Schuster, 1997).

Producer   The biography of Welles is by Frank Brady, *Citizen Welles: A Biography of Orson Welles* (New York: Scribner, 1989). Welles's *It's All True* has recently been found and edited together. It was released in 1993, more than fifty years after it was shot, seven years after its director's death. Welles's original material for *The Magnificent Ambersons* has still not come to light. Robert L. Carringer has done a "reconstruction" in print, *The Magnificent Ambersons: A Reconstruction* (Berkeley: University of California Press, 1993).

6 THE STORY TELLERS OF FILM II: THE FILM DIRECTOR

One figure remains to be discussed, arguably the most creative individual in the filmmaking process: the director. As we will see, the director's role has been a contentious one, both in the making and in the critical analysis of film, and before we discuss the work of a few individual directors, we need to examine some of this history.

EUROPEAN ORIGINS OF THE AUTEUR THEORY

Historically, European cinema was more individualized than American. Production never occurred on the scale of the Hollywood studios, even though major outfits existed, such as Shepperton and Ealing Studios in England, Gaumont and Pathé in France, and UFA (largely supported by American studios) in pre–World War II Germany. Elsewhere in the world, in Japan until relatively recently, nations had enormous production facilities. India, even now, turns out more films than Hollywood. In fact, the exotic (to Western eyes) musical-romantic-mythic-surrealistic films of "Bollywood" are now reaching U.S. audiences. In Europe, small crews and independent production were much the style. A film's director often wrote or co-wrote the script and guided the editing process. The producer was just another functionary, rarely the overriding force he is in American production. Films made abroad—especially those made for an international audience—were often more intimate and sometimes less dependent on the master narratives and stereotypes beloved of American filmmakers. It is important not to fall into a romantic overvaluation of European cinema. Some of it was different, a few directors took chances, a number of films are more intense and complex than all but a few American films. The prewar work of Jean Renoir and Marcel Carné in France, Fritz Lang and F. W. Murnau in Germany (to name only a few), and the great explosion of cinema across Europe after World War II attest to a strong, independent filmic intelligence. But two issues must be kept in mind. Films made for *internal* consumption in Europe are as grounded in clichés and narrative patterns beloved of the particular culture (as in the Indian films mentioned earlier) and as banally executed as anything made in the United States. And cinema in Europe or anywhere else in the world never achieved the variety, and only rarely the sheer energy, or—and this is a key issue in our search for the creative individual in a mass art—the popularity of American cinema. Europeans want to see American films more than they want to see their own.

The myth of the individual creator—or **auteur,** the French word for "author"—in film grew, indirectly, from political and economic issues between the United States and France after World War II, and it developed directly from the attempts of a group of post–World War II French intellectuals to account for American film and react to what they did not like in the films of their own country. The political and economic issues were of the kind that develop from time to time in all countries where the popularity of American film threatens the economic viability of the country's own cinema. France tried to solve the problem by creating a policy about how many American films could be shown in relation to the number of French films. During the Nazi occupation of France, from 1940 to 1944, no American film was permitted on French screens. After the war, a flood of previously unseen movies came into the country, and filmgoers were overwhelmed and delighted. French filmmakers hoped to compete against the welcome deluge of American movies and meet their quota of French films by making a "high-class" product. They wound up producing rather stodgy, often stagy films, many based on popular fiction or on big literary works, like Claude Autant-Lara's film of Stendhal's French classic, *The Red and the Black* (1954). That young group of film lovers—who were quickly becoming film critics and who, by the late fifties, under the title of **The French New Wave,** became the most influential filmmakers of their generation—railed against their country's movies and held American films up as a model. François Truffaut, Jean-Luc Godard, Jacques Rivette, Eric Rohmer, and Claude Chabrol wrote in disgust about the filmmakers of their country, especially in the influential journal *Cahiers du cinéma*. Jean-Luc Godard said of them, "Your camera movements are ugly because your subjects are bad, your casts act badly because your dialogue is worthless; in a word, you don't know how to create cinema because you no longer even know what it is."

Who did know? According to these Frenchmen, some European filmmakers, such as Jean Renoir and the neorealist Roberto Rossellini, knew. But most important, as far as they were concerned, a handful of American filmmakers knew best: Orson Welles and Alfred Hitchcock; John Ford, Howard Hawks, and Otto Preminger; Nicholas Ray, Raoul Walsh, Samuel Fuller—indeed names that many American filmgoers didn't know, then or now, were placed in the pantheon of great directors. For Godard, Truffaut, and their colleagues, these

American filmmakers developed and maintained that very quality we have been searching for in the last chapter: individual style. These French film critics imagined something so important about American cinema that it enabled them not only to launch their own careers in France and then internationally, but to launch film studies as a serious undertaking in the United States. What they figured out gave respectability to the movies. They decided that, despite the anonymity and mass production of the studio system; despite who may have produced, written, photographed, or starred in a film; despite the studio and despite the amount of money a film may or may not have made, continuity and coherence could be discovered across a group of films linked by one name: the director's.

THE AUTEUR THEORY

The principles of stylistic continuity were suggested by the French critics and then codified in the mid-sixties by the American film critic Andrew Sarris, who imported them to the United States under the name of the auteur theory. The principles of the auteur theory are based on the given—whether true or false—that the director is the controlling force in the structure of a film. For Sarris, that control includes three basic attributes. The first is a technical competence that marks a director's ability to understand and practice the techniques of filmmaking in an expressive way. The second is a coherent personal style, a set of visual and narrative attributes that are recognizable in film after film. Examples would be Orson Welles's use of deep focus and moving camera; John Ford's use of Monument Valley as the landscape for his imaginary West (we'll look at this in Chapter 9); Hitchcock's use of "cross–tracking," his variation of the shot/reverse shot in which a character, walking and looking at a threatening object, is intercut with that object, drawing closer, ominously, and his use of a high-angle shot to show a character in a vulnerable state; Stanley Kubrick's symmetrical compositions and careful, almost symbolic color schemes; David Fincher's dark mise-en-scène, created across the horizontal line of the Panavision screen; Oliver Stone's extraordinary montages. The Swedish director Ingmar Bergman's intense close-ups of a character in a profound state of existential despair; the German director Rainer Werner Fassbinder's framing of characters in doorways or behind doors (Fassbinder's work will be examined in Chapter 9); his colleague Wim Wenders' images of men driving the road from city to city in Germany or America are all ways of perceiving the world, of making images that mark the directors as having special ways of seeing. It is important to understand that these stylistic attributes are formal, sometimes even symbolic, expressions of ideas and perceptions. Monument Valley is for Ford a representation of the West and all the myths of the frontier that it represents from film to film. Hitchcock's camera strategies express ways of thinking about his characters and showing them in difficult, threatening, often violent situations. They

FIGURE 6.1 The intensity of the face: extreme use of close-up in Ingmar Bergman's *Persona* (1966).

are expressive of his notions of a precarious and randomly violent universe. Fincher's dark cityscapes in *Seven* (1995), *The Game* (1997), and *Fight Club* (1999) are eloquent expressions of an oppressive world in which nothing is what it seems.

Style is not decoration, but the visible creation and expression of emotion and thought through the language of cinema that is varied and repeated by a director from film to film. This "language" may consist of individual inflections of the Hollywood style, or the introduction of new ways of seeing through cinema. This leads to Sarris's third and, for Sarris, the most important attribute of the auteur: a consistent view of the world, a coherent set of attitudes and ideas. Sarris calls it "interior meaning" or vision, but it might also be called a worldview, a philosophy, a kind of personal narrative that is either unique to the specific director or a major and consistent variation of larger narrative conventions.

The French director Jean Renoir once said that a filmmaker needs to learn everything about technique, and then forget it. The ability to think cinematically, to know just the right place to put the camera, to know when to create stillness or motion in the frame, to understand how the actors are to be composed and directed, to know exactly where an edit should occur—these are the initial marks of the auteur. Technique that is learned and forgotten becomes style, because style is technique put to imaginative use. Anyone with good cinematic training can create a low-angle shot, in which the camera gazes up at a character looming above it. But only cinematic intelligence can turn this technique into a stylistic trait, and only true cinematic imagination can make it state a view of the world. Orson Welles loved to use the low-angle shot (see Figure 3.34). In his hands, and through his eyes, it became a way of expanding the horizon and distorting the world around a character. He used it to comment ironically on the strength of a character or to predict the fall of a character who might still believe in his own power. It becomes a part of Welles's vision of a labyrinthine world in which the human figure dominates only momentarily. It is matched by Hitchcock's use of the high-angle shot to observe a character in a vulnerable moment or a point of moral crisis (see Figure 3.28).

John Ford's figures in the Western landscape transcend compositional stylistics (see Figures 9.1–9.3). They articulate a changing vision of the Western myths of settlement and domesticity, of Indians as a force of the land, and of outlaws as impediments to lonely heroes in the inevitable movement from east to west. Ford's visual style fixed individuals in the landscape of a symbolic West; fixed women in the center of the domestic landscape, in the comforting interiors of homesteads, with men riding out to the peripheries, making them secure. The dynamic conservatism of Ford's cinematic inquiry into our memories and mythologies of the West developed through a variety of films, written by different hands and made for different studios. He was persistent, silent about his work, recessive; a good movie worker who developed his style and his ongoing narrative without fanfare. His concept of the West kept developing and turned to critique. His later films, such as *The Searchers* (1956) and *The Man Who Shot Liberty Valance* (1962), began questioning the very notions of frontier heroism he had originally established.

Robert Altman—the director of the original film *M.A.S.H.* (1970); *McCabe and Mrs. Miller* (1971); *The Long Goodbye* (1973); *Nashville* (1975); *Popeye* (1980); *Come Back to the 5 & Dime Jimmy Dean, Jimmy Dean* (1982); *The Player* (1992); *Short Cuts* (1993); to name just a few—uses a zoom lens almost obsessively. It is a technique that has become an expected part of his visual style (though it has been less present in his late work). He uses it as a probe, a way to move toward and beyond his characters, and a way to let us, as viewers, understand that watching a movie is, in part, a desire to come close to the image of a face, which is always slipping away from us. Altman's use of the zoom—especially when he combines it with a telephoto lens and wide-screen composition—a combination that flattens the image and makes space claustrophobic—keeps denying our desire. He plays with what we want to see, getting close, sliding away, and finally isolating our look at the characters and the connection of the characters to each other.

The zoom, along with other compositional and editing techniques, becomes part of Altman's style not merely because he uses them all the time (in which case they would just be repetitive) but because they are essential to the way he thinks about the world cinematically. They mediate, represent, and generate to the viewer his particular notions about power, the relationship of people to each other and their surroundings, the way stories get to or miss the truth, the way movies reveal and hide personal and global history.

They all prove a central point about auteurism: once you see a few films by an auteur and learn her or his stylistic traits, view of people in the world, ideas about politics, history, social order, psychology, sexuality, and power, you should then be able to identify those elements as the work of that particular director in any other of his films. The British critic Peter Wollen puts it in structural terms, suggesting that, if we take the body of work by an auteur and strip away the narrative variations that are part of each individual film, we will discover a structure of basic thematic and stylistic traits, a kind of abstract pattern of ways of seeing and understanding the world cinematically. This pattern then becomes a template that we can see generating the form and content of each film the auteur makes. Jean Renoir put it more directly. He said that a director really makes just one film in the course of his career.

At its most fruitful, studying the work of an auteur—like studying the work of a novelist, poet, painter, or composer—becomes a way of discovering thematic and formal patterns, the way similar ideas cohere or oppose each other, how images are constructed in similar ways, how a coherent idea of history and human behavior develops across the artist's work. It is a comfortable kind of discovery, because it breeds familiarity on a personal level. We can get close to a filmmaker by recognizing his or her mark; we can find—as we do in literature, painting, or music—a creative personality. Because of this, the development of the auteur theory made film studies possible as an academic discipline. When we study the novel, we never think about anonymous creativity or a collaboration, unless the novel was coauthored. The author and the work are linked. We study Melville or Steinbeck and never refer to the author of a novel as "they." Positing, even inventing, the director as auteur put film in the same league as other humanities disciplines. We could now connect individuals with their work and analyze structures of style and meaning developed by a single imagination. Connecting a singular imagination to a group of films also allowed film scholars to recuperate film from its debased state as an anonymous commercial form to the imaginative expression of a serious artist. Finally, because the French discovered auteurs within Hollywood production, establishing style and vision within the studio system, American film was redeemed from anonymity.

The success of the auteur theory was enormous. Films were rediscovered, reputations were made, methods of analysis were deployed, and a whole new discipline of study developed. Filmmakers themselves were now able to celebrate their medium. The originators of the theory—Godard, Truffaut, Chabrol, and the rest of the filmmakers of the French New Wave—began making films in homage to the Hollywood auteurs they had discovered or created. They alluded to American films in their own films—recalling a camera move from a Fritz Lang movie, a composition from a Douglas Sirk melodrama, a character gesture from Vincente Minnelli, a narrative line from Howard Hawks, a snatch of dialogue from Nicholas Ray's *Johnny Guitar* (1954). The New Wave created and honored a universe of cinema and implicitly understood what the poet T. S. Eliot said in his famous essay "Tradition and the Individual Talent." For Eliot, poems coexist and influence each other. So do films. A new filmmaker, like a new poet, responds to, is influenced by, and adds to the existing universe of films; new films absorb the old and then become part of the total film universe.

Many American filmmakers who came to artistic maturity after the auteur theory were influenced by its call to individual expression. Unlike their Hollywood predecessors, who learned their trade by coming up the ranks in the studios, these new directors went to film school and learned filmmaking by learning film history. Like the directors of the French New Wave, they celebrated their knowledge and their medium by referring to other films within their own work and, often, by taking filmmaking as one of the subjects of their films. Unlike their predecessors, who adopted the classical Hollywood style and its invisible access to story, some contemporary filmmakers—and especially those who began their careers in the late sixties and early seventies—are less likely to hide style and make us forget we're watching a film. They are more likely to foreground the presence of cinema and its methods and invite us to see the story and understand what allows us to see it. They will often make films of complexity and ideas that run against the grain.

Robert Altman

Let's return to Robert Altman for a moment. Nowhere does Altman articulate his style and his vision better than in his film *Short Cuts* (1993). Based upon a series of stories by Raymond Carver, it is one of the most powerful statements about gender inequity and the objectifying of women ever made by a filmmaker. And it is a great narrative experiment. Through a complex intertwining of characters and their stories, all taking place among mostly lower-middle-class Los Angelinos, gender difference, even gender panic, is revealed. Dozens of characters—their stories woven together through chance meetings, through amusing associations (a joke about Alex Trebeck and "Jeopardy" runs through the film)—and the restless probing of the zoom lens expose gender hostilities, both open and unconscious. The film seems to discover an almost universal thoughtlessness about feelings and inappropriate actions. A group of men go on a fishing trip and discover a woman's body floating in the water. Rather than call the police, they simply continue fishing. When one of the men returns home and tells his wife, she gets out of bed to take a bath, as if re-creating for herself the dead woman's experience as well as cleansing the wound of her husband's callousness. She goes to the woman's funeral and, when asked to sign the guest book, only makes a gesture of signing, preferring to retain the same anonymity that the dead woman held for the men.

The film is filled with serial cheating (by both sexes), long-held anger by one member of a couple toward what the other may have done years ago, and confrontations that lead to deep resentments and finally to violence. One of the men, a pool cleaner, bitterly resentful that his wife engages in phone sex to supplement their income, picks up a girl and kills her. As he does this, an earthquake occurs. The woman's murder is taken by the media as a casualty of an upheaval in nature when in fact it was actually the result of an upheaval between genders.

Short Cuts is somewhat misanthropic, casting a cold and displeased eye on relationships in general, though its sympathies are clearly with the women, who are abused in so many ways. The film is amazingly insightful into the ways gender and sexuality work to keep people cold and apart, as opposed to the melodramatic conventions of keeping them together and happy. It attempts to understand that life in the postfeminist world is no easier than it was when women were supposed to "know their place," and men were content being the dominant gender—as if it were all a given of nature. Altman knows that nothing in culture is a given of nature, especially in the realm of human relationships. His characters struggle against that fact, and his restless, probing camera pushes their struggles to the limits. *Short Cuts* is a summary film. In it are gathered all of

FIGURE 6.2 In this still from Robert Altman's *Short Cuts*, a group of some of the many characters in the film gather for a party. One of them, deeply angry over his wife's long-ago affair, dresses like the clown he is.

Altman's concerns and techniques and views of the world garnered from almost fifty years of filmmaking, a career marked by conscious efforts to undermine the conventions and narratives of the Hollywood style.

Martin Scorsese

Martin Scorsese—at least until recently—was a shining example of the new kind of filmmaker who knows film form and history and attempts always to rework it. A graduate of and part-time instructor at N.Y.U. film school during the mid-sixties, he has since become one of the best-known and most self-conscious filmmakers in the United States. He has worked across a number of genres and for many studios, developing a consistent and recognizable style. He has spun off a number of imitators, including Quentin Tarantino and many young filmmakers who make their first and second movies in homage to Scorsese's work (think of *Pulp Fiction,* 1994; *The Usual Suspects,* Bryan Singer, 1995; *Albino Alligator,* Kevin Spacey, 1996; indeed any first film involving gangsters). Even more mature filmmakers have done Scorsese imitations, such as the British Mike Newell's *Donnie Brasco* (1997). The popular HBO series *The Sopranos* is an extended riff on *GoodFellas.*

More than his equally famous contemporaries—Steven Spielberg, Woody Allen, and Francis Coppola—Scorsese has maintained an unflagging interest in exposing the grammar of film to his viewers. But, at the same time, he understands the nature of working in a popular medium. While he plays and tinkers with the classical style, often exposing its workings, he simultaneously observes the basic rules of narrative and visual construction that allow him to continue to receive financial backing for his films and acceptance from viewers. Like John Ford and Alfred Hitchcock, two of his major influences, along with Jean-Luc Godard, François Truffaut, and the British filmmaker Michael Powell, he is able to work many aspects of the system at once. He maintains commercial viability and explores and experiments. This was the kind of talent that originally defined the auteur: the director who, while working within the studio system, could also quietly subvert it, using its conventions to develop a personal style.

Scorsese began his career by making small films of consistent quality, and by varying his output. In the late sixties he made short films and a feature, *Who's That Knocking at My Door* (1968). In the seventies he made *Boxcar Bertha* (1972), *Mean Streets* (1973), *Alice Doesn't Live Here Anymore* (1974), *Taxi Driver* (1976), *New York, New York* (1977), *The Last Waltz* (1978). In the eighties Scorsese made *Raging Bull* (1980), *King of Comedy* (1983), *After Hours* (1985), *The Color of Money* (1986), *The Last Temptation of Christ* (1988); and in the nineties he made *GoodFellas* (1990), *Cape Fear* (1991), *The Age of Innocence* (1993), *Casino* (1995) *Kundun* (1997), and *Bringing Out the Dead* (1999). *Gangs of New York*, a big costume drama, large on budget and small on experimentation, appeared in 2002. Of these films only *Cape Fear* and *Gangs of New York* brought in large amounts of money, and Scorsese made *Cape Fear* exactly for that purpose as an offering to Universal Pictures, which had backed his controversial *The Last Temptation of Christ*. Otherwise, he has built both his style and reputation slowly and consciously on films that viewers remember for their extraordinary visual and dramatic sense and that influence other filmmakers.

Scorsese's films of the seventies and eighties are, as I said, made self-consciously and are, in important ways, about self-consciousness. While, on the level of story, Scorsese's films often concern small-time hoods or individuals on the edge or over the edge of psychosis, they are, on a more complex level, about style and reputation, about how it looks and feels to *be* in the world, looking at people and being looked at, seen, recognized, and hurt by the glance of others. His films—often like Stanley Kubrick's, though executed in an entirely different manner—are existential and very physical. Bodies as well as personalities are always at stake. Characters kill and get killed, beat up others or get beaten up, thrive and do themselves in by thriving, or are nobodies trying to be somebodies by doing something to their own or someone else's body.

That's what Jake La Motta does in *Raging Bull*. He tries to control his body—which is busy either damaging other people or getting fat as he tries to control the world around him by violence and jealous rages, by aggressively imposing his body on others. The film is finally a meditation on the inability to get control, or always being controlled, just as an actor is controlled by a director and a movie viewer is controlled by a movie. *Raging Bull* focuses on a boxer whose awareness of the outside world and his place in it is dim at best. He is moved by momentary, unthinking whims and responses, and winds up becoming a parody not of himself but of movie representations of a boxer, which is, after all, what Robert De Niro's Jake *is* in *Raging Bull*—an actor, playing an "actual" boxer, in a film that grows out of a fairly substantial subgenre of boxing films. In the last shot of *Raging Bull*, Scorsese appears partially reflected in a mirror, telling an aging, fat Jake, who has gone from champion boxer to a nightclub owner to a performer in strip joints, that it's time to go on stage to do his rendition of the

"I could have been a contender" scene from *On the Waterfront* (1954), Elia Kazan's film of a washed-up boxer who gets into trouble with his union. As the film ends, De Niro, as Jake La Motta, urged on by his director, playing a stage manager, does a parody of Marlon Brando playing a boxer from an older film. Jake La Motta is portrayed as a figure made up of self-contradictory parts, a reflection of a reflection. He is "real" and he is a fictional character in a film, there and not there, like film itself. Like Hitchcock, Scorsese impresses his own image on his film (like Hitchcock, he makes some kind of appearance in almost all of them). He focuses our attention on the artifice of celebrity, the illusory nature of film, and the fact that the film and our response to it are controlled by someone. The illusion totters, though Scorsese never permits it to collapse. The last scene of *Raging Bull* so fascinated Paul Thomas Anderson that he imitates it at the end of *Boogie Nights* (1997), just as Altman's *Short Cuts* is the driving force behind his film *Magnolia* (1999).

Illusion and celebrity fascinate Scorsese and his characters. Travis Bickle, in *Taxi Driver,* achieves fame without knowing it. Travis is crazy, an uncontrollable psychotic who can see the world only as a brutal, devastating place. His world is created out of an imaginative use of the most basic aspects of the shot/reverse shot and point-of-view shooting and cutting technique. Travis, like many other Scorsese characters, is menacing and sees menace around him. Paranoia rules. When Travis (or Jake La Motta in *Raging Bull*) looks at the world, the world looks back as a threatening place. One way Scorsese manages this is to generate point-of-view shots in slow motion (an effect now imitated by many filmmakers), so that the character's world appears as if it were a hallucination. Scorsese has perfected this technique so that he will literally change the speed of the

FIGURE 6.3   A fat Robert De Niro as Jake La Motta, reflected in the mirror with Scorsese's reflection just visible on the far left (*Raging Bull*, Martin Scorsese, 1980).

motion in the course of a shot. The figures seen by the main character will move slowly and then subtly speed up, until they move at a normal pace. This method, which is a refinement of Hitchcock's technique of intercutting a character in motion with an object or person that character is looking at, also in motion, is disturbing because it plays against the stability of the shot/reverse shot we have come to expect. It generates an unstable space and reflects the perceptions of an unstable character. With it, point of view and the mise-en-scène are joined in an expressive definition of character and the emotional state, the emotional *space*, he inhabits and we are asked to observe.

The result is that Travis's world is one of sharp and dark fragments, created by a mind that is both paranoid and aggressive. Travis believes that he is responsible for cleaning up the very world he imagines, first by attempting to assassinate a presidential candidate and, when that fails, by saving a young hooker who doesn't particularly want saving. In the process, he murders three people in a nightmarish episode of violence and destruction and is turned into a media hero. A number of films later, Travis is reincarnated in the person of Rupert Pupkin in Scorsese's *King of Comedy*, played by De Niro, an actor who became part of Scorsese's directorial pattern and mise-en-scène. Pupkin is not a crazy paranoid like Travis. He is an ordinary lunatic who can't be embarrassed. His goal in life is to deliver a monologue on a late-night talk show (hosted by Jerry Lewis), which he manages to do by kidnapping the star and threatening his way on stage. He gets his wish, is put in jail, and is turned by the very media he hijacked into a star.

FIGURE 6.4 A composition from *Taxi Driver* that expresses Travis's mind. He is on the phone to his "girlfriend" Betsy. Or imagining he is. The camera soon tracks, drifting to the right to the empty hallway that is an echo of Travis's impressionable psyche (*Taxi Driver*, Martin Scorsese, 1976).

FIGURES 6.5–6.6 One director sees his work through another's lens. Martin Scorsese overlays *Cape Fear* (1991) onto Hitchcock's *Strangers on a Train* (1951). The first image is from Hitchcock, where the psychotic Bruno stares out at the tennis player, Guy, holding his head steady as everyone around him follows the play of the tennis ball. In *Cape Fear* (1991), the psychotic Max Cady stares out at Sam among the viewers of a Fourth of July parade.

Blundering violently, lost in the normal world, compelled by madness, high spirits, or some obsessive-compulsive drive, Scorsese's characters, from Rupert Pupkin to Jesus Christ, try to fight the world's imposition on them and impose their own will and spirit back on the world. This question of imposition lies at the core of his characters and also at the core of the classical Hollywood style. That's where Scorsese's cinematic contention lies. Like his characters, he wants to impose his will on the structures of cinema, to undermine the impositions of the classical style by imposing his own style, his own way of seeing the world through cinema. Unlike his characters, he succeeds. He insists that we, as viewers, come to terms not only with the characters but with the way they see and are seen. He asks as well that we question our own ways of seeing movies.

One way is to remind us, even on a subtle level, that his films grow out of other films. In *Cape Fear*—not, by itself, a very subtle film—he constructs sequences that are subtly based upon Alfred Hitchcock's *Strangers on a Train* (1951). You have to be really familiar with Hitchcock to understand what's going on. Both films are concerned with apparently upright characters who become involved with, and are stalked by, figures representing their darker, corrupt natures. In each film, there are sequences in which these characters, these mirror images of dark and light, confront each other. For example, in *Strangers on a Train*, the "hero," a tennis player named Guy, sees his evil other, Bruno, staring at him from the stands as Guy attempts to play a match. All the other spectators except for Bruno turn their heads as the ball flies from side to side. Bruno just stares straight at Guy. In the companion scene in *Cape Fear*, the lawyer, Sam, goes with his family to watch a Fourth of July parade. The crowd watches the procession while in their midst Max Cady, the ex-con out to get Sam, stares straight across the street—the tormentor freezing his victim in his gaze.

Once you see the connections—and there are others—*Cape Fear* becomes an interesting conversation with an earlier filmmaker, as is *Taxi Driver*, which is in many ways a remake of *Psycho*, with allusions to John Ford's *The Searchers*. Sometimes, Scorsese can be downright weird about his obsession with drawing attention to the cinematic roots of his imagery. Early in *The Last Temptation of Christ*, Jesus goes to a tent where Mary Magdalene is performing a sex act. He sits in the audience, and the camera observes him as if he were in a movie theater, looking at a screen. At the end of the film, on the cross, his fantasy of a normal life over, Jesus dies, and Scorsese cuts to a montage of abstract colors and shapes. In the midst of this montage are images of film sprocket holes. Even his meditation on the Christ story is, finally, a meditation on film and the way it represents legend and myth.

He can be very playful, too, almost teasing us about our position as viewers of a carefully made-up tale. This is what he does at the end of *Raging Bull*, and it is the main ploy of *GoodFellas*. This latter film is a more energetic and imaginative version of his earlier *Mean Streets*. It is also an examination of just what we, as audience, think we're doing when we go to see yet another film about New York gangsters. Interestingly, in *Gangs of New York*, he gives up the examination of genre to create a large, somewhat conventional costume drama with clichéd oedipal overtones about early thugs in New York. But in *GoodFellas*, Scorsese asks us to consider who tells us stories in films, to think about whom we listen to and tend to believe—an important question in the context of a film that asks us to find gangsters amusing. Henry Hill (played by Ray Liotta), narrator and main character of the film, seems to be our guide and our eyes. His voice talks to us throughout, and we see what he sees. Or do we? One of Scorsese's favorite point-of-view techniques is to use the camera as a surrogate for one of his tough-guy characters as he moves along a bar in a club. He does this in both *Mean Streets* and *GoodFellas*.

Early in *GoodFellas*, Henry introduces us, in voice-over narration, to his gang-ster pals at a bar. The camera tracks along, pausing to look at each face, each character, who smiles and responds to Henry's off-screen presence. Everything here seems to guarantee that we are looking through Henry's eyes, sharing his point of view—until the very end of the tracking shot. The camera moves to the end of the bar, where Henry is heading to examine some stolen furs. A rack of furs appears, and so does Henry. The camera has been moving from right to left, diagonally into the frame. Henry appears on the left, opposite the direction of the camera. So, at the end of the shot, Henry himself emerges, but from the left side of the frame—not from where the camera is positioned. With this slight dis-ruption of expectations, Scorsese brings into question who is actually seeing what, whose point of view we can really depend on.

How is this possible, if we were supposed to be seeing things through Henry's eyes? Well, of course, we are not seeing through Henry's eyes. Henry is a character in the fiction, who is constructed to appear as if he were controlling the fiction. As we've seen, Scorsese is continually questioning the reality of peo-ple's control over things. It's one of his recurring themes and a major part of the formal construction of his style. Like Hitchcock before him, Scorsese plays with his characters and his audience and their imagined relationship to the char-acters. In *Taxi Driver*, for example, Scorsese limits point of view, forcing his viewers to see through the eyes of a madman a dark, violent city. Playing on the conventions of German **Expressionism** and film noir, drawing upon Hitchcock's ability to define character by how that character looks at the world and how the world looks back, *Taxi Driver* restricts our vision to that of a single, deranged sensibility. The prizefight scenes in *Raging Bull* attempt to create a mise-en-scène of noise, distortion, exaggeration of movement and sound that represents Scorsese's idea of what it must be like to be in a boxing ring. *What it might look like to someone* is a driving force in Scorsese's films. Limiting point of view, fooling us with who is seeing what, even playing with film speed, slow-ing down motion when he cuts to a character's point of view, are some of the ways Scorsese communicates shifting feelings, uncertainties, and changing re-sponses. For Scorsese, perception is a liquid, undependable, and tricky busi-ness. He uses a variety of cinematic properties to communicate this and to make us aware that film can teach us about perception, or keep us fooled.

GoodFellas plays counterpoint between Henry, who seems to be in control of the narrative, and another perspective—Scorsese's, perhaps, or a more abstract "voice" that speaks about film's ability to manipulate perception—with such in-tricacy that we are left somewhat unsettled. Henry's "story" is punctuated by freeze frames, moments in which the image is frozen while Henry meditates on what's just happened, or what will happen; by virtuoso camera movement, as in the amazing, almost four-minute-long tracking shot that accompanies Henry and Karen as they walk from the street into the Copacabana nightclub, down-stairs, through the kitchen, up to their table—all to the tune of The Crystals' "Then He Kissed Me."

At times, Henry's voice is taken over by Karen's, so that the woman's voice seems to run the narrative. Sometimes the editing takes over both and mimics the characters' point of view, as when, late in the film, frantic and high on cocaine, Karen and Henry believe they are being followed by a helicopter. The cutting is quick and nervous: time seems to speed up.

Finally, Scorsese takes over completely. It's his film, and one of the things he wishes to do with it is comment upon gangster films in general and our attraction and reaction to them in particular. He wants us to think about stories and their tellers. He makes Henry, the petty thug, the man who betrays his friends, a very attractive character, but he knows this is easy to do. Henry continually seems to take us into his confidence and remains aloof from the violence he and his friends commit. He is good looking, funny, and full of high spirits. But this shouldn't be enough to make us like a small-time criminal, and Scorsese needs to put more distance between us and his character. He does this by continually pointing to the tenuousness of Henry's authority, finally diminishing it entirely. Throughout the film, he plays with Henry's point of view and our sharing of it. Late in the film, after the mob has been busted, Henry goes to meet Jimmy (played by Robert De Niro in a relatively minor role for him in a Scorsese film). Henry is about to betray Jimmy and everybody else to the police. They meet in a diner and sit in front of the window, the camera placed so that it sees both men in profile against it.

Suddenly, perspective and space alter. Scorsese executes a simultaneous zoom and track, in opposing directions, so that the background—what's going on outside the diner window—seems to be moving in on the characters as they sit still. This is a technique that Alfred Hitchcock used to represent Scottie's reaction to heights in *Vertigo*. Steven Spielberg uses it to communicate Sheriff Brody's response to his sighting of the shark in *Jaws*, and it has since shown up

FIGURE 6.7 Like the long track in the nightclub, it is hardly possible to represent a complex camera movement in *GoodFellas*. This still is from the combination zoom-track near the end of the film. Imagine the camera tracking slowly forward while zooming slowly backward. The effect is of the world outside looming in on the characters—which is exactly what is happening in the narrative (Martin Scorsese, 1990).

in many other films. From a self-conscious device used by young filmmakers to pay homage to Hitchcock, it is rapidly becoming a cinematic cliché that can even be seen in television commercials. In *GoodFellas* it serves as a kind of outside commentary, a caution that the world created in the film is about to slip away, that the character we have been attached to has lost his moorings. Or never had any. It is an artificial gesture of camera and lens used to emphasize that everything we see through the camera's eye is artificial, in the very best sense of "artfully made."

The coup in which the director undermines the point of view of his character and our dependence on it comes in the trial sequence near the end of the film. Here, Henry simply steps out of the scene, literally walks through the courtroom set and addresses the camera, something forbidden by the Hollywood continuity style. By doing so, he acknowledges that it's all an illusion, all going on in somebody's head—Henry's, the director's, ours. As the film comes to an end and we see Henry in the witness protection program, living in some anonymous suburb, complaining in voice-over that he can't find a decent tomato sauce, he once again looks at the camera and smiles, as if to say, "We know what all this is about, don't we?" And just in case we still don't quite know, Scorsese inserts a shot of Tommy, Henry's hilariously violent friend (played by Joe Pesci), pointing his machine gun and firing at the camera. This shot doesn't come from anywhere else in *GoodFellas*. It alludes to another film, made in 1903, Edwin S. Porter's *The Great Train Robbery*. There, a shot of one of the cowboys firing his gun at the camera was put either at the beginning or the end of the film, at the discretion of the exhibitor, to excite the audience (see Figures 4.6–4.7).

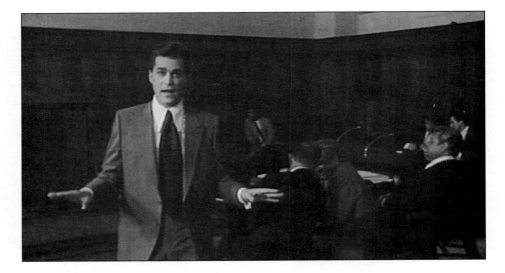

FIGURE 6.8 Henry addresses the camera, proclaiming himself the (false) narrator of the film and his status as an actor on a movie set.

So, with a wink at the audience and a nod to the history of film, Scorsese lets us know what we like about gangsters and violence. We like to watch. We like to be safe. We like to desire. And we like the delicate balance of control and fear. We also like a wise guy. In *GoodFellas,* Scorsese attaches us to a desirable character who seems to own the world, only to find that he is owned by the film we're watching, as are we ourselves. The director toys with his character and with us, allowing us in on the joke or allowing us to go off in a state of being deceived. It's only a movie, and the choice is ours.

Scorsese's desire to reflect the structures of film back at his audience, to attempt to peel away some of the illusion, is a common trait among modern auteurs. Unlike their predecessors, they want not merely to repeat the old strategies of the classical continuity style but to explore and expand them. American filmmakers such as Stanley Kubrick, Robert Altman, Steven Spielberg, Paul Schrader, Spike Lee, and Woody Allen look to their European, Asian, and Latin American forebears and contemporaries, Jean Renoir, Robert Bresson, Luis Buñuel, Jean-Luc Godard, François Truffaut, Michelangelo Antonioni, Joseph Losey, Bernardo Bertolucci (in his Italian period), Federico Fellini, Rainer Werner Fassbinder, Akira Kurosawa, Yasujiro Ozu, the Cuban Humberto Solàs, and the Russian filmmaker Andrei Tarkovsky (to name just a few), who explored and experimented. These filmmakers ask audiences to look not *through* the medium of cinema, as if it were a pane of glass, but *at* it. They never sacrifice emotion and narrative, but attempt to ask us to work for emotion by understanding how cinema itself works. Contemporary American auteurs, in various ways, attempt to communicate this approach.

Stanley Kubrick

One of these directors, Stanley Kubrick, has made films, from *Killer's Kiss* in 1955 through *Eyes Wide Shut* in 1999, that not only are great works of cinema, but, in works like *Dr. Strangelove* (1964), *2001: A Space Odyssey* (1965), *A Clockwork Orange* (1971), and *Eyes Wide Shut,* are profound insights into and prophecies of cultural and political behavior. Kubrick himself attempted to avoid completely the public life of a film director. He began working in Hollywood, and his first studio film, *The Killing* (1956), brought him to the attention of the film community and especially the actor Kirk Douglas, who had Kubrick direct him in Kubrick's first major work, *Paths of Glory* (1957). But after Douglas asked him to take over direction of *Spartacus* (1960), a film over which Kubrick had no control, he began to work in and ultimately moved to London. He rarely, and later in his life, never traveled, creating his visionary worlds on sound stages, back lots, or nearby locations (like the old North London gasworks that become Vietnam in *Full Metal Jacket,* 1987) and dealt with large numbers of people only during the actual filming process. Kubrick was the one filmmaker who tried to emulate the life of a novelist, painstakingly creating his projects—cool films, filled with strong images, carefully controlled color schemes, and tracking camera shots that let the viewer know the character's state of mind and how we are to interpret it. He flaunts conventional film-making rules (see Figures 4.21–4.22), and weaves complex themes about the cultures of violence and politics and the absolute loss of human agency. He worked long and carefully on his films that, after *A Clockwork Orange,* were completed every seven or eight years, in isolation and without any publicity. He made complex films that stay in the memory, keep yielding information on each viewing. He made complex cinema that were also—most of them—commercially successful movies that managed the great, barely possible feat of combining the popular and the difficult—high art and popular art at ease with each other, capable of causing an unease in the viewer along with a sense of elation.

Kubrick was an inquisitive prophet; his films, many of them taking place at the time of their making, some set in the past, and two set in the future, think about the limits of being human. They are not optimistic, and often verge on the misanthropic—he simply didn't think that humans had a great future ahead of them. The figures who people his films, who bear the illusion of having an emotional life, a past and a present, are actually more ideas than conventionally formed movie characters—attitudes given a movie presence. This is a difficult concept, because we are so used to characters who are created to make us simply love or hate them, to elicit admiration—even a desire to be them—or, in the case of villains, to look forward to their undoing. Kubrick's characters do not attract us. They are, very much like Hitchcock's, part of a larger pattern defined, most often constrained, by the environment he builds around them. And Kubrick never makes that pattern easy to see.

A Clockwork Orange, for example, stacks the deck so that we easily miss the joke—as did many critics, even this one when it first appeared. On first look (and listen—voice-over narration plays an important role in many of Kubrick's films), Alex is king. In his sordid, decaying world of the near future, he is a demonic force of violence and rape. Kubrick forces us to like a disgusting thug simply because he's the liveliest element of the mise-en-scène. When the camera tracks him through the record boutique where he meets two girls to take home for sex, he is completely in control. When, in clockwork fashion, his control winds down in the second part of the film, we feel sorry for him. He *tells* us to feel sorry for him. He gets his wish, and he seems to get his power returned—but as a political tool for the political party in power. He and we have both been manipulated, and when, in the midst of his last sexual fantasy, he calls out "I was cured all right," we realize that the cure may be worse than the disease.

Kubrick is that rarest thing among filmmakers, an ironist. Like Hitchcock, like many European filmmakers, he makes us look at characters and events from more than one point of view. To understand them, we have to see how they figure in the pattern of the film's mise-en-scène and how that pattern shifts and changes in subtle ways. Kubrick makes the space—and not only the space of *2001: A Space Odyssey* (which we'll look at in detail in Chapter 9)—of his films shift and change both its *and* our perspective. This is why Kubrick's films don't reveal their full meaning for many viewings, and sometimes never. How many times have you watched the last sequence of *2001* and still wondered about its meaning? It is extraordinary for a film not to have one simple meaning, but rather multiple perspectives that float around possible meanings, shifting every time you see the film. But despite the shifts, the visual structure, the spectacular, head-on, 180-degree, symmetrical shots (see Figure 3.35), the repeated vision of people losing out because they can't see beyond the internal and external repressions they've created for themselves, whether by the doomsday device of *Dr. Strangelove* that ends the world, or, after having been dehumanized by their drill instructor during training only to be done in by a female sniper in Vietnam in *Full Metal Jacket*, everyone in a Kubrick film loses. But the loss is the viewer's gain. As a prophetic filmmaker, Kubrick permits us to see beyond his own misanthropy, to examine his images, to put the pieces of the visual and narrative puzzles together, even, if we pay attention, to find the joke that lies within every film he's made.

Alfred Hitchcock

Alfred Hitchcock carefully planned every formal move in his work well before filming actually began. Cinematic form and structure, Hitchcock understood, are the means by which narrative is made and emotion generated. Nothing would be left to chance in the creation of that structure, and no one would interfere with the finished plan when shooting began. Hitchcock was pleased to say that by the time he went to filming, he never had to look through the camera, because his plan for the film and his instructions on how to execute it were complete. As a result, Hitchcock's best films—he made some 48 of them between 1922 and 1976, not counting those he directed for television—are grounded on complex structures in which each composition and cut relates a great deal of information. The space of the Hitchcockian world, seen especially in films such as *Shadow of a Doubt* (1943), *Notorious* (1946), *Rear Window* (1954), *Vertigo* (1958), *North by Northwest* (1959), *Psycho* (1960), *The Birds* (1963), and *Marnie* (1964), is created by positioning characters and camera to produce a composition that often ironically comments upon the characters' situation. He will relate figures and objects through a subtle cutting between gazes, creating an interplay between a character looking at something or someone and a shot in motion of the person or object being looked at, so carefully measured that the cutting back and forth builds a sense of threat or vulnerability. This is the cross–tracking we have been discussing.

Even without cross tracking, Hitchcock achieved extraordinary effects through the combination of composition and editing. Consider the sequence in *Psycho* when Norman invites Marion into his parlor, just before the shower murder. By cutting between the characters in their isolated worlds—their own little islands, as Marion says—and slowly increasing the visual association of Norman and his stuffed birds, including a terribly threatening, low-angle shot in which a stuffed owl looms over Norman's head, the sequence reveals much of the mystery of the plot. With its emphasis on dark and threatening spaces,

FIGURE 6.9 Norman, surrounded by the dark images of his stuffed birds. The image quietly gives away his stuffed masterpiece—his mother!

FIGURE 6.10 Norman looms into the frame, threatening Marion Crane, foreshadowing his final threat—he will, as his mother, stab her to death (*Psycho*, Alfred Hitchcock, 1960).

fear and withdrawal, its association of Norman first with passivity and anxiety and then, in a shot in which he bends forward in the frame, with a threatening look toward Marion and the viewer, the mise-en-scène of this sequence forms the nucleus of the film. Its visual structure, along with the dialogue, lets us know everything that is going on and will go on—if we care to watch and listen.

Early in *Vertigo* (a film we'll talk about in some detail in Chapter 7), Scottie goes to visit Gavin Elster, the man who will set in motion an enormous ruse that will ruin Scottie's life. Scottie is already reduced and weakened. His fear of heights has resulted in the death of a fellow police officer and his own retirement from the police force. In Gavin's offices—large, ornate, overlooking the San Francisco waterfront, with a huge construction crane moving outside the window—Scottie is made to look small, sometimes almost cowering. Throughout much of the scene, Hitchcock has him sit scrunched down in a chair composed in one corner of a frame as Gavin, standing on a raised portion of the floor in his office, dominates him and the viewer. Through the spatial arrangement developed by the construction of the set and the camera, whose placement and movement keep diminishing Scottie's presence, we are allowed to comprehend undercurrents that are not articulated in the dialogue. Gavin tells Scottie a story about how Gavin's wife is possessed by a spirit from the past. In fact, Gavin is using Scottie in a plot to kill his wife, a plot that will eventually lead to Scottie's total breakdown. Scottie will become the diminished figure we see in this sequence. Like the parlor sequence in *Psycho*, this sequence in *Vertigo* gives away a lot of the film through the ways in which Hitchcock has us see his characters as part of his eloquent mise-en-scène.

WOMEN AUTEURS

From an article by Nancy Hass, in *The New York Times,* January 31, 1999:

> *When the Hollywood studios announced their 1998 grosses earlier this month, women there raised a quiet cheer. Both Mimi Leder ("Deep Impact") and Betty Thomas ("Dr. Dolittle") had made films that earned more than $150 million domestically. It was the first time ever that two female directors had simultaneously surpassed the magic $100 million mark that certifies a blockbuster.*
>
> *But another set of numbers, released a few months earlier, made the triumph ring a little hollow. A study by the Directors Guild of America showed that in the year that both Ms. Thomas's and Ms. Leder's films were being made, the overall number of women employed on studio projects declined dramatically. Female directors worked fewer than 5 percent of the total days guild members spent on theatrical films in 1997. That represented an almost 50 percent decline from the year before.*

Clearly, and sadly, our brief listing of film auteurs has not included the names of women directors. The simple and obvious answer to this is that women are allowed to play only a small role in film production, though, happy to say, it is getting better. Sophia Coppola, for example, daughter of the man who made *The Godfather* films, is quickly being recognized as a major talent, especially with her film *Lost in Translation* (2003). But in the complex, too-often frustrating world of women's place in film, we need to discriminate between a number of issues. One is the representation of women themselves: how films "see" women, narrate them and their stories. We've discussed earlier how the basic narrative structure of intercutting shot/reverse shot, especially in the rescue narrative, is built upon men saving women. We have also seen, and will examine even more thoroughly in the following chapters, how the structure of the gaze—the looking of one character at another and the viewer at both—is directed toward women as erotic objects.

The simple point is that, as a part of the larger culture, film reflects the values of that culture and traps women with male-dominated ways of thinking and control. Commercial, narrative film persists in trapping itself within the old and worn-out master narratives of passive femininity and active masculinity, and of heterosexuality as the only means of intimacy. There have been some important exceptions to these narratives, but while a few recent mainstream films do touch upon homosexuality without stereotyping, only a few—Donna Deitch's 1985 *Desert Hearts* (a melodrama), Mike Nichols's 1996 *The Birdcage*, and Frank Oz's 1997 *In & Out* (the latter two both comedies)—have attempted alternative narratives to those that end in heterosexual union. Television has gotten into the act with the popular *Will and Grace* series and Mike Nichols's extraordinary HBO film of Tony Kushner's *Angels in America* (2003). The Hollywood story machine (of which television is an integral part) always responds, however briefly, to alternative cultural currents.

But these are narrative issues. Our discussion in this chapter is the story of women as filmmakers, the directors, behind the camera, making the images, forming the film. Women have been involved in the filmmaking process from the earliest days. They were script writers and, most often, editors. They were "script girls," the important figure who made sure physical continuity was maintained from shot to shot. They were very, very rarely directors. To begin with, we look at the avant-garde.

Women's Avant-Garde Films

In the world of avant-garde film, especially in recent years, films and videos made by women have become common, and many of them deal in more complex ways than theatrical movies with gender, race, and alternatives to the norms of society. These are directors such as Pamela Yates, who makes videos on welfare rights issues, and Christine Choy, maker of *Who Killed Vincent Chin?* (1988, originally shot in 16 mm) and one of the founders of the Third World Newsreel, a major distributor of independent political films, which, along with the group Women Make Movies, has given the opportunity to many young filmmakers who might not get their films seen otherwise. But we have to go back a number of years to find the pioneer woman avant-garde director, whose influence was widespread.

Maya Deren

Maya Deren was Russian born but lived in America since her childhood. Active from the forties through the early fifties—sometimes collaborating with her husband—her films, writings, and activities in promoting avant-garde works helped establish the genre among the intellectual underground. Never self-indulgent but always interested in the subjective, soft, but at the same time, visually hard-edged and often dark response to the everyday, Deren's short experimental films are lyrical, sometimes lyrically violent, and often surreal. In *At Land* (1944) a woman (Deren herself) climbs out of the ocean, over driftwood, at the top of which is an elegant dinner party in a room. She crawls along the table, unnoticed by the guests, and at the end of the table sees a chessboard, on which the pieces animate themselves. The images are dreamlike, whimsical, and the result of a mind that associates and connects the unexpected.

Deren's most famous work is *Meshes of the Afternoon* (1943, made in collaboration with her husband Alexander Hammid), an extraordinary work of rich dream images, using techniques, such as **jump cutting** (in which a continuous movement is cut into so that continuity is itself replaced by rapid changes in space; a cinematic version of ellipsis in prose), that were years ahead of their most famous appearance in Jean-Luc Godard's *Breathless*. In one sequence, the central figure—Deren herself—is seen mounting a staircase. But her movement is cut so that she goes up and down in a rapid montage, as if, between the cuts, she had leapt to various places on the stairs.

The film is influenced by the Spanish surrealist filmmaker Luis Buñuel and the French Surrealist poet, artist, and filmmaker Jean Cocteau. In its turn, it influenced later directors like the Swedish Ingmar Bergman, Jean-Luc Godard, and another Frenchman, Alain Resnais, as well as the American director Robert Altman, especially as it deals with the difficulties of impressing a feminine sensibility on the world. *Meshes of the Afternoon* touches upon core feminist issues of identity and ownership of the self. The central figure falls asleep in a chair and dreams of two other selves and a figure of death in black, with a mirror for a face (a figure that Ingmar Bergman brought back, without the mirror, in his

1957 film *The Seventh Seal*). A key and a knife appear as important images of openings and endings: they disappear, reappear—one turns into the other. A male figure—a lover or a husband—wakes the woman, and she goes to bed. He caresses her, and in response, the flower lying next to her becomes a knife. The mirror by the bedside shatters, and its shards fly to the sea. When the man returns, the woman is dead—of the knife or broken mirror?

The woman's death is a disturbing moment in a film otherwise dealing with the possibilities of female expression. It may be speaking to the frustration in ever getting the expression made or, on the level of avant-garde aesthetics, to an open-ended question, a lack of comforting

FIGURE 6.11 The dream world in Maya Deren's *Meshes of the Afternoon* (1943).

closure and explanation that marks off this kind of filmmaking from the Hollywood style.

Alice Guy-Blaché and Lois Weber

Maya Deren was a woman who made films that spoke to the feminine. Extremely independent, Deren's films did not depend upon the studios to finance and distribute them. Since the core of our study is theatrical narrative film, we need to consider how women have fared in that realm. The answer is simple and unhappy: not well.

Two of the earliest filmmakers were women. One was French, Alice Guy-Blaché, who, after making films in France, came to America and set up her own production company in 1910. Another was Lois Weber, who, in 1916, articulated a strong statement of auteurism. "A real director should be absolute" in her control of a film, she wrote, while she was making progressive films on contemporary social issues. Both of these women made films in which women played a more active role than usual. Weber—whose career lasted into the twenties—may have been slightly more adventurous.

Her *Too Wise Wives* (1921) starts with a lovely image of a couple against a sunset and a title that says "our story should begin that way . . . but . . . ." It then presents its heroine as a completely domesticated woman—"a martyred kind of wife who lives only for her husband. . . ." Pipe smoking, book-reading husband and his knitting wife are shown in separate shots. She cleans up his smelly pipe ashes, and he moves into a flashback in which he recalls an earlier flame who didn't mind his smoking. But, back in the present, he relents and offers to wear the slippers his wife knitted for him, which he hates. The scene shifts to another wife, selfish and calculating: "A very successful wife." She performs that role. Much intrigue follows, letters, misconceptions, and at the end, the wives perform various acts of contrition. But on the way, there is an emphasis on women's power, some reference to the politics of the day, and a lovely scene in which the two wives make up to each other—a rare sequence, even then, of women's friendship. The film is shot carefully and with the intent to focus on the women. While it may not be a large step from female stereotyping, it does at least bring its female characters to the foreground and honor their personalities.

FIGURE 6.12 From Lois Weber's *Too Wise Wives* (1921), a woman's political meeting. In the background, a woman wears the suffragette "uniform" of the day.

Dorothy Arzner

A later woman director was Dorothy Arzner, who, like many women in Hollywood production, started as an editor and a screenwriter. She began directing in 1927 and made seventeen films through 1943. Some of her works—especially *Christopher Strong* (1933) and *Dance, Girl, Dance* (1940)—speak in complex and knowing ways about women and their reduced place in the culture. They address the ways genders are shifting cultural constructs (in *Christopher Strong*, the main character, played by Katharine Hepburn, spends much of her time dressed as a boy) and how women understand their status as things to be looked at by men. In one of the most celebrated feminist moments in film, one of the female performers in *Dance, Girl, Dance* talks to her audience, expressing her outrage at being the object of their gaze. It is a rare moment when a woman is permitted to speak her understanding of what film and gender performance are about from a woman's perspective.

Ida Lupino

Ida Lupino was an actress in many films from the thirties through the fifties (some of her best are Raoul Walsh's *High Sierra* and Michael Curtiz's *The Sea Wolf*, both 1941; and Nicholas Ray's *On Dangerous Ground*, 1952). She wanted control of her work, but instead of fleeing the country and filing a lawsuit against her studio, as the actress Bette Davis had done and lost in the thirties, Lupino, at that moment in the history of the studios in the early fifties when contracts were running out and the monolithic control the studios had wielded for so many years was beginning to dwindle, formed her own production companies so that she could direct her own films.

Lupino was a canny businesswoman as well as a good filmmaker. She also understood the cultural state of the decade in which she worked. In interviews, she always played up her role as mother and family woman, and she spoke about her directing talents as being largely passive and deferential. In the fifties, a woman might conceivably find herself in a traditionally male role, but might also find it necessary to use the more comfortable discourse of the homemaker, who—in this case—just happens to be a filmmaker as well.

Lupino's films are, at first sight, very much in the manner of fifties noir. Their subjects are, often, lower-middle-class men put in bizarre situations. But there can be an interesting switch. *The Hitch-Hiker* (1953) has no female characters. It concerns two men out on a fishing trip who are kidnapped by a sadistic madman and driven through Mexico until the kidnapper is caught. In place of female characters, the two kidnapped men, Gil Bowan (Frank Lovejoy) and Roy Collins (Edmond O'Brien), are forced into passive, childlike, or—in the terms of cultural conventions—"woman"-like situations. They are almost in thrall to their crazy kidnapper, who taunts them for being "soft" and thinking about each other's welfare. At the end, freed of their captor (whom Roy finally beats up, after the madman has been handcuffed by the police), the two family men walk into the darkness. Gil puts his arm around Roy and tells him, "It's all right now, Roy, it's all right."

This is certainly not the only film by a man or a woman in which male characters show some affection and care for each other. However, it is not a male bonding film, because the characters do not work as a "team" or share their joy in the absence of women, despite the fact that no women are present. Both characters are oppressed by their condition: they cannot escape it, and they remain good, middle-class family men. Even though, early in the film, Roy wants to find prostitutes in Mexico, Gil refuses, in fact pretends to be asleep while this is all going on. It is suggested that Roy's would-be diversion is what put them in the path of the mad hitch-hiker. Precisely these kinds of subtleties mark this as a film made by a woman: that the men get into trouble because they want to chase women; because the men are reduced to passive, even weeping childlike characters; because, despite the momentary thoughts of extramarital play, they remain attached to their unseen families through the end. Within the tough, hard lines and rigorous compositions of late noir, Lupino manages to see masculine softness and vulnerability, mock these qualities just a little, and indicate a strength that comes from places other than male braggadocio and a puffed-up sense of the heroic.

There's a similar reversal in *The Bigamist* (1953), a film that shows Lupino's talents at composing and framing sequences which achieve a proximity to her characters in ways that quietly but markedly reveal emotional states. The film is structured in flashbacks as Harry (Edmond O'Brien, again, who with Frank Lovejoy were icons of the fifties ordinary man) takes two wives. Lupino creates a complexity here that belies the sleaziness of the story. Harry's first wife, Eve, can't conceive a child and turns to running Harry's business. This is a major and ugly fifties stereotype: the childless woman must transfer her maternal yearnings to "man's work" in order to be fulfilled, thereby forgoing her femininity. It is even suggested by Harry that he and his wife don't have sex anymore. But Lupino refuses to take this on face value. The Eve she depicts is a loving wife who wants to adopt a child *and* run a business. Harry, who often has to travel to Los Angeles, is shown as lonely and alienated. He falls in love with, impregnates, and marries a waitress he meets in L.A., Phyllis (played by Lupino).

FIGURE 6.13 Men: passive, under the control of a madman. *The Hitch-Hiker* by Ida Lupino (1953).

The melodramatic potential of this conflict—especially when Harry's secret is discovered by the man investigating their adoption request—is underplayed. In this film, Lupino is interested in gazing closely at both male and female faces of loss and loneliness. She condemns none of the characters and gives their neediness equal attention. Even more than *The Hitch-Hiker*, the male character is endowed with what, in conventional film, are considered female traits: shifting emotions, vulnerability, failings, even weakness. Male directors too created "sensitive" men, and we'll examine the phenomenon in detail in Chapter 7. But Ida Lupino, the only female director of the decade—of many decades—understood that gender was not something defined by the movies, only stereotyped by them. Unlike many other filmmakers, she can show sympathy to all her characters and create a film that touches upon such a taboo issue as *The Bigamist*: sympathy across the board, an understanding of what men and women might need and even get, were it not for the demands of their culture and gender.

Women Filmmakers Today

With the end of the old studio system and the rise of the feminist movement, there was a hope that filmmaking would be more welcoming to films made by and about women. There seemed to be some opening in the seventies and eighties. Some male directors—perhaps most notably Martin Scorsese in *Alice Doesn't Live Here Anymore* (1974)—attempted to portray women freeing themselves from intolerable domestic situations. But, as in *Alice*, most of these films decided that their women characters had only to find a "better" man, thereby re-creating the traditional narrative closure of heterosexual union.

There was a brief flurry of opportunity for women directors in the eighties and early nineties. Diverse filmmakers undertook a variety of approaches to women's issues, such as Susan Seidelman in *Desperately Seeking Susan* (1985) and *Making Mr. Right* (1987), a film that suggested the perfect man had to be constructed like a robot. Donna Deitch, whose *Desert Hearts* we mentioned earlier, touched on lesbian themes. Barbra Streisand, particularly in films such as *Yentl* (1983) and *The Prince of Tides* (1991), used melodrama to present images of strong women. In *Household Saints* (1993), Nancy Savoca created an extraordinary and surreal film about ethnicity and the feminine. Kathryn Bigelow, most especially in *Strange Days* (1995) (cowritten and coproduced by James Cameron), tried to alter the action genre in ways that redirected male centrality and the focus of the male gaze. *Strange Days* is set in an apocalyptic L.A. at the end of the millennium. The people are up in arms, and the cops are out of control. In the midst of this chaos she creates a technological fantasy in which a recording device worn on a person's head can record and play back experiences as if they were actually occurring. One of these recordings is of a woman being raped, with the recording device placed on her head to capture her terror. The result is a gruesome sequence, and only a woman filmmaker, I think, could have created it in a manner that downplays the inherently exploitative elements and emphasizes how horrible the act is to the woman involved.

The film's "hero" is an African American woman who is in love with a white man, who is definitely not a hero but a kind of human punching bag. In the climax of the uprising, and despite the fact that Bigelow seems to yield to convention by introducing the patriarchal figure of a good police commissioner to set the cops right, this couple emerges, suddenly and openly in love. They kiss—a kiss between a weak white male and a strong African American woman, a kiss that is simply given and revealed to the audience, without comment, without sensationalism, in a way that suggests that all the gun play, all the violence and mayhem, are actually a mask that allows the film to present this culturally transgressive act. Like the presence of an African American president of the United States in Mimi Leder's *Deep Impact* (1998), it is a kind of utopian vision of a world that, despite the violence and destruction, can somehow be better. It would be foolish to say that only a woman director could do this; we can only say that women directors did do this.

While some of the original contemporary women filmmakers, like Seidelman and Deitch, seem not to have been able to pursue their careers, or have done lesser works, others have flourished in different ways. Penny Marshall moved from television sitcom actress to the highly bankable director of engaging films *Big* (1988), *Awakenings* (1990), *A League of Their Own* (1992), *The Preacher's Wife* (1996), and *Riding in Cars with Boys* (2001). Penelope Spheeris has carved out a comfortable place making clever comedies based upon television skits and programs, like *Wayne's World* (1992) and *The Beverly Hillbillies* (1993). In 2003, she made a television documentary on the Enron Corporation, the energy company found to be totally corrupt. Amy Heckerling is in the unusual position of making commercially popular films—*Fast Times at Ridgemont High* (1982) and *Clueless* (1995), for example—the latter successfully maintaining a young woman's view of the world without sentimentality.

The Canadian-born Mary Harron has made an extraordinary transmutation of a difficult and repulsive source. In 2000, she filmed *American Psycho*, which is based upon Bret Easton Ellis's 1991 novel that turned the stomachs of most readers with its depiction of a man who mutilated women. Harron overturned the premise and realized the novel not exactly as a feminist film but as one in which the men, and *not* the women of so many conventional films, are preening, fashion-obsessed narcissists, who have something approaching a sexual experience over their business cards and are enthralled by the most banal of eighties popular music. The central character is so inward looking that he has passed directly through his own personality and come out the other side as a murderous cipher, a madman so undone by the competition of success in business (he refers to "mergers and acquisitions" as "murders and executions") that his violent attacks on both men and women may very well be fantasies. Like so many horror films, *American Psycho* presents women as its main victims; but they are victims not so much of their gender but of a lunatic's notion of gender and his complete absence of self. On its most important level, Harron's film understands that for many men or, more important for our work, for many films, women are not independent figures but the products of an overheated male sexual imagination. She has made a small-budget commercial film that quietly overturns some of the mainstays of the representations of women in film.

Julie Dash, Julie Taymor, and Chantal Akerman

In order to find films by women that demonstrate a difference not only in the kind of story being told but in the narrative means used to tell the story, we have to move out of the mainstream. Sometimes out of the country.

Television has been one place where women can work as filmmakers. When Ida Lupino left filmmaking, she went to work on TV in the sixties. One recent director, Julie Dash, an African American, made a film for the now defunct PBS series "American Playhouse" called *Daughters of the Dust* (1991). The film was financed by PBS, the National Endowment for the Arts, and various other government, regional, and corporate grants, and it received a small theatrical distribution.

The film is delicate, filled with beautiful imagery, in which color, the kind of lens put on the camera from shot to shot, the use of slow and fast motion emphasize and form a complex narrative of remembrance and forgetting, past and future, the physical and the spiritual. Set in 1902 in the Sea Islands off the Carolina and Georgia coasts of the United States, among the people called the Gullah, the film gathers together the members of the Peazant family, born into slavery and now, some of them, reaching middle class, a few about to head north. It is very much a family get-together film, but this is a family from a horrific background of slavery, who have retained not only their sense of self-possession, of coherence, but a wide-ranging religious practice, African, Christian, Muslim.

Daughters of the Dust is concerned with the fuzziness of boundaries between cultures and time, about the joining of traditions and the necessity of progress. We see this in its compositional elements, which depend to a large extent on wide horizontal shots along the beach, often observing people running across the screen. But this linear visual style is undercut by the complex interweaving of the characters' memories, by flashbacks and forwards, by close-ups of objects and faces, creating a series of interlocking stories directly told or suggested. In fact, in her commentary to the film, Dash says that she based its narrative structure on the *Griot*, the traditional African storyteller and keeper of tribal tradition. Because of this, there is much magic, much imagery of dream and remembrance. An unborn child appears through the lens of a camera set up to take a family picture. A young man, attempting to sink a powerful African statue in the swamp, walks on water.

Daughters of the Dust is in many ways an ethnographic film with touches of magic realism—a style that combines a conventional realism along with the fantastic. In other words, although a narrative fiction, it also documents a way of life along with its culture and artifacts, but it envelops that documentation with a narrative of marvelous events. It looks lovingly at the women and the men of the Peazant family, at the tensions of their past and their resolution. It is never violent, even when showing the old Indigo slave plantation, where the slaves had to make toxic dyes with their hands. Indeed, the great grandmother, a survivor of the plantation, wears an indigo dress, while most of the other characters wear white. The film proves that a human horror can be effectively communicated without being represented.

Daughters of the Dust is visually beautiful—some might argue too much so, that its prettiness overwhelms the narrative. But I think Dash is consciously attempting to break away from a current convention of African American filmmaking

FIGURE 6.14   The former slave and voice of history.

FIGURE 6.15   The children on the beach.

that concentrates on the bleak, the desolate, and the violent. She is, in this film, at least, working in a tradition of some of the great African filmmakers, like Ousmane Sembène, who look to the way cultures and religions call upon the spiritual, remain connected to their past, while staying rooted in the contemporary movements of their own and their culture's history. In this context, the characters are shown in a continuing process of incorporating and not forgetting their past. "There must be connection," says the great-grandmother in

FIGURE 6.16   Walking on water: the ancient and the modern, the mix of religions and the spiritual (*Daughters of the Dust* by Julie Dash, 1991).

Daughters of the Dust. "We came here in chains and we must survive . . . we must survive." This film is one way to trace the markings of that survival.

Dash has since tried to enter into the mainstream, making films for television that do not quite manage the sweep and magic of *Daughters of the Dust*. But this only serves to prove a point. It is so difficult for women to become directors and next to impossible for a woman of color. Therefore, a talented director like Julie Dash must work, and whether or not that work is exceptional, it provides her with the funding for a future great film.

Recently, Julie Taymor, previously a stage designer most famous for her work on the stage version of Disney's *The Lion King*, has turned filmmaker, with two extraordinary films. One, called *Titus* (1999), is a version of Shakespeare's early revenge tragedy, *Titus Andronicus*. The play is itself somewhat lunatic, including the baking of an enemy's sons in a pie. Taymor contains the hysteria by transferring it to the film's mise-en-scène in her use of color and the acting that reaches toward choreography. She does this to even greater advantage in her biography (or "biopic," as it is known in Hollywood) of Frida Kahlo, painter and wife of the muralist Diego Rivera. *Frida* (2002) takes as its visual catalyst Kahlo's own paintings—strange, disturbing, deeply personal—and her uncomfortable life, crippled by a terrible back injury and a more famous and philandering husband. The mise-en-scène itself becomes surreal and blazing with color. There is a dream sequence, created by the Quay Brothers, animators of strange, Expressionist-influenced films like *Street of Crocodiles* (1986). There is history—the assassination in Mexico of the Russian revolutionary Leon Trotsky by Stalin's henchmen. But the film is foremost the depiction, through a variety of vital cinematic means, of an energetic, creative woman artist, wrestling with her

FIGURE 6.17 The Quay Brothers animated this dream sequence in Julie Taymor's *Frida* (2002).

own physical problems and a flamboyant, famous husband. And it is created by another woman artist. Taymor does not have to turn the usual sexually driven gaze on her character, but rather allow the character's own gaze to radiate out into the film's mise-en-scène and represent to the audience her subject's own interior vision of the world.

One of the most successful attempts to question the male gaze and the entire genre of female melodrama was made by a Belgian director, Chantal Akerman, in a 1976 film, *Jeanne Dielman, 23 Quai du Commerce, 1080 Bruxelles*. The film, like many European films of the period, is very hard to find, but well worth the search. Akerman literally transforms the conventional male gaze at the female character. She makes us look, but removes the pleasure, that is, the male pleasure of gazing at a woman. The woman who is the subject of Akerman's gaze is not desirable and certainly not erotic. For over three hours, her camera spends much of its time simply watching the central character, a lower-middle-class Belgian housewife, who lives in a tiny apartment with her teenage son and practices prostitution in the afternoons to supplement her widow's pension. The camera looks, unmoving, slightly below eye level, at a distance that prevents intimacy, as this woman goes about her obsessive tasks, cooking, shining her son's shoes, making up the rooms, going to the store, looking after a neighbor's child, talking to her son, joylessly entertaining her clients. The camera looks and looks. There is rarely a cut unless there is a change of place, and the change of place is usually to another space in the apartment. Everything is slow, deliberate. The camera looks, relentlessly, but coolly.

The act of looking demystifies everything. The woman and her work, the woman and her sexuality are reduced to the routine of her doing them and our own gazing at them. She and her life become objects, just as so many women characters in film have always been. In the excesses of traditional melodrama, the assumed intimacy of our gaze, and the forward propulsion of the continuity style allow us to identify with the character. We look at her, we look with her. We want her, we want her to succeed, to be punished. Melodrama transfers desire back and forth. But in *Jeanne Dielman* there are no distractions, no excess—except the excess created by the camera's unrelenting gaze. Desire is diverted from the character back to our own looking. We either want to keep looking to see if anything will happen or want not to look. In fact, nothing happens to the woman until late in the film, when her obsessive actions begin to unravel. She forgets part of her routine, does some things over again. Then she sits in a chair for a very long time, the camera gazing at her without a cut. Later, a client arrives. The woman experiences an orgasm with him—perhaps her first—takes a pair of scissors, and stabs him. Her order disrupted, her emotions brought to the surface, she seems to have no recourse but to destroy in an attempt to get the order restored.

Jeanne Dielman is certainly not another postfeminist film about a sexually liberated woman who is really crazy and murderous in the mode of *Fatal Attraction* (Adrian Lynne, 1987) or *Single White Female* (Barbet Schroeder, 1992) or *Basic Instinct* (Paul Verhoeven, 1992). Neither is it about a dying mother, after the manner of Carl Franklin's *One True Thing* (1998), in which a career woman gives up her independent life to look after her ailing parent and dysfunctional family. Rather it is a commentary on melodrama and its attempts to sexualize and then redeem from sexuality the central female character. *Jeanne Dielman* thinks about what melodrama might look like if we were allowed to look at it without embellishment, given the distance that the classical Hollywood style forbids. *Jeanne Dielman* explores how women are represented in film and how that representation turns them into automatons. It also explores the conditions of our own watching of melodrama and—by draining that watching of all spectacle, of all excess, music, elaborate mise-en-scène, camera movement, and cutting—takes us to the bare level of the gaze and makes us very, very uncomfortable.

Now why should we watch a film that makes us uncomfortable? To understand that there are alternatives; that the language and structure of American film is not the only way films can or even should be made; that indeed film is a kind of language, but with rules that can be bent and altered. Such a film is important to show up the ways the standard language and vocabulary of film, especially when they speak of women, are not immutable. To have, in a perverse way, some fun. The last time I showed *Jeanne Dielman* to a class, they began yelling at the screen: "Cut . . . cut, already." There was nobody to hear them; it was only a film, and the shot went on and on. The melodrama had been transferred to the audience.

A woman filmmaker and her film about a lost woman made the class uncomfortable. The radical rupture of the classical style foiled expectations, and the class transferred their annoyance back to the unresponsive screen itself. This transferral was, I think, an interesting lesson in cinematic expectation and the ways we respond when we don't get what we think we should from a film. It was also a good example of why films of such radical experimentation rarely get made, and perhaps explains why women filmmakers take relatively small risks in their work. Perhaps the fear that risks might be taken is one of the reasons so few women are given directorial control.

The Hollywood of today does not "hate" women. But it is always afraid of something different and, like many other parts of our culture, of yielding male authority. Will the public accept a sharply feminist film? Will the business of filmmaking ever be comfortable with women as the directorial "boss" of a production—even as it is becoming increasingly comfortable with women as the producers and, therefore, the controllers of the budget—of a film? These are questions that move far from individual films into the large areas of culture, sociology, and the basics of power and authority.

THE AUTEUR ABROAD

Chantal Akerman was hardly the only director experimenting abroad in the sixties or seventies, and we will examine others in Chapter 9 in an analysis of how European filmmakers push against American genres and forms. The point is that filmmaking abroad was a director's medium long after the studio system took over that function in the United States, and before the French themselves invented the term. Japan, for example, produced a number of great filmmakers before and after World War II. Akira Kurosawa is the best known, but others, such as the legendary Yasuhiro Ozu and Kenji Mizoguchi, practiced long-take cinematography and alternative views of family and women. Ozu in particular—to whom we will return in Chapter 9—manifested a cultural view in the very nature of his cinematography, viewing his subjects from the low angle of the *tatami* mat that Japanese traditionally sit on. He made cool and lyrical melodramas that chronicled the movement from pre- to postwar Japan and its effects on families.

In Spain, Luis Buñuel started working in the twenties, when he collaborated with the painter, Salvador Dali, on the remarkable surrealist film, *Un Chien Andalou (An Andalusian Dog*, 1929). This film begins with what is perhaps the most notorious image in cinema: a man (Buñuel himself) slices open a woman's eye with straight razor. (Not to worry, an eye from a dead sheep was substituted in the close-up.) This, from one point of view, is a grossly misogynist moment; but from another, a key to the secret of cinema—to open the eye to things not seen before. "The screen's white eyelid would only need to be able to reflect the light that is its own, and it would blow up the universe," Buñuel said. And this remained his credo throughout his work. The fascist dictator, Francisco Franco, made life uncomfortable for him in Spain. He came to the United States in the 1940s, where he worked as an assistant in Hollywood until he moved to Mexico, where he made many films. Some were popular potboilers. Others were brilliant Surrealist films, full of strange, slow-motion dreams and bizarre occurrences, usually at the expense of the middle class. He returned briefly to Spain, where he made one of his most famous films, *Viridiana* (1961), which got him kicked out again. Back he went to Mexico, and then to France, where

FIGURE 6.18 "The screen's white eyelid would only need to be able to reflect the light that is its own, and it would blow up the Universe."—Luis Buñuel. The still is from the opening of his first film, *Un Chien Andalou (The Andalusian Dog)*, made with surrealist painter Salvador Dali in 1929.

he continued—this time with larger budgets—to direct surreal films such as *Belle de jour* (1967), about a woman who liberates herself from a tedious marriage by becoming a prostitute, like all Buñuel's work full of strange visions, unexpected occurrences, events that may or may not be fantasies. Although a foreign film with subtitles, *Belle de jour,* and subsequent Buñuel films, did amazingly well in the United States.

AUTEURISM TODAY

In the United States, the auteur theory was always a theory, a way of talking and thinking about films, much more than an accurate description of how films are actually made. It was also a way to think about redistributing the hierarchies of power in the filmmaking business. Unlike the rest of the world, directorial control has been and is very rare in the United States, at least since the early twenties when the studio system situated the director as only one among many craftspeople working on a film. American filmmaking remains so controlled by economics and audience response that its products can't be left to one person. Besides, given the studio system and its collaborative process, and the fact that filmmaking is so much a part of the cultural churn, of the thoughts, acts, artifacts, beliefs, and politics of the society in which it is made, it is difficult to reduce American filmmaking to the imagination of a single individual. But the convenience and implied intimacy of auteurism are so seductive. So are the analytical tools it offers, permitting us to understand the structure of film as the clearly coherent stylistic and thematic operation of a singular imagination. Auteurism at least gives power to the film critic and occasionally a film viewer. "You know Spielberg," I once heard a moviegoer say after watching *Saving Private Ryan,* made by the absolute master of the Hollywood style, "he gets me every time." But we may often need to sacrifice this clarity and control to the messier realities of film as part of a complex cultural mix. At the same time, it is perfectly possible to mix various kinds of analysis—auteur, genre, and cultural—in our discussion.

The actual practice of filmmaking today—despite the existence of a few directorial stars, like Spielberg, and some who have more control over their work than others, like Martin Scorsese—has pretty much reverted back to the control of the producer and the studio chief, or simply to the current versions of the classical style. The director has become a self-censor. There is little "personal" style, and with the rare exceptions of filmmakers such as David Fincher or Todd

Haynes (*Safe*, 1995; *Velvet Goldmine*, 1998, *Far From Heaven*, 2002) or Todd Solondz's wonderfully, subversively perverse *Happiness* (1998), innovation is tightly controlled. But at the same time, there are opportunities for directors that never existed before. This may be the greatest legacy of auteurism: the recognition on the part of studio executives that directors, after all, can have some imaginative say in the creation of films, even if it is limited.

African Americans, though still badly underrepresented, are finding opportunities to make movies, to find a voice within the contemporary versions of the Hollywood style. The success of Spike Lee's passionate social melodramas—such as *Do the Right Thing* (1989), *Jungle Fever* (1991), and *Malcolm X* (1992)—has led the way for strong directors of imagination, John Singleton, for instance (*Boyz N the Hood*, 1991; *Poetic Justice*, 1993; *Higher Learning*, 1995; *Rosewood*, 1997; and, on a more popular plane, *Shaft*, 2000, and *2 Fast 2 Furious*, 2003).

Spike Lee's films are deeply and passionately felt, sometimes broadly melodramatic, sometimes, as in *Clockers* (1995), understated and subtle in bringing home a point about how easy it is to stereotype and blame an otherwise deeply sympathetic character. Lee's *Summer of Sam* (1999) is his first film dealing with ethnic groups other than African Americans. It is part of the serial killer subgenre, but it expands that popular type by showing, in powerful images and big set pieces, that the murderer of women is a part of a much larger palette of a cultural violence bred of distrust and hatred, of the terror of difference.

Other minorities are being represented in small-budget films, such as Robert Rodriguez's *El Mariachi* (1992) and *From Dusk 'Til Dawn* (1996), and, with a larger budget, *Once Upon a Time in Mexico* (2003). *The Joy Luck Club* was a big-budget film, directed by the Hong Kong–born Wayne Wang in 1993, who also did a short film, *Chan Is Missing*, in 1982, and an intricate, understated film about men and families called *Smoke* in 1995. Other Asian directors are at work in Hollywood, most notably John Woo, in the big action film genre, and Ang Lee, whose 1997 *The Ice Storm* was a quiet, understated, historically and culturally acute film about early seventies suburban life. His Mandarin-language action film, *Crouching Tiger, Hidden Dragon* (2000), became a major critical and commercial success. *The Hulk* (2003) did not. But at least Ang Lee, like an auteur, is attempting various genres, trying his skills, pressing his audience to work with him as he experiments.

Other new filmmakers are attempting to mark their films with a personal style. The Warchowski brothers' *Matrix* films (1993, 2003) attempt, not always successfully, to portray alternative worlds and digital simulacra while very lightly exploring ancient philosophical problems of illusion versus reality for the digital generation. David Fincher, whose films we have looked at in other contexts, has, in some of them, explored the darkness lying below the surface of human activity. Socially and politically aware, *Seven* (1995), *The Game* (1997), and *Fight Club* (1999) create more interesting alternative worlds than the *Matrix* films, precisely because on a certain level their worlds look like our own. But like the Surrealist Buñuel, these are almost dream worlds, perhaps more accurately, mirror worlds in which we see our lives from a strange and unnerving perspective.

Whether or not any of these filmmakers will really break through the restraints of the Hollywood style is open to question. They may occasionally experiment. They are likely to remain making good, popular films that may or may not reflect their cultural backgrounds. Yet the tendency is for a filmmaker not to remain pigeonholed as a maker of African American films or feminist films or Asian films or dark, anxiety-provoking films. There is simply too much at stake: too much money, too much fame, too much power, and—not to be completely pessimistic— too much personal desire to vary imaginative approaches.

The fact remains that the commercial and cultural realities of filmmaking that largely overpower the desire to be an individual creator with a subjective style and a personal, passionate worldview can be overcome, even if only once in a while. The economic realities of production that exist worldwide and the tastes of the majority of filmgoers can sometimes be successfully challenged. It remains true that an unusual, subjective style of filmmaking rarely makes money. A passionate worldview usually comes from a passionate ego, and there is little room for a big ego in directors, whose job is usually to carry out the orders of another ego with the money, the producer. Audiences are too often uncomfortable with flights of cinematic imagination, a problem made clear in the spate of recent "independent" films, most of which are independent of neither studio money and distribution nor the conventions of the Hollywood style. We admire the idea of the artist, even though we're too often uncomfortable when an artist exercises an unusual imagination in film.

I don't want to end this chapter on a pessimistic note. For almost ten years, from the late sixties to the late seventies, a vital, sometimes experimental film culture thrived in the United States and abroad. Many of the filmmakers we have discussed here began their work during that period, and new ideas thrived and some continue to thrive. Many, many people throughout the culture were thinking and talking and writing seriously about film. The serious study of film was developed and established during this time. In the past decade, the growth of the "independent" movement has allowed some filmmakers room for experimentation, despite the fact that many distributors of "independent" films are subsidiaries of the big studios. Given the great cyclical nature of culture and creativity, where art forms continually exhaust themselves only to be revived by new talent, and given the many signs of creativity in a variety of films during the past decade, as well as the introduction of digital production, such a vital period is bound to come around again—though perhaps in different, unexpected forms.

NOTES AND REFERENCES

European Origins of the Auteur Theory   The quotation from Godard is from *Godard on Godard*, ed. Jean Narboni and Tom Milne, trans. Tom Milne (New York: Viking, 1972), pp. 146–47; new edition (New York: Da Capo Press, 1986).

The Auteur Theory   Sarris's essay, "Notes on the Auteur Theory in 1962," is in *Film Theory and Criticism*, pp. 561–64. Peter Woolen's work on auteurism is in his book *Signs and Meanings in the Cinema* (Bloomington and London: Indiana University Press, 1972). Sarris's *The American Cinema: Directors and Directions*, 1929–1968 (Chicago: University of Chicago Press, 1985) is the classic survey. T. S. Eliot's "Tradition and the Individual Talent" is widely reprinted and can be found in the collection *The Sacred Wood* (New York: Barnes and Noble, 1960).

Altman, Scorsese, Kubrick   The best book on Robert Altman is Robert T. Self, *Robert Altman's Subliminal Reality* (Minneapolis: University of Minnesota Press, 2002). See Robert Kolker, *A Cinema of Loneliness: Penn, Stone, Kubrick, Scorsese, Spielberg, and Altman*, 3rd ed. (New York: Oxford University Press, 2000).

Hitchcock   For a number of approaches to Hitchcock and *Psycho,* see Robert Kolker, ed., *Alfred Hitchcock's* Psycho*: A Casebook* (New York: Oxford University Press, 2004).

Women Auteurs   For Dorothy Arzner, see Judith Mayne, *Directed by Dorothy Arzner* (Bloomington: Indiana University Press, 1994). The quote from Lois Weber comes from Anthony Slide, *The Silent Feminists: America's First Women Directors* (Lanham, MD: Scarecrow, 1996). See also Claire Johnstone, "Women's Cinema as Counter-Cinema" in *Movies and Methods*, I. Two excellent books on avant-garde cinema are P. Adams Sitney, *Visionary Film: The American Avant-Garde in the Twentieth Century*, 3rd ed. (New York: Oxford University Press, 2002); and Gene Youngblood, *Expanded Cinema* (New York: E. P. Dutton, 1970). Professor Patty Zimmerman of Ithaca College helped me identify some contemporary avant-garde women filmmakers.

Lois Weber and Alice Guy Blaché   A biography of Blaché has been written by Alison McMahan, *Alice Guy Blaché: Lost Visionary of the Cinema* (New York: Continuum, 2002). There are various videos of their films. For the career of Ida Lupino, see Marsha Orgeron, *Making Reputations: Representation in the Cinematic Era* (Ph.D. diss., University of Maryland, 2001), pp. 292–352.

Luis Buñuel   The quotation from Buñuel comes from Freddy Buache, *The Cinema of Luis Buñuel*, trans. Peter Graham (London and New York: Tantivy Press and A. S. Barnes, 1973).

7 FILM AS CULTURAL PRACTICE

FILM IN THE REALM OF CULTURE

We have been examining film from the minute particulars of the shot and the cut to the economics of production, to the people responsible for the various parts of movie making. We have seen that film is a part of industrial production—the making of films follows principles of mass production and, in purely economic terms, is now one of the largest commercial endeavors in Los Angeles, beating out the military as the city's industrial base. We have begun to examine how film creates and satisfies its consumers' desires. But unlike other industrial goods, and conforming more closely to what we usually think of as art, movies have emotional and moral designs on us. They ask us to respond with our feelings and to think of the world in moral certainties, to assume there are clearly defined good people and bad, ethical acts and unethical ones, clearly discernible. They even suggest ethical solutions to the problems of how we should act in the world. Their characters seek redemption. Yet when compared to a novel or a painting or a symphony, the emotional demands made by most films seem shallow and unambiguous. Unlike the traditional high arts, film—with the exception of the international films referred to in the previous chapter, films by such as Godard, Bertolucci, Antonioni, Fellini, and Bergman, and others, made during the sixties through the eighties, as well as the work of some American filmmakers like Kubrick and Hitchcock—does not demand great intellectual powers to understand it. Film is too often condemned, like popular music and fiction, as being exploitative, commercial, and stupid.

While many movie studios do have units that produce "independent" films for an adult audience, who want—the producers believe—to see such things as romanticized adaptations of classic or best-selling novels, and while there exist directors in the United States seeking alternative ways of telling stories cinematically, many producers believe that the targeted audience of filmgoers lies between the ages of fifteen and thirty-five, and that they need sexual titillation and vicarious experience delivered in the most banal and violent ways. Such films feed the notion that the people, young and old, who admire and enjoy popular culture are being pandered to and willingly enjoy the bad effects of the pandering. That willingness somehow reflects a debasement of the culture. Fear that cultural standards are being lowered by popular culture and mass media causes distrust, which is followed by condemnation. But condemnation seems to have no effect. We still love movies; we still watch television and listen to rock and roll and rap. Distrust then turns to cynicism.

CULTURE AS TEXT

There is an element of truth in everything negative that is said about popular culture, although blanket condemnations are not useful in helping us understand its richness. What is useful is to attempt a broader definition that takes into consideration the negative things about pop culture, but also sees it in all its seriousness and playfulness. In this larger view, we need to start with a definition of culture and then an examination of popular culture (or, more accurately, cultures) to discover ways to fight cynicism with the understanding of unexpected complexity.

Culture can be understood as the text of our lives, the ultimately coherent pattern of beliefs, acts, responses, and artifacts that we produce and comprehend every day. Coherence, system, and order are the highlights of what constitutes a text. We usually think of a book as a text, but anything with known boundaries that produces meaning—even self-contradictory meaning, even meaning that keeps shifting—can be a text. The idea of culture as text means, first, that culture is not nature; it is made by people in history for conscious or even unconscious reasons, the product of all they think and do. Even the unconscious or semiconscious acts of our daily lives can, when observed and analyzed, be understood as sets of coherent acts and be seen to interact with each other. These acts, beliefs, and practices, along with the artifacts they produce—the music we listen to, the clothes we wear, the television we love, the films we watch—have meaning. They can be read and understood. By "read," I mean that we can understand the musical and lyrical complexities of popular music, just as we can analyze a Beethoven symphony or a Philip Roth novel. Reading as a critical act is applicable to all meaning-making entities or texts. People drive cars and select certain makes; they go to school, open bank accounts, make paintings, watch television, accept racial and sexual differences (or don't), hate Democrats or Republicans (or don't), believe in free will and a free economy (or don't), behave well or badly, love classical music or rock, and somehow make perfect sense of most of this behavior. With a little study and an open mind, we can understand the sense we make of it and the needs that are fulfilled by the choices we make and the things that entertain us. We can understand why and how our entertainments affirm or deny our beliefs. We can see that none of this is natural; it is all born of class, gender, race, education, acculturation, and the ideologies that drive us all.

Subcultures

Now, our culture—or that part of our culture that makes divisions between high and low, serious and popular art—defines culture much more narrowly than we just have. It defines as culture those serious works made by independent imaginations that are complex and acceptable only to the few who have, want, or like "culture." In other words, culture segments and segregates itself. The culture's culture is what we normally think of as the difficult, personal art we have to engage deeply in order to understand: paintings in museums, symphonies played in concert halls, poems and novels analyzed in the classroom, foreign films that used to be shown in "art houses." If other kinds of imaginative products are allowed in, they become part of a hierarchy and are referred to as "low" or "popular" culture and relegated to the margins. Popular culture is often scorned by admirers of "high" culture, and the high is often scorned by the popular. This mutual antagonism is sometimes expressed through allusions to stereotypes. Classical music, art, and poetry lovers are the effete, the intellectual elite, with all the implications of class and sexual otherness this implies. People who enjoy the popular arts are sometimes represented as working-class slobs, or women without a life, or people of color, or teenagers, all of whom threaten dominant values. The negative view of the popular is further nourished by the fact that mass culture is commercial culture ("commercialized" would be the popular, pejorative term). Movies, television, rock music, romantic novels, and newspapers are commodities, objects of commercial desire. The companies that manufacture them seek a profit. Popular culture commodities are the product not of the individual imagination but of the calculations of the large, ever conglomerating corporations that construct them to appeal to the largest part of their audience. The results are then positioned for the most appropriate segment of that audience; marketed according to age, gender, race, class; and promoted and sold accordingly. The commodities and their audience become part of the cost/price, profit/loss, asset/liability, manufacture/distribution structure that makes up industrial practice.

There are even wider, more profound, and potentially dangerous splits between subcultures who enjoy the products of popular culture itself. Religious and political differences mark divergent interests in radio programs, kinds of music, and films. People who listen to National Public Radio are identified as different from those who listen to right-wing talk shows—both by themselves and by others. People who watch action movies are seen as different—first of all by the moviemakers themselves—from those who watch adaptations of Jane Austen novels. In such divisions, the resentment and anger felt by one group toward another are marked and sometimes unsettling.

Media and Cultures

The roots of all this are complex and indicate how any narrow definitions of culture are insufficient to describe the strong and changing elements of the larger culture we belong to. What follows is a very abbreviated sketch of some complex events and movements that created subcultures within larger cultural groups, but it will give an idea of how culture keeps generating itself, how vital groups within it create its art, and how that art changes and transforms the culture.

In European culture, the "serious" production of music and painting and literature goes back to the Middle Ages, when it belonged to the royal courts. The "lower classes," illiterate peasants mostly, had cultures indigenous to their country and place, based on crafts and oral traditions, a phenomenon that is true of most non-European cultures as well. The formation of a property-owning and goods-trading middle class began in the Italian Renaissance, and it is this new group that brought high culture out of the palaces and into the villas, the homes of wealthy traders and property owners. Owning or sponsoring fine art was part of the movement of the burgeoning middle class toward owning cultural property. Well-to-do Italian merchants became patrons of the arts, commissioning painters, for example, who, in gratitude, would paint an image of their benefactor at the feet of Christ. Ownership was a sign of wealth. Owning or patronizing art was a sign of wealthy good taste. It still is.

During the eighteenth century, the property-owning middle class grew across Europe, small shopkeepers flourished, and an industrial working class began to expand. Each of these classes continued developing its own cultural forms. The novel, for example, was developed in the early eighteenth century and was originally directed at middle-class women, who read or had read to them, for example, the romantic adventures of the heroine of Samuel Richardson's *Pamela; Or, Virtue Rewarded* (1740) and *Clarissa* (1747–1748) with a devotion and identification (and, sometimes, a sense of irony) that many people still devote to soap opera. Melodrama, a popular working- and lower-middle-class form, was born of the novel, the theater, and politics, especially in the late eighteenth-century theater of post-revolutionary France. It started as pantomime with music—"melodrama" means drama with music—in response to laws that forbade traditional theatrical performances in which actors spoke their lines. Early melodrama in Europe and in the United States was broad, moral, and political, with exaggerated gestures and simplified structures of good and evil—too broad and "common" for upper-class tastes. It was broadly participatory as well, inviting emotional and even verbal response. Melodrama was a form of satisfaction and gratification, a communal expression of a class desire for stability, place, and confirmation of simple moral values. In various forms, it has thrived in many cultures in the West and the East, and its cinematic version will be examined in some detail in the following chapters.

Music Hall variety entertainments were, by the mid-nineteenth century, another working-class site of comedy, popular music, parody, and gender lampoon (cross-dressing in British variety shows remains popular and is still accepted without embarrassed innuendo). Music Hall was and is performed in a space that encourages lively audience response. Along with melodrama, the American version of Music Hall, vaudeville, was to prove an enormous influence on the development of film, as well as an early venue where film was projected.

In order for popular culture to become mass culture, storage and distribution methods had to be developed. Print culture was well advanced by the eighteenth century, and novels and newspapers enjoyed a fairly wide circulation. In the case of the novel, some transmission occurred through people reading aloud to groups. In order for the music, images, and narratives that were enjoyed by mainly working- and lower-middle-class audiences to become mass culture, other means had to be developed, which were by the late nineteenth and early twentieth centuries. The new technologies of photography, telephony, the phonograph, and the movies served everyone well, and especially those who did not have the time or the means to contemplate the complexities of high culture. These new technologies quickly became dominant. When this happened, the culture of print—with its demands of education, leisure time, and access to the quiet and solitude that reading fiction or poetry demands—ebbed.

We have examined one form of storage and distribution in some detail: the photographic emulsion on plastic strips, which, when exposed to light and developed into a series of high-resolution images, can be cut together in various ways, put in cans, and sent around the country and the world to be projected on movie screens. Electronic transmission was another important nineteenth-century development. The telephone, phonograph, and radio delivered voice and music, news and entertainment, into the most intimate of spaces, the home. When film began its gain in popularity, people had to go out of the house to see it, with all the planning and expense that entails. By the twenties, radio was omnipresent in the domestic sphere and became the dominant form of entertainment. When sound came to film in the late twenties, a vigorous interchange between the two media began. Radio carried film advertising as well as programming based on current films. Radio stars played in films; film stars appeared on radio.

One version of print media expanded along with movies and radio by becoming integral to them. Newspapers advertised and reviewed radio and film. Movie magazines and newspaper gossip columns extended the work of studio publicity by keeping the stars and their personal lives in the public eye. It would be no exaggeration to say that, by the end of the twenties, an elaborate, integrated network of popular culture had evolved in which listener and viewer had access to an intertextual web of radio, movies, magazines, and newspapers. By intertextual, I mean that all of these elements referred to one another, reproduced or represented each other. Radio broadcasts were used as narrative elements in film; films were turned into radio drama; newspapers reviewed both and printed film publicity and scandal; film music and popular music were connected so that a movie theme was available on record and on the radio. By the 1940s, a film might include a theme song composed especially so that it could be released as a single. I said earlier that a text has boundaries, but this needs to be amended by the fact that textual boundaries are extremely porous.

The only thing missing was a means of delivering moving images to the home, and that problem was solved after World War II. With the coming of television (which began development in the thirties), the web of mass-mediated popular culture was ubiquitous, available to anyone who could afford it. By the mid-1950s, almost everyone could. The intertextuality of this cultural web grew as well. Radio ceased being a medium for drama and assumed a major role, first, as a delivery system for popular music and, recently, as a site for the expression of usually right-wing political views. Film and television took immediately to one another, even though television cut deeply into film attendance and moviemakers pretended nothing but scorn for the new form.

Television became the delivery mechanism for old films and for films made specifically for television. Movie studios bought television outlets and assisted them with product. Some producers, most notably at the time of this writing, the action film maker, Jerry Bruckheimer, have added television to their roster of productions. With the advent of the videocassette and cable television in the late 1970s, movies and television became, on a very important level, functions of one another. Filmmakers depend upon videocassette and now DVD sales and rentals to round out the profits of a film. Moviegoers balance viewing at home with going to the movie theater. In fact, DVDs, along with their supplementary material, have become so popular that, in 2002, they accounted for an amazing 58 percent of a film's income to the studios. They are also—and this is certainly even more amazing—giving the studios ideas that films are worth preserving and may have educational value, two ideas that had never occurred to them previously.

Meanwhile, the domain of "high" culture shrank. It remains proscribed by class and education and finds a home in museums, concert halls, and bookstores—the few that exist outside of Amazon.com—with some airplay on radio and television. But "high" culture was always marginalized and is growing more so. The "popular," in particular the American version of the popular, is the dominant form around the world. Within it thrive many varieties and subforms, many national inflections. In almost all cultures, film is ubiquitous, and the most ubiquitous of all, the dominant of the dominant, is, of course, American film.

The New Web

I've used the image of a web to define the ways in which popular culture is spread and integrated. I've mentioned as well the various media that grew in the nineteenth century to create this web. "Web" of course not only has taken on new meaning, but has created yet another set of subcultures.

Film is the product of nineteenth-century technology that emerged from photography. It is, in fact, the first technological art. During the mid-1990s, at the same time that the digital was making its way into film production, computers were becoming a household item, and the World Wide Web was creating a new "screen" on which new communities and cultures were forming, including communities where film was the subject of discussion.

Like almost everything on the computer screen, the World Wide Web is a place of process in which everything happens but nothing is resolved. Unlike the movies, its images and words do not fall into closed, knowable fictional worlds. The narrative of the Web is in fact the story of investigation and participation, the subject's progress through an open-ended system. It is also a space that has begun to embrace film, not only for the sake of advertising—*The Blair Witch Project* (1999) was a phenomenon that was based not on an especially wonderful film, but on word of mouth that grew from its website—but as a place in which small movies can be made, shown, and discussed.

Culturally, the Web, along with computer games, has created an unusually close integration with film and television, each form interacting with the other and providing more space for participation and interactions with the viewer—and more income for producers.

Theories of Culture

Again and again, we need to remind ourselves that culture for profit—in any of its forms—does not excuse us from analyzing it. Owned or free, controlled by the user or the provider, the viewer or the studio, we are still part of it. In order to understand the place of popular culture in general and film in particular within the larger complex of cultural practice, it will be useful for us to look at some theories of cultural studies that discuss mass media and film. **Cultural studies** looks at various kinds of texts within the context of cultural practice, that is, the work, production, and material stuff of daily life, marked as it is by economics and class, by politics, gender, and race, by need and desire. Cultural studies examines the form and structure of cultural texts as they create meaning or have meaning created by the people who produce them and the people who are entertained by them. Cultural studies thinks about meaning as an ongoing process built out of complex relationships between people in their daily lives and the works of imagination they look to for emotional and intellectual sustenance and release.

The Frankfurt School

An early wave of cultural criticism that studied mass media found its subject deeply troubling, and for very good reason. The Frankfurt Institute for Social Research was founded in Germany in 1924. Its function was to integrate the study of sociology, psychology, culture, and politics. Among its members and associates—known as the **Frankfurt school**—were some of the most important left-wing thinkers of the twentieth century: Max Horkheimer, Theodor Adorno, Herbert Marcuse, Erich Fromm, Siegfried Kracauer, and Walter Benjamin. Because they were left wing and many of them Jewish, the Institute was closed down by the Nazis in 1933. Many of its members came to America, where they taught and pursued their work.

A core part of that work was the study of film and mass media. Siegfried Kracauer wrote two major studies of film, *Theory of Film: The Redemption of Physical Reality* (1960) and *From Caligari to Hitler: A Psychological History of the German Film* (1947). The latter was an attempt to describe a cultural mood, one that would lead to the cultural and political catastrophe of Nazism, by looking at the films the culture had produced. Theodor Adorno wrote books and articles on philosophy and music and coauthored with Max Horkheimer *The Dialectic of Enlightenment* (1944). A chapter of this book, "The Culture Industry," along with Walter Benjamin's magisterial essay "The Work of Art in the Age of Mechanical Reproduction," laid the foundation for future studies of media, culture, and politics. It proved to be a difficult foundation to build on. Given the society they observed, the conclusions about mass culture reached by Adorno, Benjamin, Kracauer, and others of the Frankfurt school were either very negative or ambivalent.

Germany in the 1920s was a society going through a massive political upheaval that would lead to the most brutally destructive regime in modern history. The Frankfurt school viewed the rise of popular culture in this society as part of the growing authoritarianism in Germany's political culture. Instead of a web of interrelated texts in which the listener or viewer is part of a complex structure of commercially produced and distributed music, news, images, and sound, the Frankfurt school saw a vertical structure where government and industry worked in close collusion with each other, producing mass media that was distributed downward to the people, dominating the masses with films, music, and radio. The audience for popular culture was an undifferentiated and passive mass, robbed of subjectivity and individuality by an authoritarian government, which swayed the people to its needs by manipulating the popular media.

To the Frankfurt school, the audience for the popular was in fact created, given form, made compliant, *composed,* turned into a willing tool of the ruling political party. Again, this view was based in a strong reality. Hitler's Nazi government was the first to use mass media—radio and film especially (they were busily developing television)—as a controlled means of communication, fashioning information, entertainment, and outright propaganda in such a palatable way that its audience could not, did not want to, resist.

The Frankfurt school looked upon the government and its associates in industry, journalism, broadcasting, and film as strong and controlling, the audience as weak, willing, and easily fooled. Horkheimer and Adorno wrote: "Life in the late capitalist era is a constant initiation rite. Everyone must show that he wholly identifies himself with the power which is belaboring him. . . . The miracle of integration, the permanent act of grace by the authority who receives the defenseless person—once he has swallowed his rebelliousness—signifies fascism."

The Frankfurt school understood that mass media did not have to clobber its audience into submission, that people have free will that can be easily, willingly subdued. They understood the comfort that comes with joining a group, swallowing rebelliousness, integrating oneself into the mass, and receiving authority's grace. They saw and noted how easily popular culture accepted anti-Semitism, agreed to mindless calls for sacrifice to the fatherland, to the promises of redemption from a despairing and oppressed life. Totalitarian power—along with the offerings of banal entertainment in the form of musicals, melodramas, and comedies made by the ruling powers—was hard for most Germans to resist.

Under Hitler, cultural difference, individual expression, artistic experimentation were not simply discouraged but destroyed. Serious art, modern and critical art, was declared decadent and was banished. Books were burned. Artists fled the country. Popular art was molded into the narrow spectrum of hatred of Jews and communists, adulation of Hitler, and celebration of a lower-middle-class life of home, family, and fatherland, driven by exhortations to keep sacrificing in order to perpetuate Nazi ideals. Fascism became a model for the Frankfurt school's analysis of the culture industry as a conspiracy of politics and business to form, out of the most profound and uninformed aspects of a culture's collective fears and desires, superficial entertainments that confirmed and reinforced the basest instincts of that culture. The culture seemed to yield unquestioningly.

The Critique of American Popular Culture

Unsurprisingly, Frankfurt school scholars tended to look down upon popular culture from an elitist perspective. Anything that was part of such an abominable political culture could not have any value. They took this elitist position with them when they came to the United States in the late 1930s. Theodor Adorno particularly disliked the popular and wrote often of the debasement of jazz and popular music. The worst part of Frankfurt school elitism was popularized in the United States during the 1950s and became integrated with the general concern over what some people perceived as a decay of the culture and a rise in adolescent misbehavior. The fifties were a period of serious cultural instability, during which post–World War II anxieties were heightened by the Cold War with the Soviet Union. A paranoia about being subverted and infiltrated took over the country during the first half of the decade, and popular culture became a main target of its fears.

The anti–popular culture discourse of the 1950s was carried on by many sides. Attacks by right-wing politicians and journalists were not very sophisticated, though they stirred up many anxieties. They did not present the Frankfurt school's complex portrait of a culture industry that was an interrelated process of the government and the producers of entertainment crafting their products to manipulate the willing masses. Indeed, some Cold War writers and politicians put the argument of the Frankfurt school on its head. Where the Frankfurt school analyzed a top-down control of media and the population, fifties critics of the media argued that the media—especially film and televi-sion—were elitist and left wing (some of them still do). Rather than controlling the belief system of the people, the media subverted it, destroying their values. This led to the red-baiting witch hunts in Hollywood and the blacklisting of film and media people during the McCarthy period.

Less virulent ideologues, indeed many fifties intellectuals on the left, argued that popular culture was simply too debased and shallow. If people were enter-tained by mass media, they were already diminished in intellectual and emo-tional response by contact with films, pop music, and television, or soon would be. Some critics of popular culture saw it—and some still do—as a promoter of violence and sexuality. Comic books, movies aimed at teenagers, and, near the end of the decade of the fifties, rock and roll music were deemed the worst of-fenders. Congressional hearings investigated their influence. And, of course, the explosive growth of television in the fifties was looked on with dismay. While its manufacturers, producers, and promoters saw it as a miracle that would pla-cate bored housewives and keep families together, its detractors saw it as a fur-ther degradation of cultural standards. Television was yet another sign that the culture was being reduced to a featureless, homogenized mass.

High Culture, Masscult, and Midcult

The social and cultural complexities of mass media were not as important to fifties critics as the pronouncements of decay and corruption. In the fifties and early sixties, elitist categories maintained a strict segregation of the arts and their audience based on matters as vague as taste. The film reviewer and cul-tural critic Dwight MacDonald categorized fifties culture into three parts. Creating a less ethnically and racially biased metaphor than the old "low brow, middle brow, and high brow" classification, he spoke about High Culture—the complex, resonant art for the elite—but concentrated his attention on what he called Masscult and Midcult—the first being popular culture produced for mass consumption, the second something in between, not high, not low, but pecu-liarly middle class. By splitting popular culture into two groups, MacDonald could address a decade that was entertained by a new range of entertainment from Elvis Presley records and movies to plays and films written by Tennessee Williams and live television drama.

These new categories began to introduce an element of complexity into the American discussion of popular culture. They were still derogatory and judg-mental: Masscult, MacDonald says, "is bad in a new way: it doesn't even have the theoretical possibility of being good." Midcult only reproduces the bad in a better light: "It pretends to respect the standards of High Culture while in fact it waters them down and vulgarizes them." Midcult gives the impression of seri-ousness, while reproducing the same banalities of Masscult (films made from eighteenth- and nineteenth-century novels or recent best-sellers might be con-sidered current examples of Midcult). However derogatory, these classifications at least began to recognize or point to the fact that popular culture was not monolithic, that issues of class and taste could be used to achieve a finer definition. But, without the Frankfurt school's complex ideological analysis and with the conservative bias so many of them held, the mass media critics of the fifties and early sixties mainly railed and raised alarms. These were the views from above. Meanwhile, the culture of the popular expanded.

By the late fifties, rock and roll, which began as African American rhythm and blues that was then integrated with country and western formats, became an important component of a revived, activist youth culture that began to have purchasing power to match its desire for a unique entertainment. In cinema, the influence of foreign films began nudging movies in the direction of high culture. At the same time, because of population shifts to the suburbs, movie attendance began to fall off and television viewing went up. In response, American cinema changed and began targeting specific age groups with specific kinds of movies, trying to pinpoint an ever-changing audience with both Masscult and Midcult films. Popular culture—both its products and its audience—grew more complex and needed new theories to deal with it.

Walter Benjamin and the Age of Mechanical Reproduction

New theories began to converge from many directions. The growth of film studies in the 1960s and the development of feminist theories in the early 1970s laid the ground for a growing interest in serious analysis of popular culture. Many of these theories grew from an essay by an associate of the Frankfurt school, originally written in 1936. It helped form the basis of a nonjudgmental, appropriately political, speculative, and complex meditation on popular art and its relation to the larger matrix of cultural practice. Walter Benjamin's "The Work of Art in the Age of Mechanical Reproduction" takes as its starting point the new elements of reproduction, storage, and distribution that made film and other forms of popular cultural practice possible. For Benjamin, the difference between the old art of the elite classes and the new popular art of the masses is that popular or mass art is readily available outside the usual high-culture sites of museums and libraries. The image (film is Benjamin's main object of study, though his ideas can usefully be applied to recorded music, photography, television, and now to digital media) is not a unique, one-of-a-kind event, kept in one place and viewed with awe and reverence. The image is now infinitely reproducible and available. It has lost that which makes it special, even worthy of cultural reverence, what Benjamin calls its aura.

Aura can be thought of as the uniqueness of a work of traditional high art. An original painting has aura. It is one of its kind, visible in its originality only where it is hung, looked at with the privileged relationship of viewer and the work itself. The autographed first edition of a novel might have an aura, as would the live performance of a play or symphony. Aura is the nonreproducible, the authentic, the original production from the hand of an artist or ensemble, viewed from a reverent distance. Popular, mass-produced art is without aura. The CD by a rock group that you own or song you download is the same as thousands—hundreds of thousands—that were cut from the same master or digitized over and over. The print of a film viewed in a mall multiplex in Cleveland, or on a DVD in your living room, is the same as a print viewed in a multiplex or a DVD in a living room in West Palm Beach or (except perhaps for the redubbing of the sound track) in Frankfurt, Germany. There is nothing unique about it. In fact, there is nothing palpable about it. Nothing is there but digital, electronic, or optical data; no human presence but the beholding eyes and ears of the viewer, who the producers hope will respond in the same way as every other viewer anywhere—by paying for access.

Benjamin, unlike most of his Frankfurt school associates, did not look at this development with alarm. He looked at it as historical and technological fact— something going on despite what social and cultural critics might think about it. He thought about the growth of popular culture as something to be under- stood not as an oppressive reality but as a potentially liberating one. Loss of aura and ease of access meant two things. Everyone could come into contact with works of the imagination, and everyone would be free to make of the au- raless work what she could. Curiously, the loss of aura could lead to a greater intimacy with the work. The ritual and awe that surround the creation and re- ception of original genius might be replaced by the intimate interpretation of each viewer. "The progressive reaction," Benjamin writes, "is characterized by the direct, intimate fusion of visual and emotional enjoyment with the orienta- tion of the expert." Every person becomes a critic, able to make sense and make judgments. Every person's perception becomes enlarged. "By close-ups of the things around us, by focusing on hidden details of familiar objects, by exploring common place milieus under the ingenious guidance of the camera, the film, on the one hand, extends our comprehension of the necessities which rule our lives; on the other hand, it manages to assure us of an immense and unexpected field of action." The camera, he says, is like a surgeon's knife, cutting through reality, bringing the viewer into an intimate connection with the world.

Film and other mass media offer a place of entry and participation in the imaginative representations of the world. They offer them for everyone. Certainly, Benjamin was not out of touch with the realities of mass media and politics, especially in his own country. He knew that the larger an audience, the more difficult it would be for mass art to present progressive ideas. He knew as well what the Nazis were doing with mass media and to the culture as a whole. He experienced it directly. Forced out of his country in 1940, this Jewish, mystic, Marxist intellectual, who wrote about angels as well as the mass media, would take his life while trying to escape. He understood that fascism attempted to reintroduce a false aura into the mass-produced art, turning it into spectacle and putting it into the service of political ritual and, inevitably, of war. Communism, he believed, might work the other way, by liberating the viewer and the work of art into a politics of communal action. While such a view is out of fashion at the moment, it reflects an understanding that an art of the masses can mean a par- ticipation of the masses in the political work of the culture. A utopian vision!

Benjamin was a prophet of culture, and his words, directed at film, can be applied today to the digital. He wrote in "The Work of Art in the Age of Mechanical Reproduction":

Every day the urge grows stronger to get hold of an object at very close range by way of its likeness, its reproduction. . . . To pry an object from its shell, to destroy its aura, is the mark of a perception whose "sense of the universal equality of things" has increased to such a degree that it extracts it even from a unique object by means of reproduction. . . . The adjustment of reality to the masses and of the masses to reality is a process of unlimited scope, as much for thinking as for perception. . . . [The people are] the matrix from which all traditional behavior toward works of art issues today in a new form.

The Aura of State Intervention

There have been important examples of governments working with artists to promote a popular art that involved many people on many levels, including the political. The artistic activity that immediately followed the Russian Revolution—and formed the model for Benjamin's idea of a communal, politicized art—is one successful example. The work of Sergei Eisenstein, Dziga Vertov, and other filmmakers, writers, and visual artists in the 1920s exhibited an energy and a desire to reach their audience and actively engage the audience's intellect and emotions unparalleled in the century. Stalin put a stop to all that. Elsewhere, throughout the twentieth century, there were many attempts at state intervention in the arts. Germany revived its film industry in the 1970s through state subsidies to television. Films there were made for television and also exhibited in theaters. Popular response was mixed, but most of the films made under the subsidies were excellent. By and large, public funding has helped to foster a serious and engaged, personal and political cinema—as we saw in the example of *Daughters of the Dust*. Jim Jarmusch, the independent American director of such films as *Down by Law* (1986), *Dead Man* (1995), *Ghost Dog* (1999), and *Coffee and Cigarettes* (2000) receives funding and distribution from a variety of public and private European sources. But public funding has been less successful in forging the large-scale interaction of audience, work, and culture at large that Benjamin hoped might occur in the age of mechanical reproduction, and many governments, our own included, are becoming more and more reluctant to take a financial role in the process.

The Birmingham School of Cultural Studies

Cultural studies is less a movement than a loose affiliation of intellectual agreements about how to think of culture and its productions. Started by the Germans in the twenties and thirties, coalescing around Benjamin's essay, it was developed by the British cultural theorist Raymond Williams, and given its name by the British Birmingham Centre for Contemporary Cultural Studies. It is a wide-ranging discipline, always in process, but with some important foundational principles: that the study of culture be interdisciplinary and broad. All events are seen in the context of cultural practice, and that practice is determined not only by the elite culture industry but by the activities and interventions of many subcultures, which are determined by class, race, and gender. Cultural practice involves both the production of works and their reception by an audience. Culture and all its various components can be understood as coherent, legible, interactive "texts."

These texts can be briefly isolated for the purpose of study and then placed back in their cultural context. I can analyze Alfred Hitchcock's *Psycho* or James Cameron's *The Terminator* (1984) as unique texts, as I might a novel. I can examine their formal structure, their images and narrative form. But I must also integrate them within the culture of the late 1950s and the economics of the end of the studio system (in the case of *Psycho*) or the apocalyptic consciousness of the 1980s and the melding of the superhero into the science fiction genre (in the instance of *The Terminator*). I can read parts of these films as cultural texts: the way the automobile in *Psycho* reflects an ambiguous response to mobility and security, and how the old dark house recapitulates familiar images from gothic literature and Hollywood horror movies. I can look at the way robotics in *The Terminator* is a sign of the culture's long-term attraction to and repulsion from the image of the automated human. *Psycho* and *The Terminator* can be analyzed as another entry into the popular imagination of Freud's story of Oedipus: *Psycho* talks about a child destroyed by his mother; *The Terminator* and its sequels address the unending and impossible search for patriarchal figures who destroy and are destroyed. *The Terminator* can be figured as a response to the end of the Cold War and the unknown terrors that occur when we discover that the enemy is really us and not them. Both films can be seen as ways in which the culture continues to come to terms with the modern world, with despair, emptiness, and terrors of the unknown, how it deals with issues of the feminine and masculine, with its attraction to and repulsion by sexuality, with its fascination with and fear of otherness and difference.

Reception and Negotiation

Text and context—in their usual senses of the work of art and its cultural and historical surroundings—are reconfigured in cultural studies. The individual work, the work of culture, our acts of looking, understanding, and participating, can all be read as interacting texts. The very interaction of viewer and film is a kind of text that can be interpreted. Form and meaning make sense only when we examine their intersections in all their complexity. The key is legibility, the ability to read culture and its work, to understand, dissect, and then reassemble what we have read into a coherent analysis. No one element can be taken for granted. The whole is made of its parts, and each part responds to the other.

Reading Benjamin, we introduced another principle of cultural studies that opposes many of the traditional ideas of mass media studies. Instead of positing a "culture industry"—a conglomeration of governmental, political, and business forces that determines the commodities of popular culture and conforms the culture from the top down—cultural studies sees a complex interaction of production and response and reception. The consumers of popular media are not a dumb, cowed, undifferentiated mass, repressed and oppressed by the banal homogeneity of what they see and hear. People consume in many different ways, and with varying degrees of comprehension and ability to make interpretations. Individuals, as well as small and large groups, determined by their economic and social classes, make up subcultures who negotiate (a key word for the Birmingham school of cultural studies) meanings with popular texts, much like readers of high cultural products do. Negotiation implies a relationship between the work of popular culture and the consumer, with the latter taking what she wants from a song, a television show, or a movie, and possibly not taking it at all seriously.

People have different backgrounds and different needs, which they put to use in negotiating with the text meanings that are most useful or pleasurable. People are capable of comprehension and of articulation, of struggling against the desire of the producers of the popular to inundate them with sounds and images. Everyone interprets; everyone responds. What traditional mass media studies saw as a monolith, cultural studies sees as a complex group of class-, race-, and gender-marked individuals, with desires and with intelligence. We don't merely accept what the culture industry hands down: we deal with it and use it.

Along with the process of negotiating with the text comes the work of un-packing. In Chapter 2, I spoke about the economy of the image. Films made in the classical style—as well as television, advertising, and other popular forms—pack a great deal of information into a small space. Much narrative detail is stored in a glance, a gesture, a nod, a camera movement, a cut. We understand films because we know the conventions, we know how to read and interpret. Cultural studies holds that we can move through the conventions and unpack more subtle meanings, that we decode according to what we want or need to understand about a film or a song or a television program: think, for example, how much information and emotional response about gender and the power of women is gathered from the television shows *Buffy the Vampire Slayer* or *Sex and the City*. We open the text, pick, choose, and interpret. What we interpret might not necessarily be what the producers intended. Women fans of *Star Trek*, *X-Files*, or *Lord of the Rings*, for example, write highly erotic, homosexual stories— "slash fiction"—about the heroes of their favorite programs or movies and publish them on the Web. Freddy Krueger, the evil dream figure of the *Nightmare on Elm Street* films, becomes a figure of fearful admiration for adolescents. Rap music and its lyrics provide the rhythms and narratives of African American street life. *The Terminator* moves, by means of subtle negotiation between filmmaker, audience, and movie star, from destructive monster to substitute father, climaxing, in 2003, as the governor of California. Forrest Gump becomes a role model for simple-minded courage. The class-crossed lovers of *Titanic* (James Cameron, 1997) become objects of adoration and a confirmation of teenage despair. Boy bands and girl bands provide a sublimation of desire for teenagers and icons of sexual liberation. In all these cases, many viewers and listeners respond in different ways and understand with a touch of irony and understanding the intentions such artifacts hold for them.

Judgment and Values

Perhaps not all the negotiations, unpacking of codes, and re-readings of cultural texts are for the good. Popular and high culture can turn out badly or stupidly. Some audiences may not respond wisely. During the horrible wars in the Balkans during the 1990s, Serbian nationalists dressed up like Rambo, the eighties film icon of individual heroism, and killed people. Arnold Schwarzenegger governs a U.S. state—a popular choice that might not be ennobling (or useful) for anyone. But the idea of "ennoblement" may be as much a cultural cliché as is the notion that popular culture is debasement. That some individuals or groups use culture badly is not unique or new. The Nazis made Jewish prisoners who were musicians play Mozart in the concentration camps. The point is that cultural studies attempts to be nonjudgmental while, we can only hope, maintaining a moral center. Cultural studies first seeks to describe and analyze and broaden. Judgment comes after comprehension.

This is a very complex point, because it places us between common sense, careful analysis, and wholesale dismissal. Many people still dismiss film, television, and rock as worthless and potentially dangerous. They see the Web as a hotbed of pornography or stealing other people's intellectual property. Conservative politicians blame Hollywood for ruining the culture. Study after study attempts to discover whether violent film and television provoke violence in children, and each study seems to deliver a different answer.

In the end, some judgment has to be applied. The interplay of perception and analysis, guided by methodology, that makes up critical thought must lead any critic to abstract what she finds about the culture into broad, general patterns and then analyze those patterns for subtle meaning. The description and evaluation of these patterns will be subjective, based upon the values and moral beliefs held by the critic. Some aspects of popular culture will, indeed, be found wanting, even intellectually or morally degrading, but this judgment ought not then become an all-embracing condemnation. Perhaps the key element of cultural studies is its ability to analyze broadly and make judgments discriminatingly.

Intertextuality and Postmodernism

This discrimination is difficult, largely because of the simple attractions of the works of popular culture and the desire of one part of the culture to put them down and the other to embrace them and make them their own. The works themselves make discrimination difficult because they tend to feed upon themselves, interact, and absorb one another to a remarkable extent. Films refer to other films; musical styles are filled with quotations from one another—sampling, for example, is a popular formal element of rap; television news indulges in sensationalism and fear mongering; sexuality and violence constitute the major elements of almost all mass media, substituting themselves for more rational explorations of the world. The culture seems to be enthralled with images and sounds rapidly edited together. Fragmentation rules—and not in the way either Eisenstein or the Classical Hollywood Style intended. In rock videos, the unifying elements of the classical style in film are sacrificed to the sensation of rapidity without the analytic and political energy of Eisensteinian montage. The classical style made fragments look like wholes, and while that style still predominates in narrative films, in other forms—music videos, television commercials, news reports—fragments are presented only as fragments while at the same time moving in a flow that is almost undifferentiated. Commerce, imagination, culture, and news intermingle and move us along in a process that makes analysis difficult.

This is the style of the postmodern, where hierarchies, definitions, and separations are broken down, and the quickly seen is substituted for the deeply understood. Cultural studies discovered the postmodern and, as if by necessity, adopted it. No one can look at popular culture for long and not recognize—with delight or with horror—the often indiscriminate flow of images and undigested ideas. In film and television, images of extraordinary violence become as commonplace as the sentimentality of the characters who are the targets of the violence; images of the poor, the hurt, and the starving appear indiscriminately on television news, call upon our emotions, and as rapidly disappear again. When images disappear, so does sympathy. A clothing manufacturer uses images of the dead and dying, or of prisoners on death row, to sell his goods. Everything seems to be occurring on the same plane of comprehension, or willing incomprehension. Popular culture appears to be in a steady state of assertion and denial, of claiming the importance of what is shown and then denying that it really means anything.

This must, of necessity, make media historians and critics of us all. **Intertextuality**—the interpenetration of various texts, one within the other— keeps reminding us how wise we are to the popular culture we've grown up with. The rapid association of images in film, television, and advertisements forces us to analyze and make sense of image inundation. Staccato shrieks of violins in a television commercial will make us all think about *Psycho*. A commercial for a local car dealer will play the opening of *Also Spake Zarathustra*, and we will recall *2001: A Space Odyssey*. Any episode of *The Simpsons* will contain references to a dozen movies. Everyone is wise to the sounds and images of the culture, though, perhaps, no one is the wiser.

If you detect overtones of the Frankfurt school as well as fifties critiques of the popular in this argument, it is because of the tension between the open embrace offered by cultural studies and a need to maintain some sense of what may be important and what may not be. Cultural studies insists on accepting all aspects of the popular with an understanding that individuals take from it what they feel is important to them. More traditional criticism asks for value judgment, discrimination, and a preservation of hierarchies. Some practitioners of cultural studies may applaud the undifferentiated flow of the postmodern, while other critical schools look in horror at the surrender of judgment and discrimination. As always, an intelligent compromise works best. The concept of negotiation, the recognition that the audience for the popular is not stupid, helps us understand that there may indeed be discrimination at work. A postmodern critic might argue that it is precisely because viewers and listeners are so sophisticated that sounds and images can be used in a rapid-fire, punning, intertextual structure. Perhaps it is because we have seen and heard it all before that no one accepts the old meanings, and the new ones have yet to be invented. At the same time, any critic must be aware of boundaries even as they are being broken down. Making judgments depends upon recognizing boundaries. We may not always want to keep them in place, but we must note their location, their history, and where they might be moved.

Our discussion of the form and content of film to this point has offered tools for comprehension, analysis, and judgment. Understanding the cultural contexts of film and the means at our disposal to read and account for our judgments offers the opportunity to explore another important element, the film narrative: we have seen how films tell stories, who does the telling, and now, using what we know about the contexts of form and culture, we can attempt to understand the stories that are told.

CULTURAL CRITICISM APPLIED TO *VERTIGO* AND *DIE HARD*

How do we combine a theory of cultural studies with an understanding of the formal structure of film and come up with a reading of cinematic texts that situates them within larger cultural practices and within the culture as a whole? Such a task would involve looking closely at a film and how it is put together—including its form, its narrative structure, the function of the actors and stardom in general. We would need to address the thematic structure of a film—what it is saying. We would want to place the film in the context of other films of its kind and examine its intertextual structure. We would then need to take all of this and look at the film through the eyes of the period in which it was made, as well as the period in which it is being analyzed. In other words, we would try to see the film as its contemporaries did and then see it again as it looks to us now. We would have to place all this information in line with larger social issues: technology, politics, questions of gender, race, and class, of ideology and how the film in question fits or contradicts those general ideas and images we hold about ourselves and our place in the world. We would want to draw some value judgments about the film. This should not be done mechanically, because the best criticism is written in a comfortable, integrated style, in which ideas are set forth and analyzed, grounded by the film being studied. There will be digressions along the way, but they constitute part of the complex weave of a film and its cultural surround.

I would like to attempt such a criticism of two films that could not seem more different and distant from one another. They are *Vertigo*, a film made by Alfred Hitchcock in 1958, and *Die Hard*, the Bruce Willis film directed by John McTiernan, thirty years later, in 1988, an important work in the popular action film genre. *Vertigo* is a film of great complexity and high seriousness, made by one of the few filmmakers in America whose name was as recognizable as that of a movie star. Hitchcock's popular television program, *Alfred Hitchcock*

Presents, started airing in 1955 and made his name a household word. Combined with his cameo appearances in his own films, Hitchcock's weekly introductions to the television show made him among the most recognized filmmakers in the world.

Vertigo appeared during Hitchcock's most fertile filmmaking period, right after the popular films *Rear Window* (1954), *To Catch a Thief* (1955), *The Man Who Knew Too Much* (1956), the less popular, darker film *The Wrong Man* (1956), and just before *North by Northwest* (1959) and the enormously successful *Psycho* (1960). *Vertigo* bears every sign of a careful, deliberatively crafted film by a director who attended to every last detail of his films and his career. A self-conscious artist, Hitchcock tried to gauge public taste and his own imaginative needs, to make the commercial and the subjective work together.

Die Hard appears to have come out of nowhere, like most Hollywood films. But we know by now that "nowhere" really means the anonymity of studio production. *Die Hard*'s director, John McTiernan, came to film from television commercials, a major breeding ground—along with MTV videos and the University of Southern California film school—of new directors. He had made two feature films before *Die Hard* (*Nomads*, 1986, and *Predator*, 1987). After *Die Hard*, he made two more successful films—*The Hunt for Red October* (1990) and *Die Hard*'s third sequel in 1995. In a business in which "you are no better than your last movie," McTiernan's career tottered with the expensive flop *Last Action Hero* (1993). The success of *Die Hard with a Vengeance* (1995) gave him a boost, although he has never shown quite the inventiveness that he did with the first *Die Hard* in this or any of his subsequent films. (A fourth sequel by McTiernan will be out by the time you read this.) Hitchcock is an example of a filmmaker who worked and thrived within the Hollywood system, using it to his advantage, stamping his personal mark on the films he made. McTiernan is a figure of the new Hollywood. While not a contract director, as he might have been in the old studio days, he is still typical of a decent commercial director. A better-than-average craftsperson, working as part of a large group of collaborators who are experts in the action/special-effects movie, he is sometimes able to bring together a film that is ultimately greater than its parts. With *Die Hard* he succeeded once in making a film that was successful on all counts.

The Cultural-Technological Mix: Film and Television

Analyzing films in their cultural contexts leads us into interesting, sometimes unexpected byways: we need to think about the technologies of film and television, about actors and acting styles, about the size of the viewing screen itself, because they all speak to the cultural context of the works in question. Both *Die Hard* and *Vertigo* owe a great deal to television. Both Hitchcock's and Bruce Willis's fame had blossomed because of their respective television programs, *Alfred Hitchcock Presents* in the fifties and, for Willis, a series called *Moonlighting* in the eighties. *Vertigo*'s debt to television, while playing on the audience's recognition of Hitchcock, is more indirect, more technical, and driven by economics. It has to do, interestingly enough, with screen size, which, as I discussed in Chapter 3 as an element of shot composition, becomes part of the film's aesthetic. We need to revisit this.

Hollywood film is made to immerse us in the process of its narrative. Part of that immersion is the consequence of the sheer size of the image. Larger than life, the image engulfs the viewer, overwhelms his space. Television, on the contrary, is overwhelmed by the space around it. Small, with poor resolution—though the advent of digital, high definition, wide-screen TV will be changing this—its image is not comparable to the large, sharp image projected on the movie screen. So, during the fifties, when audiences left theaters by the hundreds of thousands to stay at home and watch TV, Hollywood responded by

FIGURES 7.1–7.2 Scottie drives around San Francisco in VistaVision. The long sequence is done in traditional shot/reverse shot—Scottie and his point-of-view shot. (Alfred Hitchcock, *Vertigo*, 1958).

making movie screens larger and wider. Hollywood pretended not to get what television was all about—namely, visual narratives delivered for free in the comfort of home—and thought their films could conquer the desire for TV by further overwhelming the viewer with the image. Of course, to hedge their bets, they also bought television stations and produced films and series for TV.

The various wide-screen processes that were developed, invented, and reinvented in the early fifties brought few people back to the theaters, and, as we've seen, it has led to a lack of a coherent compositional frame for a filmmaker to use. Paramount Pictures, Hitchcock's studio during much of the fifties, developed its own wide-screen process called "VistaVision" and used it to compete with Twentieth-Century Fox's Cinemascope. All of Fox's films from 1954 to the end of the decade were filmed in 'scope. All of Paramount's films during the same period were filmed in VistaVision, *Vertigo* included.

Hitchcock turned necessity to advantage. *Vertigo* is, in part, a film about a man wandering and searching. In the first part of the film, Scottie, the central character played by Jimmy Stewart, tails a friend's wife. He falls in love with her, and when she dies, he searches for a replacement for her. Much of the first half of the film is taken up by shots of Scottie in his car, driving through San Francisco, following the woman, Madeleine, to a museum, a flower shop, Golden Gate Park. While these languid sequences of driving, looking, spying constitute a major narrative expression of Scottie's deeply obsessive personality, they are also a kind of travelogue of San Francisco, presented in VistaVision. Hitchcock was a studio director and paid his debt by filming in the studio's proprietary format. At the same time, he made the wide screen part of the film's mise-en-scène and narrative structure, using its horizontal frame to show Scottie's wanderings and also his boundaries. The screen opens point of view and limits it as well.

Bruce Willis, TV, and Movies

By the 1980s, the screen-size wars were over. Films were, and continue to be, made in a variety of wide-screen formats. *Die Hard* is in Panavision (the ratio of 1:2.35). It makes excellent use of its broad horizontal scope especially by framing its characters in the corners of large architectural spaces so they seem overwhelmed and diminished by their surroundings. *Die Hard*'s connection to television is not via the technological route of screen size, but directly through its star, Bruce Willis, who came to the film with an enormous reputation as a character on the popular television series *Moonlighting*, in which he played a snickering, wise-cracking detective—a somewhat overgrown adolescent with some conventional characteristics of self-assurance and an ability not to take himself too seriously. *Die Hard* was only his second film (the first was *Blind Date* in 1987), and it launched the second phase of his career, which followed an unusual track through the culture of American entertainment.

There is, generally, a lack of exchange of actors from one medium to the other. Some movie stars, like Willis, start on television, move to film, and almost never went back. Most stay in one medium or the other. The reasons have partly to do with old antagonisms between the two forms, despite the fact that those antagonisms are now gone on the economic front as the ownership of the companies that make or distribute television programs and movies has converged. One reason has to do with salary: movies pay more. But mostly it has to do with status. Movies, even though they are seen by fewer and fewer people in theaters, retain a higher status than television. Willis has often returned to television in small roles or guest appearances. He seems more in the British tradition, where crossing over between the two media carries no stigma.

The Actor's Persona: Bruce Willis and James Stewart

As we discussed earlier, movie stars are a combination of personality constructed by their films and their publicity. Big stars become part of the culture, recognized, identified with, gossiped about in the tabloids, their "private" lives becoming public affairs. Bruce Willis and James Stewart shared these qualities of stardom, but in very different ways.

As a television star, Bruce Willis was able in *Die Hard* to expand characterizations already familiar to millions of people. He has since gone on to try various roles, serious and comic, but keeps returning to the tongue-in-cheek adventure figure he does so well, but an aging action figure needs other outlets—despite the fact that the fourth *Die Hard* is scheduled for 2005. His usual range is quite limited, his expressions restricted mostly to sneer and smirk with a small amount of vulnerability or deadpan seriousness as in *The Sixth Sense* (M. Night Shyamalan, 1999). His is a very physical presence: he uses his body as an expression of effort and turmoil, violence and revenge. Through physical stamina and wiliness, he transmits a sense of smartness, an engaging quality at a time when many people—men in particular—are uncertain how to express themselves in the world and are liable to choose dumb rather than smart.

James Stewart, the star of *Vertigo*, was also familiar to millions, but as a movie actor who had been in films since the 1930s. Stewart's acting range was also limited, but his was a limitation that allowed him, in the course of a very long career, to become something of a cultural barometer. Stewart's on-screen persona embodied, until the fifties, variations of a passive, sweet, vaguely embarrassed and self-effacing character. His public persona was as quiet and reserved as the roles he played. That very passivity and self-effacement seemed to make him into a kind of rubber stamp, onto which could be impressed not only the characterizations demanded by a particular role but the responses of the audience as well. The illusion of simplicity and gentleness made him something of a mirror for everyone's best intentions. Until the fifties, he specialized in comedy roles, often assuming a foot-shuffling, head-down, aw-shucks characterization, whose simplicity was irresistible. His characters were nonthreatening; a viewer could feel both kindly and superior to him.

The role of George Bailey in Frank Capra's *It's a Wonderful Life* (1946) simultaneously summed up and altered this persona that Stewart, his various directors, and the audience had so carefully nurtured. Stewart and Capra added a measure of anxiety and despair to the character of George Bailey. The film's narrative is driven by George's attempt to get out of Bedford Falls and his continual frustrations in realizing this dream. The frustrations and anxieties reflect the lack of clarity about how an individual of ordinary means would make it in the new, unfamiliar world that had formed at the end of World War II, a world where old institutions and accepted ways of life were changing. *It's a Wonderful Life* is a rare Hollywood film that refuses to give its hero his life's dream and forces him instead to accept another role—almost literally forced upon him by the film. Indeed, the frustration George feels at the way his story refuses to come out the way he wants it to leads him to attempt suicide. Only through angelic intervention does he understand that, without him, the town he wants so desperately to leave would be a dark, violent, corrupt place. With this understanding, he takes the more "responsible" path and becomes a family man, a banker, and a protector of his town's interests. See Figures 8.1 and 8.2 for images of James Stewart in *It's a Wonderful Life*.

It's a Wonderful Life is one of the great postwar narratives of uncertainty about the present and the future, a statement of the culture's discomfort and yearning for fantasies of simpler times. It still strikes a chord and remains, along with a World War II film, *Casablanca* (Michael Curtiz, 1942), one of the favorites of old, black and white movies. It launched Stewart's career in a different acting direction. His roles became more serious, and that aspect of despair and moral confusion that he manifests in *It's a Wonderful Life* is played out through a succession of roles, most notably in the films he made for Hitchcock and in a series of Westerns he made for Anthony Mann, such as *Bend of the River* (1952) and *The Naked Spur* (1953).

Hitchcock began playing on the changes in Stewart's acting persona in *Rope* (1948), *Rear Window* (1954), and *The Man Who Knew Too Much* (1956). In *Rear Window*, a serio-comic film about the unpleasant consequences of being a voyeur, Hitchcock began to elicit from Stewart a worried, somewhat obsessive performance. Playing a photographer confined to a wheelchair because of an accident, the character spies on his neighbors and forces his girlfriend to investigate a murder he believes occurred in an apartment across the way. Beneath its jokey surface, the film raises serious points about the gaze, about the morality of looking and seeing what you are not supposed to see. It is a virtuoso riff on the technique of shot/reverse shot. In *Vertigo*, Hitchcock plays up further the obsessive characteristics he gave Stewart in *Rear Window*, and the two of them create one of the best portrayals of near-psychosis in contemporary film.

Vertigo and the Culture of the Fifties

To understand *Vertigo* and *Die Hard*, we have to understand what happened in the late forties and the fifties to bring about the despair in Hitchcock's film and, ultimately, the various questions about heroism we will find raised in *Die Hard*. The end of World War II did not bring a feeling of victory and power to American culture. Instead it created a churning discomfort, an uncertainty about the future and a lack of clarity about the past. The revelations of Germany's attempted extermination of the Jews and the explosion of two atomic bombs over Japan that ended the war shook the culture and confirmed how easily our myths of civility and order could fall. The communist revolution in China, the expansion of the U.S.S.R. into Eastern Europe, and the testing of a Russian A-bomb in the late forties further upset a society that had thought the second great war of the century might settle things down overseas.

At home, major changes in the economy, in race, gender, and class relations began in earnest in the early forties, continued throughout the war years, and generated anxiety for years after. Labor expressed its discontent through a number of strikes during the war. A migration of the African American population to the North responded to economic opportunities for those who had not experienced them before, while disturbing the majority white population. Meanwhile, African American soldiers fought bravely in a segregated army overseas. Attacks against Hispanics resulted in the "zoot suit riots" that spread from southern California to Detroit, Philadelphia, and New York. The outbreaks of violence not only signified the willingness of minorities to express and defend themselves but set the stage for the creation of the myth of the juvenile delinquent after the war.

By the early fifties, the culture was wracked with change and dislocation it could barely understand: suburbanization and the flight from the central cities, the formation and institutionalization of the multinational corporation, the slow, painful progress of civil rights, the continued redefinition of gender roles. However, the United States sublimated these and many other pressing issues into a struggle against a mostly mythologized external enemy (and then a wholly mythical internal one), the "communist threat." Almost every issue was absorbed into the Cold War discourse of anticommunism.

Beginning in the late forties and continuing through the fifties, the House Committee on Un-American Activities, the committees run by Joseph McCarthy, newspapers, magazines, and much of the language of political and popular culture condemned as communist almost anyone who had once held or continued to hold liberal or left-wing views. People informed on friends and colleagues. Government workers, teachers, screen and television writers, directors, and actors lost jobs. Intellectuals were discredited. The blacklist thrived. American culture and politics underwent a purge.

Women were, in analogous way, also purged from the culture. Their roles changed dramatically during the years of World War II. With most young men fighting abroad, women came flooding into the workforce, did quite well, and enjoyed financial power, many of them for the first time. While few women rose to executive positions, they kept factories and shops operating and discovered a welcome liberation from old domestic routines. The liberation was such that, when the war was over, a massive ideological retooling had to be put into place. Men were returning from battle and wanted their jobs back. Women had to be reinserted into their former passive routines. Movies, magazines, and newspapers once again extolled the importance of motherhood and family, the submissive role of women, the nuclear family in which mother was anchored to home while father was free to move like a satellite out of the home, into the office and back.

Discussions about gender got caught up in the absurd momentum of the anticommunist discourse. The political and the personal, the power of the state, the workplace, the family, the sexual all became confused and self-contradictory. The larger fears of subversion and conformity, of being taken over and changed by enemies from within and without were filtered down into the more immediate concerns of the role of men and women in the culture and the way gender determined the structure of power. Fifties culture was as much obsessed with sexuality and gender roles as our own. It tried to assuage obsession through control. The decade's most conservative desire was to maintain a perfect imbalance of male domination and female subservience, male mobility at work and female stability in the domestic space. Fear of women, fear of difference, fear of communism, and fear of conformity marked this age of anxiety.

People seemed to find security in sameness, while fearing that too much conformity would be dangerous. For example, while the growth of corporate culture was recognized as the source of secure jobs for men and a secure consumer economy for the country, it was also seen as something that interfered with the image of the free, unfettered male, who should be making his own way in the world. Voices were raised and books were written about men being unmanned by their new subservience to the corporation and the family.

Some popular literature was quite direct about this anguish over conformity, the apparent diminishing of male potency, the growth of corporate culture, and also communism. Articles in the popular *Look* magazine, gathered in a 1958 book called *The Decline of the American Male*, claimed that women control male behavior, from the early formation of men's psyches, to the kinds of jobs they take, to their competitiveness. Because women now demanded equal or greater satisfaction than the male, they were beginning to control his sexuality. The subjugation to women and the pressures brought by the culture had produced a broken shell of a man, without individuality, without power, overworked, stressed-out, unable "to love and to make moral decisions as an individual." Men were weakened and regimented, made impotent and recessive. "In the free and democratic United States of America, he had been subtly robbed of a heritage that the Communist countries deny by force." As males went, so went the country. Communism by female control.

The Kinsey Reports

Sexuality, control, anticommunism: the triad of fifties cultural obsessions. The gender problem was further aggravated by the publication of two scientific reports that became, next to anticommunism, among the most influential and disquieting cultural events of the fifties. The Kinsey Reports on male and female sexuality (published in the late forties and mid-fifties, respectively) were works of scientific analysis, presenting themselves as objective, methodical surveys. They frightened almost everyone by claiming that there was no normative sexual behavior, no controllable, conventional way of defining what people do in the bedroom. In a world where moral, cultural, and political safe harbor was becoming increasingly harder to locate the more it was demanded, the Kinsey Reports seemed to remove yet another anchor. What the Reports seemed to be saying about sex became part of the general concern about subversion—cultural, political, and gender. Nothing seemed secure.

The Vulnerable Male in Film

Many films of the decade examined questions of gender (as they did with racial issues) with some delicacy and complexity. They were able to put aside the anticommunist hysteria. Many of them created interesting narrative combinations out of the culture's fears of conformity, out of juvenile delinquency (which the culture invented as one more way to scare itself about what was happening to masculinity, while at the same time creating another fear which it could blame on the mass media), out of notions about gender that somewhat altered the old stereotypes of the rugged male hero. Some of these films, such as *A Place in the Sun* (George Stevens, 1951) and *The Man in the Gray Flannel Suit* (Nunnally Johnson, 1956), presented male characters who in their passivity, sensitivity, and vulnerability took on characteristics and attributes usually associated with female characters.

A number of postwar film actors—Montgomery Clift, James Dean, Marlon Brando, and Paul Newman, in films like *A Place in the Sun*, *Rebel Without a Cause* (Nicholas Ray, 1955), *The Wild One* (Laslo Benedek, 1953), and *The Left-Handed Gun* (Arthur Penn, 1958)—expressed a search for new ways of expression under the guise of a withdrawn sensitivity. Their acting styles were a major break with prewar movie conventions; their roles spoke to the repressed anger and sexuality of the culture at large. In *The Wild One*, Marlon Brando plays a biker with a very sensitive soul, who, in one scene, alone with his motorcycle in the night, weeps. Early in the film, a girl asks him, "What are you rebelling against?" "Whaddya got?" he asks. This film, along with *Rebel Without a Cause*, spoke to many people's feelings about the constraints and confusions of the fifties. *The Wild One* was considered subversive enough to be banned in England for many years, but its interest is really not in the rebelliousness of the male character but in his ambiguous expression of anger and passivity. Despite the gang brawling, the film's representation of masculinity plays against conventions of heroism and strength; it is, finally, the feminizing of the male that makes this and other films of its kind attractive and curious.

Vertigo is not a film about youthful rebellion. Nor is it on any explicit level about fears of conformity or communist subversion. Quite the contrary, it is about a middle-aged man who implodes under the weight of sexual repression

FIGURE 7.3 On the face of it, *The Wild One* (Laslo Benedek, 1953) is a fifties juvenile delinquent–motorcycle gang movie. But it is also a fifties vulnerable male movie, like its near cousin, Nicholas Ray's *Rebel Without a Cause* (1955). In this close-up, Brando emotes his sensitivity and despair over being misunderstood and mistreated.

and despair, bringing about the death of other people in his wake. It is more closely related to the fifties films of constricted and destroyed businessmen, films like *The Man in the Gray Flannel Suit* and Nicholas Ray's *Bigger Than Life* (1956), than to the same director's *Rebel Without a Cause* or to *The Wild One*. But it is of a piece with the decade's concerns with change and betrayal, with power and passivity, domination and servitude, and sexual panic. It quietly addresses all of these concerns and the culture's general sense of incompleteness, its feeling of unfinished, perhaps unfinishable personal business, its pervasive anxiety. It touches, in an oblique way, on the Cold War obsessions of containment. The political culture of the fifties was obsessed with containment of the "communist threat." *Vertigo* personalizes the political by creating a deeply repressed man, contained by his fears and driven by his obsessions.

Die Hard would seem to be Vertigo's opposite. It is a film about getting things done, and its hero is uncontained. The film has evil villains who are taken care of by a strong and resourceful man. *Die Hard*, unlike *Vertigo*, is about male strength and heroism, about action that is not questioned. Yet resourceful and heroic as he is, Bruce Willis's John McClane bears a relationship to the sensitive men who began appearing during the fifties. He carries pain with him. Not the vague cultural anxieties that afflicted characters thirty years earlier, John's is a much more contemporary pain—though its roots lie deep in fifties gender ideology as well as conservative 1980s notions about individual initiative. John's wife has left him, and *Die Hard*'s narrative is set into motion by his traveling from New York to Los Angeles to attempt a reconciliation. John's responses to his wife's newfound independence bear traces of the same sexual anxieties that marked his predecessors. There is even a touch of the fifties fear of corporate strength mixed in. But John McClane is a man of the late eighties. His insecurity is marked by the cultural discourse of women's independence, not male dependence, by the fact that his wife left him to take a corporate job, even to reclaim her last name. Such an event in a fifties movie would be the cause of derision, not anxiety. More accurately perhaps, it would be anxiety turned into derision. We noted the reaction in Ida Lupino's *The Bigamist* in Chapter 6.

Die Hard's John and Vertigo's Scottie do have a common lineage. Both characters are policemen. John comes from a long line of movie cops, those tough

New York Irishmen with soft hearts, figures unique to film, yet reassuring in their mythic qualities. Scottie's lineage is more local—he is a San Francisco cop—and more engaged with fifties film images and narratives of damaged men. He cannot live up to the expectations of his job. While John McClane is sick at heart over his separation from his wife and sets out to prove his masculinity, Scottie is sick in soul and mind, a sickness that manifests itself as vertigo, a paralytic response to heights and his own moral and emotional destruction. This results in the death of a colleague at the very beginning of the film, when a rooftop chase leaves Scottie dangling, paralyzed, unable to save one of his men. Scottie leaves the force and is made vulnerable to a monstrous plot by a businessman who plays upon his sincerity, insecurity, and self-doubt, and destroys his life and that of a woman with whom Scottie thinks he's fallen in love. Scottie is left at film's end alive but reduced, staring into the void. John McClane, through a series of explosively adventurous acts, saves his wife, develops a profound emotional attachment to an African American policeman, and emerges from a series of apocalyptic events alive, triumphant, but a somewhat conflicted supercop.

Scottie's despair and John's conflicted state are partly the result of gender confusions we spoke of earlier and are specific to the times of their stories. Scottie Ferguson is the timid fifties male, reduced in stature, capability, and agency in the world. There is little he can do. He is, in his small fictional container, a metaphor of all the fifties middle-class, middle-aged men, undone by forces over which he has lost control. John McClane is a collective fantasy of exactly the opposite response. By the late eighties, fear of loss of control had turned into the reality of lost control. The succession of blows to the culture's self-esteem and to the power of the individual over anything in the world had taken their toll. While there were some major victories in the sixties and seventies—gains in minority and women's rights, effective mass protests against the Vietnam War—there were greater, more profound defeats. A lingering unhappiness was the result of the Kennedy and King assassinations, the frustrations caused by Vietnam experienced by those who supported it, opposed it, and fought in it. The corruption of the Nixon administration, culminating in Watergate, the stagnation of real income, and a more subtle, yet farther-reaching realization that America had little power in an increasingly complex and fragmented world, that an individual's power over everything had diminished overtook the culture. Fifties anxiety became the helplessness of the eighties, figured in its quest for suitable heroes, reflected in the election of Ronald Reagan, the movie star hero/president.

The role of the hero, intimately tied to issues of masculinity in any cultural period, is always under question. It was being questioned in the fifties, and it was again in the late eighties. The notion of the strong, moral, righteous, and courageous man of action, who would cleanse the entire culture of corrupt and violent forces—by means of greater violence—has never held up very well when tested in reality. After World War II, the premise of heroism was examined in film across the board. The great Western director John Ford was exploring the corruption of the Western hero as far back as *Fort Apache* in 1948. In *The Searchers* (1956), Ford was pressing his and America's favorite heroic figure, John Wayne, to give a performance in a film that explored the proximity of heroism to psychopathic obsession.

This examination and debunking continued, particularly in the Western, through the early seventies and resumed in the late eighties in other genres. *Die Hard* thinks a lot about the old movie hero, and John Wayne in particular. I pointed out that the Bruce Willis character is related to the movie stereotype of the Irish cop. But there is more. His character is named John McClane. In 1952, John Wayne played the title character in an anticommunist cop film called *Big Jim McLain*. John Wayne as Jim McLain becomes Bruce Willis as John McClane. But this is not a simple substitution or even a complicated reference to the great film hero. It is an attempt to embrace and deny heroism, all at the same time. At one point in *Die Hard*, the terrorist Hans, frustrated by John's clever and heroic efforts to outsmart him, calls to him in desperation, "Who are you, just another American who's seen too many movies . . .? Do you think you are Rambo or John Wayne?"

Sylvester Stallone's *Rambo* was, just three years before *Die Hard*, one of the last action-adventure films to take its central character with deadly seriousness. Rambo became a right-wing icon. It was not until *The Terminator*, in 1984, that the action film hero began to take on some of the reflective qualities that the Western hero had in the fifties. Arnold Schwarzenegger moved his career forward by not taking his characters too seriously. There was always something safe and nonthreatening in Schwarzenegger's posturing, and it became even safer after *The Terminator*, when he began actively poking fun at his earlier characters and went on to play comic roles. His presence is invoked by John in *Die*

FIGURE 7.4   Rambo (Sylvester Stallone), the body of the eighties (*Rambo, First Blood Part II*, George Cosmatos, 1985).

Hard, who says, at one point, "There's enough explosives in here to blow up Arnold Schwarzenegger." And, if that's not enough, at one point, he dresses up to look like Rambo.

John McCla͜ is a hero and would be directly in the John Wayne–Rambo tradition if he would take himself more seriously. He fights manfully; he gets bloody (or "blooded" as some die-hard believers in trial by violence would say); and he demonstrates uncanny recuperative powers, so uncanny that they became a model for action-adventure films that follow. He finally becomes John Wayne and Rambo *and* a parody of both. *Die Hard* begins a new phase of movie violence that is now called cartoon violence. The damage being done to human bodies in film is so enormous that "real" people would never survive it. These films—which include the *Die Hard* and *Lethal Weapon* series and Bruce Willis's film *Hudson Hawk* (Michael Lehmann, 1991), as well the Stallone vehicles *Demolition Man* and *Cliffhanger* (both 1993, directed by Marco Brambilla and Renny Harlin, respectively) and have spawned films based on comic books, from another Stallone vehicle, *Judge Dredd* (Danny Cannon, 1995), to *X-Men* (Bryan Singer, 2000, 2003) through *Spider-Man* (2002, 2004) and *The Hulk* (2003)—are some of the contemporary popular movies that begin to reveal the fact that the image and the narratives made from them are not of the world but of film and other forms of popular art, and that film violence is a visual trick— a digital visual trick. The films can, of course, go only so far. Audiences do not seem to want a full-scale revelation of artifice and self-reflection. *Hudson Hawk* and the Arnold Schwarzenegger film *Last Action Hero* (1993, directed by *Die Hard*'s John McTiernan) failed partly because they did not take themselves seriously enough and revealed a sense of play that went beyond some viewers' desire for a necessary illusion. We want heroes to be self-mocking, but we don't want them mocking us.

Heroically antiheroic might best describe John McClane. He is the confused late twentieth-century man turned into a courageous, resourceful, and indestructible defender of his wife and her fellow workers. He is always a little befuddled, but always ready for action.

In order to understand more clearly where these two films and their heroes diverge and converge, we need to consider for a moment their narrative approaches, which determine the way they speak to their contemporary experience. *Vertigo*, with its dark, ironic structure, is a modernist narrative. Modernity—the movement of technological advancement, increased urbanization, rapid fragmentation of dependable, cohesive structures such as the family, religion, dominant race or ethnicity, and government, along with the falling away of individual agency and power—climaxed in the seventies and eighties. The responses to modernity are represented in various ways, including the stories the culture tells itself. Movies and television bring our fears to our attention, sometimes confirming them, sometimes attempting to assuage them with narratives about mastering our destiny, overcoming great odds, and recuperating our emotional losses. In the fifties, science fiction films spoke to our terrors of vulnerability to alien forces (allegories of the "communist threat" back then)—stories that are being retold again today, only with different enemies. Melodrama tended to confirm the loss of individual power by insisting that the family, the married couple with children rather than the individual, was the best bulwark against modernity—all the while confirming the fragility of the family. *Vertigo* is an unusual affirmation of the disintegration of both the family and the self in modernity. It has romantic elements and touches of fantasy. But it is concerned mainly with the coming apart of the modern male.

Scottie is lost, unable to act or to love. His female friend, Midge, has been unable to get him to respond to her sexually. Her simplicity and directness frighten him. So does her sense of humor. She is a designer, currently working on a brassiere ("You know those things. You're a big boy now," she tells him). The brassiere she's designing has "revolutionary uplift," based on the principle of the cantilever bridge, and it parodies the fifties fetishism of the female breast, the formulating of women's bodies into preconceived male fantasies.

Scottie's own fantasies are so powerfully conceived that women are unattainable for him, and he suffers from either impotence or sexual incompetence or complete gender panic. Immediately following the banter about the brassiere, Scottie and Midge talk about a moment, years ago, when they were engaged for three weeks. Scottie insists that Midge called it off. She doesn't respond. But Hitchcock does. He cuts twice to a close-up of her, very tight, and high enough to knock the balance of the frame off center. She simply frowns a bit and looks slightly off into the distance. It's a very typical Hitchcockian gesture, exploiting the standard grammar of the reaction shot to expand the viewer's comprehension of the situation. In this case, the reaction shot of Midge indicates to us that Scottie not only is in trouble sexually but is unaware of it. He is unaware of who he is and what he is capable or incapable of doing.

Scottie is an emotional void, into which a rich businessman pours an incredible plot about his wife, who, he says, thinks she is inhabited by the spirit of a nineteenth-century woman who committed suicide. (A major best-seller in the early fifties was *The Search for Bridey Murphy*, about a woman who, under hypnosis, revealed a past life. In 1956, Paramount, the studio that produced *Vertigo*, made a VistaVision film of the book. Hitchcock may be consciously parodying the Bridey Murphy story in *Vertigo*.) The businessman asks Scottie to follow a woman he identifies as his wife, who is actually someone pretending to be her, and report on her actions. She becomes the obsessive core of Scottie's life, which is so lacking a strong center that it barely survives. Scottie is the man of the postwar age, without power, without a sense of self and able only to re-create his desires in other people, who are not who he thinks they are.

Everything is false, a huge ruse created by the businessman—and by Hitchcock, who gives nothing away until much later in the film—to cover up the murder of his wife. But the ruse itself, as is typical in a Hitchcock narrative, is less important than its effects on the characters and the viewer. We are privy to the decay of Scottie Ferguson from someone who is already weak and afflicted to an obsessive-compulsive, to a sadomasochist, to a shell of a man gazing down at the abyss, having finally caused the death of the woman he has tried to re-create into another's image. If this sounds melodramatic, it is. *Vertigo* is in the tradition of fifties melodramas about repressed desires exploding and then imploding back onto the central character—who is usually a woman. *Vertigo* makes its figure of melodramatic suffering a man. It is unusual too because its narrative plays ironically with Scottie's perception and the viewers'. We must disentangle ourselves from Scottie. In the first part of the film, we tend to identify with him; in the second, we are asked to pull away and judge. There is no comfortable closure. Neither the character nor his world is redeemed at the end of the film. Scottie is left utterly, unrecuperably alone and in despair. In short, *Vertigo* has aspects of tragedy about it.

Modernity, and its narrative expression, modernism, speak to the loss of a center through an ironic voice with a whisper of tragedy. Postmodernity sees the center—the binding stories and beliefs of culture—as already lost and decides to get on with it through many voices, many images, spoken and shown with irony and cynicism. *Die Hard* builds its structures by borrowing from wherever it can and using or alluding to whatever fits—or doesn't. It is a ping-pong game of pop-cultural memory and contemporary cynicism. It plays havoc with any serious moral structures other than the sentimental affirmation of individual heroism. Like the postmodern in general, *Die Hard* is a roller coaster of images, a feast of the intertextual, the junk food of the indecisive and confused.

As a postmodern work, *Die Hard* tries, and largely succeeds, in being everything to almost everyone: an action-adventure movie, a political thriller, a buddy cop film, a discussion of race, an ironic commentary on movie heroism, and a study of gender conflict in the late 1980s. *Vertigo* is a movie conscious of its seriousness, a slow, thoughtful, and formally acute meditation on gender and male anxiety. *Die Hard* is a big, loud, explosive ball of fire that is built out of one of the oldest narrative structures in cinema, the alternation of scenes of pursuers and pursued, an alternation of action and reaction. It is a captivity narrative, entranced with violent action and a hero who doesn't take himself too seriously and can't be killed, who is compared to John Wayne and Rambo but thinks of himself as Roy Rogers.

Postmodern Villains

Scottie is an almost tragic figure; John McClane is confused as a hero. The villains they fight are confused even more. Scottie's enemy is none other than himself: his own weakness and insecurity. Gavin Elster, the businessman who makes up the huge lie that kills a woman and destroys Scottie's spirit, is, in a way, a reflection of Scottie himself. In *Die Hard*, the villains are clearly present and mean in the way villains of action films always are. But remember, in this film nothing is as it seems. John has flown into Los Angeles from New York to see his estranged wife, Holly, who works for a rich Japanese company, the Takagi Corporation. He visits her in the middle of the company's Christmas party, which is attacked by a group of terrorists, who kill the boss and take the rest hostage.

The 1980s were a decade of swiftly changing attitudes toward foreigners as well as women. The latter had found their voice, and men were uncomfortable with what that voice was saying. The former were creating other kinds of confusion. The Japanese were particularly frustrating to Americans. We had been victorious over them in World War II. Now their economy was booming and their products, from VCRs to automobiles, were used by almost everyone. They seemed to be buying up everything in this country from movie studios (Columbia is still owned by Sony) to golf courses to major tracts of real estate in large cities. They were held up as a model of productivity, yet demonized as a strange, alien culture. Though it was never quite spoken, they remained in memory as our dark-skinned enemies. There were other enemies as well, and *Die Hard* seems to acknowledge them all. If the Japanese seemed to be threatening us with economic takeover, then Europe and the Middle East were threatening us with terrorists: people with less than comprehensible political goals that they attempted to achieve by the most appalling violence. In all cases, we responded, and respond still, with fear and loathing to the cultures that scare and threaten us, that we did not and do not understand, or that provide diversion from the complex economic and social processes occurring at home.

Die Hard plays with these complexities and confusions and turns them inside out. Holly's Japanese company is apparently quite benevolent, and her boss, Mr. Takagi, is a kindly and paternal man. He talks gently and has the rare quality of dignified self-mockery. "Pearl Harbor didn't work out," he jokes with John, "so we got you with tape decks." In fact, the villain in the company is not the foreign boss but another paper tiger of the eighties, the yuppie Ellis. The yuppie was the eighties version of an old cultural stereotype once called "nouveau riche," and yuppies became figures of resentment and ridicule to the working- and lower-middle-class people who were not part of the eighties and nineties boom. They were the subject of a number of "yuppies in hell" movies—such as *Fatal Attraction* (Adrian Lyne, 1987) and *Pacific Heights* (John Schlesinger, 1990)—in which yuppie characters had to go through humiliating, often violent, events in order to redeem themselves.

Die Hard's yuppie is a coke-snorting, sniveling fool, who shows off his Rolex, comes on to John's wife, and betrays both her and John to the terrorists. In return, the terrorists shoot him dead—much to everyone's delight. Mr. Takagi is also brutally murdered by the terrorists, much to everyone's horror. This kindly, civil man stood in contrast to everyone else but John and Holly, and his murder clearly marks the ruthlessness of the terrorists—who turn out not to be terrorists.

Midway through the film, Hans, their leader, is discovered to be not the politically driven terrorist he pretends to be but just a thug whose gang is out to steal from Takagi's safe. Suddenly the film is stripped of the problematically political and becomes simply a struggle between good and bad guys. Even when depoliticized, Hans's gang is a strange model of cross-cultural diversity: there is a violent Russian, a number of Asians, and an African American who is both a computer wizard and a heartless murderer. This is an international cross section of the bad, and it mirrors the film's unusual treatment of race.

Ethnicity in *Die Hard*

The major reference to ethnicity in *Vertigo* is in Gavin Elster's fantastic story about his wife, who, he says, is possessed by the spirit of a nineteenth-century Hispanic woman, stereotypically marked as sensual and exotic. Scottie becomes fascinated with "the mad Carlotta" as he becomes more obsessed with her supposed reincarnation, Madeleine. Although there were a number of films throughout the fifties that did deal with racial issues, usually in very positive, liberal ways (films like Joseph Mankiewicz's *No Way Out*, 1950, and Martin Ritt's *Edge of the City*, 1957, to name only two), there existed another kind of segregation. In most cases, if race was not a central subject of the film, it was not considered at all. Therefore, in most films, people of color either did not exist or were treated as servants or, as in *Vertigo*, another reflection of the character's vulnerable imagination. By the eighties, race was a consciously pursued issue in popular culture, almost always present though treated with various degrees of sincerity and enlightenment. We will return to the matter of the representation of race in the last chapter. In good postmodern fashion, *Die Hard* plays its race card in an indecisive and noncommittal way, giving and taking, leaving us in a quandary. John is picked up at the airport by Mr. Takagi's driver, a young black man named Argyle (one might well ask why a man is given the name of a sock), who, throughout the film, sits in his limousine, listening to music, seemingly oblivious to the mayhem going on in the skyscraper above him. He threatens to be another in the long, ugly history of stereotypes of the dopey black man—until he becomes a hero by driving his limo into the van of the escaping gang.

Early in the film, as John is cornered by the gang in the unfinished floors of the skyscraper, another African American makes an appearance. This is Al, the cop. He is introduced as a bumbling, good-hearted soul, buying junk food for his pregnant wife, driving his car into a ditch when he learns what's going on in the building. However, he quickly emerges as the only representative of authority who has any sense. When the police arrive in force, their leader proves to be a dope. Two FBI men, Johnson and Johnson (one of whom is black), arrive and are pompous fools. A representative of the media turns out to be a self-serving, dangerous man, whom John's wife, Holly, finally punches in the mouth. But Al quietly endures, out on the street, in phone contact with John, remaining calm amidst the growing chaos, supporting John in his isolation, providing our point of view from the outside. The cross cutting between the two of them creates their bond and assures us that John will be saved, no matter how perilous his situation seems. Al becomes more than a black cop, and this transcendence is important, because it leaves the race issue unresolved. He becomes—after Takagi is killed—a paternal figure, John's surrogate father. He also becomes John's surrogate wife and mother, falling into the stereotype of the protective black mammy.

The Buddy Film

Vertigo is one of the most potent investigations of heterosexual panic undertaken in fifties film. Hitchcock visits the problem again in *Psycho*, where he solves it in an especially perverse way, indicating that the male personality can be entirely absorbed by the maternal female. By the seventies, Hollywood found other ways to deal with the crushing difficulties of men living up to the image of themselves produced by the culture. One was the buddy film, in which two men—most often cops—are paired in a loving union of support and good humor in which everything is possible but sex. Buddy movies always insist that the two male figures are heterosexual. They have wives or girlfriends. But the women are peripheral; true nonsexual love and unfettered pleasure are derived from the relationship between the men. It is a narrative construct that avoids the painful introspections of the fifties films of male despair, skirts issues of race by having one buddy white and the other black—providing a weak pretense of racial equality—and avoids more complex investigations of male–female or same-sex relationships.

Die Hard is a great riff on the buddy film. Al and John are given a multifaceted relationship. They are father and son, mother and child; they embrace almost like lovers. Near the end of the film, most of the villains having been killed off, John emerges from the skyscraper; he and Al recognize each other through a rapturous exchange of point-of-view shots. Al, once afraid to shoot his gun, redeems his manhood by shooting the last of the bad guys. John walks away from Holly and embraces Al passionately. Holly is marginalized on the edge of the frame as the two friends express their love.

The sequence echoes one early in the film when John has his first reconciliation with Holly in Takagi's office. Holly enters the male space where John is talking to Takagi and Ellis. There is an exchange of glances between John and Holly; they walk over to each other and embrace. In the sequence at the end of the film, the same pattern occurs, but the genders are reversed. John and Holly meet again, but now the exchange of glances and the final embrace are between two men. The bond between the buddies is sealed. Were the film to end here, interesting questions would be raised and the line between buddies and lovers might be confused. But remember, this is a film that will not allow any statement or idea to stand without presenting its opposite. And, as postmodern as it may be, it must also, finally, conform to the master narrative of domestic, heterosexual love. Al soon yields his embrace. He tells Holly to take good care of John, and the husband and wife are sent out of the picture arm in arm. John is saved, his marriage is saved, Al is redeemed, and the love between two men is strong and protected from a tantalizing suggestion that it might be something more. Al changes from potential lover to protective mother. The domestic, nuclear family is preserved. After all, the premise that begins the film is John's coming to Los Angeles to see his estranged wife and save his marriage. After so many trials, he may now assume his place as the heroic head of the family. He has proved himself. But, in the process, he has made a strong male bond with Al, the kind of bond, movies keep telling us, men need to be comfortable and

FIGURES 7.5–7.12 The romance of the buddies. These stills represent the parallel sequences of recognition and embrace in John McTiernan's *Die Hard* (1988). In the first sequence, John greets his estranged wife, Holly. Then, after his adventures in the skyscraper, he greets Al, the cop and John's new buddy (his new love? note how Holly is marginalized on the edge of the frame). The gestures and the affection are mirrored.

free; to be protected, finally, from those domestic bonds that always seem to be so difficult for men to maintain. They keep telling us. There is something so attractive and comforting about the buddy fantasy that it remains a mainstay of film and television to this day.

The End of Redemption

Scottie is not saved or protected by anyone. He wants to be the hero who saves the heroine in distress, except that the heroine is not in distress; he is. First he pursues the lie that Elster manufactures for him, then he attempts to re-create the lie by searching for a woman who never existed. In the second part of the film, Scottie discovers Judy—who was the woman who "played" Madeleine in Gavin Elster's hoax. Scottie forces her to remake herself as Madeleine. He denies her personality and tries to suck her into his. They return to the Spanish mission, and she falls to her death from the roof of the bell tower. There is no triumph over evil here, or even the triumph of good, because, unlike *Die Hard*, *Vertigo* does not externalize its moral structure into stereotyped characters. Everything, finally, is a manifestation of Scottie's lack of moral center, a lack shared by the decade of the fifties itself. Where love and friendship are offered to John McClane, Scottie is left with only his own narcissism and madness. *Vertigo*, like its title, is about an unbreakable, downward spiral.

There is much falling in both *Die Hard* and *Vertigo*. Hans falls from the skyscraper. John falls down an elevator shaft and swings out a window supported only by a fire hose. But these falls solidify his heroic stature, even as he downplays it. He returns from the struggle bloodied but unharmed, saves the captives, and appears reunited with his wife. The film quietly admits it's all too fantastic, as fantastic as Scottie's obsessive attachment to Madeleine/Judy. But *Die Hard* asks us to join in the joke. *Vertigo* asks us to observe Scottie with pity, fear, and even tragic awe as he destroys his life. The relationship between viewer and *Vertigo* is as serious as Hollywood ever demands such a relationship to be. We are asked to read this film carefully, to understand its subtleties, to stay with it as it reveals to us the secrets that aren't revealed to its central character. There are no secrets in *Die Hard*, only spectacle. Its internal confusions about gender, race, nationality, politics, and authority are meant to be taken only as passing jokes, as momentary bits of relevance, irreverence, and irrelevance.

We could conclude from this that the Frankfurt school and the fifties media critics were correct, that there is an unalterable breach between high and low culture and that, at its best, *Vertigo* barely escapes from Dwight MacDonald's category of Midcult and, at its worst, *Die Hard* is irredeemably Masscult. *Vertigo* attempts to be tragedy, though, at bottom, it is a strong romantic melodrama, well constructed, dark and complex. *Die Hard* makes no such reach and comfortably accepts its Masscult status as a simple entertainment, acceptable as straightforward action film or as a sarcastic, cynical, even ironic, play on serious issues. Its refusal to take seriously any of the issues it raises only emphasizes its lack of commitment to serious intellectual inquiry.

But our reading suggests another path. By noting the different directions the films take—and recognizing that despite their different intentions, they are very serious about using film form expressively—we discover a common base. Then, analyzing their proximity to their cultural contexts and the ways, consciously or not, they address those contexts, we see that it is possible to understand both films as serious, imaginative statements that come out of commercial intent. We could argue that *Vertigo* is a less cynical film than *Die Hard* because it is structurally and thematically more complex and makes more demands upon the attention and the intellectual and emotional responses of the viewer. Ultimately, this is a difference in address, in the way the filmmakers and their films decide

to talk to us. The address requires a difference in response, the ways in which we choose to react to the film.

This brings us back to the cultural studies position. The imagination operates in many different ways and for many different reasons, none of them completely pure or completely corrupt. The imagination of a viewer responds in different ways to different films. I find the racial and gender ambiguities of *Die Hard* extremely interesting and revealing, and the overall structure of the film irresistible in its confidence and engaging in its mixture of humor, action, and absurdity. *Vertigo* impresses me with the fine care and detail of its structure and moves me tremendously with the depth of its insight into male vulnerability. Both films are impressive in the ways they deal, subtly but pointedly, with the culture from which they emerge.

On another level, both films, fascinating as they are in their differences and similarities, clarify the ways all films tell their stories, sometimes the same or strangely similar stories in various guises, various forms. Even two such different films as the ones we have analyzed here converge at sometimes unexpected points. One reason for this is that stories are a limited resource. Another is that what we seem to want our stories to tell us is limited as well; we demand convergence and repetition. We find security by having the same stories told over and over again. Even more important, all stories can be connected, and when we look beyond the old split between high and low culture, we find that we can learn, respond to, and understand films that seem, on their surface, to be as different as Bruce Willis and Jimmy Stewart.

NOTES AND REFERENCES

Media and Cultures Two standard works on the history of melodrama are Peter Brooks, *The Melodramatic Imagination: Balzac, Henry James, Melodrama, and the Mode of Excess* (New York: Columbia University Press, 1985); and David Grimsted, *Melodrama Unveiled: American Theater and Culture,* 1800–1850 (Berkeley: University of California Press, 1987). The information on DVD sales comes from David D. Kirkpatrick, "Action-Hungry DVD Fans Sway Hollywood," *The New York Times,* August 17, 2003.

Theories of Culture There is another branch of media research known as mass communications research. This is mainly statistical and, while it may make analytic judgments about its numbers, it rarely addresses the cultural and political ramifications of what the numbers reveal. A book that combines mass media and cultural studies is James W. Carey, *Communication as Culture: Essays on Media and Society* (New York: Routledge, 1992).

The Frankfurt School The quotation is from Max Horkheimer and Theodor W. Adorno in *Dialectic of Enlightenment,* trans. John Cumming (New York: Herder & Herder, 1972), pp. 153–54; original publication, 1944; latest edition (London: Blackwell Verso, 1993).

Masscult and Midcult   The quotation is from Dwight MacDonald, "Masscult and Midcult," in *Against the American Grain* (New York: Da Capo Press, 1983), pp. 4, 37. One writer in the early fifties attempted a somewhat neutral analysis of popular culture. Although much of his work is marked by Cold War rhetoric, Robert Warshow wrote some groundbreaking analyses of the Western and gangster film genres. See his book, originally published in 1962, *The Immediate Experience* (Cambridge, MA: Harvard University Press, 2001). Another critic, Gilbert Seldes, also wrote against the grain in his book *The Seven Lively Arts*, originally published in 1924, the early, formative period of mass culture (Mineola, New York: Dover Publications, 2001).

Benjamin and Aura   The Benjamin quotation is from "The Work of Art in the Age of Mechanical Reproduction," in *Illuminations*, trans. Harry Zohn (New York: Schocken Books, 1968), pp. 223, 234, 236, 239. An excellent analysis of the relationship between Benjamin's essay and film and new media is in Lev Manovich, *The Language of New Media*.

The Birmingham School of Cultural Studies   The literature on cultural studies is quite large. Here are a few titles: Stuart Hall, ed., *Culture, Media, Language: Working Papers in Cultural Studies, 1972–79* (London: Hutchinson, 1980); Stuart Hall, *Critical Dialogues in Cultural Studies*, ed. David Morley and Kuan-Hsing Chen (London and New York: Routledge, 1996); Richard Hoggart, *On Culture and Communication* (New York: Oxford University Press, 1972); Lawrence Grossberg, Cary Nelson, Paula A. Treichler, eds., *Cultural Studies* (New York: Routledge, 1992); and John Fiske, *Television Culture* (London and New York: Routledge, 1989).

Reception and Negotiation   For a serious discussion of fans and their work, see Henry Jenkins, *Textual Poachers: Television Fans and Participatory Culture* (New York: Routledge, 1992).

Intertextuality and the Postmodern   Raymond Williams first articulated the concept of "flow" when he noticed how various television events moved together without being differentiated. See his *Television: Technology and Cultural Form* (Middletown, CT: Wesleyan University Press, 1992). A sharp, concise summary of postmodernism can be found in Todd Gitlin's essay, "Postmodernism: Roots and Politics," in *Cultural Politics in Contemporary America*, ed. Ian Angus and Sut Jhally (New York: Routledge, 1989). See also Stuart Hall, ed., *Representation: Cultural Representations and Signifying Practices* (London: Sage, 2000).

Cultural Criticism Applied to *Vertigo* and *Die Hard*   For a study of Hitchcock's popularity, see Robert E. Kapsis, *Hitchcock: The Making of a Reputation* (Chicago: University of Chicago Press, 1992).

The Cultural-Technological Mix: Film and Television   David Parker of the Library of Congress pointed out to me the connections between Scottie's driving around and VistaVision.

***Vertigo* and the Culture of the Fifties**   For a good history of the fifties, see James Gilbert, *Another Chance: Postwar America, 1945–1968* (Homewood, IL:

Dorsey Press, 1986). On the zoot-suit riots, see Stuart Cosgrove, "The Zoot-Suit and Style Warfare," in Angela McRobbie, ed., *Zoot Suits and Second-Hand Dresses* (Boston: Unwin-Hyman, 1988), pp. 3–22. There is a large literature on the work of the House Committee on Un-American Activities in Hollywood. Two excellent sources are Larry Ceplair and Steven Englund, *The Inquisition in Hollywood: Politics and the Film Community, 1930–1960* (Berkeley and Los Angeles: University of California Press, 1983); and Victor S. Navasky, *Naming Names* (New York: Hill & Wang, 2003). One of the most popular books voicing the fear of conformity in the fifties was William Whyte's *The Organization Man*, originally published in 1956 (Philadelphia: University of Philadelphia Press, 2002). The quotations about declining masculinity are from J. Robert Moskin, "Why Do Women Dominate Him?" and George B. Leonard, Jr., "Why Is He Afraid to Be Different?" in *The Decline of the American Male*, by the editors of *Look* (New York: Random House, 1958).

The Vulnerable Male in Film   One of the best recent studies of the changing ideas of masculinity in the fifties, by a scholar whose work led me to the *Look* articles, is Steven Cohan, *Masked Men: Masculinity and the Movies in the Fifties* (Bloomington: Indiana University Press, 1997). Susan Jefford's *Hard Bodies: Hollywood Masculinity in the Reagan Era* (New Brunswick, NJ: Rutgers University Press, 1994) offers an interesting political take on contemporary action/adventure films.

THE STORIES TOLD BY FILM I

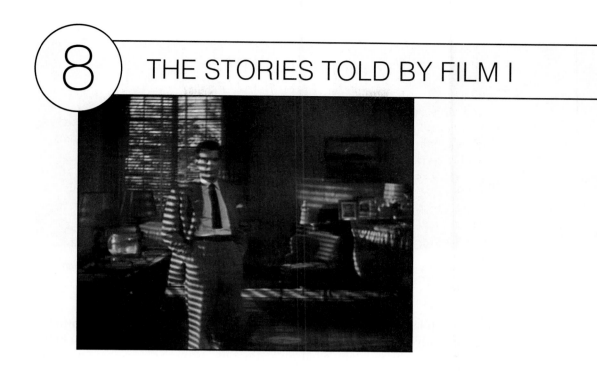

MASTER NARRATIVES AND DOMINANT FICTIONS

Frank Capra's *It's a Wonderful Life* (1946)—the Jimmy Stewart film we spoke about in the previous chapter—pulls its hero and its audience in many directions as it tries to reconcile post–World War II anxieties with a story that wants to be upbeat and morally responsible in a conventional way. In the process, the film tries to make up its mind whether it is a comedy, a fantasy, or a melodrama. It is full of high emotion but also has plenty of jokes and silly characters; angels guide the main character; and it ends, as comedies do, with a reconciliation, a reaffirmation of harmony and happiness. Everyone forgives; everyone appears ready for long-term happiness. But the film's central character, George Bailey, is not a comic figure. He is wracked with doubts; he fights against the calls of his community, wishes to break from his father, to leave the constraints of the small town of Bedford Falls. During much of the film, he is represented as a man on the verge of a nervous breakdown. He attempts suicide and is saved only because he has a guardian angel, who brings him to his senses by presenting him with a vision of the town as it would have been without him, dark, corrupt, violent—almost like the inside of George's mind.

The film, like George, is a bit schizophrenic, split between various fantasies and nightmares of its own making. Coming at the end of World War II, it tried to create a story that would bring the culture together, remind it of its responsibilities, reinstate the nuclear family headed by the working man, nurtured by the stay-at-home mother. It wanted to be a good populist warning about the

211

FIGURES 8.1–8.2   The dark side of the postwar period: anger and violence; and the happy, redeemed man and family. Two images of Jimmy Stewart in Frank Capra's *It's a Wonderful Life* (1946).

need to shift large capital out of the hands of single owners into the community. But it too fully absorbed the uncertainties of the moment, and all it can do in the end is breathlessly proclaim a happy ending. Its vision of George's conversion, and the town's sudden unity; its images of the smiling family and presumption that everyone will live happily ever after are as great a fantasy as Clarence the angel's vision of the town without George.

Closure

Despite the tensions within the film that threaten to break it down, it manages to reach closure, that conventional narrative event in every kind of fiction that stitches together the loose ends, the broken lives, the ruined love affairs, the villains still at large, the people physically and emotionally lost, all that has come unwound as a narrative moves along. More than simply ending a story, the act of closure brings back into harmony and balance lives and events that have been disrupted. That harmony and balance is always contrived to fit with what filmmakers believe to be dominant cultural values: victory over evil, as defined by the film, comfort to the previously afflicted, redemption of the lost and abused, reassertion of the family as the most valued cultural unit.

The Master and the Dominant

Despite the tensions, *It's a Wonderful Life* manages to position itself within the framework of what might be called the Hollywood **master narrative** of harmonious closure and, by so doing, positions us within it as amused, intrigued, and delighted spectators. (It is interesting to note that the word "closure," formally a critical term, is now part of everyday cultural discourse, referring to the desire to end the sense of loss following a disaster.) Like *Casablanca* (1942) before it, *It's a Wonderful Life* has become even more popular than when it was first released, not only because it tells a "universal" story, a grand narrative applicable to all people throughout time (however, keep in mind that "universal" is a culturally generated idea) but because it generates a large and inviting fantasy out of a style that carefully and invisibly propels us through a narrative of desire, sadness, fear, reconciliation, to a final proclamation of self-worth and fulfilled communal need. A master narrative contains the elements that please us with their ease of access, with the way they raise our expectations and satisfy them, generate fears and then quiet them, and conclude by assuring us that all is right with the world. A master narrative is like a template or a blueprint of stories the culture wants to hear.

Narrative is a general term indicating the construction, development, and telling of a story. We use it in many contexts. The concept of master narratives is of large culturally, historically, and economically determined constructions, many of them formed long before film. They are part of a culture's collective ideology, its generative concepts of family, order, self-possession, righting of wrongs, individuality over community, property ownership, religion, and so forth. Master narratives can be thought of as a top level of abstraction articulated by the **dominant fictions**—the reigning stories of the culture—that give words and flesh to those most comforting abstractions of love, family, sin and redemption, life and death, and our deepest fears of disruption of order, of violence and despair. As their name implies, master narratives and dominant fictions own our cultural imagination. *It's a Wonderful Life*'s story of a man who overcomes his fantasies of independence to settle down and be the center of his family and community derives from a master narrative of individual and domestic disruption and harmonious closure that is given voice by a dominant fiction of how a particular man under specific circumstances should act.

We could, stretching the point, even consider the classical Hollywood form itself a master narrative. It is not only the form that the majority of films use to tell their stories but a narrative in itself. It offers an invitation to pleasure without work, invites us to see without really having to understand what we see, and gives us an illusion of continuity and process without asking us to understand the way the links work. Through the dominant fictions that are formed by the classical Hollywood form we are asked to allow ourselves to be enfolded within a comforting space between the gazes of the characters, and it constitutes—no matter what story is being told—a tale of desire for excitement, danger, transgression, romance that is satisfied by film's end. It is the classical Hollywood form that embraces and drives the individual film, whatever the particular stories it narrates—the dominant fictions of love and hate, fear and desire, male heroism, female dependence, the liberal virtues of racial equality, self-respect, the conservative notions of demonizing and destroying selected enemies and the imperatives of "normal" domesticity, and all the other good and bad stereotypes of human behavior that films talk to us about.

Narrative Constraints

Master narratives and dominant fictions do not exist "out there," though many exist outside of film and have been constructed out of the long lineage of our culture and others. They have a history, and most important, they can be varied, told and retold, reworked at different times and for different needs. Master narratives in particular shift with the culture's ideology. Film can trace the lineage of its master narratives back to Renaissance comedy and nineteenth-century melodrama, stories of love lost and reclaimed, virtuous women attacked by corrupt men, families and other beloved institutions imperiled by greedy and immoral individuals, the sanctity of home and the order of the nuclear family, the innocence of children, the patience of women, the resolvable confusion of men.

The structure of the master narratives and the fictions that they drive are based on constraints. Cultural contexts, social norms, and dominant beliefs dictate their form and evolution. In a capitalist society, cultural constraints encourage narratives that promote close families and dependent women because this is a manageable structure that urges the woman to stay at home and care for children—future homemakers, workers, or managers—while the male is freed to be in the workplace. Socialist countries may generate narratives of communal activity rather than families and celebrate the laborer's and the farmer's work. Socialist narratives are constrained by state ideological necessity—celebration of the revolution or of workers, for example. In a commercial system, constraints are created by the need for a film to make a profit. Story and structure that push too hard against what has already been proved to work are discouraged. There are other constraints as well.

Censorship

In the history of Hollywood film, events occurred in the early thirties that further restricted the contours of its dominant fictions. Responding to pressures raised by the Catholic Church over what it perceived as licentiousness in film—especially the films of the sexy actress Mae West and the violence of the gangster films, like *Little Caesar* (Mervyn LeRoy, 1931), *Public Enemy* (William Wellman, 1931), and *Scarface* (Howard Hawks, 1932)—and faced with falling revenues caused by the Great Depression, the film business decided to censor itself before the government stepped in. The studios adopted a "Production Code" written and administered by a Catholic layman, a Jesuit priest, and a Catholic publisher. The Code essentially forbade films from showing anything sexual—even married couples had to be shown sleeping in separate beds—or allowing any crime to go unpunished. Films could not show the details of a crime or any explicit violence. There was to be no profanity or any other activity suggestive of the ordinary or the extraordinary behavior of flesh-and-blood individuals. No one in a film narrative could be allowed to get away with anything that transgressed the culture's most conservative notions of legality and morality. Nothing might be shown that wasn't conventionalized by the formalized code of cinematic representation and the restricted behavior it was forced to portray by the code. Films had to restrict themselves to the stereotypes of heroism, virtue, and reward that they themselves had imported from the Victorian stage and reworked into their native language.

If the Code had been followed religiously, movies of the thirties, forties, and fifties would have been banal to the point of being unwatchable. But screenwriters and directors created their own codes through images and editing that suggested things rather than stated them. Rain and cigarettes, for example, were often coded to signify sexuality. A look or gesture was loaded with meanings that might not otherwise have to be spelled out in dialogue. Often, screenwriters put in outrageous sequences in early versions of their scripts—a visit to a brothel, perhaps—guaranteed to throw the censors off so that they would not notice more subtle elements elsewhere.

A good argument can be made that the Production Code forced film to be more indirect, more implicit and subtle than it is now in the post-Code period. Today, even with the Code long gone—and with violence, profanity, and sexuality rampant across cinema—the stories films are telling remain largely the same. In the great majority of films, evil is still punished, the complexities of individual, communal, political, economic, and cultural behavior are largely ignored or reduced to bite-sized chunks. Redemption stands as the promise offered by almost every film and demanded by every audience: the promise that lost men will find their way, that a confused and threatened people will find clarity in the action of a male hero, that women desiring more than the culture allows will finally understand that the love of a man and the raising of a family will bring their lives to fruition, that domestic harmonies will be restored, that the right way—as defined by the dominant culture and the stories it loves—will be found.

All of this constraint and repetition must be understood within the cultural contexts of film. The ability to interpret the master narratives means that they must respond to important individual, social, and cultural needs. We respond to films because we want to; we want to because films show and tell us the things we want them to. Subtleties and variations are continually added to the dominant fictions driven by the master narratives. They have to be rearticulated at different times, for different audiences. The narratives always have to be given concrete details to create a story because master narratives are abstractions, strings of culturally accepted actions and reactions that become concrete in the dominant fictions and the individual films that give them immediacy. These concrete stories are themselves structured against the regular patterns, the recurring themes and characters of *genre,* literally the *types* of film narratives that relate the stories we want to see.

There are many layers and terms here—master narratives, dominant fictions, genres—and they are useful to help us understand how film gathers its materials and moves from the large fictions of its culture to the concrete, recognizable conventions of form and content that are repeated and varied from film to film to our continued delight. Each one of them is generated by various forms of cultural agreement or specific cinematic form. Genre is, finally, the major formal constraint within or out of which a particular film is generated.

GENRE

We invoke **genre** whenever we classify a film narrative. Video stores do it when they arrange their titles by categories such as "Action," "Comedy," "Drama." Like any generic classification, they help prepare viewers for what they will see, though the video store categories are often broad and imprecise. To better understand genre, we need to create categories that are not only inclusive but also more definitive. When we do this, we find there is a moderately stable group of major genres—comedy, melodrama, action-thriller, crime, film noir, war, musical, Western, science fiction, horror—that flesh out and individualize the master narratives and tell us the stories we like, with the variations and invention that keep them interesting.

Subgenres

From within these large groupings, **subgenres** emerge. The action-thriller genre, for example, spawns such subgenres as spy films, and chase and caper, as well as super-hero films. Under and around crime film are its satellites, the gangster movie, the detective film, the heist movie, and film noir, which began as a subgenre and quickly emerged into a full-fledged genre of its own. Road movies like *The Hitch-Hiker* (Ida Lupino, 1953), *Bonnie and Clyde* (Arthur Penn, 1967), *Easy Rider* (Dennis Hopper, 1969), *Thelma and Louise* (Ridley Scott, 1991), *Natural Born Killers* (Oliver Stone, 1994), and *Lost Highway* (David Lynch, 1997)—to name a tiny fraction of this popular subgenre—emerge from the crime genre. Comedy and melodrama often cross. *Forrest Gump* (Robert Zemeckis, 1994) is a melodrama with comedy; *Sleepless in Seattle* (Nora Ephron, 1993) is a comedy with melodrama. *Mars Attacks!* (Tim Burton, 1996), the *Men in Black* films (Barry Sonnenfeld, 1997, 2003), and the two *X-Men* movies (Bryan Singer, 2000, 2002), *Spider-Man* (Sam Rami, 2002), and Ang Lee's *The Hulk* (2003) mix the genre of comic book and trading cards with the action/science fiction genre.

Genres are often inflected and changed by gender. The Western, a genre in steep decline since the early seventies, has seen some attempts to revive it. One, *The Ballad of Little Jo* (Maggie Greenwald, 1993), makes a strong case that a generic narrative can be retold by imagining what would happen were a woman in the role usually reserved for a male. (The Western will be examined in detail in the next chapter.) The popularity of *Lara Croft: Tomb Raider* (Simon West, 2001; Jan de Bont, 2003) shows that a female superhero can, if not stretch the boundaries of the action film, at least allow them equal opportunity.

Genres, though born of constraint, can be quite supple, stretching and moving with the cultural demands of the moment. They help the viewer negotiate with the film, promising to provide certain narrative structures and character types that the viewer finds satisfying. But they have definite limits. For example, as we saw, the action-adventure film can stretch to contain a great deal of self-mockery and exaggerated, cartoon violence. But when the mockery becomes too severe, as it did in *Hudson Hawk* (Michael Lehmann, 1991) and *Last Action Hero* (John McTiernan, 1993), or too derivative, as in *The Core* (Jon Amiel, 2003), a knock-off of Jerry Bruckheimer's and Michael Bay's 1998 *Armageddon*, audiences rebel. If a film is too self-conscious, the narrative bonds are in danger of being broken. If the audience feels it is not being taken seriously enough, it may not show up.

FIGURE 8.3 Variations of this gesture, which, depending on context, could indicate fear, fatigue, thought, concern, appear in many films. The interaction of gesture and narrative context condenses meaning and lets us know quickly the character's state of mind (*The Mothman Prophecies*, Mark Pellington, 2002).

Genre and Gesture

Genres began to form as soon as films developed a narrative sense, as they moved quickly from merely showing things, such as a train leaving the station or two people kissing, to telling stories. When stories began to be told, they quickly fell into recognizable types: romances, melodramas, chases, Westerns, comedies. As we said, much of this was familiar to audiences of the Victorian stage, vaudeville, and popular fiction. Types and stereotypes of villain and hero, bad woman and faithful wife, stories of captivity, heroic action, individuals wronged unjustly and then saved, chases and rescues both comic and serious were constructed, developed, and conventionalized into film from the stage within a matter of years. Acting styles, borrowed from the stage and further exaggerated into the pantomime of silent films, established the conventions of demeanor and gesture that, modified over time, are still used and still specific to particular genres. A man or woman may no longer raise the back of a hand to the forehead to indicate melodramatic distress, but a man will bury his head in both hands and a woman will put both hands up to her mouth to show us she's shocked and frightened. Men still jut out their jaws to represent determination in an action film, and both sexes will look to the floor to show contrition, part their lips and roll their heads upward as a sign of passion in a romantic melodrama. Either will say "Oh my God!" in response to a surprising situation.

Generic Origins

Melodrama is an especially interesting case in point. The genre had its origins in the eighteenth century, when the English novel gave a voice to middle-class romantic fantasies aimed at a female audience. In the drama of pre- and postrevolutionary France and America, melodrama at first personalized great political aspirations of a middle class yearning to be free of aristocratic baggage. After the revolutions in both countries, melodrama expressed middle-class moral principles of virtue rewarded and vice punished. In nineteenth-century French and English novels—Dickens and Balzac, for example—melodrama still combined the personal and the political, addressing issues of gender and class, discovery of lost identity, strenuous pursuit of freedom from oppression, and self-sacrifice for the cause of others. These master narrative principles would become embedded in melodrama's transformation to the dominant fictions of cinema.

The transformation was made through the Victorian stage, where the passions of melodrama were played out with exaggerated abandon and the clichéd gestures that are now referred to whenever the genre is parodied. In the nineteenth century, these gestures were, in fact, codified, illustrated, and written down so that actors would know how and when to use them. Exaggeration was required in the pantomime of silent film. Intertitles, which interrupted the action with printed words, might represent the intended dialogue or summarize narrative events, but emotional continuity needed to be maintained by physical movements and facial expressions. In many countries during the silent period a live speaker might be present at a screening to narrate the events on the screen. Music also provided continuity and emotional support for the images. "Melodrama" means drama with music. Silent films were rarely shown silent. By the 1910s, orchestral scores were distributed with major film productions and were played by orchestras in urban movie theaters. In smaller theaters, a pianist might play from a score or improvise music to the film. Music provoked the emotions and made connections between what the characters on the screen and the viewers in the audience were supposed to be feeling. Music persists, now on the sound track, and it remains a major element of film in general and melodrama in particular.

The great dynamics of emotion generated by melodrama were supported by the economic dynamics of an audience willing to pay to see virtue rewarded and vice punished, to be assured that heroic men would save women from disaster and that the moral balance of the world would be restored. These dynamics were set into motion by writers and producers who worked in concert with what they intuited or analyzed as audience desire. Audience desire and creative supposition were more often in sync than not.

In literature, genres were born out of the complex interactions of form, structure, individual imagination, and social need. Forms of storytelling developed and were repeated, rules were constructed, obeyed, and repeated, in acts of collusion. An artist's imaginative needs, the audience's desire, and larger class and cultural events conspired to establish specific forms and formulas that generated specific meanings and maintained them in the social conscience. Tragedy, originally stories of kings and rulers, evoked the social profundity of the cyclical movements of power and pride, authority, self-deceit, and fall from power. The pastoral became the form for discriminating between the simplicities and complexities of a culture by contrasting an innocent, rustic world against the corruptions of the city. The epic told the large, complex story of the origination and formation of a culture and its politics from the perspective of a great hero.

In film, genres are also born out of social need and continue as long as the need is there. But while they have literary and theatrical origins, film genres rarely emerge out of the work of individual artists. In fact, some have argued that, in film, individual imagination is the enemy of generic purity. The genre transcends the artist and is therefore the perfect example of the mass production of narratives that constitutes studio filmmaking. A genre film is the result of many imaginations, including the collective imagination of the audience, the master narratives it cherishes, and the dominant fictions that nourish it. And, as in all imaginative issues relating to film production, it is economically determined.

Generic Patterns: The Gangster Film

Establishing a genre means establishing a pattern out of a blueprint, a master narrative. As in the making of a car, once the pattern is established, it is easier and cheaper to turn out many versions of the same pattern than to reinvent a new one for each unit. Here is a brief example (we will analyze other genres in greater depth): during the thirties, when Warner Brothers decided to make a gangster film—a genre that the studio came to specialize in and, with *Little Caesar, Public Enemy*, practically invented—a number of events would occur almost automatically. A basic story line would be at the ready: a young man from the slums would wander into a life of crime. Since this was the period of prohibition against alcohol, the life of crime would usually be illegal trafficking in booze. The young man would collect around him a close male friend and a girlfriend. They would all be seduced by fame and fortune, build a gang, gain riches through violence, reach for more than they could grab. The young man would become entranced by his fame and wealth, fall out with the friend, the girlfriend, or his mob, be betrayed, and finally get gunned down by the cops or a rival gang.

This narrative appealed to the Depression audience's desire to break out of the difficult, poor life many of them suffered during the decade and helped them fantasize a life of power, riches, and comfort that ran parallel to the "legal" system. At the same time, it appealed to the master narrative that spoke to the moral prohibition against easy wealth and provided a cautionary restriction on the too easy satisfaction of desire. If wealth came too easily and illegally to someone, he needed to be punished. The dominant fictions of the gangster film offered the fantasy of wish fulfillment and the reality of cultural restraints all at the same time. The audience was tempted and was redeemed from temptation, though apparently not redeemed enough to keep censors from getting nervous.

Along with the gangster narrative, the apparatus for the gangster film could be easily constructed. The studio would have everything at hand: the city street already built on the back lot, a cutout of a car placed against a rear-screen projection of a city street in motion, guns of all kinds, fedora hats, sharp suits for the men, low-cut gowns for the women. The actors were under contract: Edward G. Robinson, Humphrey Bogart, James Cagney. Writers and directors, also under contract, could be assigned to the latest gangster production. In short, all the elements were there and ready to make a genre film. As long as the audience and the censors remained receptive, the economies for this kind of production were sound and returns on investment guaranteed. Unfortunately, the censors soon cracked down on the studios and so they modified the genre, sometimes turning the actors who played gangsters into FBI agents, repeating the patterns but with the "good guys" in the foreground.

But the gangster genre has prevailed. It was reborn in the forties and became a major element in film noir. We love the outlaw; we wish to see him prevail; we know he must fail. But the genre—as all genres must—changed with the times. After the war, with the growth of corporate power and the advent of the American mafia, the gangster moved from lone hero to member of a "syndicate," and a number of films, like Raoul Walsh's *White Heat* (1949), began to show the gangster as a fading figure, destroyed by modern technology, or, in the case of one of the most extraordinary films of the genre, Abraham Polansky's *Force of Evil* (1948), becoming part of organized crime. The gangster as heroic figure and—of all things—strong family man emerged again in the first of Francis Ford Coppola's *Godfather* films. In the second, the gangster as a man diminished by the burden of his success reemerged.

But the *Godfather* films, along with Italian director Sergio Leone's *Once Upon a Time in America* (1984), brought the gangster genre into the ranks of big-budget, sweeping narratives of male bonding, the inevitability of corruption in a corrupt world, along with a certain amount of sentimentality for strong men in a world of power. And the gangster genre lives on, in action-adventure films, in films like *The Heist* (David Mamet, 2001), and *Ocean's Eleven* (Steven Soderbergh, 2001, a remake of an earlier film). Even the ethnic gangster survives in television's *The Sopranos*. These days, now that organized ethnic crime has gone through a change in the culture itself, various films feature the Russian Mafia in place of native gangsters, even gangsters in a Kung-Fu film like *Bulletproof Monk* (Paul Hunter, 2003). (For images from early gangster films, see Figures 3.16–3.18. One of the gangster film's spin-offs, film noir, will be discussed at length later in this chapter.)

Genre and Narrative Economy

By the thirties, as the studios geared up production, many of them releasing a film a week (six major studios and a number of smaller ones averaged over 300 narratives a year for about twenty years), originality in story line was not a practical or affordable quality. Genres—fed by adaptations from existing novels, stories, plays, or other films—allowed this vast production of narratives to go on with ease. The question of originality was rarely raised. Audiences became habituated to seeing variations on a theme with apparent ease. The studios continued the variations on a theme with obvious ease. Each part of the process—production and reception, filmmaker and audience—remained in contact through genres. The studios negotiated generic form and content with an audience that signified its acceptance of the contract by buying tickets.

In the days of the studios, executives would hold previews in the Los Angeles suburbs. The film's director and producer, perhaps even the studio head himself, would travel to a theater and, from the back of the house, watch the audience watching the film. Afterward, they would collect note cards from the audience. Depending on the audience's reaction during the film and on their written comments after the screening, the executives might order retakes, demand an alternative ending be filmed, ask to have more funny lines added, or have the entire film recut to increase or slow down its rhythm. Based on audience response, the film would be reshaped, the variations on a theme reworked.

Previewing still goes on. Some moviemakers hold focus groups, in which a representative collection of people are invited to discuss their attitudes about a particular film or about film in general. But currently the main negotiating power of the audience is mediated through the money they pay in film admissions and DVD rentals. The most important "preview" is a film that makes a great deal of money. If a film is successful, it becomes a model for films to follow. The audience resides mostly inside the gross receipts a film earns. On the basis of those receipts, writers, agents, producers, and directors attempt to guess what variations on the successful genre or story might make them more money still. They guess wrong more often than right. But every right guess usually pays for the wrong ones. Think of how that single variation of the old thirties action-adventure film, *Raiders of the Lost Ark* (Stephen Spielberg, 1981), led to a string of imitations. When *Batman* (Tim Burton, 1989), a variety of the heroic thriller and comic book film, came along, filmmakers seized the opportunity to combine comic book action, heroism, fantasy, and elements of the science fiction film in a variety of ways. There were the sequels of the films themselves (two for *Raiders: Indiana Jones and the Temple of Doom*, 1984; *Indiana Jones and the Last Crusade*, 1989; both directed by Spielberg; and three for *Batman:* Burton's *Batman Returns*, 1992; and Joel Schumacher's *Batman Forever*, 1995; and *Batman and Robin*, 1997), and there were spinoffs from both films like Robert Zemeckis's *Romancing the Stone* (1984), Sam Raimi's *Darkman* (1990), *The Crow* (Alex Proyas, 1994), *The Shadow* (Russell Mulcahy, 1994), *Stargate* (Roland Emmerich, 1994), The *Lora Croft* films, *The Hulk*, and even *Daredevil* (Mark Steven Johnson, 2003), to name a few.

But we cannot simply blame the studios for churning out generic clones. In fact, no one entity is to blame. The key to genre is the circulation of stories, and as long as audiences enjoy the product and pay for it, the circulation continues. As long as the stories keep shifting and changing shape, the studios keep making them applicable and acceptable to a large enough audience, and audiences keep reading them and making them applicable to themselves, a large enough generic community will be achieved. The films will be successful and the genre will thrive.

DOCUMENTARY

At first thought, documentary—sometimes called nonfiction—film seems to stand outside the usual categories of film genres: Westerns, science fiction, action-adventure, comedy, romantic comedy, melodrama, thriller, gangster film, and so on. It stands outside because it is not fiction, not "made up," and therefore not driven by the large narratives and dominant fictions of make-believe. The master narrative of documentary is supposed to be its truthfulness, a faithful gaze at the world and the lives of the characters it observes. Observation is the guiding force of documentary, and the illusion of neutrality of the documentary filmmaker makes up its central generic element.

In fact, the history of documentary, which is as long as the history of fiction film, proves otherwise, and the documentary turns out to be not only a genre but, like narrative film, host to a number of subgenres. Earlier we spoke about the old notion that fiction film derived from the work of the Lumière brothers, who often set up their cameras and simply recorded the events in front of it, while Georges Méliès crafted fictions inside his studio. In fact, Méliès also filmed historical events and the Lumières set up little fictions to film. Between them, they set the complexities of documentary filmmaking that all the way through *The Blair Witch Project*—a fiction film made to look like a documentary—have made it a difficult genre to define with any certainty.

Newsreels and Television

Documentaries break down into a number of subgenres. Originally, documentaries were made to observe and record events that might have gone on even without the camera's presence. Newsreels were one manifestation of this kind of documentation. They were a part of almost every filmgoer's experience from the thirties throughout the fifties. In cities, there were theaters devoted to showing only newsreels. One major hybrid of newsreel documentary was *The March of Time*, a weekly newsreel produced in the thirties through the early fifties by Louis de Rochemont and *Time Magazine* (*The March of Time* is parodied in the "News on the March" sequence in *Citizen Kane*). *The March of Time* rarely depended on newsreel footage alone and, like many turn-of-the-century silent newsreels, would boldly create sequences in order to achieve maximum dramatic effect.

Today, television has taken over the work of the newsreels that were common in theaters, and while the re-creations of events are less radical than the theatrical versions, TV news skews and shapes the events it observes in other ways. Television news loves to show blood and tears, and it is the major outlet for prepackaged political messages. While much of the footage is of events that have actually taken place, the footage is edited for maximum emotional effect, like a movie. And because everyone from politicians to special interest groups is now quite savvy about the power of television, events—especially political ones—are more often than not staged by their participants to be filmed in a certain way. If *The March of Time* pointed the way to the mixture of fact and fiction to produce what appeared to be fact, television news turns fact into fiction and attempts to control viewer attention to maximize viewership itself.

TV news—especially local news—is also the great fear-monger to the culture. Unlike film, in which the convention is to avoid a direct gaze at the camera, the TV newsman makes direct eye contact with us, telling us of disaster, murder, and disease. Invading our private, domestic space, the face on the screen can pretend intimacy and evoke a narrative of participation and proximity, an invitation into a fantasy world of threat and violence (the news) or desire and pleasure (the commercial), which flow together seamlessly.

Early Masters of the Documentary

Newsreels, news footage, and television news and "reality" programming—shows like *Dateline, 20/20,* or *Survivor,* which take banal events and shape them into heartrending melodrama or faked action—are in fact a special and one might say especially corrupt aspect of documentary filmmaking. Much more prominent and lasting are films made by a variety of independent filmmakers whose purpose is to show an aspect of human activity, promote social programs, or record societal problems. Some of these filmmakers worked entirely on their own. Others—especially in the thirties and forties, in Russia, the United States, and Great Britain—worked for government agencies and created some of the most important and exploratory films that we have.

Dziga Vertov and Esther Shub

We have examined, through the work of Sergei Eisenstein, the powerful, structurally complex political films that were made after the Russian Revolution. Other filmmakers of the period made films that were documents of events before, during, and after the revolution. Dziga Vertov, best known for his inventive celebration of filmmaking, *Man with a Movie Camera* (1929), also made a long series of films about daily life in the postrevolutionary U.S.S.R. The *Kino Pravda* films were instructive, observant, and playful. They would, for example, demonstrate the making of a loaf of bread by running the process in reverse, from the loaf to the bakery, the flour mill, the field of wheat. Vertov's "kino eye" made the camera a kind of reality probe to show people how the world worked.

FIGURE 8.4 The "kino eye" (*Man with a Movie Camera*, Dziga Vertov, 1929). Compare this with Figure 6.18.

Esther Shub, on the other hand, rarely filmed out in the world and instead made her films out of found footage. Called **compilation films,** nothing is

FIGURE 8.5 Found footage of the revolution, *Fall of the Romanov Dynasty*, by Esther Shub, 1927.

shot specifically for the new work, which is created in the editing room. Like so much of postrevolutionary Russian film, Shub's compilations are about editing, about choosing available images and so ordering them that they are given new meaning. Unlike Eisenstein's muscular, dynamic montages, Shub's *The Fall of the Romanov Dynasty* (1927) is amazingly linear, a history lesson moving across revolutionary time.

Robert Flaherty

The American Robert Flaherty still holds a place as a founding figure of the documentary. In fact The Flaherty Seminar for Independent Video and Cinema is held regularly as a forum for discussion and exhibition of documentary and experimental work. Flaherty was a perfectionist and a creative force, pulling together his material, the people whose lives he was documenting, and literally arranging their environment to create the perfect scene and effect that, though often staged, would bring home the points he was making about his subjects even better than unmanipulated observation. His most famous film, the silent *Nanook of the North* (1922), despite its mildly patronizing attitude and stereotyping of the "simple savage," creates a kindly, engaged, and often lyrical observation of daily Inuit life in the twenties. Flaherty loves to look into the faces and actions of his characters with both an anthropologist's curiosity and a desire to find the homely and comprehensible attributes of what, to an outsider, is an exotic culture: Nanook listens to (and tries to eat) a phonograph record, the family gives medicine to a child, the group builds an igloo, or they simply engage in play. In some of the film's most famous sequences, we observe Nanook fishing (he kills the fish with his teeth) and his capture of a walrus and a seal.

The latter event is a fake. Flaherty had a dead seal placed beneath the ice. But this production history does not take away from the power of the sequence and representation of authenticity of the film as a whole. Flaherty's talent at placing his camera at exactly the right place to compose the person in the landscape, and the time he allows for events to take their course, mark the film as a kind of touchstone for documentary filmmaking to come. Unfortunately, Flaherty's own career did not fare well. Film was a perfect vehicle for the culture's desire for the exotic: foreign people in strange lands who fit stereotypes of the primitive and childlike. *Nanook* fit that desire well enough that the studios attempted to cash in on it. Flaherty went to work for Paramount on a variety of projects, often with a codirector whom the studios either trusted or—in the case of the German filmmaker F. W. Murnau, who collaborated with Flaherty on *Tabu*

(1931) until the latter abandoned the project—apparently thought would add to the exoticism and make it more sentimentally attractive.

These films barely adhere to anything but the vaguest requirements of documentary, and it wasn't until Flaherty turned to government and corporate sponsorship that his talents shined again. He made *Man of Aran* (1934) for the British, and it is one of his best and least compromised works. The rawness of the life of a fisherman in an inhospitable environment is presented with little flinching; the brutal landscape and hopeless labors of its inhabitants are represented with little sentimentality. Flaherty ended his career with *The Land* (1942), made for the U.S. Information Service, and *Louisiana Story* (1948), sponsored by Standard Oil. Somewhat compromised because of its sponsor, which wanted a film to show what a good environmental neighbor it was, the film is a lyrical glorification of both place and alleged corporate goodwill.

Pare Lorentz

Documentaries are never big moneymakers, and filmmakers often have to turn to government and corporate support in order to make their films. This does not, of course, mean that the films are automatically more ideologically charged than films financed by the studios, or that they have to toe a particular line. *Louisiana Story* survives as a well-made documentary apart from its corporate sponsorship. There have been periods in the history of film when many governmental bodies understood the importance of film in representing the culture, creating images for it, and, yes, propagating some important ideas that the sponsoring bodies wished to have known.

The U.S. government under Franklin Roosevelt in the thirties became, briefly and through various agencies, the funder and producer of some of the best documentaries we have. Pare Lorentz, for example, made two films about the work of the government in land reclamation—*The Plow That Broke the Plains* (1936) and *The River* (1938)—in which a precise photographer's eye composes the shots (indeed Lorentz used prominent still photographers to film his work) and an editor's rhythm, heavily influenced by the montage practice of Sergei Eisenstein, drives the films forward with grace and purpose. Indeed, it is the visual rhythm of *The Plow That Broke the Plains* that turns a powerful statement about the reclamation of the thirties' dustbowl into a splendid piece of filmmaking with political urgency. Its precise montages of land and people, of the deadness of the first threatening the lives of its inhabitants, make it a strong prelude to the saving of the land by government intervention.

Leni Riefenstahl

Lorentz was one of many American documentary filmmakers in the thirties who used government sponsorship to provoke their political and aesthetic imaginations into visually stimulating cinema. There were also many European documentarists, perhaps most famously Joris Ivens, who worked through a

FIGURE 8.6 Leni Riefenstahl's staged Nazi documentary, *Triumph of the Will* (1934).

variety of subjects, including *The Spanish Earth* (1937), a film about the struggle of the Spaniards against the right-wing insurgency of Francisco Franco, with a commentary by Ernest Hemingway.

One filmmaker, however, did not use her government sponsorship well. Or perhaps she did—too well. Leni Riefenstahl remains, even after her death in 2003 at 102, one of the few prominent women filmmakers across the history of world cinema and one of the most controversial. She was the filmmaker of the German Nazi Party. Her two best-known films, *Triumph of the Will* (1934) and *Olympia* (1938), were financed for and made in the service of Adolf Hitler and his Minister of Culture, Joseph Goebbels (the man who was reported to have said, "When I hear the word 'culture,' I pull out my gun"). *Triumph of the Will* is a film about a gigantic Nazi rally that was staged precisely so that Riefenstahl could film it. The purpose of the film is to provide visual and ideological stimulation to the viewer of people in large, geometric masses, marching, saluting, looking at and listening to Hitler, the object of their adoration. A part of the hypnotic effect lies in Riefenstahl's cutting, which proved so tight that filmmakers were unable to extract footage from *Triumph* to compile an *anti*-fascist film. Stimulation is not the same as stimulating, however. The incessant parading and the huge massing of people, along with Hitler's harangues, may have had a hypnotic effect on a willing and ideologically committed fascist audience. Today the film is long, noisome, and tiring.

FIGURE 8.7 Riefenstahl's composition is imitated by George Lucas in *Star Wars* (1977). Why celebrate the triumph of good by imitating a film about evil?

Curiously, the film maintains some kind of perverse influence. For reasons best known to himself, George Lucas imitated not the cutting but the compositions of *Triumph of the Will* to celebrate the victory of the heroes at the end of the first *Star Wars*. Perhaps there is something in the composition of geometrically massed people that attracts an innocent (or not so innocent) cinematic eye.

The film, obviously, has remained in the global cultural consciousness and has sparked many arguments about aesthetics versus politics. This controversy reaches as far back as the nondocumentary film *The Birth of a Nation* (1915), D. W. Griffith's groundbreaking work that celebrates and led to the renewed popularity of the Ku Klux Klan. With Riefenstahl's *Olympia*, which at casual glance really does give the impression of an artful recording of sports events, the aesthetics versus politics controversy grows stronger. The film appears to be a "neutral" documentary of the 1936 Olympic Games in Berlin, in which Riefenstahl even had the authority to include the humiliating (for the Germans) win of Jesse Owens, the African American Olympic athlete. The climactic high-diving sequence of *Olympia* is among the most delirious and expertly cut visions of the body in motion. But here is where the problem lies, and it ties in with much of what we are talking about in regard to film throughout this book. The cultural, political context of the film, its maker, and its intended audience bring it under suspicion. If *Triumph of the Will* is a paean to the totalitarian massing of fascist forces, *Olympia* is a celebration of the Nazi cult of the body: the perfect Aryan body, which—with the brief, begrudging exception of Jesse Owens—is what Riefenstahl concentrates on the most. Hers is a politicized erotic gaze of the body under stress and sacrifice, two major elements of Nazi ideology. The very structure and image content of her films make them part of the ideology of destruction, no matter what those images seem to show.

John Grierson and the British Documentary Movement

Leni Riefenstahl proclaimed her innocence to her dying day, insisting that her interest lay in art not politics. She has even become the subject of someone else's documentary, Ray Müller's *The Wonderful, Horrible Life of Leni Riefenstahl* (1993). She remains, perhaps with D. W. Griffith, among the most interesting, unredeemable figures in film history.

Happily, while she was making Nazi films in Germany, John Grierson, a Scotsman with large humanist-socialist leanings, began overseeing a complex filmmaking process in England through funding first by the Empire Marketing Board and then—more in keeping with his notion of film as a means to disseminate information—through the General Post Office. Though Grierson directed only two films himself, he produced or oversaw many, many others. The films were as varied as they were brilliantly made. Harry Watt and Basil Wright's *Night Mail* (1936), with its narrative written by the poet W. H. Auden and music by Benjamin Britten, showed how the British mail system worked. The same director's *Song of Ceylon* (1934) demonstrated the growing and production of tea. All of the films represented information through a synthesis of word, sound, and imagery photographed in bold, large compositions, edited with an Eisensteinian imagination, a rhythm that drives the viewer through and with the film's information.

If this weren't enough, Grierson went to Canada in the late thirties and founded the Film Board of Canada, which was in its time a major and influential government filmmaking agency. Grierson also wrote. He invented the very word "documentary" in a review of Robert Flaherty's *Moana* (1926) and propagandized the social power of the documentary film with grace and persistence:

> The "art" of documentary is, as always with art, only the by-product of an interpretation well and deeply done. Behind the documentary film from the first was a purpose, and it was the educational purpose . . . to "bring alive" to the citizen the world in which his citizenship lay, to "bridge the gap" between the citizen and his community.

World War II

During World War II, the U.S. government, through the Office of War Information, continued the production of documentary films, all of which were "propaganda" films in the sense that they propagated the rightness of the American cause and pushed, sometimes to extreme racist proportions, the horribleness of the Germans and, most especially, the Japanese. Many of these films were produced or directed by major Hollywood figures: Frank Capra, for example, oversaw production of a large number of films grouped into two categories, *Why We Fight* and *Know Your Enemy*. These films combined narration, war footage, reenactment, and animation (supplied by Walt Disney) in films that compelled the viewer into an assent to the rightness of the war.

Other directors of great stature also made wartime documentaries. John Huston, for example—the director of films such as *The Maltese Falcon* (1941), *Treasure of the Sierra Madre, Key Largo* (both 1948), and *The African Queen* (1951)—made two dark, troubling nonfiction films about the war and its aftermath. *The Battle of San Pietro* (1945) is something like an engaged (though partially reenacted) newsreel with a probing, troubled intelligence behind it, so troubled that the army itself was uncomfortable with its unrelenting images of destruction and cut it for public release. Similar trouble confronted Huston's *Let There Be Light* (1946), a documentary of emotionally disturbed soldiers in an American rehabilitation facility. In this case, it was fear of revealing the identities of these emotionally disturbed prisoners of war that kept the film out of circulation until a few years ago.

Cinéma Vérité

Later in this chapter, we will be discussing a kind of film that emerged in post–World War II Italy called "neorealism." Neorealism was fiction film, but its use of actual locations and nonprofessional actors gave it the air of documenting life in the streets and tenements of a war-ravaged country. As we will see, the influence of Italian neorealism was enormous, and extended to the documentary as well.

Much of early documentary was carefully planned and structured. Flaherty's films, as we pointed out, contained staged sequences, and the best of the thirties and forties documentaries were composed and edited more artfully than fiction films. There was a tendency in many studio-made documentaries to use voice-over narration, providing a shell of words to envelop the images. The term "voice of god" was coined to describe the stentorian tones of the narrator of the *March of Time* series, imitated in the newsreel sequence of *Citizen Kane*. But the influence of neorealism led to a change in these documentary structures. Beginning with the work of Jean Rouch in France in the fifties—and moving to the United States in the films of Richard Leacock, D. A. Pennebaker, Frederick Wiseman, and David and Albert Maysles—a surge in new documentary, often referred to as **cinéma vérité**, occurred in the sixties. Cinéma vérité is marked by the absence of voice-over narration and strives to achieve a perfect illusion of ongoing life, casually observed by the camera. Vérité is meant to appear seamless: in other words, it attempts to imitate some aspects of the Hollywood continuity style. But this continuity is meant to communicate the ongoing process of everyday life, of people doing their work, conducting their personal affairs.

For example, David and Albert Maysles' *Salesman* (1969) follows a Bible salesman on his door-to-door rounds, watches and listens to him give his pitch to prospective customers, talk to his colleagues, and ruminate about his profession. The film attempts to represent a neutrality, which, given the very nature of its subject and his work, it cannot quite manage. While not melodramatic, and never reaching for the large emotions of that other great work about salesmen, Arthur Miller's 1949 play *Death of a Salesman*, the film cannot avoid pulling our emotions toward the comprehension of a rather small, sad life devoted to the selling of religion. It also cannot avoid a very careful editorial structuring of events. The film's sequences may actually have been recorded as they occurred, but they are arranged to create a particular and affecting narrative flow.

It was another Maysles brothers film, *Gimme Shelter* (1970), that brought the vérité movement to its climax. One of a number of rock music documentaries following in the wake of Michael Wadleigh's *Woodstock* (1970, one of whose editors was Martin Scorsese), *Gimme Shelter* contained a major difference: it showed a murder. The film documents the infamous Rolling Stones' Altamont concert, for which the band hired Hell's Angels as guards. The Angels fought with the crowd, and one of them stabbed to death a man brandishing a gun. In the film, the Stones are very aware that trouble is afoot; they ask the audience to "chill out." But in a sequence staged for the observing camera, the Maysles sit the members of the rock group in front of an editing machine and show them the footage of the fight. Mick Jagger asks, "Can you roll back on that, David?" And in slow motion the stabbing is clearly seen.

From one point of view, *Gimme Shelter* is a perfect documentary in that it shows us events happening that even the crew shooting them were unaware of at the time. At the same time, it is so edited that the discovery of the murder becomes the film's climax, and the filmmakers' presence is clearly announced. The Maysles argued that it couldn't have been done otherwise, given the notoriety of the event. However, it does demonstrate how carefully a good documentary is structured and crafted, given form not by the passing of the daily world in front of a neutral lens but by the creative intelligence of the filmmaker.

Gimme Shelter and the *cinéma vérité* movement spurred documentary filmmakers to further experimentation, including the often strange, hypnotic, and surreal documentaries of the German filmmaker Werner Herzog, one of whose films, *The Great Ecstasy of the Woodcarver Steiner* (1974), consists of long, slow-motion shots of a skier, his mouth opened in a strange oval of awe at his own flight. In his documentaries and his fiction films, Herzog's images of people, animals, and landscapes, often taken at unusual distances or with a disconcerting combination of lenses, greatly influenced the nature films so prominent on Public Television. His own vision of a strange, hypnotic world extended into his fiction films as well, such as *Aguirre: The Wrath of God* (1972) or *Hearts of Glass* (1976), during the making of which the actors were literally hypnotized.

Other filmmakers, in particular Errol Morris in *The Thin Blue Line* (1988) and *Mr. Death: The Rise and Fall of Fred A. Leuchter, Jr.* (1999), pushed harder and harder against the generic principles of documentary. In *The Thin Blue Line* he uses the policemen and the accused in a murder case to reenact the incidents and, in the resulting film, prove the innocence of the accused. *Mr. Death* is an example of how the talking-head style of television documentaries can be put to insightful and even subversive ends. The film consists mainly of interviews with its subject, a former inventor of and consultant for human execution devices, who becomes, through his own obsessive behavior, a Holocaust denier—that is, someone who claims that the Nazis did not kill six million Jews. The latter part of the film intercuts the interviews with images of Leuchter endlessly chipping away at the walls of a Polish concentration camp, gathering samples to prove that gas was never used. Another interview, with someone who actually knows what he's talking about, completely demolishes Leuchter's theory, and the rest of the film allows Leuchter to reveal himself as a kind of innocent, amoral idiot, who seems simply to have followed ideas without actually having any. The film joins with the great documentaries of Marcel Ophuls—*The Sorrow and the Pity* (1971) and *Hotel Terminus* (1988)—which allow past and present participants in human atrocity to expose themselves before the gentle, ironic, and completely knowing eye of the documentarists. Recently, Errol Morris made a film, *Fog of War* (2003), about Robert McNamara,

FIGURE 8.8 Modern documentary may reveal truths by composing images that best represent what the filmmaker wishes us to see. (*Mr. Death: The Rise and Fall of Fred A. Leuchter, Jr.*, Errol Morris, 1999).

the Secretary of Defense during much of the Vietnam war, using news footage, but, again, mostly allowing his subject to expose his actions by letting him talk.

Morris and others have themselves proved that neutrality and the illusion of objective observation are not generic givens. Some documentarists, like Michael Moore in *Roger and Me* (1989) and *Bowling for Columbine* (2002), and in his television work, make themselves the center of observation, the agents provoking actions that *wouldn't* have occurred without the camera's presence. Moore's *Fahrenheit 9/11* (2004), a film about the Iraqi war and the Bush administration, demonstrates not only a maturing of the filmmaker's talents, but a profound return to the social and politically committed documentaries of the thirties. Its power and clarity, giving us images of war long suppressed and interviews exposing both heartbreak and subterfuge, allowed it, given the political climate of the time, to become the first documentary to win the top prize at the Cannes Film Festival. It went on to become the top grossing documentary film in its American release (which was briefly threatened when its original distributor, the Disney organization, got political cold feet and pulled out). *Fahrenheit 9/11* proves, perhaps, what Hollywood has tried to spend much of its time disproving, that politics and art do mix, and may, in fact, be inseparable.

Television Documentary

Television has done a bizarre perversion of *cinéma vérité* in those endless series of network voyeur programs, the "reality" shows that prove that, just as with fiction film, we love to look at what other people are doing, no matter how dull they are and how inconsequential, or vulgar, their acts may be.

Grierson's drive toward the well-made educational and civilizing documentary has, today, devolved into the talking-head mode of Public Television nature, science, and history documentaries. In the thirties, there was a notion that governments could help produce progressive and artistically adventurous films that could influence for the good a good many people. And, certainly in Great Britain and the United States, this proved true. But American ideology hardened after World War II, and the notion took hold that art and politics should never mix and the government should not have a large hand in the making of art. We see these battles being fought to this day. Public Television, partially funded by the government, has therefore had to prove itself a neutral party. In both script and execution, the concentration on still images, newsreel, or nature footage, and close-ups of uncontroversial scholars, PBS and its cable imitators create documentaries apparently free of ideology—of the driving force of a cultural or political idea. In fact, because no work of the human imagination is without ideology, these remnants of the Griersonian ideal tend toward a centrist position, carefully treading the potentially dangerous waters of governmental interference (including the withdrawing of funding) by keeping away from issues that some might consider "controversial"—a word that usually means that someone might disagree with what they see.

THE GENRES OF FICTION FILMS

The malleability of the documentary appears, potentially at least, to be greater than the fiction film genres we are familiar with. Fiction films seem more bound by the rules and conventions imposed—self-imposed—very early in the history of film than the more independent (and—until *Fahrenheit 9/11*—much less seen) work of documentarists. Even most so-called independent filmmakers adhere to generic rules if they want their films to be well distributed. But these restrictions can sometimes be superficial. Many filmmakers expand, manipulate, or otherwise subvert generic expectations in ways that refresh the genres or, sometimes, destroy them. However, before change or destruction can occur, we, as well as the filmmakers themselves, need to understand the structures that might be changed. To do that, we need to move backward in film history when genres were a bit more straightforward.

Genres are such complex things that I want—for the sake of clarity and in order to see in strong detail how their structures, themes, and variations work—to focus on just a few of them: melodrama, film noir, the Western, and science fiction, while also referring to a number of others. One of the genres, melodrama, is, as we've seen, very old and predates cinema. Science fiction literature and film are almost contemporaneous. Film noir is relatively new and particular to film. The Western is an interesting case of a genre that has all but died. These case studies will allow us to examine a range of structures and meanings across the history of film and understand further the relationship between culture and film form.

Melodrama can be understood as a genre and a master narrative, an overarching narrative form that controls all films that aren't comedies and that had an existence before film was invented. It is so important, in fact, that I'll be returning to it again in the next chapter in order to understand not only its power, but how it can be bent and reworked. Film noir, on the other hand, is original to film and is also a kind of hybrid. It developed out of detective fiction, the gangster film, thirties French cinema, the thriller, and melodrama itself. Film noir occurred at a very specific moment in the history of film as a response to specific cultural events. Its uniqueness has made it one of the most imitated forms in current cinema, and its name is one of the few terms from French criticism that have entered common usage. Curiously, at the time of the creation of noir in the early forties, nobody knew they were inventing what would become one of the most celebrated of genres. The Western, like melodrama, predated cinema, but was also born with it. Cowboys and Indians, cowboys and outlaws, rode after each other from almost the moment the first camera cranked. Science fiction, like film itself, is a product of the technological revolution of the nineteenth century.

Melodrama

As we noted earlier, melodrama is not original to film. As an old and popular form, it is even represented by a popular stereotype. Because it is the dominant serious dramatic and narrative form of so many cultures, it contains within it the seeds of its own parody. In popular usage, "**melodrama**" is often used to describe an exaggerated, emotionally overblown situation. But in this case, parody turns out to be a form of flattery (or self-protection) because melodrama has never lost its power to make grown people cry. It is the central cinematic form that creates empathy and identification. In its once most popular guise, as radio and then television soap opera, it demanded the attention of millions of listeners and viewers around the world.

Melodrama is about feeling or, more accurately, about provoking emotions, perhaps more intense than what are called for by the story being told. The desire to provoke emotions, and, for the audience, to have them provoked, was a driving force in the development of American cinema's classical style. Its formation and the development of film melodrama went hand in hand. Knitting the viewers' gaze within the narrative space of a film; emphasizing glances, faces, hands (D. W. Griffith especially liked close-ups of women's hands, wringing, twisting); and finding ways to mold the viewers' response into a narrative flow of despair, loss, anxiety, hope, and eventual triumph, suffered or instigated mainly by women, helped filmmakers establish a style of visual, narrative, and emotional continuity. Exaggerated as they might seem to us now, the gestures of silent film melodrama were in fact a refinement, even a rethinking, of their stage originals, providing an emotive language of look and gesture that created and maintained a connection with viewers. An intimacy between the audience and the representations of actors on the screen was greater than that achieved when live figures gesticulated on a distant stage. These looks and gestures and the way they were edited together became conventionalized codes that triggered conventionalized responses, predictably, time and time again. In their predictability lay their security. It lies there still. The gestures and looks are less broad now, but still codified. It must be so, because melodrama is about security, about the safe expression of overwhelming passion, safe because confined within the known bounds of cinematic codes. Circumscribed, predictable, closed, the codes of melodrama can permit extravagant stories to be told, stories that articulate deep, subjective passion and terrors, which are always contained within the bounds of the master narrative.

Broken Blossoms

D. W. Griffith was as central a figure in the development of the contours and contents of film melodrama as he was in the development of the classic style itself. He was a man of conservative, populist,

FIGURE 8.9 A close-up from D. W. Griffith's *Intolerance* (1916). What may look like a grossly exaggerated expression was common in silent film—and actually only toned down a bit in contemporary movies. Acting styles, like everything else in film, are built on convention.

Southern character, and his background and ideology colored his films. His racist film *The Birth of a Nation* (1915) not only expanded the narrative scope and running time of theatrical film but celebrated and managed to revitalize a then dormant Ku Klux Klan. Griffith spent much of the rest of his career attempting to atone for the appalling social-political results of his "masterpiece." His racial attitudes were matched only by his attitudes toward gender (though it should be emphasized that these attitudes were shared with large parts of the contemporary culture). Women, in most of Griffith's films, fulfilled conventional roles of wives and mothers. They were weak and got into trouble, often at the hands of desperate, angry men. They needed saving by good, virile men. One of the essential, primary structures of narrative film, the cross-cutting editing pattern that links a sequence of captivity and a sequence of rescue, is based on this response to gender difference. The pattern was not invented by Griffith, and it was used in comedies as well, but he fully exploited it, made it essential to melodramatic construction, and climaxed it, in fact, in the great rescue scene of *Way Down East* (1920) where the woman—passive, trapped, stranded on rapidly dispersing ice floes—awaits rescue by her man, who is desperate to arrive before she dies.

Griffith helped institutionalize this formula—made it a permanent part of the language of melodramatic cinema—and he could also reverse it. In *The Mother and the Law*, a film made right after *The Birth of a Nation* and included as one of the stories in *Intolerance* (made in 1916, the first of the films he made to atone for the racism of *The Birth of a Nation*), it is the woman who leads the rescue of her son, imprisoned because he is wrongly accused of labor violence (Griffith's populism occurs in other films, like the 1909 short film *A Corner in Wheat*, where he takes the side of labor against business). Such a reversal in gender expectations is nowhere as startling as in *Broken Blossoms* (1919), a melodrama in which gender positions are set askew, and both the male and female characters suffer an

FIGURES 8.10–8.11   Two stills from the famous rescue on the ice in D. W. Griffith's *Way Down East* (1920). Of course, as the heroine almost goes over the falls, the hero rescues her from the ice floe.

enormous amount of repression. *Broken Blossoms* was another film made to help Griffith redeem himself for *The Birth of a Nation*, and it sets some basic patterns for the family melodrama that have persisted, with much variation but little fundamental change, to the present.

Griffith's overt theme for the film is a rather weak-willed wish for "universal brotherhood." What the film crucially investigates is miscegenation (interracial sexual relations) and brutality to women. The central male character is a Chinese man, played by a white actor (Richard Barthelmess), who is referred to in the intertitles as "The Yellow Man." He comes to London—a mythical movie-set London, a place removed from any reality, a perfect mise-en-scène for this fantasy of domestic terror—on a religious mission to calm the savage white man. He lives an isolated life in the East End ghetto. He takes no part in the pursuits of opium smoking, which Griffith portrays in an extraordinary tableau, showing men and women lounging sensually in a smoked-filled opium den, and maintains a spiritual aloofness as a small shop owner. His revulsion from violence, his features and gestures, the very way he holds his body are strongly marked as female. That is, they are marked by what the culture recognizes as feminine—small, mincing gestures; hands and arms drawn close to the body; a nonaggressive personality.

"The Yellow Man" is doubled by the film's female character, Lucy. In gesture and demeanor she is his mirror image, and they are even composed by the camera in similar ways. Though white, Lucy is also an outcast, a poor, withdrawn, helpless creature of a monstrous father, the prizefighter "Battling Burrows," who beats her with ferocious violence. The melodramatic triangle set up by these figures is fascinating in its complexity and in the ways it reveals basic principles of the genre. Lucy is oppressed by a paternal figure of such violence that she attempts to escape him by turning to the gentle, feminized male—a

FIGURES 8.12–8.13   In *Broken Blossoms* (1919) vulnerability and sensitivity are marked by gender and race. The two main characters are drawn to each other in an impossible attraction. They become reflections of each other.

vulnerable, regressive figure like herself—for comfort. But the comfort she receives is also threatening in its otherness.

Melodrama must create a world of threat, not only to its characters but to its audience, before it resolves itself. Filled with desire of his own, "The Yellow Man" turns Lucy into a fetish object, making her up to look like an Asian doll and placing her on his raised bed. This really frightens her—and us. In one close-up from her point of view, "The Yellow Man's" face moves toward her filled with lust—a shot that will be echoed later when "Battling Burrows's" face moves toward Lucy, filled with violent hatred. But "The Yellow Man" has sublimated his lust and is no threat to her; he worships her. The look on his face actually reflects her own fears. Everything, the erotic in particular, remains repressed. In melodrama, sexuality and desire must be sublimated into something else. In *Broken Blossoms,* their sublimation results from the cultural prohibition against miscegenation and the fact that protection is stronger than the need for sexual satisfaction.

The sublimation turns "The Yellow Man" into a maternal figure, a strangely desexualized but somehow still erotic figure who both worships and cares for the battered Lucy. But this adoration and care is no match for "Battling Burrows." The tension of the narrative is built when he finds his daughter. The brutality of the crazed patriarch will destroy the apparently innocent pleasures of this odd couple. He drags Lucy back to their hovel and beats her to death after she flees to the confines of a closet. "Battling" breaks down with an ax the walls she hoped would protect her, the camera capturing Lucy's entrapment and exposure through a sequence of point-of-view shots that is chilling and unrelenting. It is a scene so grueling and so expertly done that Hitchcock does homage to it in the shower scene in *Psycho,* as does Kubrick in *The Shining* (1980) when Jack breaks down Wendy's door with an ax.

It is typical of melodrama to create an experience of such extremity, a cruelty so enormous that it seems impossible to correct it. But it must be corrected, because without closure, without recuperating the situation, the internal melodramatic world would be in perpetual disruption. It might be useful to think of melodrama spatially, as a kind of bell-shaped curve. The narrative starts out with a forced and weakened harmony between the characters. Events become complicated as when, for example, an abused white woman and an Asian man seek affection for each other. These complications raise the emotional graph to sometimes unbearable peaks. But these excesses must be themselves subdued—melodrama is always about subduing the excess it creates—and a kind of harmony is reestablished by the film's end. Often, when the narrative situation appears to have no probability of closure, the film will simply kill off its participants, which is what happens at the end of *Broken Blossoms.* Griffith tries to create a standard intercut sequence of rescue. But "The Yellow Man" doesn't arrive in time to save Lucy. She is murdered, and he shoots "Battling Burrows" and then himself.

Melodrama is structured on the containment and release of desire. It calls for the end of repression and then reimposes it at the end. That is because melodrama is essentially a cautionary form. Yes, it says, people live constricted and hurt lives. They want more, should have more. But too much more will damage the fragile emotional equilibrium, the sets of oppositions, the dominant and regressive states that the culture needs to survive. So melodrama always enacts, at its end, a process of recuperation, bringing its characters back to a kind of cultural health or, more accurately, a "health" prescribed by the dominant values, and the dominant fictions, of the culture. Melodrama is an expression of the master narrative of closure and equilibrium, of bringing characters and culture into a manageable steady state; and if it cannot recuperate its characters into a steadier state than the one in which they began, or if they cannot be recuperated because they have transgressed too far, it will enforce an equilibrium through their absence and kill them off, usually in the name of their being too good or too bad or too damaged to survive.

As a dynamic genre, depending upon a close interaction with the people who view it, we can almost say that melodrama has a life of its own. "It" can do things to characters and to viewers. All genres can do things, because they are prescriptive mechanisms. Within a genre, certain actions can and *must* be taken by or occur to certain characters, and the narrative that directs their lives must follow a prescribed and proscribed path.

Broken Blossoms deals with one of the ultimate cultural transgressions, miscegenation. And while the film pretends a tender understanding of how "The Yellow Man" and Lucy find comfort in their bizarre, asexual union, it cannot possibly allow that union to prevail or endure. Melodrama is self-censuring. It always assumes to know how much passion and transgression the audience, within its cultural constraints, will or should manage. In the process of built-in censure, it will also gauge the maximum emotional capital it can cause the audience to use in exchange for the images they are watching. So, while Griffith has his three characters killed off because the triangle was simply more than cultural reality in the late 1910s could bear, he manages to wring from his viewers as much sympathy, or even empathy, as they can muster or commit.

Caution and exploitation are two of melodrama's main attributes. If tragedy—the dramatic form that preceded melodrama—asked of its audience a profound recognition of great human achievement undone by greater human limitation, melodrama asks for a less lofty but more emotional recognition of the necessity to contain all aspirations within comfortable and known boundaries. "Asks" is wrong, though. Melodrama demands. For melodrama to work, an audience must be told what to feel and when to feel it; viewers must be hooked and reeled in. Narrative movement must be unstoppable and not allow any questions to be asked. If, at any point, melodrama permits an opening through which the viewer can look and say, "This is ridiculous, such events, such suffering could or should never occur," the structure would fall to pieces. Melodrama demands continuous assent and uses all the force of the continuity style to get that assent. It sutures the viewer into its fabric and makes the viewer's emotional response part of that fabric's pattern.

The pattern is often enough based on very primal stuff. Simple human need for emotional comfort in the face of outrageous brutality is the baseline of *Broken Blossoms*. But elaborated into a narrative of interracial romance, gender diffusion, and a grotesque representation of an abusive father, the baseline is built up just to the point of collapse. Griffith's delicacy and restraint (not qualities he shows in many of his other films) and the constant fascination of his mise-en-scène—the mythic constructions of East End London streets; the conversion of "The Yellow Man's" room into an exotic, erotic temple; the oppressive grunge of "Battling Burrows's" room—keep the viewer contained within the narrative. The simple cutting, the connections of gaze and response, ease the viewer into this mise-en-scène of gender hysteria. The sexual ambiguities, the continual threats to Lucy of violence and rape, even her ghastly attempts to smile at her beastly father by pushing up the corners of her mouth with her fingers, fascinate because of their very outrageousness. Melodrama turns the outrageous into the plausible and asks us to believe that plausibility is close to reality.

Now, Voyager

Melodrama throws pain and dissatisfaction in our faces, insists we can do better, and then, in the end, takes it all back, assuring us that we'll be fine if we only modify desire and deflect pain somewhere else—or end it with death. In 1942, Warner Brothers made a rich and complex melodrama called *Now, Voyager*, directed by Irving Rapper. With Bette Davis, one of Warner's major players, as its star, it combines an Oedipal narrative with the story of Cinderella to create the classic structure of melodramatic proposal and denial. A superb example of the classic Hollywood continuity style, *Now, Voyager* knits its pieces together within a narrative of such perfect continuity that the viewer is compelled across its parts into an illusion of a seamless flow of events. *Now, Voyager* substitutes an oppressive, upper-class mother for *Broken Blossoms'* brutal working-class father. Mother is always shown rigid and dominating the frame, even if it is only her fingers, ominously taking up the foreground of a composition, impatiently tapping on a bedpost. The subject of her oppression is her daughter, Charlotte Vale, seen early in the film as a mousy, gray, emotionally arrested, neurotic middle-aged woman.

The film plays out the introduction of Charlotte as long as it can, in an interesting display of the intimacy filmmakers knew existed between viewer and film. Audiences already knew very well what Bette Davis looked like from her many other films: she was a major star who had gained even wider recognition by unsuccessfully attempting to break her contract with the studio because she did not like the roles she was being given. Viewers could be depended upon to have read stories of her lawsuit and also to have read publicity that stressed how ugly she was made to look early in the film. Therefore, *Now, Voyager* takes its time introducing her and, when it finally does, shows her legs first, descending the stairs, to further heighten expectation. In a similar way, Warner Brothers' *Casablanca* (Michael Curtiz), made at about the same time as *Now, Voyager*, and retaining some of the political structure of melodrama's origins, also withholds the appearance of its star, Humphrey Bogart, building audience expectation and defining the character through his surroundings.

Now, Voyager posits two men who come to Charlotte's rescue, each one a "foreigner," each one offering a different kind of assistance and release. One is a psychiatrist, a figure with a mixed history in American film. The cinematic role of psychiatry and psychiatrist reflects the profession's mixed reputation in the culture at large. Feared and admired, looked to as someone to deliver us from emotional pain, or as a personification of individual defeat and help-lessness, or as the embodiment of evil influence, the psychiatrist can help or destroy. In *Now, Voyager* psychiatry is salvation, and its incarnation in Dr. Jaquith—a wise, ironic, and self-contained Britisher—enters Charlotte's mother's house at the very beginning of the film and rescues Charlotte. He is an asexual individual, emotionally potent but no romantic threat. Because the sex-ual is so foregrounded in melodrama and placed as a primary cause of most of the characters' activities, the genre often needs clean divisions between those for whom sex is a central issue and those for whom it plays no role. These non-threatening figures (very often represented as the friend of the central character, like Sam in *Casablanca*) are mediating forces. They act a bit as our presence in the film, guiding, threatening nothing, seeing everything, assuring the success of the main character. In *Now, Voyager,* Jaquith figures as a pleasant, though aloof, patriarchal counter to Charlotte's mother—understanding, supportive, curative where she is negative, mean, and destructive. Though the film does not show the details of her cure, Charlotte is indeed transformed by her stay at Dr. Jaquith's sanitarium and emerges, as if from a cocoon, to appear as the glam-orous Bette Davis everyone in the theater would have been familiar with—as familiar as now we would be with Julia Roberts.

Jaquith helps execute the Cinderella myth embedded in this particular melo-drama. The genre demands, however, more than physical and emotional trans-formation. Sexual transformation must occur as well. Jaquith provides the paternal guidance. Jerry, an architect with a European accent, provides the sex-ual awakening. Charlotte meets Jerry on a cruise. This is an important moment in her life. In a flashback to an embarrassing moment in her past, on another cruise, we learn the reason for her repression: her mother caught her making love to one of the ship's crew. The incident is coded to indicate that the mother's oppression of Charlotte's sexual awakening had lasting effects on her sexuality, constricting her, bringing her to that condition so abhorred by melodrama—and the culture that melodrama addresses—of being an old maid.

In melodrama, repressed sexuality is a standard starting point, liberated sex-uality its apparent goal, moderated sexuality its favored closure. *Now, Voyager* pursues this path with relentless determination. In Brazil (Latin America being a stereotyped place of the erotic in classic American cinema), Charlotte and Jerry fall in love and make love, in the spaces of a fade-out between a glowing fireplace and its afterglow embers—a lovely substitution for the physical con-tact the censors forbade showing on the screen. Their affection is signaled by one of those great Hollywood inventions that hooks a film into our imagination. Jerry begins a habit of lighting two cigarettes in his mouth. One is for himself; the other he hands to Charlotte. The gesture is repeated many times in the film, and, with the recurring theme music on the sound track, it becomes a correlative of the couple's passion. The critic Thomas Elsaessar points out that in film melodrama, music and mise-en-scène often express the excess of emotion experienced by the characters. The lighting of the two cigarettes in *Now, Voyager* and the swelling sound track that accompanies it are excellent examples of gesture, movement, and sound that express to us a world of emotion.

As if in response to her daughter's romance, Charlotte's mother feigns illness and a crippling fall in an attempt to reclaim her daughter, who wavers momentarily and, out of touch with Jerry, thinks she will marry a local Bostonian of good family. She also discovers that Jerry is married. This decline and dangerous reversal are an important part of melodramatic structure, which depends upon graphing our emotions in predictable patterns. Having shown Charlotte a way out of her misery, melodrama insists on letting her—and the viewer— know that a return to the darkness is not far out of sight. Suspense and fear for the central character are constructed by means of comparing where she was, how far she has come, and how tentative her liberation remains. The female character of melodrama is always on a precipice, with the narrative line acting as a kind of tightrope, and we are depended upon to agonize over the chances of her falling back to where she was.

So tentative is Charlotte's situation that she winds up back in Dr. Jaquith's sanitarium, where a series of events occurs that is less important as a matter of story than indicative of what melodrama must do to recuperate its characters, even at the expense of strained credulity. The intolerable paradox of melodrama is that the liberation of its characters is also their transgression. To make themselves free they break culture's rules and have to pay. Through Jaquith's intervention and Jerry's intimacy, Charlotte achieves a degree of sexual freedom and emotional maturity. But a narrative and cultural tension is thereby created. As

FIGURE 8.14 Cinderella in melodrama. Charlotte, in her ugly, repressed state, with Dr. Jaquith.

FIGURE 8.15 Charlotte liberated, beautiful, romantic with Jerry (*Now, Voyager*, Irving Rapper, 1942).

far as our identification with the character in her narrative is concerned, her freedom is a relief and our emotions soar with her. Charlotte has become an independent agent. But in terms of what is culturally allowable, what she has done is impossible.

In film, and perhaps still in the culture at large, a woman cannot express an independent, joyful sexual freedom outside of marriage without paying some price. Certainly, in the early 1940s, when restrictions on the representations of sexuality in film were stronger than they are now, Charlotte could not be permitted to go much further in her explorations of independence. But, in fact, little has changed. In the wake of the feminist movement there have been many films about liberated women. Most of them always compromise their female characters in one way or another. If such a film is a comedy, the strong-willed woman will be convinced that marriage is the only final outlet for her energies. This is not surprising, given the fact that, as a genre going back to Shakespeare and earlier, comedy ends in marriage. Marriage remains the ritual representation of harmony and rebirth in most cultures, the joyous reproduction of the family, and the unstated representation of sexual containment. If the film is a melodrama, the unrepressed woman is as often as not depicted as crazy or evil, threatening the man and his family. Think about three Michael Douglas films, *Fatal Attraction* (Adrian Lyne, 1987), *Basic Instinct* (Paul Verhoeven, 1992), and *Disclosure* (Barry Levinson, 1994), films made as part of the backlash against feminism.

Crazy if repressed, crazy if unrepressed, melodrama catches women in a double bind and allows few escapes other than death or a falling back into some barely tolerable compromise. The latter is what happens to Charlotte in *Now, Voyager*. In Jaquith's sanitarium, she meets a depressed little girl, the double of Charlotte in her former state. She nurses the child back to mental stability and discovers she is Jerry's daughter, product of an unhappy marriage in which Jerry nobly remains because his wife is an invalid. The metaphor of sickness and health overwhelms the film. Disease is melodrama-friendly, because it represents people in extreme states. Curing disease, or succumbing to it, parallels melodrama's accordionlike structure of repression or restriction, expanding outward to emotional or physical health and then collapsing again into a more culturally acceptable situation of moderated health and constrained emotional activity, or death. James L. Brooks's *Terms of Endearment* (1983), which seems to begin as a romantic comedy, ends with the onslaught of fatal disease that reawakens a mother's love for her daughter. Karl Franklin's *One True Thing* (1998) coaxes a daughter away from an independent life to care for her dying mother. The local fiction of any given melodrama is less important than the dominant fiction of sickness in body or mind that produces sacrificial acts on the part of one family member or another.

As the reigning metaphor of *Now, Voyager*, the cycle of sickness and health is passed from one character to another—to Charlotte, her mother, Jerry's wife, and his daughter. Charlotte gets well. But her cure is entirely local. She's happy, but her happiness does not satisfy the film's or the culture's melodramatic requirements. Individual happiness is never sufficient for melodrama. Perhaps because it has never completely shaken off its class origins, perhaps because audiences find insufficient gratification in a character whose happiness is complete, melodrama must do something to temper events. A selfish indulgence in sexuality might do well for Charlotte the fictional character, but it does not satisfy cultural demands for self-sacrifice and moderate behavior, qualities found if not always in life then in the ideal representation of life in melodrama. Melodrama mediates between desire and social probity, what we want and what the culture thinks it should allow. Its characters must conform to the impossible demands to be free *and* restricted, liberated *and* domesticated, sexual *and* chaste. For Charlotte, and all her predecessors and heirs throughout the history of film worldwide, a series of internal mediations is the only means to salvation. She must bring her desires down to a manageable level and recontain her passions in a semblance of respectability.

She will not marry Jerry. She will not return to her mother's domination. She chooses to become a surrogate mother. She will care for Jerry's daughter, sublimating her passion for him through the child. Sex is out. Marriage is out. Sacrifice is the key. Liberation from emotional repression is gained by means of another kind of repression. "Don't let's ask for the moon," Charlotte tells Jerry, after he lights two cigarettes and asks if she will be happy, "we have the stars." Why ask for passion, when our ideal love is mediated through the innocence of a child and the perfection of being close and separate at the same time? This is not happiness, only its perpetual promise. The music swells.

Melodrama's insistence on self-sacrifice or self-denial is a trait even more remarkable than its excessive emotions or piling up of incredible coincidence. It is more remarkable because self-sacrifice is largely an invisible trait. Hysteria and passion can be made visible in the mise-en-scène and audible on the sound track. Self-sacrifice is an internal condition, the external manifestation of which is usually *not* doing something rather than taking a visible action. Therefore, unless the act of sacrifice is the ultimate one of dying, melodrama asks us to build our own response to the negative gesture of the character, to Charlotte's withdrawal from adult contact in order to love Jerry through his daughter. Sometimes, if a film is part of a larger social movement, the negative sacrifice can be given positive, even political overtones.

Casablanca

I mentioned that *Casablanca* has parallels to *Now, Voyager*. Rick gives up his beloved Ilsa (Ingrid Bergman) to Victor Laszlo (played by Paul Henreid, who is Jerry in *Now, Voyager*) and turns to Captain Renault (Claude Rains, who plays Dr. Jaquith) for the greater good of the war effort in *Casablanca*. As in its companion film, sexuality is again repressed, but here in the name of political allegiance. Rick is very much the melodramatic figure in this film. He suffers for his love, overcomes—or represses—it in the name of getting involved in the French Resistance against the Nazis with his old enemy and friend, Captain Renault. "Our problems don't amount to a hill of beans in this crazy world," he tells Ilsa, as he allows her to fly to safety with Victor and he goes off with Renault to fight the good fight. Like Charlotte, Rick represses his love for a cause, though in this case a global, political one.

But women still prevail, despite the occasional appearance of vulnerable and sensitive men, as the main sufferers in melodrama. Charlotte, after freeing herself from her mother's domination, willingly falls under Jerry's by becoming his daughter's surrogate mother. Women sacrifice their desires for freedom and self-expression by reclaiming a cultural respectability that affirms the gross imbalance of conventional gender behavior. Ilsa, in *Casablanca*, gives up her love for Rick to support her husband, even as Rick gives up Ilsa because he knows Victor's cause is bigger than his own emotions. Even in contemporary melodrama, where the conventional ideologies of family and self-sacrifice have become ever more strongly posited, we see women gaining freedom and then returning to the family fold. Women are still seen as instigators and victims of distraught and failing femininity. Other contemporary melodramas return to the vulnerable male syndrome we saw operating in the fifties. James L. Brooks' *As Good as It Gets* (1997) has a deeply flawed, profoundly neurotic male character at its center, a writer suffering obsessive-compulsive disorder. To this nerve-wracking center is drawn a simple waitress who must give herself to the man's often obnoxious behavior in a great act of self-sacrifice. Through her sacrifice, the man softens: he is—and this is a typical melodramatic trait—"redeemed," which has become Hollywood language for "behaving a bit better."

Because Hollywood and the rest of world cinema is never finished with melodrama, neither are we. To end the final chapter of this book, I will compare three melodramas, each based on the same idea, made in three different periods by three very different directors. They will serve, in a sense, to summarize all we have been talking about regarding film, form, and culture.

Film Noir

In the mid-1940s a new genre developed, though it might be more correct to say that it invented itself. The genre, which was named film noir some years after it appeared, changed some elements of melodrama and disrupted some Hollywood stereotypes about gender and the inevitability of sacrifice and suffering. Hollywood didn't know it was making a new genre as the elements of noir were put into place. Neither filmmakers nor film viewers were aware, at least on a conscious, articulate level, that a new story was being told to them in a new visual style. It was the French in the 1950s who finally recognized that something was happening and gave it a name. But this does not mean that film noir was born out of nothing. Like any other genre, it came forth as a response to cultural need and developed out of cinematic elements already in existence.

During the Nazi occupation of France (1940–44) there was an embargo on American films. *Citizen Kane* wasn't seen in Paris until early in 1946, five years after it was made. At war's end, American films flooded into France, a country that has had a deep and serious love of cinema since its invention. An eager group of young intellectuals—including François Truffaut and Jean-Luc Godard, who would go on to be immensely influential filmmakers, the French New Wave—began watching these films with an intense interest. They had a good location in which to do this, the Paris Cinémathèque, run by Henri Langlois, who showed whatever films he could get his hands on, twelve hours a day. They watched everything they could and especially loved American films, the spoken language of which they couldn't understand. They learned what they needed from the visual narrative, the images and their construction. They noted across the films of the mid-forties a darkening of visual style and a darkening of thematic content. After a series of French detective stories called *Série noire*, one of these critics gave the name "film noir" to this new kind of film. But noir went far beyond the detective genre.

Expressionist Roots of Noir

Three main currents fed into the development of noir: German Expressionism, the hard-boiled detective fiction of the thirties, and the cultural turmoil of World War II. Noir's visual style harks back to the Expressionist movement in German film, literature, theater, and painting that flourished after World War I that had a major influence on the Universal Pictures horror films and on Welles's *Citizen Kane*. I described this influence in Chapter 3, but it is important to repeat that Welles's dark and deep mise-en-scène, its combination of **chiaroscuro** lighting and deep-focus cinematography that creates a mysterious world in which space is both inviting and threatening, had a major influence on noir.

Because its story was too closely modeled on the life of the newspaper magnate and millionaire William Randolph Hearst, who tried to have the film destroyed, and who refused to advertise it in his papers, *Citizen Kane* was not a commercially successful film. But even though its popular appeal took many years to form, its appeal to movie professionals was immediate. Directors, cinematographers, and production designers were taken by its radical style, which depended so much on the visual structures of Expressionism. The influence of Welles and his cinematographer, Gregg Toland, on the style of forties cinema was enormous. Darkness descended on Hollywood filmmaking.

Hard-Boiled Fiction

Citizen Kane was the main conduit into film noir, fed by the tributary of German Expressionism as well as some late thirties French film. Another source of influence came from literature. In the 1930s, a popular school of detective-fiction writers emerged, the most famous of whom were Raymond Chandler and Dashiell Hammett. Their work became known as the hard-boiled school of detective fiction, and they were masterful at creating visions of a dark, corrupt underworld of dopers and robbers, of sexual exploiters and an omnipresent immorality infiltrated by their cynical but morally secure detective characters—Hammett's Sam

Spade and Chandler's Philip Marlowe. Their detectives were unheroic, ironic, self-aware, but also persevering, cunning but flawed and vulnerable, barely surviving their exploits with their moral centers intact.

A third figure connected with this school did not write detective fiction. James M. Cain told stories of sleazy, lower-middle-class families falling apart under the pressures of infidelity, murder, and general moral corruption. Almost all his novels—*Double Indemnity, Mildred Pierce, The Postman Always Rings Twice*—were made into films in the forties. Cain's work and that of the hard-boiled school did not fit well with the Hollywood of the thirties, however, burdened as it was with its self-imposed censorship code and need to provide ideological uplift for a Depression-ridden culture. But this wasn't for lack of trying. Warner Brothers had acquired rights to Hammett's *The Maltese Falcon* very early on and filmed it twice during the thirties, once as a Bette Davis vehicle. They didn't actually get it right, though, until 1941, when John Huston directed the film with Humphrey Bogart as Sam Spade. During the thirties, MGM was more successful with Hammett's *The Thin Man*, which the studio made as a series of **screwball comedies**—bright, fast-paced narratives about an upper-class married couple who drink a lot and verbally spar with each other while they do a bit of detective work on the side.

The Maltese Falcon

The 1941 version of *The Maltese Falcon* was not a comedy, though it did have a more ironic and wry tone than its predecessors. It is also somewhat slower paced and more intensely composed and cut than most films of the thirties. It maintains much of Hammett's tough-guy dialogue, and it catches the sense of an infinitely corrupted world that was difficult to do in thirties studio film. Visually, while the film was darker in tone than was usual during the preceding decade, it did not employ the deep chiaroscuro that would occur in films after the appearance of *Citizen Kane*. That darkness began to take over about 1944.

Murder, My Sweet; Double Indemnity; Scarlet Street

The third current that made film noir possible occurred outside of film. The darkness of noir owes much to the darkening mood of the culture during and right after the war. Noir's themes of male isolation and weakness, of female treachery and murderousness, grow out of a multitude of insecurities occurring in the American psyche—events we discussed in Chapter 7. These themes infiltrated film noir through both form and content. The genre's visual darkness and its obsessive, damaged men reflected the culture's anxious postwar state.

Three landmark films solidified the look and the thematics of the new genre in 1944 and 1945. RKO, the studio that made *Citizen Kane*, produced an adaptation of Raymond Chandler's novel, *Farewell My Lovely*, directed by Edward Dmytryk, that they called *Murder, My Sweet*. Presumably the name was changed because the film was a vehicle for Dick Powell, a lead player in musicals, who

FIGURE 8.16 The palpable slats of light from the venetian blinds become a visual convention in forties cinema. Note how the play of light becomes a prominent part of the composition, the human figure turning into an aspect of the mise-en-scène (*Double Indemnity*, Billy Wilder, 1944).

was attempting to broaden his acting capacity; the studio feared that audiences would think the original title would be interpreted as another Dick Powell musical. *Murder, My Sweet* is among the best of the Chandler adaptations. Powell delivers Philip Marlowe's voice-over narration with a grim irony, while the world the characters inhabit is bathed not in thirties light but in darkness only occasionally relieved by light. "I'm a little man in a dirty job," Marlowe says at one point, a comment that exemplifies the reduced existential circumstances of the noir male in a world he cannot quite see through, cannot accurately detect.

In the same year, 1944, the German director Billy Wilder made *Double Indemnity* for Paramount. Based on a James M. Cain novel with a screenplay by Raymond Chandler, it synthesized noir's essential generic elements—bitterly ironic dialogue, a weak male character who falls prey to a female predator, and a mise-en-scène not quite as dark as *Murder, My Sweet* but unrelentingly gray and claustrophobic. The film contains some rare (for its time) exterior footage: a nighttime city street is pierced by the headlights of a careening car and the spark of a workman's blowtorch; a gray suburban Los Angeles street, its cracks filled with veins of black asphalt, adds to the pervading atmosphere of limited, sleazy lives. Interiors are dusty and gray. The living room of Phyllis Dietrichson—the woman who lures the poor insurance salesman, Walter Neff, to murder her husband and finally shoots him and is shot by him in turn—is cut through with light coming from behind venetian blinds. The light makes palpable the swirling dust in the air. The image of the shadowy slits of light from venetian blinds occurs in almost every forties film from this point on.

Double Indemnity can be read two ways. It is either a misogynist film about a terrifying, destroying woman, or it is a film that liberates the female character from the restrictive and oppressed melodramatic situations that render her helpless. Feminist critics are divided in their views of the film and the noir genre as a whole. If it is in fact a film that gives its female character more strength and control, it no longer situates her as the secure center of the family but its destroyer; it marks a shift in the dominant fiction that speaks of women's passivity. However, the fact that both she and her doomed male prey die at the end diminishes its radical potential. What is unambiguous is the film's attitude toward such sacred cultural institutions and generic mainstays as the protective family and the brave, heroic, self-possessed male.

Walter Neff is dying from the very beginning of the film, which is narrated in flashback as, slowly bleeding to death from Phyllis's gunshot, he dictates his sorry tale onto a recording machine in his office. And while Neff is never self-pitying and remains verbally dexterous and self-deprecating in his story, he is also clearly a loser, whose lust for Phyllis undoes his reason and self-control. Phyllis, we learn, creates families in order to destroy them. The family into which Walter comes, as an insurance man trying to make a sale, are a bunch of snarling whiners. Phyllis's husband is fully worthy of the death she plans for him. She manipulates first him and then Walter through a morally (and visually) gray world of cheap houses, crowded office buildings, supermarkets, and dark railroad tracks where Walter dumps the husband's body. There is as little sentimentality in this narrative as Hollywood could allow.

The following year, Fritz Lang, another director from Germany and an important figure in the Expressionist movement, made a film called *Scarlet Street*. Here, a meek, henpecked husband, Christopher Cross (played by Edward G. Robinson, an actor from the early gangster film days, who plays Walter Neff's boss and would-be friend, Keyes, in *Double Indemnity*), becomes sexually in thrall to a young woman named Kitty. His enthrallment is climaxed by the kind of image Hollywood loves to use to indicate male debasement: he paints her toenails. Painting is a major issue in this classic noir film. Chris Cross is a would-be painter, and Kitty has her boyfriend, Johnny, pass off Chris's work as hers. Chris kills Kitty in a rage, and Johnny is sentenced for the crime. The meek man is given power only through his reaction to being played a chump, and though Johnny deserves killing for many reasons, his execution is the cause of overwhelming guilt, borne by the ironically named Chris Cross.

This grim little narrative is given considerable substance by Lang's ability to reproduce the desire and paranoia, the failure and miserable triumph of his meek and hopeless main character. The narrative is given existential portent in its climax, as Chris becomes a kind of eternally guilty everyman. He becomes a street person, wandering a city that is empty of other people. He is the only man alive, carrying his despair alone.

Scarlet Street announces a universal anxiety and a reduction of individual agency that are usually associated with great modernist literary fiction. The point is made over and over again by film noir. The world is dark and corrupt. Women are predators. Men are either violent and brutal or the passive, unwary prey of the violent or the sexual. Any way out is hard to see. As one film noir character says, "I feel all dead inside. I'm backed up in a dark corner and I don't know who's hitting me." All of this is remarkable in a cinema usually devoted to the bright and harmonious or to the safe excesses and reassuring closures of melodrama. While none of the filmmakers had a term for the genre that rapidly took over production across the studios, the darkness reigned, and by the mid-forties, most films from Hollywood that were not comedies shared some noir characteristics, even if only the core image of a room banded by shadows of light coming through venetian blinds.

Anthony Mann

One figure stands out in film noir's mature period in the late forties. Anthony Mann, collaborating with his cinematographer John Alton, created among the darkest, most misanthropic films of the genre. His characters are cold and merciless; extraordinary acts of violence explode unexpectedly; and his mise-en-scène is the darkest, his compositions the most disorienting until Welles's *Touch of Evil*. Mann took noir seemingly as far as it could go, turning the screen in films like *T-Men* (1947), *Raw Deal* (1948), *Side Street* (1950) into a tunnel of despair and anxiety. He even made a film noir Western, *The Furies* (1950), before he turned to color cinematography and a string of Westerns we'll discuss in the following chapter. He ended his career making sword and sandal epics, and was Kirk Douglas's director on *Spartacus*, before being replaced by Stanley Kubrick.

Noir's Climax

In a Lonely Place

Noir lasted through the early fifties, climaxed by four films that were very self-conscious of what they were doing. Nicholas Ray's *In a Lonely Place* (1950) combines elements of noir with the male melodrama we discussed earlier. Humphrey Bogart, who had helped form the male noir character in *The Maltese Falcon* and *The Big Sleep* (Howard Hawks's 1946 adaptation of Raymond Chandler's novel, screenplay co-written by William Faulkner), constructs a figure of repressed rage, a screenwriter who lives in the shadows of his own uncontainable violence. He is recessive and aggressive at the same time, and when he emerges into the light and falls in love, he is undone by his rage. *In a Lonely Place* is as complex and moving an analysis of male angst and the turmoils of gender as exists in the canon of American cinema. This is the rare American film that allows the fact—indeed, the "reality"—that love may not, actually, conquer all; that differences in gender response may be insuperable; and that the central characters and their narrative may not be resolved.

The Wrong Man

Alfred Hitchcock's *The Wrong Man* (1956) took a "true story" and created a quasi-documentary style to narrate the events of an ordinary family man accused, arrested, and tried for robbery. His wife sinks into madness as a result of the events. Much of the film—visually as dark and claustrophobic as Hitchcock ever made—doggedly follows the process of its central character's incarceration and trial. It has a slow, almost trancelike pace and refuses to mitigate its characters' unrelenting misery. Even more than *Scarlet Street*, made over a decade earlier, it uses the structures of noir to address the loss of individual power and identity in the post–World War II world.

Loss, powerlessness, the inability to pull out of oncoming chaos—the elements of a bad dream drifting from the individual unconscious into the culture at large—had marked noir from its beginning. Now near the end of its first cycle, these noir elements spoke to the fifties with even more immediacy. In a decade characterized by extreme governmental interference into the intellectual freedom of the country, by big corporate growth, by the construction of a myth of a super enemy ready to infiltrate the very fabric of the culture, fifties paranoia was addressed quite profoundly by film noir as it was addressed somewhat less profoundly by the alien invasion science fiction film, a major fifties genre we will look at in the next chapter.

Kiss Me Deadly

Robert Aldrich's *Kiss Me Deadly* (1955) used the private detective version of film noir to address Cold War issues directly. The film is based on a novel by Mickey Spillane, who wrote vulgar, violent, woman-hating detective fiction that was enormously popular during the fifties. Aldrich's screen version of Spillane's detective, Mike Hammer, removes much of the vulgarity, turns the sexual violence into a peculiar kind of sexual reticence, but leaves the physical violence much intact. *Kiss Me Deadly* is about the search for a mysterious box that contains nuclear material. When opened, the box roars, screams, and glows with a deadly light: Quentin Tarantino got the idea for the mysterious suitcase with the golden light in *Pulp Fiction* from the mysterious box in *Kiss Me Deadly*. The box is discovered and opened by a curious woman—the film plays on the Pandora myth with a special fifties misogyny—and it blows up the world.

FIGURE 8.17   An example of intertextual allusion. The blinding light of an atomic device hidden in a box in Robert Aldrich's *Kiss Me Deadly* (1955).

FIGURE 8.18 Quentin Tarantino is thinking about Aldrich's bomb when he has Jules open the mysterious suitcase in *Pulp Fiction* (1994).

Noir is usually about implosion rather than explosion. But as the poet T. S. Eliot pointed out in the twenties, the end of the world does not have to come with a bang. A whimper is more likely, and a whimper is what's heard in *Scarlet Street* or *The Wrong Man* or *In a Lonely Place*. *Kiss Me Deadly* turns the whimper back into the more conventional bang. When light pierces through the noir darkness, the world comes apart. When the detective finds out the secret he's been looking for, he gets fried. This is the peculiar double-edged paranoia of the fifties. Men will collapse into lonely isolation, or, if they really find out the world's secret, they and everything else will be destroyed.

Touch of Evil

Between implosion and external destruction, there is another possibility. Create a world that appears as an ongoing nightmare of dizzying perspectives, long, dark streets, bizarre individuals careening around an unstable landscape of strip joints, hideous motels, oil fields, barren gray intersections, and open sewers. In other words, update the Expressionist vision to address the modern age. This is what Orson Welles does in *Touch of Evil* (1958), the last film noir of the genre's first cycle. It is fitting that this climactic film should be made by the director who originated the genre seventeen years earlier. Welles had been away from the United States, making films in Europe, for almost eight years and returned to find a project based on a second-rate novel about corrupt police, starring Charlton Heston as a Mexican cop. He took the challenge and created the most intriguing and inventive film noir to date. Filming mostly in the streets of Venice in Los Angeles, and inside actual buildings, Welles turned the "real world" into a bad dream of a border town trafficking in corruption, a local cop who plants evidence to catch his man (the cop is played by Welles himself, puffed up, limping, and growling), and a sappy, moral Mexican official out to save his country's name and protect his American bride.

Touch of Evil is, in part, an outsider's view of mid-fifties America just coming out of the grip of Joseph McCarthy and the anticommunist, evidence-fabricating witch hunts—a morass of moral and political corruption. It is also an ironist's attempt to play sympathy for the devil. Welles's Hank Quinlan, the corrupt cop—a Joseph McCarthy surrogate—is, in fact, weak and spiteful, out for revenge against "my dirty job." The world Welles creates for these characters, on the other hand, is of his imagination only, insinuated by his camera, which tracks, cranes, cants, sinks far below eye level and then rapidly cranes high above the characters. The long opening shot of *Touch of Evil* tracks a car moving through the dark labyrinth of a Mexican-American border crossing. The shot lasts for almost three minutes and is one of the most famous long takes in contemporary cinema. The camera articulates the characters and the audience's perceptions of them by means of dizzying, off-center compositions and enfolds them in its dark, nightmare world. It is the definition of how mise-en-scène can be created.

Noir's Rebirth

There was not very much further one could go past *Touch of Evil* in creating a dark, decaying, Expressionist mise-en-scène. The genre was spent, and films were beginning to respond to television in ways that made noir obsolete. The deeply shadowed black and white of the forties was giving way to a more evenly graded spectrum of gray tones in the fifties. Then in the sixties, black and white gave way to color. Since film noir was so essentially dependent on the dark end of the black and white spectrum, a move to color would seem to mark the end of its visual life, despite at least one notable noir color experiment,

FIGURE 8.19   The apotheosis of film noir. The urban landscape: dark, vertiginous, threatening (Orson Welles, *Touch of Evil*, 1958).

Henry Hathaway's *Niagara* (1953). But color turned out to be a very flexible medium. To understand why, a review of the short history of color film is necessary.

Film had always been tinted and toned in the silent period, with a red tint signifying passion, blue standing for night, gold for day. Experiments with a more "realistic" color stock began in the early twenties, and the three-color Technicolor process was introduced in the early thirties. Color remained a specialty process until the early sixties, used mainly for musicals and fantasy films (that's why the Oz portions of the *Wizard of Oz*, 1939, are in Technicolor). Realism required black and white. We have been discussing all along how convention-alized film is, how it is based on repeated patterns and recognizable structures. This is nowhere more apparent than in the fact that "reality" for film before the sixties meant black and white cinematography. Of course there is nothing in-herently "realistic" in either color or black and white. The latter was considered "real" only because it was the dominant mode and color wasn't. But that changed in the sixties. By the early sixties, television began to broadcast in color, and, because the final distribution point for any film is the television screen, by the end of the decade, all films had to be made in color.

The influence of film noir was powerful, and young filmmakers, many com-ing out of film school in the late sixties and early seventies, felt a response sim-ilar to that felt by those French intellectuals in the early fifties: the discovery of something extraordinary in the style and content of American film from the for-ties and early fifties. They began to revive noir, rethink it in color, and use noir as a way to make color cinematography responsive to their imaginative needs. Arthur Penn made a key film in the noir revival in *Night Moves* (1975), and Martin Scorsese was at the center of the revival. *Taxi Driver* (1976) captures the dark Expressionism of original film noir, with its creation of an urban landscape that reflects the paranoia of its main character more thoroughly than any film since *Touch of Evil*. Many films are now referred to as noir that are not, though the call of darkness and helplessness seems to come from deep within our mas-ter narratives and continue to be given form—and now even parody—in the dominant fictions of film. The genre named by the French became, by the sev-enties, a genre recognized by many filmgoers. By the eighties, *TV Guide* was re-ferring to film noir in its listings. In 1984, there was a nightclub sequence in *The Terminator*. The club is named "Tech Noir."

Notes and References

The Master and the Dominant   The term "dominant fiction" is suggested by Kaja Silverman in *Male Subjectivity at the Margins* (New York and London: Routledge, 1992). For a theory of the *end* of master narratives in the postmodern age, see Jean-François Lyotard, *The Postmodern Condition: A Report on Knowledge*, trans. Geoff Bennington and Brian Massumi (Minneapolis: University of Minnesota Press, 1984). An ideological reading of genre can be found in Robin Wood, "Ideology, Genre, Auteur," in *Film Theory and Criticism*, pp. 717–26. See also Terry Lovell, *Pictures of Reality: Aesthetics, Politics, and Pleasure* (London: BFI, 1980).

Censorship   David Cook presents an excellent history of Hollywood censorship in *A History of Narrative Film*, 4th ed. (New York: W. W. Norton, 2004), pp. 236–39.

Genre and Gesture   François Delsarte was a nineteenth-century Frenchman who codified dramatic facial expressions and gestures in the nineteenth century.

Generic Origins There is some interesting discussion about the tension between genre and individual expression in Leo Braudy's *The World in a Frame* (Garden City, N.J.: Anchor Press & Doubleday, 1976), and by Robert Warshow in his essay "Movie Chronicle: The Western" in the collection *Film Theory and Criticism*, pp. 703–16. A good theoretical discussion of film genre is done by Steven Neale, *Genre* (London: British Film Institute, 1983). See also Robin Wood's "Ideology, Genre, Auteur," in *Film Theory and Criticism*, pp. 717–26.

Generic Patterns: The Gangster Film A lively history of the Warner Brothers gangster film and biography of its stars is in Robert Sklar, *City Boys* (Princeton, NJ: Princeton University Press, 1992).

Documentary A useful history of documentary is Richard Meran Barsam, *Nonfiction Film: A Critical History* (Bloomington: Indiana University Press, 1992). A strong analysis of Leni Riefenstahl's work is in Susan Sontag's essay "Fascinating Fascism," in *A Susan Sontag Reader* (New York: Vintage, 1982). For current theory on nonfiction film, see Bill Nichols, *Representing Reality: Issues and Concepts in Documentary* (Bloomington: Indiana University Press, 1991). The quote from Grierson comes from *Grierson on Documentary*, ed. Frosyth Hardy (New York: Praeger, 1971), p. 289. For an interview with the Maysles brothers, see my "Circumstantial Evidence" in *Sight and Sound* (Autumn 1971), pp. 183–86.

Melodrama There are two excellent anthologies of essays on melodrama and film: Marcia Landy, ed., *Imitations of Life: A Reader of Film and Television Melodrama* (Detroit: Wayne State University Press, 1991); and Christine Gledhill, ed., *Home Is Where the Heart Is* (London: BFI, 1987). The standard essay is Thomas Elsaesser's "Tales of Sound and Fury: Observations on the Family Melodrama," reprinted in *Home Is Where the Heart Is*.

Film Noir So much has been written on noir, but the best remains an essay by the screenwriter (of *Taxi Driver*, among others) and director Paul Schrader, "Notes on Film Noir," *Film Comment* 8 (Spring 1972). A good visual analysis is offered by J. A. Place and L. S. Peterson, "Some Visual Notes on Film Noir," in Bill Nichols, ed., *Movies and Methods*, vol. 1 (Berkeley and Los Angeles: University of California Press, 1976), pp. 325–38. See also Frank Krutnik, *In a Lonely Street: Film Noir, Genre, Masculinity* (London and New York: Routledge, 1991); and James Naremore, *More Than Night: Film Noir in Its Contexts* (Berkeley: University of California Press, 1998). For a feminist reading, see E. Ann Kaplan, ed., *Women in Film Noir* (London: BFI, 1980).

Expressionist Roots of Noir The best work on German Expressionism is Lotte Eisner's *The Haunted Screen*, cited in Chapter 3. An interesting cultural study of the thirties horror film is in David Skal, *The Monster Show* cited in the same chapter.

Double Indemnity Walter Neff is played by Fred MacMurray, until this time an actor in light comedy. Like Dick Powell, he used a noir film to change his style. Phyllis is played by Barbara Stanwyck. For discussion of whether noir elaborates a destruction of the women-based family or merely recuperates it, see Claire Johnston, "Double Indemnity," in the previously cited *Women in Film Noir,* pp. 100–11; and Joyce Nelson, "Mildred Pierce Reconsidered," in Bill Nichols, ed., *Movies and Methods,* vol. 2 (Berkeley and Los Angeles: University of California Press, 1985). The quotation "I feel all dead inside . . ." is from Henry Hathaway's *Dark Corner* (1946) and is quoted in Frank Krutnik's *In a Lonely Street: Film Noir, Genre, Masculinity,* p. 101. The implied destruction of the world at the end of *Kiss Me Deadly* is apparently a studio addition. In a recent "director's cut," the detective and his girlfriend escape.

Touch of Evil   There is a wonderful sequence in Tim Burton's film *Ed Wood* (1994) in which the momentarily dispirited director of very bad films goes into a dark bar in the middle of a bright Hollywood day. He finds Orson Welles sitting in a corner working on a script. "Tell me about it," Orson tells Ed Wood. "I'm supposed to do a thriller at Universal, but they want Charlton Heston to play a Mexican!" The long take at the beginning of *Touch of Evil* is lovingly parodied in the opening of Robert Altman's film *The Player.* Altman makes his shot even longer, and the characters who move around in it keep referring to Welles's film.

9 THE STORIES TOLD BY FILM II

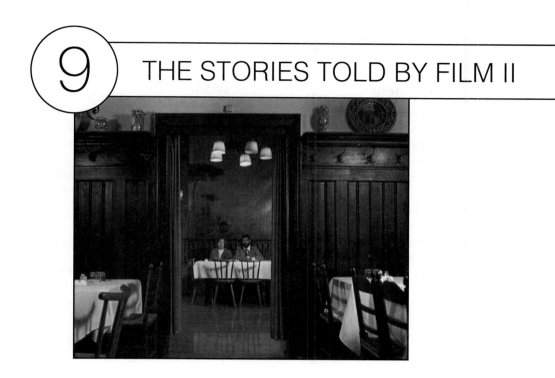

OTHER GENRES: THE WESTERN

Film grows out of ideology and cultural desire and feeds back into them. Sometimes, when the ideology shifts radically or the desire is redirected by history, a genre can either vanish or go into a recessive state. The Western film is an interesting example of a genre that bent and then snapped under shifting ideological pressures, perhaps because it was the genre most tightly connected to our country's historical legends.

The Western began practically at the same time as narrative film and went on to become one of its most popular genres. It was invented and continued composing our myths of the American frontier and the white man's destiny, an embodiment of the 1840s' doctrine of "Manifest Destiny"—the inexorable movement of European civilization westward to the Pacific, destroying everyone in its path. Western films drew on the nineteenth-century literature of the West, but quickly established their own generic patterns. The Western's settings of chaparral or desert, of small, dusty frontier towns bordering on vast, open land, created a representation of the culture's wilderness fantasies that may have existed, but were set in memory through movies, and they became part of its visual conventions. Narratives of white settlers fighting savages, of heroic gunmen protecting small communities from outlaws, were rapidly set and confirmed our belief in the rightness of expansion and in the structuring authority of law and order. They confirmed for us as well that there were always enemies that threatened "our way of life." Gender was another structuring principle. The creation of the civilized community in the heart of the wilderness, so essential to the Western narrative, involved the melodrama of women creating the cultural hearth in a barren land where men broke horses and shot Indians and outlaws and then returned to the domesticity they helped secure. All of this seemed to reassure the audience that our movement West was close to a divine imperative. After all, settling the West made our current life possible.

Many pre-fifties Westerns were anonymous studio products, some with unusual casting, like Warner Brothers' *The Oklahoma Kid* (Lloyd Bacon, 1939) with Warner Brothers' stock gangsters of the time, Humphrey Bogart and James Cagney, playing cowboys. There were Gene Autry and Roy Rogers movies—the singing cowboys who were fixtures of the genre. There were serials—ongoing Western narratives (among others), presented in one episode a week. There were studios, especially Republic Pictures, that specialized in the Western, repeating its stereotypes and clichés on a regular basis and all but inventing one of the classic Western codes, the hero in the white hat and the outlaw in black.

Landscape

Among the most important generic codes of the Western is its visual location, representing history and nation by means of visual space. The desert was at its center: open spaces, a big sky with large clouds—those "wide open spaces" that beckoned the cowboy hero, who wanted his freedom and in which he could act out his obligation to help create a safe domestic space. These are the same spaces that still lure our imagination, even as they quickly shrink. The counter to the open Western landscape is the enclosed town, and within it the closed domestic space—which finally closes the cowboy in as he becomes part of the very domestic sphere he fights to create and preserve. In some Westerns, the free spirit of the open range cannot be held within domestic bonds (unless the cowboy marries the schoolmarm) and so the genre winds up creating a space that makes him even more of a loner.

Therefore, two basic kinds of composition create Western spaces: the cowboy on the desert or plain, often fighting off Indians and outlaws, and the frontier community, often concentrating on its representative, the saloon in the town that needs cleaning up and made safe. Beyond the domestic space is a place of misrule and violent action, the saloon is the place in transition, and making both safe is the story the Western tells us. Its dominant fictions come from not only master narratives of national expansion, but also those that insist that the enemies of order (and therefore of expansion) must disappear.

The Obstacles to Westward Expansion

The Western posited a gender and racial basis of continental extension. The women of the West were largely the passive representatives of the *need* to pacify the western territories. Therefore two varieties of passivity are engendered in

the women of the West. Stereotyped as the "schoolmarm," they were the hold-
ers of knowledge and domesticity. The "schoolmarm" herself contains stereo-
typical remnants of the quiet, retiring woman who can thrive and teach only
when lone, heroic males cleared the wilderness. Therefore, passive by nature,
she had to have her very environment pacified—perhaps feminized—in order
for her and domesticity to thrive.

The racial basis of the Western is superficially simpler: Indians. The Western
wilderness took many forms: the desert itself, whose inhospitable barrenness
needed to be made green and secure; outlaws—white men who took the wilderness as land open for their violence—and the Indians. There is a large literature
on who the Indians actually were and what white people did to them. But until
the late 1960s movie Indians mostly conformed to old, cultural stereotypes of
the vicious savage, a flesh and blood representation of the wilderness itself, acting in opposition to the dreams of expansion. They were the "Other," barely
human, existing mainly to be destroyed. And therefore, from the beginning, the
Western represented the Indian as a violent obstacle that had to be obliterated.
"Circling the wagons" has become a cultural cliché, and it is repeated visually
in almost every Western film as a generic convention in which the travelers or
settlers must protect themselves from savage onslaughts.

The Western Star and the Western Director

Robert Warshow, one of the rare 1950s critics of popular culture to take film seriously, said that for a genre—the Western especially—to remain pure, it could
not be altered by an individual's style that tinkered with its conventions.
Warshow's argument is particularly cogent. Because a genre is made up of conventions negotiated between filmmakers and audience, tinkering with them,
adding personal touches, stretching their generic bounds, only complicates the
negotiating process that is essential for a genre to work. Too much tinkering and
the audience may simply refuse to negotiate.

Warshow imagined an ideal genre represented by what he considered clas-
sics of the form. He singled out William Wellman's *The Ox-Bow Incident* (1943)
and Stuart Gilmore's *The Virginian* (1946), and out of them built his ideal of the
West. The fact is that, although many directorial hands and many actors attempted Westerns, with varying degrees of success, the genre was dominated
by two men, the actor John Wayne and the director John Ford. They shaped it,
and Ford eventually pointed the way to its change and its ultimate move to a
recessive place. But that is getting ahead of ourselves. The point is that the
Western is a genre that owes much not only to the buildup of conventions, but
to the ways in which those conventions were inflected, shifted, and changed by
two individuals. At the same time, it confirms the fact that film is a complex mix
of collaboration and individual imagination.

Let's first consider the actor. John Wayne has been among the most admired actors during *and* after his life. His self-assuredness, swagger, and on-screen heroism and bravura made him the perfect film action hero. He was not the first

FIGURE 9.1 John Wayne's spectacular entrance in *Stagecoach* (John Ford, 1939). This filmstrip attempts to simulate the power of the tracking shot.

such—during the silent and early sound periods, Douglas Fairbanks emerged as perhaps the first universally admired action hero and there have been many since in a variety of films. Wayne himself starred in other genres, mainly war films, but he is best known as the moral and muscular figure in the Western landscape. His figure is part of the genre's landscape. His best director was John Ford.

Ford, too, directed other film genres, most famously such melodramas as *The Informer* (1935), *How Green Was My Valley* (1941), and *The Grapes of Wrath* (1940). He began his work in the Western as far back as *Cheyenne's Pal* (1917), gained renown with *The Iron Horse* in 1924, and solidified his connection with the Western with *Stagecoach* in 1939. *Stagecoach* launched John Wayne into stardom. He had a minor career before meeting up with Ford, but with this film, the two of them together began defining the West and the Western hero, and quite consciously and conspicuously. Wayne's first appearance in the film is by means of a fast dolly in, so fast that the camera goes briefly out of focus. Wayne's character, The Ringo Kid, is an "outlaw," but in a film that attempts to work out the right balance of morality in the West, he is an outlaw who protects the outcast and fights the Indians. His importance is marked by the way Ford introduces him.

Stagecoach is a Western road movie in which a collection of people—a gambler, a crooked banker (who is given a long, suspicious close-up when he mouths the cliché "what's good for the banks is good for the country," a comment bound to get a rise from a depression-era audience), a drunken, kindhearted doctor, who redeems himself by delivering a baby, a whiskey salesman, a "proper" lady, a whore with a heart of gold, who is being driven out of town, and Ringo—all traveling together on the coach, fighting Apaches, working out their moral differences, creating a small universe of character types that have to be reconciled with the new world of the West and have to reconcile that world to their own differences.

What were quickly becoming the genre's conventions are solidified, although the play on the outlaw as ultimately a moral hero already marks Ford as a director thinking about other directions he could drive those conventions. Ford's film not only presents stereotyped Indian savages, but fights sanctimony and fake moral virtue, taking another "outlaw" (the prostitute) to its heart, and then articulates that major generic element of settling down and creating domesticity in the wilderness.

Beyond the plot, other elements mark this as an important example of Ford's command of the genre. Much of the action is set in Monument Valley, which constitutes Ford's West throughout his filmmaking career. Here, as in all of his Westerns, he composed it from varying angles and with all the variations of lighting that were possible. He also treated interiors differently, putting ceilings on his sets, allowing the light to show the dust in the air. His compositions led Orson Welles to say that *Stagecoach* was his textbook before filming *Citizen Kane*. "I ran it over forty times."

Among the most important aspects of Ford's Westerns is the ways he kept pushing the genre. This is precisely what Warshow was worrying about—adulterating the genre by the intervention of individual imagination—and pre-

FIGURE 9.2 Of all the images in John Ford's films, this composition, from *My Darling Clementine*, his telling of the gunfight at the O.K. Corral (1946), can stand as his archetypal image. Just on the edge of town, a new church is being built: religion and the country (represented by the American flags) come together. In the background are the rocks of Monument Valley. The townspeople are joining together in a dance, which figures prominently in most of his Westerns. The new community, the frontier, the promise of harmony (through the dance) are all present in the frame.

cisely why Ford defined the genre and kept it exciting and meaningful as long as he could. He took the conventions, questioned and refreshed them. He rarely undid them, but he did make them respond to changes in the culture, particularly after World War II. He was able to take, if not an ironic, at least an ambiguous view—as in *Fort Apache* (1948), which pits a soldier (Wayne) against his superior, a rule-bound and ultimately dangerous man (Henry Fonda, playing against his usual nice guy type). The Indians are here depicted as more knowing than the military leader, part of their land and wise to its ways. The inability of the officer to understand Indians except as hateful brutes results in a rout of his troops. The military is brought into question—but only to a point. Wayne gives a rousing defense of the military at film's end.

In a late film, a kind of indoor Western, *The Man Who Shot Liberty Valence* (1962), the John Wayne character has settled the town and lives in the desert outside it. One vicious outlaw still reigns, however. A politician from the East comes to town and shoots him. Ford shows this event at two points, from two points of view, in the film. The story is being narrated by the politician, Ransom Stoddard (played by Jimmy Stewart and called "Pilgrim" by Wayne's Tom Doniphan), to a newspaper man, and he finally understands that it was not he but John Wayne who shot the outlaw. He insists the newsman tell the truth. The man refuses: "When the legend becomes fact, print the legend," he says. And this was the motto of all Westerns, until the legends no longer worked.

A few years earlier, Ford had made a film with Wayne called *The Searchers* (1956), which has become the most influential movie made in the United States, second only to *Citizen Kane*. The film is mirrored in Scorsese's *Taxi Driver*, in Lucas's first *Star Wars*, in Tarantino's *Kill Bill 2* (2004), and in almost every film by Steven Spielberg. The reason lies in its complexity and simplicity; its ability to question generic assumptions and confirm them simultaneously; its affirmation of the domestic enclosure against the wilderness; and, most important, the power of its images. The cyclical nature of the film, the door opening on the desert at the beginning and closing on it at the end, stays in memory like few others.

Some background is needed. Ford had already begun rethinking the genre in his late 1940s films. While still presenting the cavalry as heroic, he questioned some assumptions of the Western, even as he had done as far back as *Stagecoach*.

FIGURE 9.3 The opening shot of Ford's *The Searchers* (1956). Outside the cool dark of the homestead is the burning desert—Monument Valley, of course—out of which rides John Wayne's Ethan Edwards.

By the fifties, the Western film had reached the zenith of its popularity. The Western almost seemed necessary in order to confirm the culture's always tenuous faith in its rightness and strength. The genre sometimes became overtly political, as in the anti-McCarthy Westerns *Johnny Guitar* (Nicholas Ray, 1954) and *High Noon* (Fred Zinneman, 1952). In *High Noon*, the townspeople are cowards who refuse to help the sheriff face down the outlaws; they reflect the passivity of the country in the face of McCarthy's bullying. Ray's film is more complex. It too presents a community easily swayed by a leader with a grudge and turns lynching into a metaphor for the ease with which McCarthy could accuse and condemn his imagined enemies. Both these films also had women who were stronger and more active than their male counterparts. In *High Noon*, the sheriff's wife helps him gun down the outlaws as the town cowers. Johnny Guitar is a passive man, and the town's feud is between the two women characters. In fact, many fifties Westerns began to change the contours of the Western hero, though none as radically as *The Searchers*—this despite the fact that Ford was no liberal and, in fact, made documentaries for the CIA!

John Wayne's Ethan Edwards rides from out of the desert with a shady past and an obsessive hatred of Indians. When his family is wiped out and his niece taken captive, he swears revenge. Worse, he considers his niece no longer human because she has become a "squaw." His racism (he was a member of the Confederate army) is overwhelming and he spends five years hunting down her and her captor. The film is driven by one of the oldest master narratives, the captivity narrative. Its master narrative is the nation held captive by a stronger power. In the dominant fictions it creates, a woman (occasionally a man) is held captive by a vicious, murderous "other." The captivity narrative is played out in literary fiction and in film from its beginnings. It is carried out in the narratives of history itself, and has never lost its power. We have seen it at work in D. W. Griffith's films. The culture saw it in action during the Nazi takeover of Europe and destruction of the Jews. Master narratives can be played out in the everyday world. In *The Searchers*, it is turned to a fiction of obsession in which the hero is close to psychotic and even closer to the "savage" he claims so much to hate. Ethan's hatred of Indians seems to echo the obsessive anticommunism the culture was going through at the time: mindless and bordering on the criminal and insane.

Of course, when Ethan finally discovers her captor—an Indian who is almost his double—and finds his niece, he doesn't kill her. This was the fifties, after all, and like all of Ford's attempts to rework the genre, he allowed himself to go only so far. But the power of his revision, along with the power of the images he uses to create it, marks the film as the apex and perhaps the climax of the Western as it was to then.

The Western after the Fifties

By the end of the fifties the Western had perhaps been tinkered with too much; by the sixties, fact began to interfere with legend. A number of things happened to the Western that finally destroyed it. One was the series of extraordinary films made in Italy by Sergio Leone. *The Good, The Bad, and The Ugly* (1966) and its sequels and his huge homage to every Western ever made *Once Upon a Time in the West* (1968) exploded generic conventions to the proportions of grand opera, with huge, long held close-ups (see Figure 3.39), actions drawn out past any normal stress point, forcing the viewer to think about how we look at Westerns, not to mention how we think about cinematic time. Here, Warshow is almost proven right. A genre cannot take such self-examination.

The Western, so sensitive to history, was under attack from the outside by a growing awareness of the realities of America's expansion and by contemporary events that challenged Western myths. By the sixties, we could no longer, in good faith, hold on to old narratives of the savage Indians raping and pillaging. Indians were not "savages," but rather deeply spiritual builders of complex nations and laws. The truth of "Manifest Destiny" was that it was merely raw imperialism and destroyed the original inhabitants of the country. The Indians were not the bad guys. We were. The Vietnam war also put a temporary hold on those captivity narratives that drive us as a country to want to free the "oppressed," even when the oppressed are the liberators and we are not. The war against insurgents abroad reflected back on our stories of war against the original inhabitants of our own country.

Three films of the late sixties and early seventies—Sam Peckinpah's *The Wild Bunch* (1969), Arthur Penn's *Little Big Man* (1970), and Robert Altman's *McCabe and Mrs. Miller* (1971)—took these new realities, shifted the genre's conventional myths of male heroism even more than *The Searchers*, questioned the role of Indians, and even the place of women, on the frontier. They turned tables on the genre.

The Wild Bunch declared the end of the all-male community of gunfighters propounded by the Western and showed the violence of gunfighting as a terrible tearing up of the body. It also did what few earlier Westerns attempted: it examined the politics of violence, the male bond, and the taking of sides. *The Wild Bunch* was the most violent film since *Bonnie and Clyde*, two years earlier. Blood spurts in slow motion and its climactic sequence is a grand ballet of slaughter. But this is violence for a purpose. The film's heroes are old men at the end of the West. The best they can do is rob an army train to supply guns for the Mexican government fighting a peasant uprising. The parallels with Vietnam are clear. And, when the Bunch realize their mistake, all they can do is wipe out the Mexican fort and be destroyed themselves.

Little Big Man turned the relationship of Indian and white man on its head, declaring that the "savages" were really the "human beings" and the white men crazy. General Custer is depicted as a raving lunatic, and the Battle of Little Big Horn a righteous cause for the Indians. *McCabe and Mrs. Miller* showed the Western community as a cold place of mutual betrayal, the hero as the joke of his own legend, and women as the marginalized, self-protective maintainers of rationality and sexuality. McCabe is a bumbler in a town that is not enclosed in the open spaces, but in the constrained, freezing rain of the Northwest (see Figure 3.7). The film has an Indian and two outlaws, but they are the "hit squad" of the mining company that wants to take over the town. McCabe—who everyone in the town decides is a gunman—does, in fact, kill the three and is himself shot. However, the town church, which everyone had ignored, catches fire. In a sequence worthy of Griffith stood on his head, Altman cuts between the townspeople fighting the fire to save the town and McCabe dying alone in the snow, having saved the town. But unlike Griffith, the two parts of the editing structure do not come together. McCabe is buried in the snow; Mrs. Miller, the madam who literally has a heart of gold, the box in which she collects her money, withdraws to an opium den. As we noted in Chapter 6, Altman pulls and twists genres, taking them far past their borders, and creates worlds in which his often desperate and more than sometimes stupid heroes can't exist.

Both *The Wild Bunch* and *McCabe and Mrs. Miller* are elegiac films. They mourn the very genre they are taking apart. And it would be too strong to say that these and other films of the period destroyed the genre by themselves, but only that they were reflecting cultural changes that no longer allowed the Western to exist in its old forms. Certainly it has popped up again from time to time, most notably in the hands of Clint Eastwood. But Eastwood came to fame in Sergio Leone's operatic Westerns, and the influence is from them more than from the classic genre. That is gone and will never return. A genre exists only as long as history, culture, and the viewers who are the products of both can maintain belief in their conventions.

FIGURE 9.4   The smoke of modern weaponry, blood, and pain mark the end of the old West in *The Wild Bunch* (Sam Peckinpah, 1969).

FIGURE 9.5 "Whatever else you can say about them, it must be admitted you cannot get rid of them. . . . There is an endless supply of white men, but there has always been a limited number of human beings." With words and images like these, it was no longer possible to represent Indians as bloodthirsty savages (*Little Big Man*, Arthur Penn, 1970).

SCIENCE FICTION

Science fiction is another example of a genre that came from literature and appeared early in film, but, unlike the Western, it has been able to remake itself from decade to decade. One reason is obvious. Science fiction is about speculation—about the future, about alternatives to the present, about technology and its use and misuse. Science fiction is also, like the Western, open to allegory. It can tell one narrative that is wrapped around or infiltrated by another, which may be of cultural concern or political import. But, unlike the Western, its allegories are changeable from moment to moment. Like any other film, no matter when its narrative is supposed to take place, science fiction is about the present.

The generic conventions of science fiction are not as simple as the Western, partly because the genre pulls in so many elements. Some are from the outside: science fiction depends upon technological imagery, speculation on the use and misuse of science, images of outer space, and, of course, robots, computers, and aliens. When the latter are involved, we come to a complex mixture of genres: science fiction and the horror film. Think of Frankenstein and his monster: originating in an early nineteenth-century novel by Mary Wollstonecraft Shelley— wife of the poet—which addressed contemporary notions of creation, science, consciousness, and imagination. Frankenstein entered movies as early as 1910, when the Edison studios did a sixteen-minute adaptation. Of course, it's the 1931 Universal Pictures version, directed by James Whale and starring Boris Karloff, that has become part of film history. This film and Tod Browning's *Dracula*, made the same year, with Bela Lugosi as the blood sucker, are considered horror films, even though *Frankenstein* verges near to science fiction. They concern beings not quite of nature, horrors from the laboratory or the crypt. As we've seen, they and their many sequels throughout the decade and after drew heavily on German Expressionism, with its looming shadows and distorted spaces.

Fritz Lang's *Metropolis*

In 1927, in Germany, Fritz Lang made one of the first full-fledged science fiction films, *Metropolis*. Expressionist in set design and acting style, it is a politically complex film that seems at first glance to take the side of the oppressed workers, forced to live in a grotesque underground city, but concludes with a reactionary notion of joining the "head" of the owners with the "heart" of the workers. The film was written by Lang's wife at the time, who went on to write films for the Nazis.

Metropolis introduces important elements that, with its intersections of gigantic machinery, a mad scientist, and a robot, would become inseparable from the science fiction and the horror film. The term "robot" had only recently been introduced in 1920 by the Czech playwright, Karel Čapek, in his play *R.U.R.* (*Rossum's Universal Robots*), and quickly adopted after that. *Metropolis* is science fiction because it speculates on the future, creates what has been called a "visionary architecture" in its city of the imagination, and imagines the capabilities of science to create a robot and then make that robot humanlike. It is a horror film because the mad scientist, Dr. Rotwang, like Dr. Frankenstein, plays with nature and creates an inhuman form that then takes the life of a human being and creates tremendous discord.

Alien, *Blade Runner*, and *Dark City*

If we move forward many years and consider Ridley Scott's two extraordinary films, *Alien* (1979) and *Blade Runner* (1982), we see how the genres become inextricably mixed. *Alien* is a science fiction monster film in which the spaceship becomes a version of one of the major conventions of horror films, the Old Dark House, that place of mystery, threat, and fear that we find in a variety of places from Dracula's castle to Norman Bates's house in *Psycho*. In the unknown spaces of the spaceship the monster roams, devouring everyone except Commander Ripley (believe it or not), one of the few women heroes of the genre. *Blade Runner* develops in a direct line from *Metropolis*. It depicts a city, specifically Los Angeles, of the future—but, as is always the case in science fiction, a future based on the present. As we saw in the example of *Die Hard*, a reigning cultural myth of the eighties was that the Japanese were taking over the United States. Scott takes this contemporary myth and creates a Los Angeles that is all but a huge Asian slum, so overpopulated that "off world" colonies are created for those who can afford to escape.

In this fetid world, in a huge building like a modern version of an Aztec pyramid, a scientist has created robots—Replicants—to guard the colonies. Like Frankenstein, the Replicants gain self-consciousness. They are also given memories and a limited life span, which causes their rebellion as their consciousness develops. One, Roy Batty, kills his maker by taking out his eyes—seeing is an important metaphor in this film, seeing memories that may or may not be real or implanted. But also, the scientist is the "father" of the Replicants and Roy Batty, the longest lived and most self-conscious of them, takes his revenge in reverse Oedipal fashion. Rather than taking out his own eyes, he destroys the sight of his maker. Roy finally does epic battle with a policeman, whose job is to round up the errant robots, and Batty proves to have not only self-consciousness, but a soul and poetry.

To complicate things further, *Blade Runner* pulls in elements of film noir, with its dark city, its detective searching for evil and discovering—perhaps, though it's barely hinted at—that he's a replicant himself. Like Alex Proyas in *Dark City* (1998), a science fiction film whose very title comes from a 1950 film noir, and also has its root in *Metropolis*, Scott pulls genres into a mix that remains science fiction but revitalizes it with other conventions that merge together nicely.

Proyas's film *Dark City* turns the noir city of dreadful night into a dream of alien mind control, which turns out to be the unrealized desires of the city's inhabitants, themselves quite possibly the dreams of the aliens. All of noir's attributes, from the encompassing darkness to a nightclub scene that is almost a prerequisite in any forties noir, as well as specific borrowings from Fritz Lang's early Expressionist films, are at work in *Dark City*. It is one of the many "virtual world" films of the 1990s and early 2000s which, picking up on the virtual and immersive reality games of the digital world, and the parallel universes posited by science fiction literature (and quantum physics), as well as old master narratives of illusion versus reality, question the very trustworthiness of perception. Of course *The Matrix* films are the primary examples of this thread, but all the threads lead to the uncertainties of knowing and seeing, which constitute the very questions of cinema itself and which are taken up by many filmmakers, like Scott, and Kubrick in *2001: A Space Odyssey*, who concentrate their images on the fragile veil between what the astounded eye may or may not be seeing.

Science Fiction in the Fifties

Like the Western, science fiction bloomed like a flower in the desert during the 1950s, and it did so for very specific cultural/political reasons. My metaphor is not so fanciful, given the fact that the desert was the location of so many of these films, and the culture itself was living in a dry, scary place of political fear and accusations, of blacklistings and firings because of political views. This was the fertilizer for the genre's popularity.

The fifties Western responded to the culture's need for reaffirmation of its greatness and rightness. It took over from the war film an examination of the hero and his role in nation building and began to question it. Science fiction, conversely, responded to the culture's terrors. As we saw in the discussion of *Vertigo*, the fifties were burdened by a fantasy of communist infiltration. Between the hearings of the House Committee on Un-American Activities and the hateful, destructive games played by Joe McCarthy, the culture was scared. The fear was literally of *alien* invasion—an *alien* ideology that would destroy our souls—so it was relatively easy to represent this fear by making the aliens come from outer space rather than the Soviet Union.

Historically, the fear of space-borne alien invasion started at least as far back as Orson Welles's infamous 1938 radio dramatization of H. G. Wells's novel *War of the Worlds* (1898), concerning a Martian invasion. The radio play, presented in the style of a newscast of "breaking events," broadcast on Halloween, at a time of great anxiety over the growing unrest and imminent hostilities in Europe, caused people to panic and take to the roads to escape the Martians. This was certainly one of the most visible early examples of the effect mass media could have on its public.

The real deluge of alien sightings began shortly after World War II in 1946 and was spurred on by the presumed crash of a UFO in Roswell, New Mexico. Without arguing the validity of any of this (okay—I don't believe it), I think the point should be repeated that World War II left a culture full of anxiety, that the atomic bombs that ended the war provoked a fear of science's unknown dangers, and that the birth of anticommunism at around the same time added the final fear to the mix. The new round of science fiction film was spawned.

Three films started it: Irving Pichel's *Destination Moon* (1950) was a nonalien, prointerplanetary discovery film, using clay animation to represent astronauts performing extravehicular activity. Robert Wise, the man who edited Welles's *Citizen Kane* and *The Magnificent Ambersons,* and who became a prolific director, whose films included *The Sound of Music* (1965), made *The Day the Earth Stood Still* in 1951, a brilliant piece of work, and perhaps the only "liberal" science fiction film of the decade. A Christlike alien visits Washington, D.C., to warn earth about its "petty squabbles" and its danger to a peaceful universe. He is accompanied by his own anti-Christ, a spectacular robot named Gort, whose laserlike eye incinerates whatever it touches.

The film is especially media savvy, understanding even this early in the fifties how television—it uses actual broadcasters of the time—influences public perceptions. It is "liberal" in the sense that Klaatu, the alien visitor, wishes to bring the warring parties of the postwar world together and is destroyed for his pains and resurrected by Gort. But, as an indication of things to come, the film pulls its punches and introduces fear. In his parting speech, Klaatu warns the scientists, gathered by a figure representing Albert Einstein, that the world, if it doesn't solve its "petty squabbles" will be destroyed by the race of omnipotent robots, of which Gort is but one. "The test of any such higher authority is, of course, the police force that supports it," Klaatu tells the assembled group. Not exactly a progressive sentiment after the United States had fought a war against a nation that believed the same thing. But despite this curious ending, its noirish mood and style and its polished effects point the way for much science fiction to come.

FIGURE 9.6 Robots and monsters in fifties science fiction. Gort in *The Day the Earth Stood Still* (Robert Wise, 1951).

The third film in the opening trilogy is *The Thing*, also known as *The Thing From Another World* (1951), "produced" by Howard Hawks and "directed" by Christian Nyby. The film essentially belongs to Hawks, who was a veteran Hollywood director and whose style and narrative of men in groups, bonding in stressful situations and permitting a strong-willed woman to enter their enclave, is very much evident in this film. But it is prophetic of the rather low esteem in which science fiction would be held in fifties Hollywood—despite its popularity with filmgoers—that he gives directorial credit to his editor. *The Thing* is a monster movie in which the alien beast is a vegetable—a bloodsucking vegetable which invades an arctic military outpost. The film is roughly but craftily made, noirish in its use of shadow, with the dark corridors of the arctic military base becoming the threatening spaces of horror film's old dark house.

Three figures stand out in the film (other than the monster, who is played by James Arness, who would go on to star in one of television's longest running Westerns, *Gunsmoke*). One is Capt. Hendry, whose calm and humor under pressure keeps his men in line. Another is the woman, whose fifties common sense, her understanding of how to cook a vegetable—boil it, steam it, fry it—leads to the monster's destruction. The third is the mad, slightly effeminate scientist, Dr. Carrington, who wants to study the Thing, make friends with it, make it feel welcome. He is the film's representation of fifties anti-intellectualism, precisely because he is an intellectual whose curiosity leads to more deaths, retards the work of the "real men"—the military—and who represents the fifties fear of doubters and conciliators, of those who did not believe the Red tide of Russian aliens was about to flow over the country—"egg heads." He is a curious version of a great man, Adlai Stevenson, a smart, witty, and knowledgeable politician, who twice ran for and lost the American presidency because he too was an "egghead."

The Thing sets the tone for the genre in the fifties: low budget, dark, desolate, fearful, and provoking of fear. It is a film of people huddled together against a monstrous unknown until they find a way to defeat it. The variations in the many films that followed were few, because almost all involved some kind of alien threat, even, as in the case of Don Siegel's *Invasion of the Body Snatchers* (1956), where the aliens were invisible, coming to Earth as seed pods to take over our bodies, turning us into emotionless zombies—as the communists might do. Almost all of them involved this danger of losing our souls to an alien force;

FIGURE 9.7   Before the bloodsucking vegetable gets fried, the scientist tries to reason with him (*The Thing*, Howard Hawks, Christian Nyby, 1951).

almost all of them depended on the military to save us. There were a few exceptions. MGM made a big-budget science fiction film, Fred Wilcox's *Forbidden Planet* (1956), which was based on, of all things, William Shakespeare's play *The Tempest*, with a good measure of one early twentieth century intellectual who was especially popular in the fifties, Sigmund Freud.

The film is in color, as opposed to the dull gray of most low-budget science fiction, and the visuals, especially the **matte paintings** of the planet Altair, are beautiful. Many moments in the film had a direct influence on both *2001: A Space Odyssey* (1968) and *Star Wars* (1977). An old scientist, Morbius (Shakespeare's Prospero), who traveled to this distant brave new world, has lived with his daughter, Altaira (Shakespeare's Miranda), alone, since the rest of the colonizers were killed. They are served by one of the greatest (and friendliest) of screen robots, Robbie (Shakespeare's Ariel), built like a fifties juke box, productive of all needs, and protective of his owners. *Forbidden Planet* eschews the anticommunist politics of its generic relatives and instead addresses issues common to science fiction literature and usually diluted in films: alien worlds with enormously intelligent beings.

But the beings of Altair, the Krell, are dead. They weren't merely intelligent, but too intelligent. Their huge machines and fantastic energy sources overpowered their unconscious, which, repressed, forced itself back as "creatures from the Id," the film's version of *The Tempest*'s Caliban. Once again, fifties anti-intellectualism raises its anti–egg head. By the time the planet is visited by a military rescue crew, Morbius has himself fallen victim to these monsters—which are magnificently drawn by Disney animators—and eventually dies. The level of inquiry in *Forbidden Planet* is not terribly deep, but deeper than most other representatives of the genre. As I said, it was influential, though not immediately. Lucas borrowed some of its visuals and also transmuted Robbie the Robot into

FIGURE 9.8 Robbie the Robot, surrounded by Dr. Morbius (the famous actor Walter Pidgeon, nearing the end of his career) and Commander Adams (Shakespeare's Alonso, a very young Leslie Nielsen) (*Forbidden Planet*, Fred Wilcox, 1956).

R2D2 and C3P0 in *Star Wars*. And Stanley Kubrick, maker of what is still the most spectacular and complex science fiction film, *2001: A Space Odyssey*, had, I'm sure, *Forbidden Planet* in the back of his mind when planning his film.

2001: A Space Odyssey

2001 is the climax and the rebirth of the science fiction genre. It appeared after the boom of the fifties had died down and in its turn influenced the revival of the genre some ten years after its own appearance—revived it with such intense visual power that there is hardly a science fiction film made since *2001* that does not carry some of its traces. *2001* itself carries all the traces of science fiction film that came before it and gives them depth and resonance. The film deals with three basic generic issues: the loss of human emotion, "aliens," and the robot/computer. Kubrick's characters have already been taken over by the boredom of modernity. They are without affect, emotionless, but not because of an alien takeover. The spectacle of the film that awes us, as viewers, has no effect on the characters in the narrative itself. They are oblivious. Space and the possible existence of alien life is, for them, as ordinary as the everyday is for us. They are as empty as space itself.

The emotion that does occur in the film lies within and is caused by HAL, the computer who runs all operations on the spaceship bound for Jupiter, and who has consciousness. He is Kubrick's Frankenstein monster, and the only one on the voyage who has been told the source of the "aliens," the monoliths which push the narrative forward. Only he has full knowledge of the mission, which he deems too important for humans. He tries to kill all of them off, and almost succeeds. One survives and dismantles the computer's higher functions. HAL's

FIGURE 9.9   "Dave, I can feel it. . . . " Dismantling HAL. Note how the memory modules look a little like the monoliths (*2001: A Space Odyssey*, Stanley Kubrick, 1968).

expression of fear is the closest thing to a human response we get in the film, and it is unnerving.

I've been putting the word "aliens" in quotation marks, because they constitute the film's biggest question. Like all of Kubrick's films, everything has multiple layers, ambiguous meaning. They force us to see things from multiple points of view. The film's famous monoliths seem to have been placed at strategic times and places first to push proto-humans in the "Dawn of Man" sequence to discover that bones can be used to kill, and later, on the moon, to push men to further exploration of space, where HAL kills most of the crew members. A monolith appears at the foot of the bed of the strange hotel room of the mind inhabited by the surviving astronaut. He ages before our eyes in a series of over-the-shoulder shots in which he sees himself at different stages of his decrepitude and then, through a point of view shot, seems to pass through the monolith to emerge as a fetus circling the Earth.

Does Kubrick believe that aliens have guided our destiny? No. The monoliths are visual metaphors of obstacles in the development of human intelligence that must be overcome. But the obstacles are not, and this is typical of Kubrick, overcome for the better. The apes at the beginning of the film experience the monolith and learn to kill and, as mentioned earlier, the spectacular cut from bone-weapon to spaceship indicates a perpetuation of violence throughout human history (see Figures 4.14–4.15). The movement to "Jupiter and Beyond the Infinite" results in HAL killing the hibernating astronauts. This journey is also a

FIGURE 9.10 The end of old humankind as the old man is about to be reborn—because of the monolith; because the monolith is a representation of the speculative imagination? This image is also an excellent example of a wide and high angle, 90-degree composition that puts the viewer in a strange and uncomfortable situation (*2001: A Space Odyssey*, Stanley Kubrick, 1968).

fantasy of a human going beyond the known and returning back in an uncanny, strange rebirth, as a fetus entrapped in the universe's womb.

No science fiction film before or after *2001: A Space Odyssey*, with the possible exception of *Blade Runner*, has realized the genre with the complexity that usually belongs to science fiction literature. But the genre survives, because our imagination for the monstrous alien, our need to develop fictions to explain science, to tell stories of the threats of computation and cloning, which make up such a large part of the genre today, and our fantasy, our master narrative, of creating life outside of normal biological methods, remain undiminished and therefore perpetually filmable.

GENRE RESILIENCE

The key to genre is its ability to be reworked, to renew itself. But there is a point beyond which generic boundaries cannot be stretched, or they will break and the genre will fall apart. Still, they are malleable and can infiltrate one another. The Western, along with the war film, was refigured in *Star Wars*, for example. Sometimes, as in film noir, genres can stretch the boundaries of the master narratives and revise their dominant fictions. For some filmmakers, testing the boundaries and even pushing them beyond the breaking point are ways to define a subjective approach to filmmaking, to move beyond the classical American style. By working from a generic base, filmmakers can find their voice, change viewer perceptions, change the genre, and, perhaps, change cinema.

This is true for a number of American filmmakers—we saw it happening to the Western—but it is even more apparent in film from abroad, from a cinema much more open to individual style and interpretation and therefore a questioning and probing of genres, not merely testing their limits, but going beyond them.

EUROPEAN AND OTHER CINEMAS

Italian Neorealism

American cinema is the dominant form across the world, which is why we are paying so much attention to it. Given this domination it should not be surprising to find that when filmmakers in other countries seek their own style, their own methods of seeing the world in cinematic terms, they begin by thinking about American film and how their work might be different. We saw this happening among the postrevolutionary filmmakers of Russia and see it again in post–World War II Italy, where a new style of filmmaking emerged that changed cinema the world over for many years. Italian neorealism was born of many economic, social, and political factors—not the least of which was the fact that the Italian economy and the very physical structure of the country were in ruins in 1945. Filmmaking as usual was neither possible nor desired. Italy was destroyed by the fascist regime, a dictatorial structure of corporate state control that managed and brutalized all facets of life, including filmmaking. (Italy's main studio, Cinecittà, was inaugurated by dictator Benito Mussolini.)

After the war, Italian filmmakers linked the commercial cinema of prewar Italy with all that was bad about the fascists. They also saw a link to Hollywood film in those fascist comedies and melodramas about romance among members of the upper middle class—called "white-telephone" movies because of their overdone decor. They knew that all of this production, with its reliance on elaborate sets, stars that were removed from the life of ordinary people, stories that addressed the lives of people who could not possibly exist in the day-to-day world—the whole artifice of middle-class fantasy—had to be overthrown. In its place would be a new genre of film that addressed poor people in their daily lives, peasants in the countryside, workers in the streets and in their apartments and meeting halls.

Stars and studios, sets, and the elaborate tricks Hollywood used to fabricate complex, unreal images would be jettisoned. Gone too would be stories about doomed love affairs among the rich and the indulged emotions of bored women and heartless men. Instead of the studio melodramas, films would be made on the street, on location, amid the buildings, traffic, and the people of the cities, or in the countryside. Instead of movie stars, ordinary people or semi-professional performers would be used. Their faces would not be familiar or associated with other films. Hollywood cinema, and the cinema of fascist Italy, were seen as altogether an act of evasion. People went to movies to see movie life, not the life of the world. Do away with these conventions, strip generic formulas and generic responses, get to the people, and film would in turn communicate back to the people images of life as it is.

It's important to repeat that the neorealists were not interested in making documentaries, even though they influenced documentary filmmakers. They wanted to continue using fiction as a means to structure an ordered narrative. But for them, the narrative and the mise-en-scène would appear to grow out of the present circumstances of history and place. Many of the films they made had an immediacy and texture, a visual quality quite unlike anything ever seen before. Roberto Rossellini's great war trilogy, *Rome, Open City* (1945), *Paisan* (1946), and *Germany, Year Zero* (1947); De Sica's *Bicycle Thieves* (1948), *Miracle in Milan* (1951), and *Umberto D.* (1952); and Luchino Visconti's *La Terra Trema* (1948)—one of the few films ever made that addressed the poverty and hopelessness of disenfranchised rural life—in this case the life of fishermen—were raw, sometimes unpolished films of great power and clarity. They spoke about Italian life during and after the war and all of them have a roughness and directness that move the viewer beyond the form of the film to the movement of its story and its characters. But unlike Hollywood films, which also take us beyond their form and into their content, neorealism addresses poverty and desperation, the social life of the poor, and the difficulties of forming supportive communities in a way Hollywood genres rarely permit. Unlike the classical Hollywood style, these films demand our visual attention. By filling the screen with images of a shattered and destructive world, they ask us to observe what we have never seen in film before.

Bicycle Thieves

And yet Italian neorealism is, basically, melodrama. Hollywood melodrama is about the politics of subjective suffering—individuals oppressed by gender, domesticity, unrealizable desires to escape. Italian neorealism is about the suffering brought on by political and economic events, as well as the lives affected by them. The characters of neorealism are deeply oppressed, not by domesticity or gender but by war and poverty. *Bicycle Thieves*, for example, has a simple premise: a very poor man gets a job putting up advertising posters. In a key sequence, he pastes up a poster of the famous late-forties movie star Rita Hayworth. It is a kind of symbolic act that demonstrates his distance, and the film's, from the world of Hollywood glamour. In order to do his job, he needs a bicycle to get from street to street. To get the bicycle, he hocks the family's linens. But to indicate that his desperation is not an individual one, the camera observes huge shelves upon shelves of linens, hocked by various other people in as much economic trouble as he.

Ricci, the main character, played not by an actor but by an actual laborer, is happy at his new job. Then his bicycle is stolen by someone in even worse economic and physical shape than he is. The rest of the film follows his search around Rome in a hopeless attempt to find the bike and restore his life. Ricci is seen amidst family and comrades in the houses and streets of Rome. The camera will often move away from him to observe passersby and the life going on around him. At one point, when he is putting up his posters, two beggar children wander by and the camera casually stops looking at Ricci to follow these two along the street.

The American continuity style insists that narrative and visual focus remain at all times on the central figures of the story. The world around them is often only suggested or caught in quick cutaways. In neorealism, the world that surrounds the characters is given equal space with the characters themselves. Neorealism's mise-en-scène is created by the interplay of city or countryside, people, and the central characters who emerge from the community. Ricci's is one story among others. But his story, finally, is about anguish and hope, which are irresistible. De Sica, no matter how he tries to link Ricci with his surroundings, still finds that he must focus on his character's emotional state, though he never lets us forget that it is tied to the class and economy in which the character lives. He communicates these emotions and creates empathy in his audience by one of the most standard of melodramatic means, triangulating the viewer between the main character and his little son, Bruno. The child clings to Ricci's hand throughout his search for the stolen bicycle. His misery and tears echo his father's despair and amplify it, as when Ricci himself attempts to steal a bike, only to be chased by the crowd. Hand in hand, father and son disappear among the sea of humanity.

These films finally entrap the audience as much as any other with melodramatic devices like death or a dog, which De Sica uses in his later film, *Umberto D.* (1952). *Bicycle Thieves* raises the melodramatic stakes, by universalizing its character's plight—at least within his particular historical and economic context.

FIGURE 9.11 The figure and the street. A typical neorealist composition (*Bicycle Thieves*, Vittorio De Sica, 1948). See also the still from Satyajit Ray's *The World of Apu*, Figure 2.10.

This is not to undercut the power of the neorealist movement or the extent of its influence, which was enormous. It is important, though, to stress how genres, especially melodrama, are so powerful that they can maintain their hold on a filmmaking movement whose original aim was to overthrow the structure and ideology of cinema's past.

Neorealism in America

Neorealism was absorbed into American filmmaking very quickly because of its melodrama and because its style of exterior shooting was so novel and, as we'll see, economically feasible. It influenced—of all things—the gangster genre. By the late forties, some films were being promoted as shot "on location," where the action "actually takes place." *The Naked City,* filmed in 1948 by Jules Dassin, was not a neorealist film by any means. Neither was it filmed entirely on location. There was still the need to manufacture images in the Hollywood style. But it used exterior sequences to a somewhat greater degree than many previous films, and it led the way for gangster films and films noir to use the streets more than the back lots, to generate images out of the material of the world rather than putting them together in an optical printer.

The exterior shooting influenced by neorealism also reflected some economic realities. Italian neorealism emerged from the wreckage of the postwar economy and political culture. A more subtle wreckage occurred in the United States after the war. What Hollywood faced was a decline in movie attendance, and therefore a falloff in revenues, the end of many binding contracts between studios and their personnel, accompanied by the blacklisting of many key creative personnel—including Jules Dassin, who directed *The Naked City,* and Albert Maltz, who wrote it. The power of the studio, manifested in its total control of the filmmaking process, and its control of distribution, was waning. Filmmakers began to form independent production companies and to shoot their films outside the studio. One of the results was a movement out onto the streets. Shooting on location in the United States was partly a matter of aesthetics and a search for novelty, but probably never, as it was in Italy, a question of ideology.

The French New Wave

Exterior shooting was the closest American filmmaking came to the neorealist movement. The young French critics—the same ones who discovered film noir after seeing many American films from the late forties—looked also at *Rome, Open City; Bicycle Thieves,* and the other neorealist films coming from Italy. They recognized in both forms a departure from the classical Hollywood style and new ways to imagine cinematic space. When they made the move from film viewers and film critics to filmmakers, they found that, by combining the gangster/noir style with neorealism, they could shake up the very foundations of genre and the way we think of film. They shot on the streets, using new, little-known actors. While they did not make their films about the working class, like the neorealists, they did look at the lives of the dispossessed and the marginal. Some then moved on to the overtly political. With them we return to a basic truth about genres: individual directors will intervene and sometimes radically change them.

Jean-Luc Godard

Most of these young directors started their careers by making interesting variations on the American gangster film. François Truffaut, the best known of this group of innovators, made his second film an homage to noir called *Shoot the Piano Player* (1960). Jean-Luc Godard, who became the most influential filmmaker since Orson Welles, made his first full-length film a celebration of the gangster genre called *Breathless* (1960). But this was no ordinary gangster film. Its main character is a smart, disenfranchised admirer of Humphrey Bogart. He is a creature of the movies as much as his creator was. He is reckless and, when necessary, violent. In appropriate film noir fashion, he is betrayed by a woman.

But more important than plot—and for Godard, as for any great filmmaker, plot was the least important item—was the visual form of the film. *Breathless* was shot outdoors and in actual apartments, in long takes (Godard would actually put his cinematographer, Raoul Coutard, in a wheelchair with a handheld camera and have him pushed or pulled, following the characters), or cut with a nervous, elliptical style that gained the name "**jump cut**," removing excess movement like the three dots we put into a quotation to leave out the parts we don't need. The jump cut fractured space and moved the narrative through the point of view of its character, whose attention never focused for long an any one thing. Godard would go even further—Godard was always going further—and in 1965 made *Alphaville,* a film that places the noir detective inside the science fiction genre and has its tough-guy hero travel the universe in his Ford Galaxy. The tough guy confronts all the standard science fiction conventions: a mad scientist, a city of the future—actually Paris in 1965—run by a computer. The detective confronts and destroys the computer and the City through a series of dialogues with the machine. "What separates light from darkness?" the computer asks him, and he answers: "Poetry." The computer is made aware of its own self-consciousness and finally destroys itself, as the detective and his girlfriend drive back across the galaxy in his Ford Galaxy.

Godard was not idle between *Breathless* and *Alphaville.* He made seven feature films and a number of short ones before his brief venture into science fiction. Every film, and all that followed, experimented with genre, narrative form,

FIGURE 9.12 Driving through the galaxy in a Ford Galaxy (*Alphaville*, Jean-Luc Godard, 1965).

and all the basic conceptions and preconceptions of cinema. For Godard, and the movement he was part of, these films were neither imitations nor parodies. They were homages, energetic celebrations of the American films that nourished their directors' imaginations, and they were vehicles for rethinking how genres work and how audiences respond to them. Their films interrogate the ways genres operate and, further, the ways in which films told their stories and developed mise-en-scène. For Godard, the gangster of *Breathless* or the private eye of *Alphaville* become figures of existential anxiety, not that far from Chandler's Philip Marlowe, who seeks out identity and speaks philosophically about who he is and how he is to be known.

The latter becomes the key question for Godard: how do we *know* what we see in a film and learn about characters? What is the nature of the cinematic image and the genre-driven cinematic narrative? When we see the same characters in roughly the same story, with basically the same outcome in film after film, are we lulled into a sense of acceptance, of ideological complicity with the filmmakers and their work, both of which request our uniform response? Can genres be altered in a way to make us ask questions rather than respond with the same feelings?

Godard's answer to these questions, like Robert Altman's in the United States, was to take genres, the cinematic image, and the narrative apart, in order to make us look and understand that what we were seeing was just an image. "This is not a just image," Godard would say, "this is just an image." And these images are freighted with ideological and cultural baggage, which he tried to unpack. His films break all the rules: they give up straightforward continuity editing, avoid over-the-shoulder shots, gaze at length from a position directly in front or in back of the characters, who talk not only to one another but to the audience. His narratives shift mood and direction, closure is not promised, and loose ends, popping out all over the narrative, even in the music that accompanies the images, need not be tied up at the end. His films grow in complexity and in political energy, questioning why we look, what we look at, how representation itself is an act of power that we, as viewers, can counter by examination, by keeping our distance, by learning and interpreting.

Michelangelo Antonioni

Other filmmakers followed suit in the sixties and seventies, continuing to ask questions about the Hollywood style and Hollywood genres and answer them in their films. If they didn't use the gangster film as their object of interrogation, they turned, as always, to melodrama. In Italy, following the neorealist movement, filmmakers examined the world inhabited by their characters, now more often middle rather than working class. They articulated the spaces around the figures, the architectural structures they lived in that defined their social and emotional life. Michelangelo Antonioni, for example, investigated the melodramatic mise-en-scène so that the world surrounding his characters not only expressed their anxieties but manifested the repressions that caused them, in a strange and powerful combination of Expressionism and neorealism. Antonioni was the great modernist poet of urban space in which architectural geometry delineated the barriers of the spirit. His quiet, oppressed women and jumpy, unfocused men wander through landscapes that don't so much dwarf them as carry on a visual dialogue with them.

Unlike the classic American cinema, Antonioni does not privilege the human figure in the frame. He insists that composition be about the relationship between the human figure and her surroundings and that emotion emerge from that interaction. His camera is a distant, sometimes disembodied observer, whose movements make us wonder who authorizes the gaze in a film. Who is looking at whom, and why? His films rely on the eloquence and articulateness of the image more than those of almost any other filmmaker. They are the poetry of the figure in the urban landscape.

Antonioni—in films such as *Il Grido* (1957), *L'Avventura* (1960), *La Notte* (1961), *The Eclipse* (1962), *Red Desert* (1964), and *Blow-Up* (1966)—breaks many rules. He substitutes composition for the cut, forcing the viewer to look *at* the frame rather than across it from one action to the next. When he does cut, it is off the rhythm and visual perspective of the Hollywood style. He changes the internal dynamics of melodrama. Instead of transposing excess emotion from the individual to mise-en-scène and back again, he makes the individual part of the mise-en-scène and asks the viewer to inspect both very carefully. Emotional excess is replaced by a shifting visual dynamic. Emotion emerges from our comprehension of these dynamics and is never removed from an intellectual awareness of what the film is asking of us. The cinema reclaims its obligations to the visible, and melodrama is restrained by an active engagement of the viewer's eye and mind (see Figure 3.37).

Yasujiro Ozu

Antonioni was not the only filmmaker to force the viewer's eye to observe composition and make the human figure only one aspect of a complex mise-en-scène. Orson Welles and Stanley Kubrick do the same. Hitchcock does it and, subtly, often without showing his hand; so does John Ford. In Japan, Yasujiro Ozu made many domestic melodramas that addressed the quiet change of culture in that country after the war. Films as moving and beautiful as their titles— *Late Spring* (1949), *The Flavor of Green Tea Over Rice* (1952), *Tokyo Story* (1953), *Early Spring* (1956), *Late Autumn* (1960)—examine the Japanese middle-class family from an ironic, quiet distance. Ozu places his camera in the "tatami"

FIGURE 9.13 The middle-class Japanese family, viewed from the "tatami" position—that is from a mat placed on the floor (*Tokyo Story*, 1953).

position, low on the floor, emulating the traditional seating of a Japanese at home on a tatami mat. But this emulation does not define the point of view of a particular individual in the frame. It is, rather, a cultural gesture, looking at the world from a domestic, Japanese perspective. That perspective includes a respect for space, an interest in rooms and surroundings that is not confined to the narrative of a particular film but speaks the narrative of the culture as a whole.

As I indicated earlier, American films rarely maintain interest in or focus on spaces that have no human figures in them. Ozu loves these spaces, because, even though no figure is present, they were humanized, made by people to live in; and therefore they retain and define human presence, even in their absence. His camera gazes at a room before someone enters it and after she leaves. He cuts away from the main narrative line to create a montage of the city, a train passing, a rock garden, clothes hanging on a line. Ozu's world is defined by its particular cultural articulations.

But there is no mistaking the melodramatic base of Ozu's films. They are about families in turmoil. Parents die, daughters marry, fathers get drunk, sisters are mean, the domestic center does not hold. None of these situations is addressed with the hysteria and overstatement beloved of American melodrama, nor is the viewer asked to deliver emotion on the basis of a character's death or the redemption of a misguided soul. The viewer is asked only to observe and put things together and to recognize within Ozu's mise-en-scène a harmony that transcends the particular upheavals of the domestic.

Douglas Sirk, Rainer Werner Fassbinder, and Todd Haynes: One Genre, Three Ways

Always, in the end, as in the beginning, there is melodrama. This is the most flexible genre, and the most international. Even though I said earlier that it is very hard to break its conventions, they are resilient and able to be molded by individual filmmakers, forcing them into new configurations without actually changing them. So we end our investigation of genre with three versions of a single melodramatic concept: one original and two remakes.

Remakes are a standard method of ringing the most out of a successful film. If a film is well received, why not do it again? Even a great director does this: Alfred Hitchcock filmed *The Man Who Knew Too Much* in 1934 and 1956. In the studio days, it was not unusual for the production of a remake to put a **moviola**—the old standard film editing machine—on the studio floor and copy the older version of the film frame by frame. Less usual are multiple versions of a single film, from different hands—indeed, in our case, from different countries—each approaching the film's subject from different personal and cultural points of view. When this happens, we have the unusual opportunity not only to see three ways of creating a similar narrative, but to understand how creation is inflected by period, country, culture, and the temperament of the filmmakers involved.

The films are *All That Heaven Allows*, directed by Douglas Sirk in 1955; *Ali: Fear Eats the Soul*, made in Germany by Rainer Werner Fassbinder in 1974; and Todd Haynes's critically and commercially successful *Far From Heaven*, 2002. Studying these films reveals not only how genre works, but how it is responsive to time, place, and culture.

The Filmmakers

If Ozu saw a greater cultural harmony emerging out of local family melodrama, the German filmmaker Rainer Werner Fassbinder looked for melodrama to deliver insight into history and politics and to discover in the family a microcosm of large power structures in the culture. Fassbinder was one of the more remarkable figures to appear in European cinema during the 1970s, the period of a long-delayed post–World War II rebirth of German film. He began in the theater and started making films in 1969, directing some thirty-nine of them—including multipart series for television—before his premature death in 1982. He experimented in many genres, and even made a "Western," *Whity* (1971). A large, punk, openly gay man, Fassbinder brought together a remarkably talented stock company of cast and crew, who set out to rethink American film melodrama as a mode of addressing the politics of the family and the state.

After a period of imitating Godard and other European filmmakers, Fassbinder discovered Douglas Sirk. A German émigré to America, Sirk, in the fifties, working for Universal Pictures and producer Ross Hunter, directed over-the-top, bigger-than-life melodramas that pushed the genre to its limits, making the viewer aware of how the excesses of emotion, and the spilling over of those excesses into the mise-en-scène, were the marks of the genre's artifice rather than illusory imitations of life. Sirk knew that melodrama was not a reflection of life, but a concentrated, stylized representation of it. He was a commercial director who was smart enough to give an audience the tears they wanted while at the same time stretching melodramatic boundaries, but only so far. Fassbinder took the genre's conventions and reflected them back in on themselves, exploiting them not as reflections of the personal anguish, but as larger statements about a culture and its politics (which, in fact, is where melodrama started). Sirk showed him the way, his films giving Fassbinder a visual and thematic methodology he could both imitate and turn upside down. Many of Sirk's films were comments on the fifties' social failings and selfish excesses.

Fassbinder pushed this commentary by making the social and the political state of postwar Germany unmistakably intertwined.

Todd Haynes's work veers less to the overtly political than to the gently satirical. More than Sirk or Fassbinder, he seems genuinely to like his characters, even when they are Barbie Dolls, as they were in his first major film, *Superstar: The Karen Carpenter Story* (1987). This has become one of the few films that can seriously be called "cult," because it was, literally, occulted—removed from view by the Mattel Corporation—Barbie's owners—who, disliking the way their major profit item was used, enjoined the film from ever being shown. It now exists only on underground videotapes. Haynes's subsequent films are varied in subject and style. *Safe* (1995) is almost Kubrickian in approach, concentrating on a woman who, believing she is sensitive to allergens, winds up allergic to the very material and emotional stuff of the contemporary world and withdraws into isolation. *Velvet Goldmine* (1998) is an energetic film about the London Glam Rock movement, full of music and general high spirits. *Far From Heaven* was his most commercially and critically successful work.

This is curious. *Far From Heaven* is a moving, understated, quietly filmed melodrama, set in the fifties. It has none of the elements that usually make up a contemporary popular film, except for good acting and a quietly effective mise-en-scène. Perhaps because it touches upon some vital social issues by filtering them through the past, allowing us a certain superiority to the very problems that still plague us precisely because they are made to appear old problems, viewers could feel comfortable, believing, perhaps they no longer exist. Maybe its popularity was based on the fact that it is a well-made, emotionally complex film.

The Common Thread

A driving force of our discussion throughout this book is that plot is a product of the film narrative, not the film itself. A film cannot be reduced to plot, because plot is only one thing that the narrative—the construction of story by the form of the film—produces. However, when dealing with three films, two of which work and rework each other, we do have to find the common threads before we see how they are woven and rewoven, how their patterns and meanings change each time, and this involves abstracting plot from the narrative. *All That Heaven Allows*, *Ali: Fear Eats the Soul*, and *Far From Heaven* are each about a woman who makes a romantic choice that is outside the realm of the social and cultural norms of her time. In Sirk's film, an upper-middle class suburbanite and widow, Cary Scott (Jane Wyman), falls for her nurseryman, Ron Kirby (Rock Hudson). He is a free spirit, with friends who read Thoreau and talk of no longer living lives of quiet desperation. In Fassbinder's, Emmi (Brigitte Mira), an elderly Polish housekeeper, widow of a German, both of whom were members of the Nazi party, falls in love with and marries Ali (El Hedi ben Salem), a Moroccan *gastarbeiter*—literally "guest worker," an immigrant brought in to do the low-paid work the country's citizens won't and who are reviled for it. Todd Haynes's Cathy Whitaker (Julianne Moore), of the same suburban class as her Sirkian forbear, is attracted to her nurseryman, Raymond Deagan (Dennis

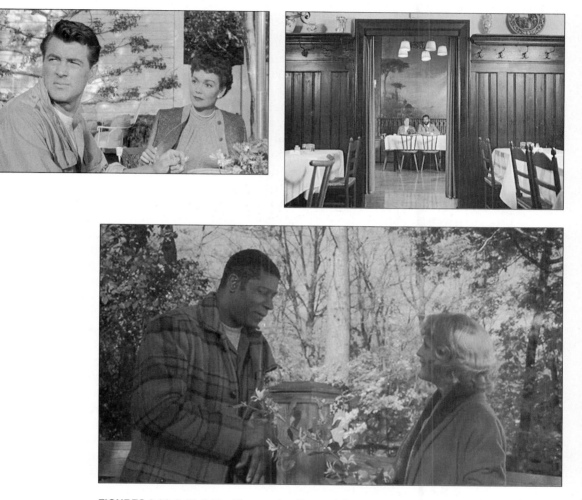

FIGURES 9.14, 9.15, 9.16   The couples: Ron and Cary (Rock Hudson and Jane Wyman) in Sirk's *All That Heaven Allows* (1955). Emmi and Ali (Brigitte Mira and El Hedi ben Salem) in Fassbinder's *Fear Eats the Soul* (1974). Cathy and Raymond (Julianne Moore and Dennis Haysbert) in Haynes's *Far From Heaven* (2002).

Haysbert), who is African American. To complicate matters, her husband, Frank (Dennis Quaid), realizes he is gay and leaves her.

All of this is the stuff of romantic melodrama, particularly the fact that each film presents a woman acting on desires forbidden for various social reasons. In each film, the characters undergo extreme emotional turmoil, and in each film, their environment, the people around them, indeed the film's entire mise-en-scène serve as containers for the excess of the turmoil. Yet each film is remarkably different, and together they act as resonant echo chambers, each one playing against the other, opening up their ideas and their styles when seen side by side.

All That Heaven Allows and Far From Heaven

The two American films are closest, by virtue of the similarity of their characters and the familiarity of their surroundings and social concerns. *All That Heaven Allows*, on one level, is quite straightforward in its melodramatic import: Cary suffers terribly for her romantic and sexual desires. She is spurned by neighbors and children, and closure is reached with the appropriate sacrifice on her part. The mise-en-scène, however, is extraordinary. Like most of Sirk's films of the period, the colors are rich, saturated, and often completely unnatural in ways that a black and white image on the page can't communicate. In one scene, where Cary is talking to her daughter, the light comes in as if through a spectrum, bathing them in red, green and blue lights as her daughter whines about her mother ruining their lives by marrying the gardener. Not completely adverse to fifties' stereotyping, the daughter is portrayed as a glasses-wearing intellectual, spouting Freud, and sounding ridiculous. Of course, she finds a husband and comes to her senses (and wears scarlet red clothes). When Cary's son berates her, he steps behind an elaborate screen, creating a composition that broadly represents how purposefully he cuts himself off from his mother's feelings and needs.

Mirrors and screens figure prominently in Sirk's compositions, either visually representing a blocking off of feelings, as when Cary's son steps behind a screen when expressing his disapproval of his mother, or reflecting the characters back to themselves, making us see them twice, doubling their passion. The most telling use of a mirror image occurs when Cary's children forget their passionate anger at her choice of a lover. As the film progresses, the grown children get involved in their own affairs, but not before they've forced her to give up her plans to marry Ron. The son is off for a new job overseas. The daughter, dressed in scarlet, has discovered her own sexuality, which she denied to her mother, and found a husband. They leave Cary alone with the Christmas present they've gotten for her: a television set. We have to remember that even in the mid-1950s, television was, like so many things, both embraced and distrusted. It was sold as the lonely housewife's companion. In fact, the salesman who delivers the children's present promises Cary she will now have "life's parade at your fingertips." The irony is bitter—Cary is given a replacement for passion by the children who were so violently against her passion to begin with. The TV is rolled in and Cary's own reflection is given back to her. The TV screen receives nothing but the image of her own loneliness.

Such exaggerated images, reflections, and colors serve not only to heighten the emotion but to allow us to step back from them. There is enough artificiality in Sirk's films for us to understand that what we see is an artful representation of life and its turmoil; through the images, there is enough commentary on the wretched behavior of people toward events and feelings to allow a fifties—and a twenty-first century—viewer to understand that film was not life but an image representing it. Sirk wants it all ways. He absorbs a fifties audience into his characters' melodrama and, simultaneously, creates distance from it, by means of the emotional and visual exaggeration, in order to allow them to understand that life is not what's happening on screen, only a Technicolor representation.

Far From Heaven, on the other hand, is visually more subdued than *All That Heaven Allows*. Haynes captures a great deal of the Sirkian style, but in a lower key, with only occasional flashes of fall color to brighten an autumnal and winter light, metaphorical of the fall and decline of the main character. There are the mirror images and even the exaggerated fifties décor, but less flamboyantly displayed. There is a reason for this. *Far From Heaven* is *All That Heaven Allows* seen through a glass darkly. Seen through a number of glasses, in fact. Made in the early twenty-first century, it is set in the same period as Sirk's film and has Fassbinder's film on its mind as well. The issues faced in the film are articulated by the way we know them now and the way they may have been experienced then, more accurately, the way Sirk, Fassbinder, and their audiences experienced them *through Sirk's film*. By setting the film in Sirk's period, Haynes can't openly bring the fifties up to date to the early 2000s, the way Fassbinder does by setting *Ali* in 1970s Germany. Haynes can use the fifties as a mirror for the early 2000s and create a kind of ping-pong effect directly with Sirk's film and indirectly with Fassbinder's. *Far From Heaven*, therefore, changes its characters and its narrative in quiet and often highly ironic ways.

Race

For example, Cathy's attraction to her gardener remains a focal point. However, the gardener is African American. Two things are happening. There are no African Americans in Sirk's film. They do not fit into the lily-white Connecticut suburb in which his film is set. This is not to say that either Sirk or the fifties ignored racial issues. Amidst the crushing repression of that decade, the one thing that Hollywood can be proud of was its progressive treatment of race—and not only progressive: one film, Joseph Mankiewicz's *No Way Out* (1950), borders on the revolutionary. Sirk himself attempted a liberal reading of racial issues in *Imitation of Life* (1959, itself a remake of a thirties film), in which a white woman and her maid become close and confront the maid's daughter's attempt to pass as white. But in *All That Heaven Allows*, it was enough for Sirk merely to have Cary have sexual feelings for a white man below her age and class in order to start tongues wagging and misery to ensue. For Haynes, Cathy and Raymond are attracted out of mutual gentleness and loneliness, amidst a sea of racist hatred, which is alluded to in various ways. At a party, a guest jokes that there is no racial problem in their town because there are no Negroes. Haynes cuts to the African American waitstaff quietly looking on. In one gruesome scene, where the family vacation in Miami, an African American child innocently steps into the hotel pool. He is pulled out as the guests look on with horror and disgust.

The interracial relationship between Cathy and Raymond is played out quietly, between them, at least; but when it surfaces, they have both been so reviled and even physically threatened that Raymond chooses to protect his daughter and himself, leave town, and leave Cathy miserably alone. The scenes between

Raymond and Cathy are among the most moving in the film, even though some interesting touches are given to her character that modify her gentleness. She's startled whenever she comes across an African American, even after she gets to know Raymond. She's strict and unpleasant with her children. But when she becomes comfortable with Raymond, their relationship is created in a straight-forward way, usually in two shots, to indicate their closeness. Unfortunately, whenever they are together with other people, the potentials for a deeper inti-macy are always suppressed. Whenever people are around, they are the subject of merciless stares; they seem filled with a predetermined sense of loss and al-ways the objects of hatred. It is typical of Haynes's women that they are perpet-ually vulnerable and isolated. In *Safe*, suburban wife Cathy White—also played by Julianne Moore—is globally vulnerable, so alone, so inward, that the outside world becomes a total threat, rendering her helpless. *Safe* is an allegory of a woman's difficulty in asserting herself and inserting herself into the world. The world, in its turn, attacks her and renders her helpless. *Far From Heaven* is a melodrama of a wife who cannot hold her center—which, in the fifties, as today, means her family—together. One reason is her transgressive attraction to a man of another race. Another is a subject that Sirk could not possibly touch.

Gender

Far From Heaven enters the subject of homosexuality into the narrative variation of the two previous films. There are few gender issues that create more cultural dissonance and downright violence than this one, and Haynes treats it not only with great delicacy, but also by placing it in the past. In the fifties, in fact throughout the history of film, gays could not be portrayed on screen except un-der the subterfuge of a usually fussy, comic character, or a wink and nod joke. Outside of film, the fifties were particularly hard on gays in the culture, often harassing them as subversives. But the fact is that, despite the negative major-ity attitude toward homosexuality, it has always existed. Perhaps, because gay women and men have, until quite recently, had to live an underground exis-tence, it has indeed been subversive. This is true in the arts, where many cre-ative people were gay and, happily, if mischievously and secretively, made their presence felt.

This sets up an intriguing set of reasons for the entry of a gay character in *Far From Heaven*. Todd Haynes is openly gay. Douglas Sirk's producer, Ross Hunter, was gay; Rainer Werner Fassbinder was gay; and perhaps the most subversive element coursing through the three films, if only by inference, Rock Hudson, who plays the nurseryman in *All That Heaven Allows*, was gay. Rock Hudson was a major Hollywood star in the fifties and early sixties and in television dur-ing the seventies. His homosexuality was known throughout the film business, and his studio, Universal, tried with the greatest success to keep knowledge of his sexuality from his adoring public. He almost always played macho charac-ters—he even played an Indian in, of all things, a Douglas Sirk Western, *Taza, Son of Cochise* (1954)! We must not forget that Sirk was a studio director and took the projects that came his way, forging them with his personality only when he was able. And, of course, Hudson's role in *All That Heaven Allows* is as a strong, self-sufficient, totally independent, yet gentle, man, gentle enough to tend to plants; strong enough to build a dwelling for Cary and himself. Under Sirk's hands, if I may play on a cliché, Hudson's "feminine" side was often allowed to appear—and he appeared in five Sirk films.

Hudson's gayness was not known to the public, at least until the early eighties when he had HIV-AIDS and, in the television series *Dynasty*, was visibly wasting away. It is this very secrecy that allows Haynes to make homosexuality a point of focus in *Far From Heaven*. He had a delicate job. By the 2000s, though still reviled from many quarters, homosexuality was, after much struggle, pretty much open. Television shows and some movies dealt with it if not matter-of-factly, at least as a societal and cultural given. But Haynes's film is set in the fifties, when the question was not openness but furtiveness. He does two things to take care of the problem without making it less problematic.

He casts Dennis Quaid, an actor best known for smirky, macho roles, as Cathy's husband. He is made up to look quite unattractive, given an ugly nose and directed to act with a kind of sorrowful, depressed air of hopelessness (see Figure 5.1). If Rock Hudson was the fifties gay man pretending to be straight in romantic melodramas and comedies, Quaid, the laid-back tough guy, becomes a fifties gay man in a 2003 film, trying hard, but failing, to be a good father and provider. Before yielding totally to his sexuality, he goes to a psychiatrist to get "cured" of his homosexuality—which was, until relatively recently, considered a disease—and has clandestine affairs with pick-ups in his office late at night, until he is caught by his wife.

The result of all of this is continuing and growing despair on Cathy's part, caught between two—both for the fifties and for the early 2000s—impossible loves. She discovers her husband's "secret" and is as helpless before it as he is. When, finally, both he and Raymond leave (Raymond is threatened by other African Americans and his daughter attacked by white children because of his friendship with Cathy), she is left utterly alone. At the train station, waving goodbye to Raymond, she walks into the stark late winter street. The camera, reversing its opening movement, where it imitated the beginning of *All That Heaven Allows*, cranes up to a branch in early blossom. But everything else on the street is so gray, Cathy is in such a hopeless situation, that this sprig of hope can't even close the melodrama with more than a suggestion of nature's ongoingness as opposed to people's meanness and sorrow.

Cary, in *All That Heaven Allows*, suffers a different kind of repression. The only question reigning over this melodrama is exactly how much will heaven allow? We know already from our previous discussions of the genre that it allows only so much, which Haynes acknowledges by showing just how far his characters' lives are from heaven. In Sirk's film, Cary's friends and relatives forget their cold rebuff of her romance, which she has already broken off. She is forced to a doctor to see about her headaches—a nice fifties displacement for sexual repression. She decides to return to Ron, only to see him fall from a snow drift and become seriously injured. As a result, she must become his caretaker, his nurse. A doe appears outside the window where Ron lies ill and Cary sits by him and it promises a return to gentleness and perhaps even a recuperation of their love. But on what terms? Fifties terms. Cary assumes a maternal role; Ron the passive "son." No notion if they will become lovers again. Melodrama thrives on sacrifice. "Don't let's ask for the moon . . . we have the stars."

Fassbinder—*Ali: Fear Eats the Soul*

Sirk takes melodrama and presses its limits, as Ford pushed the limits of the Western in *The Searchers* or Welles climaxed film noir by exaggerating its dark images in *Touch of Evil*, as Kubrick pushed science fiction beyond the universe in *2001*. In 2002, Haynes remakes Sirk's film and creates a melodrama in which emotional escape is offered only as an impossible desire as everyone loses the protection of a domestic center.

When Fassbinder made *Ali: Fear Eats the Soul* in 1974, he was working not only at the peak of his own imaginative energy, but at a peak of creativity in cinema worldwide for an audience looking forward to films that experimented, that took genres and stood them on their heads. This is exactly what Fassbinder did with Sirk's films.

Fassbinder took the essential banality of Sirk's premise—the romance of an older woman with a younger man beneath her class—and turned it into political and social allegory. I've noted that the social and political is already present in Sirk's film, that *All That Heaven Allows* is a kind of mirror of fifties repression and prejudice, but Fassbinder goes further. He takes an overt, contemporary political problem in Germany at the time, the country's importing of foreign workers, whom native Germans both needed and hated, and makes it the driving engine of his work. He's not merely working through social and political issues, but talking—and not very indirectly—about social policy.

But there is much more happening here. Fassbinder opens up the latent social commentary of Sirk, and also takes the melodrama of *All That Heaven Allows* and subverts it, down to its very mise-en-scène. In place of Sirk's opulence, his gorgeous and carefully integrated color scheme, Fassbinder moves between the plain and the garish. Since his subjects are poor Germans and Moroccans, there are no fancy houses, but cramped apartments, dull streets, and a seedy bar (Haynes imitates a scene from *Fear Eats the Soul* when he has Cathy and Raymond dance in a bar beneath a Champagne ball). Fassbinder indeed uses lighting for effect. Like Sirk, he will play with red to indicate passion or, ironically, its impossibility. But mostly he uses fairly stark, high-keyed lighting in this film. Everything is brought to light. He also plays upon a Sirkian camera strategy for particular effect. I noted how Sirk loves to photograph his characters through things, framing them behind screens or observing their reflections in mirrors, for example. Fassbinder almost always frames his characters, most usually in doorways or the room dividers of apartments. He will put his camera at a distance, staring at his characters, isolating them in our gaze and the gaze of others, and sometimes allowing the characters to stare directly back at us.

The Influence of Bertolt Brecht

This leads us to consider an important influence on Fassbinder and many of his contemporaries, especially Jean-Luc Godard, who was, in turn, an influence on Fassbinder also. Fassbinder does not only invert melodramatic principles and turn them inside out; he does this to show how they can be made to work, to expose their mechanisms by showing their artificiality. Instead of absorbing the political into the personal—or absorb the viewer into the melodrama—Fassbinder shows how personal suffering and emotional repression can be understood as political events on both the micro and macro levels. He frames his characters, for example, to show that these are characters framed in a film, and also are subject to the constraints, the pressures of the world that reduces them.

He also shows how melodrama can be made to work on an intellectual level, usually fatal to the genre, by inviting the viewer to step back a bit and look with some detachment—as when he frames characters at a distance through doorways, inscribing frames within the movie screen frame. Fassbinder was influenced by the important left-wing German playwright Bertolt Brecht, who said that the work of art should not mystify or make itself invisible but rather open itself up to interrogation. For Brecht, the more invisible the form and structure of a work, the more the viewer is fooled into believing the illusion. The more fooled, the more she is taken advantage of. The more visible the form and structure, the more the viewer understands how form and ideology operate, and are in fact inseparable. Made visible, the work of art becomes a tool for understanding larger structures of power in the culture. Brecht would have the playwright and, by extension, the filmmaker build into his work effects that create distance between it and the viewer and thereby make its workings and its reception visible.

Fassbinder frames his characters in doorways and within rooms so that we become conscious of the framing of the camera and how that framing comments upon the characters and their situation. He creates outrageous narratives with characters who are physically unattractive by Hollywood standards. This is a major break with Sirk—and even Haynes can't quite carry this one through: his actors are mostly attractive people. Instead of an attractive upper-middle-class matron as the central female character, Fassbinder presents us with an old German washerwoman, Emmi, a widow who was a member of the Nazi party ("everybody was, back then," she says without thinking about her words). Instead of a handsome young nurseryman, there is Ali, a homely, bumbling Moroccan, an immigrant worker, who suffers the indignities, scorn, oppression, and diseases faced by people of color who are brought in by a rich culture to do the dirty work. Here, of course, is an elision made by Todd Haynes in his version: the nurseryman is an African American who suffers a similar scorn as Ali—his daughter is stoned by her classmates—and like him, is the object of everyone's cruel gaze.

The old German woman and the young, black immigrant fall in love and marry. Fassbinder makes this all so touching that we have to shake ourselves to realize how perfectly absurd it is. It simply couldn't happen. And this is part of the Brechtian moment. In "real life," the conventional absurdities of ordinary melodrama could never happen. The narrative structure and events of *Ali: Fear Eats the Soul* only point up these absurdities and make us examine our assumptions about them. The film invites us to come to understand how much we take for granted in melodrama, and how much goes unexamined. And this is itself a distancing device. At the same time, Emmi and Ali's love is as emotionally touching an event as any melodrama can present, and as impossible.

There are other Brechtian effects. Fassbinder will literally stop dramatic action and have his characters look up and stare at the camera, forcing us to recognize the artificiality of the scene. After their marriage, Emmi and Ali go to a fancy Munich restaurant—she does not fail to mention to Ali that it was Hitler's favorite! They are condescended to by the maître d' and confused by the menu. It is an appallingly embarrassing sequence. The sequence is ended with a cut outside the doorway of the restaurant, the camera framing and staring at the poor couple, who simply stop acting and stare back, for a long time, at the camera . . . at us (see Figure 9.15). A bit later, in the film's most emotional scene, Emmi and Ali sit in an open-air restaurant, she weeping over the hatred they receive, both of them isolated by the gazes of the people around them. Fassbinder tracks far from them as, again, they stop acting and simply stare at one another.

The Gaze

The gaze itself becomes a distancing device. Everyone stares at Ali and Emmi, and Haynes picks up on this device in *Far From Heaven*. These benighted characters become objects, the Other—in other people's eyes. Of course, film is all about the gaze. When we discussed the Hollywood continuity style, we spoke about how shots are built by characters looking and the audience shown what they are looking at. We examined the gendering of the gaze, the look by male characters at women. In Fassbinder's and later in Haynes's eyes, the gaze is turned into both a narrative device—a way to tell us about hatred and fear—and a reflection of the cinematic act itself. They make it an attention drawing effect that forces us to think not only about the cinematic gaze in general, but of the larger cultural conditions that make people outwardly or implicitly stare at those who are different, and the effect on people who are turned into objects by the stare.

FIGURE 9.17 The poisonous gaze in *All That Heaven Allows.*

Fassbinder's Narrative

Like Cary and Ron and Cathy and Raymond, Emmi and Ali—the unlikely couple—are visited by a string of humiliations, even more exaggerated than their cinematic predecessors and heirs. Emmi's neighbors scorn her; her family reviles her. They take out their anger on her and her possessions. Recall how in *All That Heaven Allows,* Cary's children buy her a television set to keep her mind off the loneliness for which they are largely responsible. Emmi's son—after a slow panning shot of her children staring at her and Ali in disgust—kicks in her television set to show his anger at her impending marriage. It is part of the climax of rejection: her neighbors shun her and call the police when she has Ali's friends over to the apartment. The local grocer won't sell his food to Ali. And everyone stares. The destruction of the television is just one displaced act of anger, violence to a possession instead of against the transgressing parent. (In *Far From Heaven,* incidentally, television functions quietly but persistently: Cathy's husband works for a manufacturer of television sets.)

Then Fassbinder reverses the situation. After all, a major component of melodrama is a sudden, often coincidental turn in events. Suddenly, Emmi's children realize that mother is a good resource for babysitting; the neighbors want Ali to help them move furniture;

FIGURE 9.18   In *Ali: Fear Eats the Soul*—which is full of people staring—Emmi's family glowers at her and Ali. Fassbinder is the second from the left.

FIGURE 9.19   People at an art exhibition stare at Cathy and Raymond in *Far From Heaven.*

the grocer, realizing that his business is being hurt by supermarkets, welcomes Emmi back to his shop. But as outsiders change their tune to fit their needs, Ali and Emmi go through a reverse change and become their own exploiters. Emmi humiliates Ali by showing off his muscles to her neighbors and refuses to allow his friends to visit the apartment. He, in turn, flees to the arms of the woman who runs the local Moroccan bar. Earlier, Emmi was cast out by her coworkers. Now she joins them in taunting and isolating a foreigner who has joined her cleaning crew at the office. Fassbinder makes a special point of this by literally rhyming a shot. Earlier in the film, his camera looks at Emmi sitting alone on the stairs, eating her lunch, as her coworkers group together making fun of her. She is composed between the spokes of the banister, as if imprisoned. Later, when Emmi joins her coworkers taunting the newcomer, this poor soul is framed by the camera in exactly the same way that Emmi was. Oppression returns like rhyme.

Happiness Is Not Always Fun

For Fassbinder, oppression is not merely internalized. Repression is not only sexual. Unhappiness is not always the result of a bad romance or a failing marriage. Repression and unhappiness are social and political phenomena; they are about power and one-upmanship (an exercise of power)—about how someone with a little power exercises it by oppressing someone with even less. This cycle of oppression and hurt is itself contained within a larger cycle of power and repression exercised by the state, in which the powerful continually manipulate those with no power. With the promise of a melodramatic renewal of romance, Emmi and Ali have a reconciliation. They meet at the bar for Middle-Eastern immigrant workers where they first found each other, and they dance. A happy ending threatens—but Fassbinder has warned us by means of the epigraph to the film, itself taken from Godard's film *My Life to Live*: "Happiness is not always fun." In the middle of the dance, Ali collapses.

All That Heaven Allows ends with Cary assuming a maternal position at Ron's bedside, while a doe plays in the snow outside. He may get better if she gives him her all-devoting care. Ali's collapse has nothing to do with Ali and Emmi's reconciliation. He is suffering from an ulcer. The doctor at the end of *Fear Eats the Soul* offers no hope and tells Emmi that Ali will never get well. His condition is a common physical response of immigrants to the terrible conditions and humiliations they face in their host country. He is a victim, finally, of state power and cultural prejudice. The humiliations and the ulcers will keep occurring until he dies. The film ends with the image of Ali in his hospital bed. There is no deer at the window, only the cold light of a Munich afternoon. As in *All That Heaven Allows* and *Far From Heaven*, the women are left alone, turned into nurse and nurturer in Sirk's film, into completely isolated figures in Fassbinder's and Haynes's.

FIGURES 9.20–9.21 The television reflects Cary's image in *All That Heaven Allows*. Her son smiles smugly at her. Emmi's son just kicks in the TV to express his anger.

FIGURES 9.22–9.23 In *Ali: Fear Eats the Soul*, repression returns like a rhyme, as the foreign worker is imprisoned in the same composition as Emmi was, locked in the stares of her coworkers. In the second shot, Emmi becomes one of the starers.

BRIEF CONCLUSIONS

I hope I have indicated the great sweep of film, its possibilities to repeat itself endlessly and also to renew itself with insights that are engaging and, dare I say, entertaining. There is much to say for and against the classical Hollywood style. After all, it has been around, hardly changed, for almost a century. There is also much to be said about directors who experiment, because only those filmmakers who push cinema to and beyond its limits keep it alive. There may not be many, and their works may not be commercially popular. But they serve to keep cinema alive, to enrich its form and enliven the great melodrama of our culture.

NOTES AND REFERENCES

The Western   See Philip French, *Westerns: Aspect of a Movie Genre* (N.Y.: Viking Press, 1974); Edward Buscombe and Roberta E. Pearson, eds., *Back In The Saddle Again: New Essays On The Western* (BFI Publishing, 1998).

Landscape   For the idea of the cowboy hero creating a domestic space he can't inhabit, see J. A. Place, *The Western Films of John Ford* (Secaucus, N.J.: Citadel Press, 1974).

The Western Star and the Western Director   Robert Warshow's "Movie Chronicle: The Westerner" can be found in *Film Theory and Criticism*, 703–16. The best book on John Wayne is by the historian, Garry Wills, *John Wayne: the Politics of Celebrity* (London: Faber and Faber, 1999). There are literally dozens of books and articles on John Ford. The J.A. Place book cited above might be a good place to start.

Science Fiction   *Visionary Architecture* is the title of a book by Ernest E. Burden (New York: McGraw-Hill, 1999) and is used by Annette Michelson to refer to the future visions of science fiction film. See also J. P. Telotte, *Science Fiction Film* (New York: Cambridge University Press, 2001) and Vivian Sobchack, *Screening Space: The American Science Fiction Film*, 2nd ed (New Brunswick: Rutgers University Press), 1997. For a responsible, brief history of UFO's, see the website http://www.angelfire.com/co/Area51info/shthistory.html.

European and Other Cinemas   A good survey of postwar European and international cinema is in Robert Phillip Kolker, *The Altering Eye* (New York: Oxford University Press, 1983). Now out of print, it is online: http://otal.umd.edu/~rkolker/AlteringEye).

Italian Neorealism   On Mussolini, Cinecittà, and the history of neorealism, see Peter Bondanella, *Italian Cinema: From Neorealism to the Present* (New York: Frederick Ungar, 1983).

The French New Wave   The best discussion of the movement remains James Monaco's *The New Wave: Truffaut, Godard, Chabrol, Rohmer, Rivette* (New York: Oxford University Press, 1976).

Fassbinder   Some of Fassbinder's crew are now active in America. His cinematographer, Michael Ballhaus, works for Martin Scorsese and has filmed such diverse projects as *Goodfellas* (1990), *The Age of Innocence* (1993), and *Gangs of New York* (2002). The influence of Brecht Brecht's theoretical writing is collected in *Brecht on Theatre*, trans. John Willett (New York: Hill and Wang, 1979).

GLOSSARY

180-degree rule   This rule holds that, from one cut to another, the camera does not cross an imaginary line drawn behind the characters.

90-degree rule   The camera may never be placed 90-degrees facing the subject, but rather set off the center to give an illusion of depth.

actualitès   Events filmed as they were happening, events that would be happening even if the camera weren't there.

ambient sound   See "room" and "world tone" below: the sound added to a sequence to provide aural atmosphere.

anamorphic processes   The camera lens "squeezes" an image onto the film. When unsqueezed by the projector lens, the ratio of the image is 1:2.35. Panavision is the most common proprietary anamorphic process.

aspect ratio   The relationship of screen width to height. There are four ratios. "Standard" ratio existed from the early 1930s through the early 1950s and is 1:1.3. Two wide-screen ratios are 1:1.6 and 1:1.85. Anamorphic wide screen (Cinemascope, Panavision) is 1:2.35.

aura   Critic Walter Benjamin's term for the uniqueness of a work of art which is lost when, as in film, it is mechanically reproduced.

auteur   French term for the film director who places a personal style on his or her films.

automatic dialogue replacement (ADR)   A method, largely digital, of dubbing in dialogue after the film is completed. See "looping."

avant-garde   Often used to explain works of artists that are personal, experimental, and not aimed at a wide audience.

backlighting   Lights behind the characters that set them off from the background.

back story   Filling out the "plot" with a related story or action.

blue screen   Characters are photographed against a blue screen; the background is photographed or digitally rendered separately. The two (or more) parts are then joined digitally or photographically—the blue background is dropped out—to create the illusion of a complete image.

captivity narrative   One of the major master narratives of the United States, expressing its fear of being dominated. Its dominant fictions show women in distress, held by vicious men, and in need of rescue by a strong hero.

chiaroscuro   A term from art history that refers to the use of deep shadow in the mise-en-scène.

Cinemascope   Patented by Twentieth-Century Fox, one of the first modern anamorphic processes that squeezed a wide image onto 35 mm film, which was then unsqueezed by the projector.

cinematographer (director of photography)   Working with a film's director, the cinematographer lights the scene, chooses the appropriate lenses and film stock, and therefore carries a large responsibility for determining the look of a film.

cinéma vérité   A version of documentary developed by the French in the late fifties and sixties that attempted to capture the ongoingness of everyday life without narration.

Cinerama   A wide-screen process that originally used three cameras to capture the enormous width of the image.

classical Hollywood style or **classical narrative style**   The classical Hollywood or narrative style refers to a complex collection of formal and thematic elements that became basic to Hollywood filmmaking by the early 1910s. Continuity cutting—including shot/reverse shot and over-the-shoulder cutting—the 180-degree rule, happy endings, psychologically motivated characters, villains getting punished, women becoming wives and mothers are all associated with the classical Hollywood style. The continuity style is a subset of the classical Hollywood style.

close-up   The actor's face fills the screen. Also, medium close-up, where the actor is seen from the upper torso.

coding   Conventions that telegraph a lot of information economically, as in older films where the way a coffee cup was held or a cigarette smoked told the audience much about a character.

compilation film   Films made by editing footage from other films.

composition   The arrangement of characters and surroundings within the boundaries of the screen frame.

computer graphics imaging (CGI)   The variety of backgrounds, foregrounds, digital animations, and effects created on the computer and transferred to film.

continuity style/continuity editing   Smooth, seamless editing that links shots so that the cuts appear invisible to the viewer.

coverage   Filming enough variations of a scene to allow the editor to put it together with perfect continuity.

crane   An apparatus that can lift the camera into the air and is therefore responsible for a crane shot.

cross cutting   Editing shots, representing different places, to give the illusion of simultaneity. Also called "parallel editing."

cross tracking   A variation of shot-reverse track in which what a character in motion sees is also shown in motion. Often used by Alfred Hitchcock.

cultural studies   A wide-ranging critical approach to works of imagination that exami_ _s them in light of the cultures they are part of and that create them.

culture   The sum total of the intricate ways we relate to ourselves, our peers, our community, our country, world, and universe.

deep focus   In deep-focus cinematography, all objects from front to rear of the composition are in sharp focus.

direct cut   One shot follows another without any optical transition like a dissolve.

dissolve   One shot fades out and another fades in. If the two occur simultaneously and we see one shot fading out as the other fades in, we have lap dissolve.

documentary   A film that records actual events, often creating dramatic impact through editing.

dolly   An apparatus that holds the camera but can, itself, move in, out, or from side to side. A dolly-in or dolly-out refers to a movement toward or away from a figure.

dominant fictions   Particular stories that articulate a culture's **master narratives**.

editing   The process of cutting film footage and assembling the pieces into an expressive, narrative structure.

editor   The person who assembles the shots of a film into its final shape.

establishing shot   Before a cutting pattern can begin, there must be a shot that establishes the whole space. Examples of establishing shots are the initial two-shot of characters in a dialogue sequence, or the image of an entire roomful of people, or of the city in which the film takes place.

Expressionist   This term originally referred to the style of film and theater in post–World War I Germany, where the mise-en-scène expressed the exaggerated, neurotic psychological state of the characters. Now it is used to refer to a mise-en-scène that is dark, distorted, and menacing.

eye-line match   Continuity editing dictates that, if a character is looking in a certain direction in one shot, she should be looking in the same direction in the following shot. This is crucial in the over-the-shoulder pattern, where the characters must seem to be looking at one another (even if both actors are not physically present at the same time when the shots are made).

fill lighting   Lights that fill in the scene, creating accents, removing or adding shadow.

film noir   A genre of film developed in the 1940s. Noir has a literary heritage in the hard-boiled detective fiction of Raymond Chandler and Dashiell Hammett and the novels of James M. Cain. Its cinematic lineage is German Expressionism and Welles's *Citizen Kane*. It is marked by a mise-en-scène of heavy shadow and narratives of weak men destroyed by predatory women.

flashback   When we see something a character remembers.

flat wide screen   A nonanamorphic process in which the film is matted top and bottom to create the illusion of wide screen.

flow   A notion developed by the British cultural scholar Raymond Williams to define the ways that disparate and incoherent elements, commercials, promotions, and the shows themselves move together seamlessly on television.

foley   Foley design and the foley artist create the sound structure of a film. The name comes from a sound effects pioneer, Jack Foley.

frame   The borders of the screen that, along with the composition of the shot, determine the limits of what we see.

Frankfurt school   Short for the Frankfurt Institute for Social Research, founded in Germany in 1924, much of it devoted to the study of popular culture and its productions.

French New Wave   A group of young film critics who turned to filmmaking in the late fifties and changed the language of cinema. Among the group were François Truffaut, Jean-Luc Godard, Eric Rohmer, Claude Chabrol, and Jacques Rivette.

genre   A "kind" of story or narrative, made up of character types, plot lines, and settings common to all its members. Science fiction films and Westerns are genres, for example.

high-key lighting   Creates a bright, evenly lit scene.

image track   As opposed to the sound track, the series of images that contain the film's visual content.

intertextuality   The way texts are interwoven or refer to each other in film, music, and the other arts. "Sampling" in rap is a kind of intertextuality.

iris shot   Shrinking or expanding the frame by a dynamic, circular black mask; mostly used in the silent period.

Italian neorealism   Developed by the Italians at the end of World War II, a genre that defied studio conventions by filming on the streets, using nonprofessional or semi-professional actors to define a working class ruined by the war.

jump cut   The result of editing out unnecessary transitions so that continuity is replaced by rapid changes in space.

key light   The main overhead light that lights the faces and is reflected in the eyes.

location   A place outside the studio—such as a city street, the desert, an actual house or apartment.

long shot (long takes)   A shot that lasts a long time without a cut.

long take   In an average film, shots last six to nine seconds. A long take may last sixty seconds or more and contain rich narrative and visual information.

looping   An older term meaning the post-dubbing of dialogue. A section of film was looped over and over again to allow the actors to synchronize their voice to the lip movements in the shot.

master narratives   The abstract narrative ideas retold in any culture in various kinds of stories.

matte painting   A detailed, photo-realistic painting of a background over which images of characters in the film are placed.

matte shot   A method of shooting characters against a colored—usually blue or green—backdrop. Then, other elements are added to the shot replacing the colored background.

mediation   All of the events—visual, political, personal, conventional, cultural—that stand between ourselves and the world. We, in fact, do not know the world directly. Every perception is mediated.

medium close-up   Character is shown from the shoulders up.

medium shot   Character is shown from the waist up.

melodrama   With comedy, the major genre of film, providing large arcs of emotion, often spilling into the music and mise-en-scène, and ending with the death of a beloved character or a closure in heterosexual marriage.

mise-en-scène   The use of space within the frame: the placement of actors and props, the relationship of the camera to the space in front of it, camera movement, the use of color or black and white, lighting, the size of the screen frame itself.

mismatched cut   The shots on either side of the cut don't match—the movement may be out of sync, the characters may be in the wrong place, etc.

montage   A style of editing that juxtaposes shots to build dramatic tension. Sergei Eisenstein used montage as the basic structure of his films.

Motion Picture Association of America (MPAA)   One of the most powerful political lobbyists is also responsible for the various ratings—PG, R, etc.—that presumably tell audiences what kind of sexual or violent content a film has.

moviola   For many years the standard machine for editing, now largely replaced by digital editing.

narrative   The construction of a film's story.

one-shot   A shot in which a single character is shown, often inserted into the over-the-shoulder cutting pattern.

optical printer   A synchronized projector and camera that allows exposed film to be recorded on another piece of exposed film to create a process shot.

optical sound track   An "image" of the sound waves that, converted and amplified, reproduces the recorded sound of the film.

over-the-shoulder cutting pattern   A major component of the classical Hollywood style. A dialogue sequence (two people talking to each other) begins with a two-shot of the participants and then proceeds to cut from over the shoulder of one speaker to over the shoulder of the other. Occasionally a shot of one of the participants talking or listening will be cut into the pattern.

pan   The camera pivots on its tripod or dolly, side to side.

panning and scanning   The only way to show the entire width of a widescreen film on television is to matte the top and bottom of the screen with black bars (the process is called letter-box format). Because many people believe they are seeing less of the film in this format (they are actually seeing more), television broadcasters and videotape distributors blow up the image to a square and move the focus around in that image to find what they think are the important elements.

parallel editing   Two scenes occurring at different places shown one after the other, creating the illusion of simultaneity. See "cross cutting."

point of view Simply, the representation of what a character sees. But it also refers to the dominant "voice" of the film, the teller of the tale, similar to third-person point of view in fiction.

post-studio period Since the late fifties, when the studios no longer controlled every aspect of a film's production.

principle photography The major shooting of a film.

process shot Any shot, some of whose elements are added optically or digitally, after the initial shot is made.

producer The individual who administers the making of an entire film, and often puts together its financing.

production designer Conceives and elaborates the setting's rooms and exteriors that help give a film its visual texture.

rear-screen projection The background of a scene is projected on a screen from the back, while the actors play their roles in front of the screen. Actors and the projection are photographed by a camera in front of them and the screen.

release print Prints made by the film distributor to send out to theaters.

reverse shot Cutting to the opposite side of the previous shot. In a dialogue scene, a reverse shot occurs when a cut is made from over the shoulder of one character to over the shoulder of the other character. If a character is seen looking at something and a cut is made to what she is looking at, that is a reverse shot.

room tone A sound effect that creates ambient sounds of people talking in the background of an enclosed space.

rotoscope A method in tradition or digital animation in which live action is drawn over to create an animated effect.

scene A unit of action or a segment of a story.

scopophilia Literally "love of looking."

screwball comedy Films of the 1930s in which both members of a romantic—often married—couple carried equal weight with dialogue of wit, strength, and self-possession.

second unit A small crew that is sent out to shoot locations that will be intercut with the studio footage or as part of a process shot.

sequence A related series of scenes or shots.

shallow focus Figures in foreground are in focus; background is very soft.

shot An unedited, or uncut, length of film.

shot/reverse shot Any pair of shots in which the second shot reveals what is on the other side of the previous shot. If, for example, the first shot is a hat and the second shot is a character looking at something, the character constitutes the reverse shot and we assume that character is looking at the hat.

silent era From the beginning of film to the late 1920s, there was no recorded sound accompanying the image. Nonetheless, films were never shown without sound. A piano or, in a big movie palace, an entire symphony orchestra played a score that was often created especially for a particular film.

sound track Either an optical or a magnetic strip along the side of the film that contains the recorded sound for the film.

stop action   The camera is shut off, elements of the scene changed, and the camera restarted, creating trick effects. Stop **motion** refers to photographing an object one frame at a time, as when creating animation.

studio system   Beginning in the early 1920s, the film studios developed a production process—with the producer at the head on any given film—and a style of shooting and editing that, despite many variations, remains to this day.

subgenre   Films that use major elements of an established genre along with other conventions. The heist film is a subgenre of the gangster film, as are many road movies and even **film noir.**

suture effect   A critical theory that addresses the way the viewer is "stitched" into a film's narrative.

take   A shot made during the production of a film. A scene in a film is the result of editorial choices made from many differing takes.

Technicolor   A proprietary color process that used three strips of black and white film, each one exposed to either red, blue, or yellow light. These strips were then used to transfer color dye to impart a rich color to film that did not fade with age.

The New Wave   A group of French filmmakers—Jean-Luc Godard, Claude Chabrol, François Truffaut, Eric Rohmer, Jacque Rivette—who started as film critics, became filmmakers in the late fifties, and briefly revolutionized the look of cinema.

three-point lighting   The basic lighting pattern of key light for the face, back light to set the figure from the background, and fill light to create the appropriate shadow and bright spots in the frame.

track   The camera moves on a transport mechanism like a tripod or dolly. This mechanism is put on rails so that the camera will move smoothly. A lateral track moves horizontally. The result is a tracking shot.

trailer   Industry term for "coming attractions."

two-shot   A shot composed of two people.

VistaVision   Patented by Paramount, a nonanamorphic wide-screen process that originates on 70 mm film moving horizontally through the camera and is then printed vertically for the 35 mm release print.

voice-over narration   Either a character in the film or a voice not associated with a camera tells some of the story and fills in some of the blanks. In the hands of some directors, notably Stanley Kubrick's, the voice-over narrator is not dependable.

wide shot   A shot that takes in a large amount of space, often created with a wide-angle lens.

wipe   An editing device, now defunct, in which one shot is removed by a diagonal line sweeping it off the screen.

world tone   A sound effect of traffic and other street sounds to accompany a sequence taking place outside.

zoom   Changing the focal length of lenses by moving them while the camera is stationary creating the impression of movement from near to far or the reverse.

INDEX

Note: Page numbers in *italics* indicate material in illustrations and their captions; page numbers followed by *n* indicate material in chapter endnotes and references.

U

V